The Death and Life of American Journalism

THE *Death* AND *Life*
OF American Journalism

*The Media Revolution That
Will Begin the World Again*

ROBERT W. McCHESNEY
JOHN NICHOLS

NATION
BOOKS

A Member of the Perseus Books Group

Designed by BackStory Design
Set in 12 point Minion Display by the Perseus Books Group

Cataloging-in-Publication data for this book is available from the Library of Congress.

First Nation Books edition 2010
ISBN: 9781568586052

Published by Nation Books
A Member of the Perseus Books Group
www.NationBooks.com

Nation Books are available at special discounts for bulk purchases in the U.S. by corporations, institutions, and other organizations. For more information, please contact the Special Markets Department at the Perseus Books Group, 2300 Chestnut Street, Suite 200, Philadelphia, PA, 19103, or call (800) 810-4145, ext. 5000, or e-mail special.markets@perseusbooks.com.

10 9 8 7 6 5 4 3 2 1

For Bill Moyers and David Austin

Contents

Preface

Barack Obama put this book in context in September 2009 when, in response to a question about the decline of American newspapers and the tenuous state of journalism, the President of the United States said: "I am concerned that if the direction of the news is all blogosphere, all opinions, with no serious fact-checking, no serious attempts to put stories in context, that what you will end up getting is people shouting at each other across the void but not a lot of mutual understanding."[1]

The president is no alarmist. Nor are the many members of Congress, commentators and citizens, from across the political and ideological spectrum, who have of late engaged in hand wringing and wailing about the collapse of newspapers and the decline of journalism. The crisis is real and, as the fresh research and analysis in this book confirms, it is of the highest magnitude. How Americans respond to it is no academic matter. The outcome of every debate of consequence, from those involving education, health care, social justice, climate change and the economy to questions of war and peace will be determined by how the challenge of rejuvenating the news is resolved.

Obama's recognition that a crisis for journalism is also a crisis for democracy distinguishes him from recent presidents and their supporters, who have tended to complain about what they regarded as the unfair nature of press coverage. But the current president's recognition of the connection between vibrant journalism and vibrant democracy is not unprecedented. The founding presidents, Washington, Jefferson and Madison in particular, understood the linkage as essential, and they endeavored to assure that the new American republic would have the most diverse, contentious and easily accessed media the world had known.

While Ronald Reagan, Bill Clinton and the George Bushes pursued more favorable coverage, they assumed, as generations of Americans had assumed before them, that there would be journalism. Now, for the first time in modern American history, it is entirely plausible that we will not have even minimally sufficient resources dedicated to reporting and editing the news and distributing the information and informed analysis that citizens require. Journalistic attention to all levels of governance has declined to a fraction of what was understood as necessary just a generation ago. And, unless there are interventions to alter clear patterns of decay, matters will only get worse. Already much of governmental activity is conducted in the dark. Investigative journalism is on the endangered species list.

A world without journalism is not a world without political information. Instead it is a world where what passes for news is largely spin and self-interested propaganda—some astonishingly sophisticated and some bellicose, but the lion's share of dubious value. It is an environment that spawns cynicism, ignorance, demoralization, and apathy. The only "winners" are those that benefit from a quiescent and malleable people who will "be governed," rather than govern themselves.

The troubling evidence of a debauched and deteriorating journalism is all around us at present. This is about a lot more than misspelled words, misnamed sources or missed school board meetings. To some extent we see the consequences of what happens when journalism deteriorates and disappears in taken-for-granted corruption, endless foreign wars, crumbling infrastructure and social services, and vast increases in inequality. These pathologies are metastasizing, rapidly, and the end result of this evolution could well be disastrous.

That's a frightening prospect and, any way you slice it, these are frightening times. We are entering uncharted waters, as not just our media system but the underpinnings of our republic experience restructurings so fundamental and so sweeping that we can say with certainty that the future will bear little resemblance to the past. We can also say that what will be will not necessarily be better. It depends upon what we as citizens do, and in this time of crisis it is imperative that our options extend far beyond the limits of old media and outdated thinking.

This book reflects our concern about changes that are occurring. But we offer little in the way of nostalgia. In fact, it is the opposite. It is a cry for action to shape inevitable change in a manner that assures that America will have the journalistic institutions, practices and resources necessary to maintain what can credibly be described as a self-governing society. We do not know the precise character or content of the news media that will develop; but we do know that without *bona fide* structures for gathering and disseminating news and analysis, the American experiment in democracy and republican governance will be imperiled.

That peril was understood by the founders. They wrote a constitution that, as the Supreme Court has repeatedly confirmed, is predicated upon the assumption of an informed and participating citizenry. If no news media exist to make that a realistic outcome, the foundations of the republic will decay and ultimately crumble.

We are not the first to write about this crisis; we honor and embrace the lessons learned from those who have come before us. But this book is different from most if not all books about the collapse of journalism. What we offer here is a deeper and more historical analysis of the crisis, one that goes beyond blaming the Internet and the Great Recession for the collapse of traditional news media business models. New technologies and a scorching economic crisis clearly shape our moment, but this is a crisis decades, not years, in the making. The issues that are now so much in play have roots in a deep-seated and longstanding tension between commercialism and the public good that is journalism.

The approach we have taken with this book allows us to respect what is being lost—whole newsrooms, competing voices, institutional memory, news outlets that take seriously their responsibility to cover the powerful and that have the authority to do so—without getting overly romantic about Woodward, Bernstein and tattered copies of the *Washington Post*, circa 1973.

We have no great faith in the past. Nor do we share the faith of those who hope that new technologies, billionaire philanthropists or untried and often impractical new business models will solve the problem and magically generate the quality and quantity of news a self-governing society requires. We review these options closely, and wish them well, but find slim evidence supporting hope for a panacea.

Americans who want journalism and democracy have to get beyond nostalgia for what was *and* utopian fantasies about what might be. This book makes common cause with those who are ready to toss off rose-colored glasses and start looking at the past and the future of journalism in a more fundamental and critical manner. That examination leads quickly to the recognition that the existing policy toolkit—which pretty much begins and ends with calculations of ways to make the news profitable—is all but worthless. Journalism must be understood as a public good. It is something of value to society that the market might once have produced, with strengths and limitations. But the circumstances that made possible that production no longer exist and the market is ceasing to nurture or sustain substantial journalism. That does not mean that the United States can no longer have journalism, or even significant amounts of commercial journalism. But if Americans want sufficient journalism to make our constitutional system work, it means we need a massive public intervention to produce a public good.

We know that this argument contradicts the widely accepted contemporary understanding of the First Amendment and the American free press tradition. In the dominant view, there is no role for the government in the news media except to stay out of the way. The less government, the better, and no government involvement at all is supposedly what the Founders intended. This understanding of the First Amendment was elevated during the period when this country's free press tradition evolved to accommodate the corporate commercial news media system that dominated communications for much of the 20th century, the very system that is now dying. We need to send this dogmatic understanding of a free press to the same graveyard that will receive the corporate news media system.

Let's be clear about this: the bedrock principle that government must not censor or interfere with the content or journalistic operations of news media is non-negotiable. Though the commercial system has placed a high value on this principle, it is neither a corporate nor a commercial construct. Rather, it is a core value of journalists and small "d" democrats.

It is not, however, the only core value. Opposition to government censorship of journalism is one significant component of the American free press tradition, but it is not the entirety of that great tradition. While the

First Amendment prohibits state censorship, it does not in any sense prohibit—or even discourage—the public from using their government to subsidize and spawn independent media. The Supreme Court has confirmed this reading of the constitution again and again. And for good reason. This is in both history and in theory the other foundational component of the American free press tradition.

During the commercial era this central aspect of our free press tradition was easily forgotten, because commercial interests found it to their advantage to provide the resources to subsidize news media. Now the commercial era is collapsing, creating a crisis where no one seems to know what Americans should do to renew and sustain journalism. This book cuts through the confusion and suggests that the solution can be found by returning to our democratic roots.

We demonstrate in this book that the entire press system of the United States was built on a foundation of massive federal postal and printing subsidies that were provided to newspapers during the many decades that forged the American experiment. The first generations of Americans understood that it was entirely unrealistic to expect the profit-motive to provide for anywhere near the level of journalism necessary for an informed citizenry, and by extension self-government, to survive. The very idea was unthinkable. The subsidies that these adherents of the enlightenment developed were themselves enlightened; their purpose was not to enrich publishers but to broaden the marketplace of ideas and to provide a journalistic check and balance on those who might threaten fragile freedoms. It is not too much to say that without these huge subsidies to journalists our nation would not have evolved as it did; indeed, it might not have evolved at all. So it is that tradition, the tradition of Thomas Jefferson and James Madison, that we to turn to as we address a 21st-century crisis.

Ours is not a nostalgic exercise, however. This book proposes specific new methods for using public subsidies to generate a high-quality, uncensored, competitive and independent news media. These methods are founded on an understanding of and respect for the new technologies that make possible a journalism that is more adventurous, more exciting, more participatory and more valuable to society and democracy than any

American has ever known. We recognize that the point of enlightened policies is to establish subsidies that support news media independent of government control or influence. This is a difficult task that often times gets policymakers into a gray area of indirect effects; but the complexity of the task should not, indeed cannot, be equated with impossibility. The current practice of other democracies and our own history provide successful examples of enlightened subsidies. Our public universities, where one of us draws a paycheck, demonstrated long ago that public money could subsidize institutions while protecting academic freedom from politicians' interference. (Thank goodness that is the case, or much of the research contained in this book would have been thwarted.)

We do not advance specific ideas with the purpose of providing the final word on the matter of renewing American journalism, but rather to begin to make tangible the imagining of what a truly democratic news media system could look like in the 21st century. We seek to kindle and encourage bold thinking and we understand that the ideas of others may deliver us not just *from* the current crisis but *to* a finer journalism and a finer democracy. We are not rigid in our thinking, except on the fundamental point that it is necessary to rip off the shackles that have made it so difficult to think of American journalism as anything but the private preserve of Wall Street and Madison Avenue.

We are optimists by nature. But our optimism is not of the pie-in-the-sky variety, honed exclusively in a seminar room or on a barstool. It is based on the hard political work we have done over the past decade working on media policy issues in Washington and across the nation, particularly in conjunction with Free Press, the media reform group we cofounded with Josh Silver in 2002. We have worked with politicians from both major parties and all political philosophies on successful campaigns to stop media consolidation and government secrecy and to promote an open uncensored Internet and viable independent public media. We have learned, as Saul Alinsky put it, that organized people can defeat organized money, and that Americans from all walks of life, when given an opportunity, care deeply about this issue. They get it.

We are convinced that the approach we outline in this book will gain support as the conventional wisdom continues to disintegrate under the searing light of reality. As 2009 drew to a close, for example, the Knight Foundation as well as the Columbia School of Journalism—in a paper it commissioned Leonard Downie Jr. and Michael Schudson to prepare— released extensive and thoughtful research reports on the crisis of journalism. These valuable studies acknowledged the severity of the crisis and the limitations of the conventional response.[2] They both offered up reforms that complement the direction we advocate herein, in a manner that might have raised the eyebrows of their august institutions only a few years ago.

As encouraging as these reports are, it will take more than our leading universities and prestigious foundations to win the battle for journalism. Genuine reform will only occur if Americans understand that they can demand, and indeed create, a journalism and democracy worthy of this country's promise. We hope this book will serve as their manifesto.

For more than a decade, we have been researching and writing together. This book draws from that work. But it really began with a cover story we wrote for *The Nation* magazine early in 2009. The reaction to that article was so overwhelming that we determined to write a book that would expand on the information and ideas contained in the article. Unfortunately, time was not on our side. The crisis was evolving far more rapidly than were ideas for responding to it. So we established a timeline for completing this book that was unreasonable in its brevity and overwhelming in the demands that we had to place our on colleagues, compatriots, friends and families. To write an adequate book in such a time span we required the assistance and feedback of scholars, journalists, elected officials and activists from across the United States and around the world.

The following people gave us research assistance, provoked insights on key points, and in some cases actually read and commented upon chapters of the book. Their contributions to this book are beyond measure, as is our regard for them. Many of these people rank among our closest friends and all of them are true comrades. It is a doozy of a line-up. This book could not possibly exist without their contributions although we alone are responsible for the arguments we make and any flaws in the final product.

Here goes: Craig Aaron, Pat Aufderheide, Marvin Ammori, Ben Bagdikian, C. Edwin Baker, Dean Baker, Randy Baker, Gerald Baldasty,

Patrick Barrett, James Baughman, W. Lance Bennett, Sue Blankman, Frank Blethen, Ryan Blethen, John Robinson Block, Jay Blumler, Mary Bottari, Sister Miriam Brown, Roane Carey, Tim Carpenter, Jessica Clark, Steve Cobble, Bob Cohen, Jeff Cohen, Ana Cohen-Bickford, Jim Conaghan, Congressman John Conyers, Mark Cooper, FCC Commissioner Michael Copps, Matt Crain, James Curran, Sean Michael Dargan, Phil Donahue, Laura Dresser, Diane Farsetta, Laura Flanders, Linda Foley, John Bellamy "Duke" Foster, Laura Frank, Bob Garfield, Ed Garvey, Amy Goodman, Linda Gordon, Glenn Greenwald, Peter Hart, Chris Hedges, Edward S. Herman, Hannah Holleman, James Holm, Brent Hueth, Arianna Huffington, Shanto Iyengar, Richard John, Mark Jurkowitz, Rick Karr, Richard Kielbowicz, Richard Kim, Naomi Klein, Deepa Kumar, Barbara Lawton, Chuck Lewis, Mark Lloyd, Gary Lucas, Bernie Lunzer, Loren Lynch, Adam Lynn, Ben Manski, Josh Marshall, Christopher Martin, Robert W.T. Martin, Mark Crispin Miller, Ralph Nader, Victor Navasky, John Nerone, Eric Newton, David Nord, Geneva Overholser, Jeffrey Pasley, Sandy Pearlman, Michael Perelman, Victor Pickard, John Randolph, Michael Ravnitzky, Mark Ritchie, Niel Ritchie, Joel Rogers, Matt Rothschild, Senator Bernie Sanders, Jeremy Scahill, Jan Schaffer, Michael Schudson, Ben Scott, Josh Silver, Caroline Sinclair, John "Sly" Slyvester, Patti Smith, J. H. Snider, Matt Sobek, Norman Solomon, Audrey Sprenger, Paul Starr, John Stauber, Vince Stehle, Inger Stole, David Swanson, Rod Tiffen, Derek Turner, Katrina vanden Heuvel, Gore Vidal, Christopher Warren, David H. Weaver, Mark Weisbrot, Aidan White, Bruce Williams, Granville Williams, Scott Wilson, Dave Zweifel.

R. Jamil Jonna did the hard research and prepared the charts in the book and authored Appendix III. He worked insane hours over the summer to help us complete the book. We cannot thank him enough.

Bob thanks Dr. Dale Brashers, his colleagues, and the terrific staff at the Department of Communication at the University of Illinois at Urbana-Champaign for supporting this research. John does the same for Katrina vanden Heuvel and his colleagues at *The Nation* magazine and Dave Zweifel and his colleagues at *The Capital Times*. Without institutions with a commitment to fostering a broader and better discourse, books of this sort would not be possible. We are fortunate to be employed by them.

We thank the extraordinary staff of Free Press for leading the fight for journalism, and making this book more than an academic exercise.

We thank our families: Inger Stole, Amy McChesney, and Lucy McChesney for Bob; Harrison and Mary Nichols and Mary Bottari and Whitman Genevieve Nichols Bottari for John. They sacrificed much of 2009 to the words you hold in your hands.

Carl Bromley recruited us to Nation Books, embraced this project and ably guided it to completion. He was the first to see the promise of this project. John Sherer of Basic Books took a personal interest in the book early on, prodding us to be even more ambitious in imagining its potential. Marco Pavia oversaw production and demonstrated a passion for producing a beautiful look. Caitlin Fitzpatrick and Michele Jacob have graciously crafted the marketing and promotional plans for the book. Cait, in particular, went far beyond the call of duty as she pieced together our 2010 North American book tour.

This book is dedicated to two people. David Austin supported not just the cause of media reform but every endeavor (sound or crazed) in which we have engaged over the past decade with an organizer's flair for pitching in before he was asked, asking wise questions and providing steady support grounded in an understanding that love and solidarity are the same thing. David helped launch each of our books and it saddens us beyond words that his untimely death robs us of the opportunity to share this one with him.

This book is also dedicated to the greatest and most courageous television journalist of our times, and one of the finest persons we have ever known. We desperately need a media system that strongly encourages, rather than discourages, the type of independent, principled and brave journalism he does. As we engage in that battle, his work demonstrates what can be done and what we are fighting for. Indeed, when we are asked to provide an example of the journalism we seek, we respond not with a long list of prerequisites but with a single name: Bill Moyers.

Bob McChesney & John Nichols
Madison, Wisconsin
October 2009

Introduction

AMERICAN CRISIS;
American Opportunity

America was called into being by a journalist. When Virginia plantation owners who would become presidents were still pondering petitions to King George III, when a Boston lawyer who would also be president was fretting about the excesses democracy might unleash with the replacement of colonial rule, good Tom Paine argued in the *Philadelphia Journal* that Americans had a right to govern their own affairs. Within weeks of his arrival on American soil in the fall of 1774, months before "the shot heard round the world" was fired at the North Bridge in Concord and a full year and a half before the penning of the Declaration of Independence, Paine outlined "the essence of liberty" as self-governance by informed and empowered citizens. It was Paine, that ink-stained wretch and citizen of the world, who convinced uncertain patriots that "the sun never shined on a cause of greater worth" than the revolt of 13 small colonies against the mighty British empire—inspiring the continentals to fight not for gain or glory but "to begin the world over again."[1]

Having experience with the power of the press—he was the most widely read writer in revolutionary America —Paine would eventually observe: "Whoever has made observation on the characters of nations will find it generally true that the manners of a nation, or of a party, can be better ascertained from the character of its press than from any other public circumstance."[2]

America, like any country that would be democratic, requires not merely a free press but a functional press— media that regard the state secret as an assault to popular governance, that watch the politically and economically powerful with a suspicious eye, that recognize as their duty the informing and enlightening of citizens so that they may govern themselves in a republic where, as Paine observed, power rests "inherently with the universal multitude."[3]

These radical notions are the essential underpinnings of the American experiment. They have been well regarded and widely respected across two centuries. Yet, a free and functional press does not merely occur. While Paine argued that there is a natural right to liberty, the journalism that sustains it does not naturally follow. A media system that sustains journalism of consequence is willed into existence and maintained by a people and by their representatives.

Without a civic counterbalance to the vagaries of the market, it is entirely within the realm of possibility that journalism could wither and die. Its replacement would be not a void but the sophisticated propaganda, be it private or public, of a modern age in which it is possible to tell people much of what they need to know to consume products and support spurious wars but nothing that they need to know to be voters and citizens. This is the fear that the founders sought to guard against when they established a free press with protection in the Bill of Rights. They threw the full weight of the American government into the work of creating and sustaining a diverse, competitive, skeptical and combative media system for a nation that would rest power with an informed people rather than an enthroned magistrate. The makers of the American experiment knew precisely what they hoped to avoid. "A popular government without popular information or the means of acquiring it," explained James Madison, "is but a Prologue to a Farce or a Tragedy or perhaps both."[4]

For the better part of 15 years, we have argued that the existing and evolving commercial news-media system has contributed to the collapse of quality journalism in America, creating precisely the circumstance

Madison feared.We don't claim to be pioneers in the criticism of consolidated, downsized and dumbed-down news. We discuss herein the long tradition of criticism of the problems for journalism wrought by commercial control.

The systematic deterioration of journalism has, for many years now, been observed and chronicled on the margins, among journalists, media scholars and activists. But it has until the current moment been largely ignored by the political mainstream and, not surprisingly, by the commercial news media. To some extent this neglect was grounded in the fact that the largest news-media firms were raking in colossal profits as they grew bigger and fatter over the past three decades. If firms were making money, the thinking (in what will be looked back upon as a period of capitalism-on-steroids) suggested, they had to be serving the public.

But when the money flow slowed and the speculators began to jump ship, leaving journalism to sink with the wreckage of newspapers, it suddenly became clear even to those who had once sung the commercial system's praises that no service had been rendered.

By the end of this first decade of the 21st century, the crisis of journalism is obvious to all. Daily newspapers are in free-fall collapse. The entire commercial news-media system is disintegrating. Wall Street and Madison Avenue are abandoning the production of journalism en masse. Our nation faces the absurd and untenable prospect of attempting what James Madison characterized as impossible: to be a self-governing constitutional republic without a functioning news media.

This book outlines the dimensions of the crisis and explains how and why it came to be. In Chapter 1, we explain why the Internet has been a central factor in the collapse of the commercial news media, but also why leaving the analysis there is misleading. This is a deep-seated and long-term crisis that was created by media owners who made the commercial and entertainment values of the market dramatically higher priorities than the civic and democratic values that are essential to good journalism and a good society. Simply remaking business models to squeeze a few more dollars out of newspapers, or to find a few on the Internet, will not solve the crisis. A radically unsettling circumstance, for journalism and for democracy, demands radical policy solutions.

But they must be solutions sufficient to the task at hand.

In Chapter 2, we review the two leading "fixes" that have been at the center of most discussions to date: to use the authority of government to rewrite existing rules in order to allow old and dying commercial media to get even bigger and possibly establish a cartel on the Internet; or to simply relax and wait while entrepreneurs cobble together a new journalism system on the Internet. We are neither old-media stalwarts nor new-media fabulists. Our brief is a journalistic one that is less concerned with the print-versus-digital debate than with the construction of platforms that will sustain journalism and democracy in the 21st century. To our view, neither the "can't we just rewrite the rules one more time?" nostalgia of the patrons of print nor the "let's just find the answer on the Internet" utopianism of the denizens of digital is sufficient. In fact, both approaches are, upon scrutiny, revealed as structurally and practically unsound. Americans have to face the hard and cold truth: journalism is a public good that is no longer commercially viable. If we want journalism, it will require public subsidies and enlightened policies.

In Chapter 3, we tackle the behemoth myth that is handcuffing Americans as they attempt to respond to the current crisis: that American news-media institutions are and always have been operating in a "free market" system, run to maximize profit, and that the proper and necessary role of the government has been to stay completely out of the picture. We demonstrate that this is inaccurate. The vital and nonnegotiable prohibition on government censorship of media content has been blown up to make it the beginning and ending point of any discussion about what role government can play in preserving and ultimately extending the public's right to know. We demonstrate that the government in fact created the free press throughout American history with aggressive and often enlightened policies and subsidies. Without this massive government role, it is unlikely that U.S. democracy would have survived, let alone blossomed.

We argue that Americans need to embrace this tradition as they respond to the present crisis. Unless Americans develop enlightened and extensive government policies and subsidies to spawn an independent journalism, it will not exist. And democracy will again be imperiled.

In Chapter 4, we offer our vision of the types of policies that will produce a powerful independent news media and journalism that realizes the revolutionary potential of digital technologies. We offer these proposals not on the assumption that the stating of wise ideas will conclude the debate but rather to begin the serious conversation our nation needs about journalism and media policies; we have little doubt that what we propose can and will be improved upon once Americans get the full might of their collective talent applied to the task.

Our central premise is that in this crisis moment Americans need to understand that the goal of democrats ought not be to simply patch up the old corporate news-media ship and sail it deeper into the storm. The goal must be to create a vastly superior news media that dramatically enhances the constitutional system and representative democracy.

What we know from our experience in politics and policymaking over the past two decades is that these are extraordinary times and that this crisis demands extraordinary solutions. Ideas that would have been taken off the table in the recent past are moving to the center of the debate, because the status quo and the conventional wisdom are bankrupt and discredited. If Americans do nothing, matters will get worse, dramatically worse. But if Americans act, this can be a moment of revolutionary advance. The American people are at a rare historical juncture where they hold their fate very much in their hands. They do indeed have it in their power to begin the world over again.

We discuss the real-world, here-and-now politics of media reform in our conclusion.

Make no mistake; the work of salvaging journalism is rapidly becoming one of the central political issues of this era. The first indication that the political culture is awakening to the crisis came in spring 2009, when both branches of Congress held committee hearings on the matter. In May, Massachusetts Senator John Kerry, one of the most media-savvy of our legislators, convened the latter of these hearings. It featured much earnest discussion and recognition of the severity of the crisis. Senator Kerry quoted, affirmatively, from the brass plaque on a wall at Columbia University's Graduate School of Journalism, which bears the words of legendary newspaper publisher Joseph Pulitzer: "Our Republic and its press will rise or fall together."[5]

Even as it clarified what is at stake, the Senate hearing was largely lacking in plausible solutions, or even a sense of how to proceed.

"Is there any government role at all?" Kerry asked. "I don't know the answer to that."[6]

This book provides Senator Kerry and anyone else asking the same question with an answer.

Chapter 1

THE CRISIS IN
Journalism

Amerian journalism has a future.

It has a face, and a name: Kate Giammarise.

At 27, Kate has proven herself as a reporter, writer and savvy interpreter of the news. She took all the right journalism courses, worked for the college paper, interned and freelanced and then grabbed the first "real" job she could find: joining the staff of Ohio's oldest daily newspaper, *The Chillicothe Gazette*, circulation 15,000. Kate excelled at the *Gazette*. She broke big stories in a small town—digging into scandal stories that would ultimately end the career of a local congressman. Kate got noticed and moved to the award-winning *Lorain Morning Journal*, where she started collecting her own honors for incisive coverage of government and environmental issues. Then she got the call that every young journalist awaits. It came from the editors of *The Toledo Blade*, a great Midwestern daily that had just collected a Pulitzer Prize for sending investigative reporters from Ohio to Vietnam in pursuit of a story of atrocities that had almost been lost to history. They wanted Kate to join the same city desk that had trained top reporters for *The Chicago Tribune*, *The Washington Post* and *The Wall Street Journal*.

Like generations of American journalists before her, Kate was making her name as a smart, enterprising reporter who was prepared to work the night shift, ready to sit through the long meeting to make sure that the folks who could not hire an expensive lawyer were treated fairly by the county commissioners, willing to climb the flight of stairs in the building with the broken elevator in pursuit of the perspective on a real-estate report that would not otherwise be revealed. She covered the tough, wrong-side-of-the-tracks stories: homegrown terrorism trials, priests who almost got away with abusing kids and, above all, poverty and homelessness. Kate hung out with hungry children and wrote stories that made everyone in town care about getting those kids their next meal. She crawled under bridges to interview homeless veterans of the Iraq war. To get to the bottom of the debate over whether food-stamp allocations were sufficient, she lived for a week on a $21 food-stamp allotment and then told the tale so well that it was recognized by U.S. Senator Sherrod Brown, a Democrat from Ohio.

Kate wasn't just good at what she did. She was great.

And she loved her job. If she saw a problem, she wrote about it. If a low-income family was getting lost in the bureaucracy, Kate called a city council member or a state senator or a member of Congress to ask why government was making things so hard on those who needed it most. She was practicing journalism with the purpose Finley Peter Dunne championed: "The business of a newspaper is to comfort the afflicted and afflict the comfortable."[1]

Editors looked at Kate and said, "The girl's got journalism in her blood."

Not just any journalism. Print journalism. Old-school. Ink-stained. The kind where a recent college graduate—whom grizzled veterans can't help calling "kid"—runs up the steps of an old brick building in the downtown of a city that might be just a little down on its luck and tells an editor with a seen-it-all face that she is ready to read police reports on a Saturday night, sit through six-hour planning-commission meetings and hold the hand of a mother whose child has been killed in a distant war. The kind where Humphrey Bogart, as crusading editor Ed Hutcheson in the movie *Deadline USA*, holds up a telephone in the pressroom of the *New York Day*.

"What's that sound?" demands the politically connected mobster who has used violence and intimidation to try and kill a story that will blow the lid off a corruption scandal that has left a trail of bodies and broken lives strewn across the streets of a big city.

"That's the press, baby. The press!" shouts the journalist that every American with a heart and soul wanted to be. "And there's nothing you can do about it. Nothing!"[2]

It turns out Ed Hutcheson was wrong.

Deadline USA was made in the middle of the 20th century that newspapers defined—and survived.

But as the first years of the 21st century ticked away, newspapers, while still in many journalistic senses definitional, were not surviving. And neither was the craft of gathering and telling America's story. Major daily newspapers collapsed into bankruptcy, venerable chains teetered on the brink of collapse, publications that had survived depressions, wars and the centuries that went with them—*The Christian Science Monitor*, Denver's *Rocky Mountain News*, Seattle's *Post-Intelligencer*—were stopping the presses, permanently.

Even where journalists and journalistically inclined publishers kept the bankers at bay long enough to put another edition out, the "product" that was rolling off the press was a thin, lifeless shadow of the newspapers of old. And so were the newsrooms. Buyouts, layoffs, downsizings, reductions in force, all the terms of art of the great shrinkage, had left them feeling like morgues.

At *The Toledo Blade*, Kate Giammarise began to hear the rumblings in the fall of 2008, as she hustled to keep on top of the hunger, homelessness and poverty beat she had staked out in a factory town where unemployment was creeping into double digits. Layoffs might be coming. The *Blade*, a family-owned newspaper that had resisted the ugliest cuts in an industry that began to dwindle long before the financial markets tanked that September, was struggling to balance the books.

Kate began emailing mentors, friends and family members.

She was a reporter. She wanted to get the story out. Her story—and that of an industry that was taking a dire turn.

On December 13, 2008, Kate hit the "Send" button on her computer.

"They laid off 25 people, including me," the message read. "My last day is Dec. 26."[3]

But it wasn't just the 25 at the *Blade*.

Kate Giammarise is the face of journalism's future. There's no doubt about that.

But at the end of 2008, she was something else: a statistic.

As the stories of laid-off journalists like Kate Giammarise turned from tales of individual loss to mass displacement, the stories of dead or dying newspapers went from romantic reflections to the drab accounting of the toll. Newspaper journalism, an endeavor colorful enough to have spawned movie and mystery-novel genres, was itself becoming a statistic.

When we are assessing the fate of the fourth estate in a great republic, *statistic* seems a particularly ugly word. It suggests a bureaucratic calculus that is more mechanical than human, more of ledgers than of the individuals who report, write and edit the stories of the American experience. Unfortunately, the current crisis of journalism has, for the most part, been presented as a matter of mechanics and ledgers rather than one of turmoil for journalists and danger for democracy.

While it is essential for reasons of humanity and practical perspective to keep conscious of the individual and institutional elements of what is transpiring, it is also necessary to recognize the broad dimensions of the current crisis. No individual story of a newspaper printing its last edition, of a continent going uncovered, of a Washington bureau shuttered or even of a Kate Giammarise taking one last look at the sprawling second-floor newsroom in the *Blade*'s castle-like building in downtown Toledo can begin to convey the scope of the change that is taking place in American journalism.

A media system—constructed across centuries; woven into the very fabrics of our communities, our states and our nation; once muscular enough to begin wars and make presidents shudder; steeped in tradition yet irresponsible enough to employ the word *tabloid* as both a noun and verb; overlaid with a veneer of romance so thick it could obscure a particular publisher's corruptions of greed and personality; still huge in its pretenses and ambitions but entirely uncertain about what to make of itself—is collapsing.

So it is that Kate Giammarise's experience becomes part of the big story of journalism in our time, a dramatic, rapidly unfolding series of events that must be understood if we are going to have a serious discussion about journalism in the 21st century. This chapter examines the broad dimensions—and the explanations—for the crisis that cost Kate Giammarise her job. Our purpose is to get clear about what has gone wrong because it is the essential first step in the process of getting things right—for Kate, for journalists and, most important, for the democratic life of the United States.

Farewell to Newspapers, Farewell to Journalism?

That newspapers are in crisis, and may soon become extinct after being central to the American experience through the country's entire history, is a fact now broadly accepted. In 2009, *TIME*'s Walter Isaacson described the situation as having "reached meltdown proportions" and concluded, "It is now possible to contemplate a time in the near future when major towns will no longer have a newspaper and when magazines and network news operations will employ no more than a handful of reporters."[4]

This is not a routine crisis. It fundamentally brings to a head the long-simmering tension between journalism and commerce. For a very long time, since the mid–19th century, this marriage, though at times rocky, generated sufficient resources to sustain journalism. At its best, the marriage provided a measure of independence and freedom, allowed for innovation and helped dissident voices to be heard. At its worst, the marriage promoted monopoly, supported privilege and put commercial interests ahead of the public interest. We confess a certain attachment to what newspaper journalism has produced on the positive side of that ledger—encouraged by our familiarity with so many outstanding American reporters, columnists and editors past and present—but we are well aware that even at its best the tension with commercialism was always gnawing away at the democratic potential of the enterprise.

That long-standing tension is becoming almost moot today, however. The corporate community has determined that commercial journalism as we have long known it is a nonstarter, and they are abandoning the field at a breakneck pace. The business model is dying and soon to be buried forever, or at least for the imaginable future. News media are being shuttered, resources that are vital to remaining news media are being slashed and commercial pressures are gaining ever more leverage over journalistic values. On this point, we agree with Wall Street: forget about the old "penny press," newspaper shares are now "penny stocks."[5] The question for us, as citizens, is what we are going to do about it.

Nowhere is the crisis more striking, or more frightening, than in the daily-newspaper industry, which is imploding before our eyes. The industry is attempting to act like a magician and explain how it can somehow metaphysically survive and prosper. But, as with a magician, one is advised to watch the hands, and ignore the words.

Here are the words: the Newspaper Association of America, the trade group that chirps about how "newspapers are reinventing themselves to focus on serving distinct audiences"—translation for "print publications: shrinking"—announced in the spring of 2009 that it was mere myth-making to suggest that: "Newspaper readership is tanking." In reality, NAA President and CEO John F. Sturm declared with no indication that he recognized the absurdity of his claim: "Average weekly newspaper readership declined a mere 1.8 percent between 2007 and 2008, and about 7 percent since its peak in 2002. Compare that to the 10 percent decline seen in the prime time TV audience in 2007 alone."

"This is not a portrait of a dying industry," declared Sturm.[6]

Actually, a rapidly accelerating loss of readers that is now acknowledged to be approaching 2 percent annually used to be considered a serious matter. And comparing the fate of newspapers to that of prime-time television, which is itself in a crisis of survival, is anything but reassuring.

What is particularly peculiar is Sturm's use of the phrase *average weekly newspaper readership*, a mushy old newsroom dodge from the era of Barnum & Bailey. The primary measure of any daily newspaper's success or failure has always been found in actual circulation data—not estimates of weekly readership. And, no matter what Mr. Sturm says, that data provides a portrait of an industry that, if we are uncomfortable with the term *dying*, must surely be described as withering. From October 1, 2008, to March 31, 2009, according to a survey of 395 of the country's top daily newspapers, weekday circulation declined 7.1 percent. That represented a dramatic acceleration from the rate seen during the two previous six-month reporting periods, when daily circulation fell 4.6 percent and 3.6 percent, respectively.[7] There is no way to put a positive spin on these figures, which the Poynter Institute's media-business analyst, Rick Edmonds, correctly characterized as "not very good, and probably a little worse than expected."[8]

Want to see a portrait of a dying industry? Try this: Mired in debt and rattled by revenue shortfalls as advertisers cut back and young readers show no interest, the managers of corporate newspaper firms seek to "right the sinking ship" by cutting costs, leading remaining newspaper readers to ask why they are bothering to pay for publications that are pale shadows of their former selves. Older readers are giving up on papers they had once relied upon. Advertisers have also gone elsewhere. Print display advertising fell a historically unprecedented 29.7 percent at daily newspapers in the first quarter of 2009.[9] In the second quarter of 2009, newspaper revenues fell a whopping 29 percent from a year earlier, the greatest quarterly drop since the Great Depression. It marked the 12th consecutive quarterly decline in revenues since 2006.[10] This is a portrait of the daily newspaper death dance-cum-funeral march.

We understand that some newspapers remain profitable, largely as a result of their local monopolies. Profit margins have been so high traditionally that even a sharp decline will not pull some firms below double-digit returns, at least not for a while. But none of these newspapers, as far as we can tell, are expanding their editorial budgets, or expanding their readerships. To the contrary, they are making cuts, accepting declining circulation and developing exit strategies. The most popular strategy is to maximize their profits in the foreseeable future by emptying out their newsrooms. In 2008 McClatchy Company newspapers earned a 21 percent profit margin, but the company still reduced its workforce by nearly a third, as it attempted to pay off the loan it required to purchase the remains of the Knight Ridder chain in 2006. Gannett's newspapers enjoyed an 18 percent profit margin in 2008, with some papers earning as much as 42 percent. Nonetheless Gannett slashed 3,000 jobs (10 percent of its overall workforce), demanded that remaining employees take an unpaid weeklong furlough and imposed a pay freeze. The cuts continued in 2009, when another 1,400 jobs were eliminated and a 139-year-old newspaper, *The Tucson Citizen*, was closed despite concerted efforts by residents of Arizona's capital city to preserve it.[11] There was some good news for Gannett, however: Their executives received six-figure bonuses in 2008.[12] Is this a great country or what?

The inescapable conclusion is that these guys are not serious about the future of journalism; they are serious about cashing in as many chips as possible before closing time. They will be the ones who turn out the lights.

For perspective, let's consider a pair of simple extrapolations:

1. If newspapers continue to lose circulation at a rate of 7 percent every six months, they've got less than eight years to go before no one is reading them.
2. If the circulation losses continue to accelerate—from 3.6 percent to 4.6 percent to 7 percent—it's probably closer to six years. In view of the ongoing cutbacks that make daily newspapers less and less attractive, this is not an unreasonable projection.

Only a few weeks before the NAA made its wild claims about the health of newspapers, a more convincing assessment was made by the longtime owner of *The Buffalo News*, a fellow who has made a good deal of money in the industry and knows it reasonably well. Warren Buffett said he would not buy most of the newspapers in the United States "at any price." He said the changing media environment meant newspapers had "the possibility of unending losses" and he did not "see anything on the horizon that causes that erosion to end."[13]

So the "This is not the portrait of a dying industry" line is not just pathetic. It is destructive. Like the Minnesota mother who took flight with her sick son rather than have his cancer treated—providing one of the major "news" stories of the spring of 2009—the NAA is still claiming that newspapers will be saved without modern medicine. They're wrong, and their denial—even if it is so evidently aimed at keeping advertisers on board—does a dramatic disservice to the cause of journalism.

It is journalism, not newspapering, which is our real concern. We argue that it is wrong to regard the current mess as merely a crisis for newspapers—even if they are in demonstrably deep trouble. This is a crisis moment for journalism, and therefore for self-government. We place so much emphasis on daily newspapers, not out of a romantic attachment to ink and newsprint, but because they account for so much of original journalism. It may strike readers under the age of 50 as bizarre, but three or four decades ago many people expected television to usurp print's historic role and become the primary source of journalism. That never quite happened, as over the past few decades the commitment to television journalism has stagnated and declined. Taken over by large media conglomerates in the 1980s and 1990s, network television news became a bit player in entertainment empires, and increasingly was subject to the same commercial principles as quiz shows and comedies.[14] As a result it has remained a minor contributor to overall news production. To a very large extent, arguably a larger extent than two decades ago, broadcast journalism takes its cues on what stories to cover and how to cover them from daily newspapers.

Local television stations, identified by a majority of citizens as their primary source of news about civic life, are covering less political news than they did a decade ago. And over a decade ago, a New York Times Magazine writer had already concluded: "Most anyone in the press and academia who has given it much thought has concluded that while there are exceptions, local television news is atrocious."[15] A study of the coverage of the recent election seasons, conducted by University of Wisconsin researchers, concluded that "local television news viewers got considerably more information about campaigns from paid political advertisements than from actual news coverage." The survey also said that "Local newscasts in seven Midwest markets aired four minutes, 24 seconds of paid political ads during the typical 30-minute broadcast [before the election] while dedicating an average of one minute, 43 seconds to election news coverage."[16]

Moreover, local TV news has been clobbered by cuts over the past two years, along lines similar to those seen at newspapers. One study determined that 1,200 TV newsroom jobs were lost in 2008, a 4.3 percent drop.[17] The difference is simply that the figures are hidden in the larger employment numbers for the stations.[18] At any rate, few observers expect local TV commercial news to have much of a future, if it has one at all. And local radio news, a significant producer of local journalism in the 1960s and 1970s, when nearly all AM stations had news directors and often reporters, has all but disappeared, a casualty of "deregulation." Chart 1 demonstrates the employment in broadcast news between 1982 and 2008, illustrating the number of broadcast journalists per 100,000 people.

Cable television news channels, the one growth area, have come to play an important role in the national debate over the past two decades, and especially in recent years. But we should not exaggerate the amount of original journalism done there. The same corporate pressures that afflicted network broadcast news and daily newspapers have affected them. In many respects the great contribution of Fox News was not to demonstrate the commercial viability of a more aggressively partisan approach to the news; it was in demonstrating that when one went more aggressively partisan, it was easier to dispense with actual (and costly) journalism because viewers focused on celebrity hosts and political operatives who pedaled spin for free. The specialty of these channels is to take a particular story and blow it into a huge topic, generating tremendous heat, but little light. To be fair, sometimes programs on these stations draw public attention to important stories. But even then, as often as not, the producers rely on print journalists for their hard digging and genuine expert analysis. This makes these channels more profitable in their own right, but less important as sources of journalism.

The Internet certainly devotes more attention to politics and, as we discuss in Chapters 2 and 4, it is the unquestioned future of journalism. Already, it is playing a crucial role in keeping mainstream journalism honest, and it has created quality content far beyond its limited resources.[19] But, to a significant extent, Internet news sites are aggregators of the news gathered by old media rather than producers of news content. The information discussed online is still gathered by newspaper and broadcast reporters, and while a few high-profile journalists have begun to migrate from old-fashioned newsrooms to the blogosphere, they tend to arrive as commentators rather than collectors of news. The leading news Web sites are almost all affiliated with the "old media," and much of what the bloggers blog about comes from

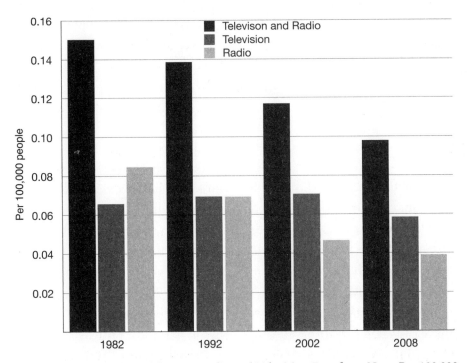

CHART 1. Estimated Workforce in Radio and Television Broadcast News Per 100,000 People, Selected Years 1982–2008[20]

the old media in digital form. As these old-media Web sites dry up be-cause newspapers are making massive cutbacks, the amount of original journalism on the Web is going to stagnate or decline. The Web has yet to emerge as a distinct journalistic force—let alone one that speaks with the authority at the local, state or regional level of a traditional daily newspaper. While the Internet may someday be home to sites that generate the revenues needed to pay reporters and editors to pro-duce journalism, that day has yet to arrive in a meaningful sense.

Harvard's Alex S. Jones estimates that 85 percent of all professionally reported news originates with daily newspapers, and that he has seen credible sources place that figure closer to 95 percent.[21] A scientist friend of ours once told us that if a couch could be made to magically disappear, we could possibly be able to still see for an instant the outlines of the couch from all the microscopic organisms that had been attached to the couch. In many respects, daily newspapering is the couch of American journalism. If it disappears, the organisms, regrettably all too microscopic, living on it will be undermined as well. Hence our emphasis on the crisis in daily newspapers as central to the broader crisis in journalism.

"Out of Print"

And what a nightmarish crisis it is! The most conservative estimate of the collapse in newspaper employment, that of the American Society of News Editors, suggested that 5,900 reporters, columnists and editors lost their jobs in 2008, for an 11.3 percent decline in newsroom employment. That was the largest annual drop ever recorded in a survey by the 87-year-old ASNE, and it more than doubled the loss seen in the previous year. It was enough to cause ASNE president Charlotte Hall to moan, "The loss of journalists is a loss for democracy."[22]

True. But the figures distributed by Hall's group early in 2009 did not begin to give a full measure of the decline in journalism employment. The ASNE survey was based on self-reported figures from just 931 of 1,405 daily newspapers. There's no accounting for the job losses at the remaining dailies, or at the more than 6,500 weekly, biweekly and tri-weekly newspapers nationwide, even though they too are shedding jobs at a historic rate. From our research it has become clear that this crisis is happening so fast, is so widespread, that no one has authoritative figures. And as soon as someone thinks they have the numbers in alignment, a new wave of closures, buyouts and layoffs blows them out of the water. It is like trying to play badminton in a hurricane.

Before we can go any further we have to get a better handle on exactly what is taking place with newspapers.

Perhaps the best way to grasp the crisis as it has unfolded is through the experience of Erica Smith, a multimedia and print designer at *The St. Louis Post-Dispatch*. Smith got riled up after reading a special report on journalism's dire straits ("As Cuts Trim News Pages and News-rooms—What Gets Lost?") that appeared in the industry's bible, *Editor & Publisher*, in 2007. So Smith, who says, "I love breaking news alerts," started talking it over with fellow journalists. Everyone agreed that things looked bad—the *Post-Dispatch*, after its 2005 sale to the financially shaky

Lee Enterprises chain, had by 2007 seen 180 staffers take buyouts, and the great mid-American daily was on the verge of a round of layoffs of news editors, bureau chiefs and reporters that veteran *PD* reporter Florence Shinkle would describe as having "breached some critical boundaries for the health and stability of the newspaper."[23]

Yet, it struck Erica Smith that the evidence of the crisis, though jarring, was still largely anecdotal. "I was curious to know how many layoffs and buyouts there were, but couldn't find a total anywhere," she recalls. "So I started a list, which evolved into this blog on April 9, 2008." The fan of breaking news alerts didn't know what she was getting herself into with her "Paper Cuts" blog.[24] Soon she was getting "alerts" from across the country in the form of tips, copies of publisher memos and layoff notices, links to news articles on buyouts and all the other sources of data for a Web site Smith was updating daily, then twice daily and more in order to stay ahead of the flood of bad news. She started creating maps of the United States with electronic "pins" in them to record job losses—white for 1–24, yellow for 25–49, blue for 50–74, green for 75–99, red for 100 or more. By the end of 2008, there were was a sea of colored "pins" on a map that was the very picture of an industry on the skids. Worst of all were the black pins, which represented newspapers that had experienced serious cuts but that had not revealed exactly how many. These were the "unknowns."[25]

"So with all of those 'unknown' posts, does that mean the total isn't really, you know, the total?" Smith was asked. "It does," she replied. "It means that the actual number of people who have been laid off is higher than what I have listed. That's why there is a plus sign after the 'total' number." But if the outer limits of the crisis remained uncharted, there was no question that "Paper Cuts" was providing the clearest reflection of its scope. And it was horrifying. When Smith put the pin in the map for Toledo—the one with Kate Giammarise's name on it—the total number of job cuts and buyouts recorded for 2008 was already over 15,000.

By the time Smith had totaled all the numbers from the year, they added up to 15,970, and that was without the "unknowns."

2008 was a golden age compared with what came next. By October of the following year, Smith's firm figure for 2009 layoffs and buyouts had surpassed 14,000. At this rate, the job-loss total for 2009 will be around 17,000—roughly 1,000 more than the "record" year of 2008.

Unfortunately, the news about the news gets worse.

As the miserable year of 2008 wore on, Smith found she needed to add a new map to her site. It was titled: "Out of Print."

More than four dozen newspapers folded in 2008. Most were weeklies, such as Newbury, New Hampshire's 185-year-old *Argus Champion* and the 100-year-old *Orfordville Journal and Footville News* in Wisconsin. But venerable dailies began shutting as well. The 86-year-old *Albuquerque Tribune*, which won the 1994 Pulitzer Prize for national reporting after revealing how the federal government injected plutonium into 18 human beings as part of a "Dr. Strangelove" experiment at the Walter E. Fernald State School, closed in February; *The San Juan Star*, a 49-year-old English-language daily that once employed Pulitzer Prize–winning author William Kennedy as its managing editor, gave up the ghost in August; *The Eureka Reporter*, whose evolution from a Web site into a freewheeling print daily had sparked an unprecedented newspaper war on the Redwood Coast of Northern California, folded a few days after the 2008 presidential election. When the *Reporter* closed, a keen observer of the Eureka scene bemoaned its disappearance. The *Reporter*, he explained, had forced the dominant paper in town, the *Times-Standard*, out of the complacency that can dumb down a small-city daily. "There is no question that the competitive environment made the *Times-Standard* a better newspaper," declared Dean Singleton, with no sense of irony. Singleton is the owner of *The Times-Standard* and the founder of MediaNews Group, the fourth-largest newspaper company in the United States, and an outspoken champion of corporate newspapering. MediaNews Group is the corporate overseer of *The Denver Post*, *The Detroit News*, *The Salt Lake Tribune* and 50 other dailies.[26]

The dailies that closed in 2008 were, for the most part, the sort of papers that had been closing for years. The mortality rate was accelerating, to be sure, but the victims were predictable: afternoon dailies pegged to a pre-suburban nation; upstarts with dreams bigger than their wallets; smart, well-edited papers that lost their fights not on the newsstand but when they ended up on the losing end of the Frankenstein's monster of "newspaper preservation": the network of urban joint operating agreements (JOA) that merged the non-journalistic operations of supposedly competing papers into messy monopolies. The JOA experiment was initiated in 1970's Newspaper Preservation Act by then-president Richard Nixon at the behest of Hearst newspaper chain CEO Richard Berlin.[27] *The Albuquerque Tribune* was the weak sister of the "Albuquerque Plan," a Depression-era stretch of anti-trust laws that laid the outlines for ensuing JOAs.

By 2009, however, even the big dogs of JOA experimentation—which critics had long seen as a scheme to enrich big publishers rather than a real "Newspaper Preservation Act"—began to crumble, eliminating the great newspapers of America's largest cities.[28] The final edition of *The Rocky Mountain News* rolled off the presses February 27, 2009, with the flourish of a front-page "Goodbye, Colorado" editorial that noted the paper was "just 55 days shy of its 150th birthday." It wasn't only the front page of the *Rocky* that noted the news; the story "played" on the front pages of newspapers across the country. "Part of Denver's Past, The Rocky Says Goodbye,"[29] announced *The New York Times*, which returned several days later to report, in a piece headlined "In Denver, Residents Lament the Closing of a Newspaper,"[30] a story in which only the names would need to be changed as it began to unfold in cities across the country:

> 230 members of the paper's editorial staff hastily packed up their desks and discarded files that had been meticulously kept for decades on the state's most powerful people and companies, Coloradans who had not bought a newspaper in years scoured news racks for The Rocky's last edition.
>
> "I want one for sentimental value," said Jason Perez, 36, a salesman, who said he had not subscribed to a Colorado newspaper in several years. "The Rocky has always been more integrated in the community than The Post. It's the paper that talks straight to you. The Post is the more academic and aloof observer."
>
> Chatting with neighbors at the Stapleton Starbucks, Terrance D. Carroll, a Democrat who is the speaker of the Colorado House of Representatives, said he hated that Denver would not have two fiercely competing big dailies—even if The Rocky's politics rarely squared with his.

"I'm afraid of the echo chambers that are emerging because more people are choosing to get their news only from sources that reinforce what they want to believe," he said.

The spring of 2009 would create a lot of echo chambers.

When *The Seattle Post-Intelligencer*—which had once counted Franklin and Eleanor Roosevelt's daughter, Anna, as an editor and novelists E. B. White, Frank Herbert and Tom Robbins as writers—printed its last edition on March 17, *The New York Times* ran a feature story on the symbol of the paper. The 30-foot neon globe wrapped in the slogan "It's in the P-I" that decades earlier had been placed atop the newspaper's waterfront building as a reminder that Seattle was and would always be a two-newspaper town spawned a nice headline: "In Seattle, the World Still Turns, a Beacon in Memory of a Lost Newspaper." "The Globe's long-term fate is unclear: for now, it will remain where it sits, spinning. In the end, of course, the Globe is only an inanimate object; it doesn't live and breathe, say, the way a newspaper does," *Times* writer Dan Barry gracefully noted.[31]

It fell to Ruth Teichroeb, an investigative reporter who had just lost her *P-I* job, to explain what disappears when a corporate bean counter closes the books on a living, breathing newspaper—even as its owners promise "an Internet-only news source . . . with a news staff of about 20 people rather than the 165 it had" as some kind of replacement. "The thing that's always been closest to my heart is the P-I's coverage of the underdog, people who are invisible," mused Teichroeb, eerily foreshadowing the quotes to come as the foldings of *The Tucson Citizen, The Ann Arbor News, The Claremont (New Hampshire) Eagle-Times* and historic dailies and weeklies in cities across the country made the death of individual newspapers so commonplace that they were no longer all that newsworthy. "Those people who have the least voice in society are losing access to another part of the mainstream media."[32]

Erica Smith kept the record, sticking black electronic pins in cities on her "Out of Print" map on the "Paper Cuts" site—more than 70 inserted from January 1 to November 1 of 2009, with more guaranteed to come. And she added an "industry news" feature, with headlines like "Dark

Days at the *Baltimore Sun*" and "Will Philadelphia Be the Place Where the American Newspaper Dies?"

No one had to tell Smith her site was depressing. "Trust me—I know," said the woman who on May 22, 2009, posted the news of 39 more layoffs at her own paper, the *Post-Dispatch*.

What had begun as "a curiosity" had become something painfully real. "Now co-workers, friends and other journalists and newspaper employees I know are being laid off," noted Smith. "So, as cheesy as it sounds, I do the project for them and for the working journalists."[33]

As journalists were laid off and newspapers cut back or shut down, the implications came into focus. *Editor & Publisher* published a special issue on the threat to the newsroom way back in 2007. Joe Strupp wrote,

> With thousands of job cuts in recent years, costly news coverage that includes two foreign wars, and ever-escalating demands for Web content, newspapers these days are being forced to do more with less. For some editors, that means cutting back coverage of some lower-tier stories. For reporters, it often means taking time that was once spent digging for stories or networking with sources and instead using it to crank out or update the latest Web scoop. Newsrooms are facing larger workloads, increased stress, and more hours spent in the office for the same old pay, all the while hoping that the increased demand, amid decreased help, does not result in a huge editing gaffe—or major missed story. So with newsrooms shrinking and corporate demands growing, the question inevitably must be asked, "What Gives?"

Editor & Publisher interviewed several dozen reporters and editors who described in often painful detail how the current pressures—both economic and journalistic—are affecting them.

> Some editors claim the reduced workforce and increased needs are not hurting newsrooms, just requiring better organization and planning. Others admit they have had to abandon some beats entirely, and in a few cases, eliminate whole sections—not to mention foreign bureaus—to allow for the smaller staff and online push.[34]

By 2009, the optimistic editors who had tried to find some justification for the leaner, meaner look of their newsrooms had given up on looking for silver linings; in fact, many were, themselves, looking for jobs.

Investigative journalism was first on the endangered species list; it cost a great deal and required patience and experienced journalists to be done properly. "What it takes is time and money," legendary investigative journalist Seymour Hersh explains. "I strike out one time in three." "A skilled investigative reporter can cost a news organization more than $250,000 a year in salary and expenses for only a handful of stories. Single projects can sometimes take months or even years," notes Harvard's Jones. "This kind of reporting also often means incurring legal risks and the wrath of powerful interests."[35] This is anathema for media owners in the current situation, with, at times, life-or-death implications.

In 2009, for example, the Innocence Project, the extraordinary group that uses DNA testing to free prisoners, conceded that its entire approach was imperiled. It had depended upon professional journalists having the institutional credibility and resources to do the hard digging to turn up the evidence that would qualify a prisoner to have his or her case reviewed. Since 1992, 238 people in the United States, some of whom were sitting on death row, have been exonerated of crimes through DNA testing. "It's extremely troubling; some of the leading investigative journalists in this country have been given golden parachutes or laid off," said Barry Scheck, the Innocence Project's cofounder. "When procedural mechanisms begin to fail, the press is the last resort for the public to find out the truth." Without effective journalism, it was far more difficult, if not impossible, for the Innocence Project to advance cases. The consequences can only be regarded as barbaric.[36]

The success of the broader criminal justice system is premised to no small extent upon the existence of a press system to monitor trials and battle secrecy and injustice. "For the last four decades, maybe longer, citizens have been able to rely on small, medium and large news organizations, mostly newspapers, to fight their access battles on their behalf," said Lucy Dalglish, the executive director of the Reporters Committee for Freedom of the Press. These days, such work has "dried up." A recent Supreme Court brief stated, "The days of powerful newspapers with ample budgets appear to be numbered." *The Press-Enterprise* of Riverside, Cal.—a newspaper long renowned for its campaigns to force trials to be open to the public—was so strapped for cash by 2009 that it no longer distributed free copies to its own city room employees while they were at work.[37] The lights are going out in the halls of justice.

Science journalism also met the guillotine. To a greater extent than most areas of reporting, this one requires extensive training and a rare ability to translate complex concepts into popular prose and easily understood imagery. It is also of the utmost importance for citizens in explaining essential stories about the environment, technology, energy, public health epidemics (and pandemics like the recent swine flu outbreak) and healthcare in general. When CNN eliminated its entire science, space and technology unit in 2008, the field was left almost entirely to newspapers and magazines. Unfortunately, print publications were following the CNN route. As Sabin Russell, the award-winning medical writer for the *San Francisco Chronicle*, said about his cohort when he was laid off in March 2009, "We have not left journalism; journalism has left us." When the *Houston Chronicle* laid off the space reporter who covered the Johnson Space Center (JSC) in 2009, one wag noted "there are now more people in space than there are reporters in the JSC newsroom."[38] The elimination of science beats and the abandonment of the expertise possessed by those who once worked those beats strikes a significant body blow to journalism and democracy. Even the best of the remaining (overworked) general-assignment reporters are ill-equipped to wade through the competing scientific and technical claims not only of scientists, but also of sophisticated public-relations operatives and the corporate interests they represent.

Whole sectors of our civic life, some long-neglected, some until recently well-covered, began to go dark in 2008 and 2009. Newspapers that years before had closed their foreign bureaus and eliminated their crack investigative operations began the warp-speed shuttering of their Washington bureaus. They called home, and in many cases laid off, the correspondents who had once prodded the politically powerful to answer questions from the whole of America regarding farm policy, industrial development, labor relations, higher education and all the issues that are so easily lost in the groupthink and gossip-mongering of the capital.[39] The Cox chain, publisher of *The Atlanta Journal-Constitution, The Austin American-Statesman* and 15 other papers, padlocked its D.C. bureau on April 1, 2009—a move that followed the closures of the respected Washington bureaus of Advance Publications (*The Newark Star-Ledger, The Cleveland Plain Dealer* and others); Copley Newspapers and its former flagship, *The San Diego Union-Tribune*; and the once strong regional dailies of Des Moines, Hartford, Houston, Pittsburgh, Salt Lake City, San Francisco and Toledo.

At the state level, where so many of the decisions about education, transportation and social services are made, it was just as bad. "Statehouse coverage is the bread and butter of a newspaper: unsexy and repetitive, but one of the foundations of a nutritional news diet," observed media writer Belinda Luscombe in May 2009. "But unlike bread and butter, however, it can be expensive. Reporters have to monitor long, complicated funding debates—about schools and roads and health care—many of which do not result in front-page news. Uncovering corruption, incompetence or waste takes an inordinate amount of time and effort. As newsrooms and newspapers have become smaller, coverage of state politics has been among the first to get cut."[40]

According to the *American Journalism Review*, the number of statehouse reporters in capitals across the country dropped from 524 in 2003 to 355 in 2009.[41] Forty-four states had fewer reporters covering their governments. In California, a state with a scorching budget crisis, eight of the 15 papers that had covered the capital cut back on reporting. Copley News Service, *The Bakersfield Californian* and *The Stockton Record* simply shut their bureaus. In Illinois, where the governor was impeached and removed from office as part of a scandal that made national news, six of 10 papers with capital bureaus made cuts; three papers simply closed their bureaus. In Delaware, there is just one full-time statehouse bureau reporter left. In South Dakota, there are none.[42]

Similar patterns are playing out at county-government and city-hall bureaus, where the cuts have been deep. David Simon, who left his job as a *Baltimore Sun* reporter to make television shows like *The Wire*, told the U.S. Senate in May 2009: "The next 10 to 15 years will be halcyon days for local corruption. It's going to be a great time to be a corrupt politician."[43] Princeton media historian Paul Starr makes the same point: "Goodbye to the Age of Newspapers," his piercing essay in *The New Republic* is titled, "and hello to a new era of corruption."[44] The question that demands an answer: can we allow our politicians to go unaccountable if Wall Street has decided there isn't enough money to cover the activities of our elected officials and government agencies?

Even this does not do justice to the gravity of the situation, as it may suggest to some that the problem is primarily local in character or that it is largely in front of us. In fact, we are far along on this crisis of unaccountable leadership, secrecy, corruption and hollowed-out democracy, with the news media having played all too complicit a role. This crisis is represented by industrial bailouts that receive scant scrutiny by members of Congress, let alone the voters, and wars launched on the basis of fantasy rather than fact. It both creates and responds to a demoralized and disengaged citizenry, the very existence of which is an affront to our news media and its self-image as a democratic institution. If what remains of our news media disappears or survives in flaccid form, matters will get worse, possibly much worse, but enough of the crisis is already present to make this concern anything but hypothetical.[45]

Why the Crisis?

If we are going to get out of this mess, we had better figure out how we got here in the first place. What is killing newspapers and, more broadly, all of commercial journalism as we have known it? The conventional wisdom emphasizes two factors. First, and by far the most important, is the emergence of the Internet to revolutionize communication and blow up the business model of newspaper publishing.[46]

The Internet undermines newspapers in many ways, the argument goes, and in combination they prove fatal. First, the Internet is taking away classified advertising, until recently a large source of income for newspapers. In 2000, daily newspapers received nearly $20 billion from classifieds. Even in a shrinking revenue pie, classifieds fell from 40 percent of all newspaper-advertising revenues in 1999 to 22 percent in 2009. At the present rate of decline—classified-ad revenues fell 42 percent in the first quarter of 2009—classified advertising will barely exist for newspapers in 2012.[47]

Second, the Internet has taken away readers, who can find online, for free, much of the newspaper journalism and media content they might want. A whole generation is used to getting its journalism this way . . . and not paying for it. A study by Harvard's Thomas Patterson published in 2007 determined that a measly 16 percent of Americans aged 18–30 regularly read a daily newspaper, well under half the percentage of over–30 Americans who were regular newspaper readers.[48] There is no reason to expect any of these young people to begin paying for print newspapers after they turn 30.[49] (Indeed, we are certain that updates in the years to come will document a steady decrease from 2007 levels.) The parents and grandparents of the digital generation are getting in on the act, too. This means that traditional display advertising is also jumping ship, especially since advertisers had no commitment to supporting journalism per se.

Third, the Internet is a radically less expensive means of production and distribution; once the revenues begin to fall, it is awfully hard to justify raising enormous sums simply to produce hard copies of what can be produced at a fraction of the expense online. But since you can't sell the product or make a profit online, daily newspapers are cooked.

By this logic, the fate of newspapers, and all "old media" commercial journalism for that matter, is irreversible due to the technology. It is only a matter of time. Newspapers are the horse and buggy, and the Internet is the automobile. "Newspapers are going to die," Jeff Jarvis writes. "We are undergoing a millennial transformation from the industrial, mass economy to what comes next. Disruption and destruction are inevitable."[50]

The second factor that is getting a lot of blame for what ails newspapering is the economic recession/depression. Hard times did not create a new crisis for publishers; rather, they collapsed a process that might have taken many more years into many months. Advertising tends to be a cyclical business expense; during boom times it grows faster than the economy and during slumps it comes to what seems like, to newspapers, a screeching halt. The timing could not be worse. Newspapers find their advertising revenues plummeting, and many of them have taken considerable debt to pay off the acquisitions they made in recent years, based upon assumed values for the acquired newspapers that were far greater than the values of those media today. It has been a recipe for disaster.

We examine this issue of the future of advertising and journalism in greater detail in Chapter 2; for present purposes, note that *The New York Times'* advertising revenues plunged 45 percent from 2006 to 2009.[51] In those three years, the ratio of advertising revenue to circulation income fell from 2 to 1 to 1 to 1. By the second half of 2009, in what the *Columbia Journalism Review* deemed a "landmark event," circulation revenues topped advertising income for the *Times* for the first time in the newspaper's august history. And it is not like circulation is exactly shooting through the roof.[52] The concern, probably closer to a conviction, is that when the economy finally begins to grow again—if the recovery is strong, which is a very a big "if"—many advertisers will not return to those newspapers that remain.

The economic crisis contributed to the country's great regional dailies— *The Chicago Tribune, The Los Angeles Times, The Minneapolis Star Tribune, The Philadelphia Inquirer*—all declaring bankruptcy. And the talk was no longer of restructuring papers to meet the new challenges of the 21st century; the speculators in many cases were really just interested in selling off the scrap (downtown buildings and printing plants, television stations and sports stadiums) that could be pulled from the wreckage. Even the "quality" companies were preparing to shoot the wounded. With *The San Francisco Chronicle* losing a reported $1 million a week, Hearst Newspapers talked about closing the 12th-largest paper in the country and leaving one of the nation's leading media markets without a metropolitan daily.[53] The New York Times Company, having spent far more than it could afford to buy *The Boston Globe*, briefly threatened to shutter the *Globe*, the 14th-largest paper in the country.[54]

By fall 2009 the optimists were pointing to signs that the effects of the recession were lessening and suggesting that there would soon be an uptick in advertising buys, albeit a tepid one.[55] What was striking, however, was that the same newspapers that featured headlines about economic recovery were continuing to layoff reporters. There is little sense that any significant number of news media will begin to hire back laid-off journalists; the hope is mostly that the rate of lay-offs might slow down or, in a best-case scenario, stop for a while, maybe until the next recession.

But that seems to be a false hope. Consider the recent history of the aforementioned 144-year-old *San Francisco Chronicle*, one of the nation's largest and most well-known regional dailies. In 2007, the Hearst chain that owns the paper announced that it would cut 25 percent of the remaining newsroom staff at a paper that had already been downsizing. Tom Rosenstiel, the director of the Washington-based Project for Excellence in Journalism, described that slashing of jobs as "one of the biggest one-time hits we've heard about anywhere in the country." "That's not just trimming fat, that's an amputation. That's losing a limb," added Rosenstiel, who explained that "25 percent of what goes on in the Bay Area won't be covered. It will happen in the dark..." And it just kept getting darker. In August, 2008, plans were announced to eliminate 100 more jobs. "They're cutting deep into muscle, sinew and bone now," said Newspaper Guild representative Carl Hall. By the spring of 2009, a newspaper that had started the decade with 575 newsroom employees was down to 275. It was getting even darker. Then, on September 1, 2009, *Editor & Publisher* magazine reported that *Chronicle* managers had met with Guild representatives to discuss plans for a new round of job cuts, and there were predictions that the newsroom would finish the decade with only about a third of the reporters and editors it had at the start. And if that's not dark enough, the owners of the paper were still suggesting that they might just close it down altogether—leaving, as we mentioned above, one of the nation's largest media markets without a metro daily newspaper or a newsroom sufficient in size to tell its stories.[56]

By the logic of the conventional wisdom, if the Internet had never come along and our economy was flush, newspapers and commercial journalism would be doing just fine, thank you. In fact, the evidence is very much to the contrary. Newspapers and much of commercial journalism have been in a pronounced and growing crisis for at least two decades. It is only because the crisis was not apparent in corporate profits that it received inadequate attention. What the Internet and the economic downturn have done is simply make the final push against an already tottering giant.

We should be clear: eventually the Internet and digital revolution are going to bring ink-and-paper newspapers and all traditional commercial news media to their knees. It is in the process of doing so to all major media industries, from book publishing and recorded music to radio and television.[57] But the way it is happening now, and therefore what we have to be mindful of as we address the crisis, owes significantly to the long-standing tensions in commercial journalism.

In Chapter 3 we chronicle the historical development of commercial newspaper publishing, and the strains that are built into the process. We'll discuss the origins of professional journalism, a recent development intended, in part, to make the marriage of commercialism and journalism in the public interest successful. For the purposes of this chapter, we need only to emphasize one reality about the commercial system: central to it has always been a strong tendency toward concentration—i.e., one-newspaper towns or, at best, duopolies—which produced massive profits but also a certain editorial lethargy. (As one economist puts it, "Economic theory predicts that when two opponents face off, the winning strategy for both entails their becoming almost identical."[58]) From 1904 to 1947, newspaper circulation rose 56 percent in America, with growth continuing even as radio took shape as a major force and television began to appear on the horizon. From 1947 to 1998, newspaper circulation fell 44 percent. Few doubt that television was a factor. But even before television took hold, newspapers were consolidating and sales were declining. The number of newspapers sold per person in the United States has been in decline since the late 1940s, and real circulation numbers, after remaining relatively steady from the 1950s to the 1980s, have been trending downward since 1987. Fewer Americans read a daily newspaper today than in 1950, yet the population of the United States has more than doubled.[59]

Chart 2 demonstrates daily newspaper circulation per 100,000 people from 1950 to 2008. Chart 3 demonstrates the percentage of all media advertising that went to daily newspapers from 1950 to 2009.

These charts confirm the severity of the present crisis, but they also demonstrate that the problems have been building for decades, and were already striking long before the Internet was imagined. Consider youth newspaper readership. Before the 1970s, people aged 18–30 read daily

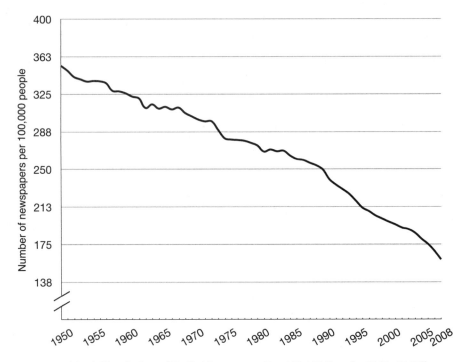

CHART 2. Total Circulation of Daily Newspapers Per 100,000 People, 1950–2008[60]

newspapers at close to the same levels as did older Americans. The percentage of under–30 newspaper readers began to fall around that time
and was a well-established fact long before the World Wide Web.[61] "The
Internet cannot be faulted for the decline in news interest by young Americans," concludes Patterson.[62] In other words, newspapers were losing
their hold on readers young and old for other reasons. The turn to radio
and television is part of the answer, of course, but that fails to explain
why many western European nations did not see similar declines.[63]

A crucial part of the answer can be found by actually looking at newspapers. Go back and read a daily newspaper published in a medium-
size American city in the late 1960s and 1970s, and you will be surprised
by the rich mix of international, national and local news coverage and
by the frequency with which "outsiders"—civil-rights campaigners, antiwar activists and consumer advocates like Ralph Nader—ended up on
the front page. Newspapers often actually exposed readers to new ideas,
different perspectives and real possibilities—as opposed to weather re-

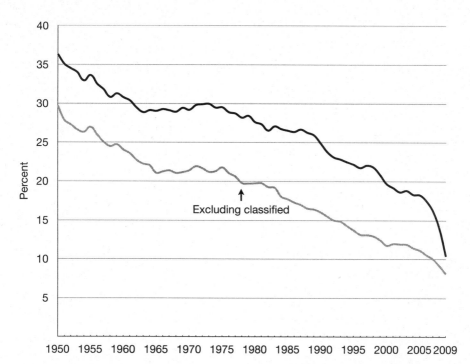

CHART 3. Percentage of All Media Advertising Going to Newspapers, 1950–2009[64]

ports, celebrity gossip, syndicated fare and exercise tips. By the early 1990s—before the Internet was a factor—the same newspaper likely would appear lifeless by comparison.[65]

What happened? The big change came in the late 1970s and 1980s, when large corporate chains accelerated the long-term trend to gobble up daily newspapers. Family owners sold for a variety of reasons and corporations came in to milk the cash cow. The corporations paid top dollar to get these profit machines, and they were dedicated to maximizing their return. They quickly determined that one way to increase profits even more was to slice into the editorial budget; in a monopoly there is little pressure to do otherwise, and with the money flowing, who has time to worry about the long-term implications? David Simon explained to the Senate in May of 2009:

When locally based family-owned newspapers like the Sun were consolidated into publicly owned newspaper chains, an essential dynamic, an essential trust between journalism and the community served by that journalism was betrayed. Economically, the disconnect is now obvious. What do newspaper executives in Los Angeles or Chicago care whether readers in Baltimore have a better newspaper, especially when you can make more money putting out a mediocre paper than a worthy one? Where family ownership might have been content with ten or 15 percent profit, the chains demanded double that and more. And the cutting began, long before the threat of new technology was ever sensed.[66]

It was then, at a point when they were still swimming in profits, that managers began to balance their books and to satisfy the demand from investors for ever-increasing returns by cutting journalists and shutting news bureaus. Stock prices built up expectations for continually massive earnings so there could be no letup, or a CEO might walk the plank. As far back as 1983, legendary reporter Ben Bagdikian warned publishers that if they continued to water down their journalism and replace it with less-expensive but also less-necessary fluff, they would undermine their raison d'être and fail to cultivate younger readers. But corporate newspaper owners abandoned any responsibility to maintain the franchise. By the late 1980s and early 1990s, prominent journalists and editors like Jim Squires, Penn Kimball, John McManus and Doug Underwood were criticizing the field and sometimes leaving it in disgust at the contempt corporate management displayed toward journalism.[67] By the end of the decade, the exodus was more like a torrent.

This point deserves elaboration. The 1990s were a period of tremendous profitability for newspapers (and broadcast networks) and of relatively rapid growth for the economy. It was also a decade of considerable population growth. The Internet was a huge deal on Wall Street but had yet to do much more than hypothetical damage to journalism business models. Yet from 1992 to 2002 the editorial side was marked by the reduction of 6,000 broadcast and newspaper jobs.[68] At the dawn of the new century, leading editors and observers were vocal, at times almost apoplectic, in their alarm at the policies that were devastating newsrooms.[69] In 2001 a team of leading journalists and scholars concluded, "Newspapers are increasingly a reflection of what the advertisers tell the newspapers some of us want, which is what the financial markets tell the newspapers they want."[70] It was clear that this was a recipe for disaster; at the least it had no long-term future.

The collapse of coverage of so many vital areas of our public life that we now recognize actually began to accelerate in the 1990s. For instance, that decade was especially devastating for science journalism. "The conglomerates had a different plan—more revenue, low cost, rising stock prices," a report on the state of science journalism observed. Between 1989 and 2005 —before the Internet-Great Recession crisis — the number of daily newspapers with weekly science section shrunk from 95 to 34. And, as the report observes, "many of the remaining sections shifted to softer health, fitness and 'news you can use' coverage, reflecting the apparent judgment that more thorough science or science policy coverage just doesn't support itself economically." The authors warn, "For a disturbing glimpse of what to expect from a media world with vastly fewer trained science journalists, we need only recount how much of the press managed to bungle the most important science-related story of our time: global warming."[71]

Bagdikian started talking about what he saw as a tipping point, where newspapers needed to start lowering profit projections and raising quality if they wanted to survive. He won a following among media critics and smart commentators, but not among media-company executives. As they measured the indicators of the implosion, former *Washington Post* executive editor Leonard Downie Jr. and *Post* associate editor Robert Kaiser put a practical spin on Bagdikian's warning: "A great news organization is difficult to build and tragically easy to disassemble."[72] But no one in the business listened because, of course, when the speculators took over it ceased to be anything but a business. The great disassembling went into full swing. By the end of the 1990s the number of foreign correspondents working for American newspapers and television networks had already been decimated, as had the number of investigative reporters.[73] (And, in 2010, 1999 really does look like the *good* old days!)

To be more concrete, consider the findings of the Project for Excellence in Journalism in 2006 on the changes in Philadelphia's journalism over the past three decades:

In some cities, the numbers alone tell the story. There are roughly half as many reporters covering metropolitan Philadelphia, for instance, as in 1980. The number of newspaper reporters there has fallen from 500 to 220. The pattern at the suburban papers around the city has been similar, though not as extreme. The local TV stations, with the exception of Fox, have cut back on traditional news coverage. The five AM radio stations that used to cover news have been reduced to two. As recently as 1990, the *Philadelphia Inquirer* had 46 reporters covering the city. Today it has 24.[74]

What that translates to is this: if we assume that *Inquirer* reporters work normal schedules, there are substantial portions of any given week when fewer than five journalists provide the primary coverage for a city of 1.4 million people. Major news stories are going untold. Vast stretches of a metropolis are being neglected. And the reporter-to-population ratio will soon worsen, as plans are implemented to cut up to 17 percent of remaining editorial jobs. More significant, as Ed Herman, professor emeritus at the University of Pennsylvania's Wharton School and an expert not just on the media but on Philadelphia, told us, the sense of civic connection that should be nurtured by a great newspaper is instead fraying. "Newspapers were once thought to bring communities together. That's not the case anymore," he said. "People aren't stupid. They recognize when their local newspaper loses interest in them as anything but consumers of advertisements."[75]

By the beginning of the 2000s newsrooms were already well into a downward spiral of demoralization. Harvard's Howard Gardner led a team of researchers that published a long-term study of journalists in 2001, finding that journalists were "overwhelmed" by the commercial pressures on their craft, and regarded contemporary journalism a "nightmare." They despaired because they were not "allowed to pursue the mission that inspired them to enter the field."[76] *The Columbia Journalism Review* published the results of a survey of TV news directors at the same time that concluded that, due overwhelmingly to commercial factors, "pessimism rules in TV newsrooms."[77]

David Simon, who holds out less hope than we do for Web-based reporting to fill the void, does not blame the Internet. "Anyone listening carefully may have noted that I was brought out of my reporting position in 1995," he explained to the Senate, adding:

> That's well before the internet began to threaten the industry, before Craigslist and department store consolidation gutted the ad base, before any of the current economic conditions applied. In fact, when newspaper chains began cutting personnel and content, the industry was one of the most profitable yet discovered by Wall Street. We know now, because bankruptcy has opened the books, that the *Baltimore Sun* was eliminating its afternoon edition and trimming nearly a hundred reporters and editors in an era when the paper was achieving 37 percent profits.
>
> In short, my industry butchered itself, and we did so at the behest of Wall Street and the same unfettered free market logic that has proven so disastrous for so many American industries. Indeed, the original sin of American newspapering lies in going to Wall Street in the first place.

When the Internet came along as a significant force, newspapers were already heading due south. And they were doing so by downsizing journalism. People, especially young people, were not irrational when they elected to stop (or never start) reading papers. The Internet only accelerated the process and gave it an inexorable logic.

The late syndicated columnist Molly Ivins reflected on the demise of her industry near the end of her life. "What really pisses me off," she said, is "this most remarkable business plan: Newspaper owners look at one another and say, 'Our rate of return is slipping a bit; let's solve that problem by making our product smaller and less helpful and less interesting'."[78] Legendary journalism professor Philip Meyer recalls how he endeavored

> …to convince the owners and managers of newspapers of the futility of cutting the quality of their products in an attempt to maintain monopoly profits after their monopoly was gone, It was an argument that might seem obvious to news-editorial people, but it was not so apparent to accountants and advertisers: that product quality is necessary for sustained profitability.[79]

Whether we can place the blame on dumb or greedy owners is irrelevant at this point. It seems more logical to blame a system that makes it rational to pursue near-term profit maximization and let some other chump sacrifice sure-thing profits to grow the readership for risky down-the-road profits. At any rate, nearly all the major news-media owners pursued the same course, so the point is moot. (In the 2009 second edition of *The Vanishing Newspaper*, Meyer concedes "that horse has left the barn. The destruction of the traditional mass-market newspaper could be irreversible."[80]) We do not doubt that if we could have replaced all the corporate-media CEOs with different people, they would have pursued essentially the same approaches, with more or less the same consequences—and if they deviated from the course, they would have lost their jobs.

The one thing we do know is that at the same time as they gutted newsrooms and dumbed down their own papers, the corporate-media CEOs were fattening their personal bank accounts big-time. Chart 4 chronicles how the ratio between the average salary of a leading news-media CEO to a reporter/editor changed from 1970 to the present, tracking the same 13 major newspaper and broadcast newsrooms across four decades, and accounting for their newer and larger corporate owners.

The colossal megadeals of 1999 and 2000 inflate the average salaries for that period, even using five-year averages. Put another way, the average media CEO salary in 1976 for the firms we tracked was $300,000. In 1986 it was $1 million. In 1996 it was $3.4 million. In 2006 it was $11.4 million. In fiscal 2009 it was $15.5 million. Had media CEO salaries risen from 1976 to 2006 at the same rate as the average salary of reporters and editors increased over those three decades, we would be living in a very different world. In that case the media CEO would have enjoyed a salary of $780,000 in 2006. It is also worth noting that the widening gap between average CEO compensation and average worker salary took place across the entire private economy during these years, though it was more severe in the news media industries since the mid 1990s. The overall average CEO-average worker compensation ratio was 29–1 in 1970, and grew to 275–1 in 2007.[81]

During this period journalism increasingly became a province of large corporations. Chart 5 demonstrates the increase in the number of Fortune 500 firms that had significant broadcast news, newsmagazine or

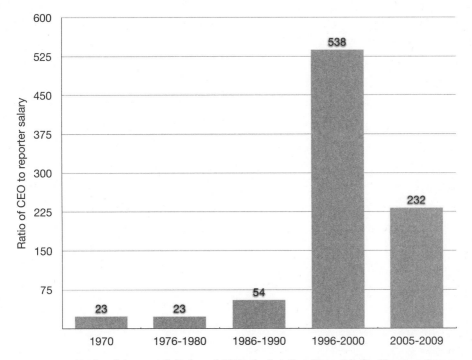

CHART 4. Ratio of Average Salaries of CEOs in Leading News Media Firms to Average Salaries of Editors and Reporters, 1970–2009 (Five-year averages, except 1970)[82]

daily-newspaper operations since 1960. The growth in the 1970s and 1980s was followed by decline and stagnation since 1990. This is a bit misleading as more firms with news media holdings rank among the 100 largest firms today than has been the case ever before.

Media conglomerates also found money to pour into campaign contributions and lobbying for federal policy shifts that would allow them to merge with competitors to have more monopoly power. The NAA and industry lobbyists have been pushing for years for the elimination of the Federal Communications Commission's newspaper/broadcast cross-ownership ban, which prohibits ownership by a single firm of a newspaper and television and radio stations in the same market. Newspaper owners argue that with the ban lifted, they could cut costs by having the same journalists produce online and print reports and appear on company-owned radio and TV news programs. In the few cities where the cross-ownership model has been tried, however, there is no evidence to suggest that it produces better journalism or a more informed public.[83] Instead

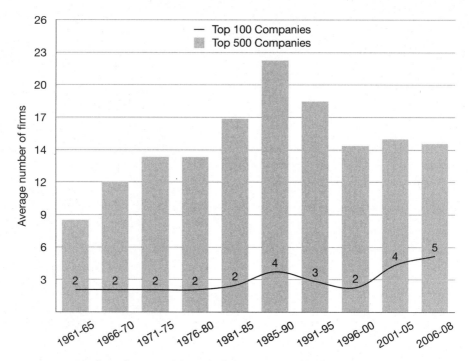

CHART 5. Number of Top 500 Firms with Interests in Broadcast News, Newsmagazines or Daily Newspapers, 1960–2008 (Five-year moving averages)[84]

it makes the few remaining reporters busier, leaving them with less time for what *Washington Post* veteran and Pulitzer Prize winner David Maraniss says is the most important work of journalism: thinking.[85]

The development of corporate newspapering undermined one of the strongest defenses of the commercial media system: that it would provide the structural independence necessary to let the press criticize the government and politicians without fear of punishment or retribution. Corporations like Gannett would boast that the larger and wealthier they became, the more leverage they had to protect the free press from the government's sword of Damocles. The evidence is now in on this argument: instead of greater independence it has created a fantastic conflict of interest. Although this "independence" claim has greater credibility for smaller private firms in competitive markets, giant monopolistic media corporations are closely tied to the government in numerous ways, and depend upon the state for policies, regulations and subsidies that directly and substantially affect their profitability. The track record shows that profits come first, and journalism finishes a distant second. We are willing to bet that for every dollar the news media–owning corporations have spent battling against government secrecy, or to support a campaign to get an independent journalist released from some foreign prison, they have spent hundreds, perhaps thousands, of dollars to bankroll politicians, produce public relations and lobby for favorable commercial regulations. So much for the independent Fourth Estate.

In the next section we discuss the long-standing tension between the editorial integrity of the newsroom and the desire of news media owners to maximize profits. In the corporate era a new twist was added to that tension: for the first time journalism was housed in enormous corporations with vast holdings across mass media and sometimes non-media sectors. There emerged patterns of periodic corporate pressure to see that news division promote the broader profit interests of the parent corporations with their myriad of holdings, even if the editorial integrity of the news operation was compromised. Sometimes this pressure leads news operations to go easy on an administration or politician the corporation needs to be on good terms with to secure the policies and subsidies it desired.[86] Exhibit A in this regard is corporate media coverage of the run-up to the invasion of Iraq in 2002 and 2003.[87] Sometimes it means going easy on some dubious venture the corporation is involved in, or otherwise assisting its chances for maximizing profits. The pressure is applied subtly; more often than not, successful editors and reporters tend to internalize the necessary values so no pressure is necessary. At other times, the pressures can be explicit.[88] The effect is that the news is altered, unbeknownst to the public, in a manner it would never had been had the newsroom been independent and freestanding.

In the summer of 2009, this problem was brought into the open by a scandal that involved some of the biggest names in cable news. News Corp. Chairman Rupert Murdoch (owner of Fox News) and General Electric Chairman Jeffrey Immelt (owner of MSNBC) reportedly agreed after a private summit meeting not to have some of their news programs criticize each other's programs and the activities of the parent corporations. Murdoch was apparently concerned that MSNBC's Keith Olbermann routinely criticized Fox's Bill O'Reilly for his casual relationship to the truth, in a manner filled with sarcasm and contempt. It is worth noting that this criticism, as far as we can tell, was almost always accurate, and Olbermann's program did much to educate viewers about what bad journalism, hypocrisy and propaganda look like. This type of blunt deconstruction of lousy journalism had been all but absent from commercial TV news prior to Olbermann. It was also popular with viewers and commercially lucrative for MSNBC. Olbermann had been one of the only commercial cable journalists to take on the Bush Administration's lies directly during the mid-decade period when most of the media was still giving the former president a pass. Along with his fellow MSNBC host Rachel Maddow, Olbermann was proving by 2009 that corporations could produce critical cable journalism without any strings attached, as long as the profits kept flowing.[89]

O'Reilly did not respond to Olbermann's criticism by defending his work, which would have possibly generated a valuable public debate over journalism. Instead, O'Reilly elected to criticize GE as an unpatriotic firm, pointing to its work in Iran, much to Chairman Immelt's displeasure. (Although General Electric warrants much more critical analysis than it receives in the news media, O'Reilly's criticism was of the opportunistic potshot variety, as far as we can tell.) Immelt's office was being flooded with criticism from irate Fox viewers —some of whom descended upon a GE shareholders meeting—which Immelt did not regard as helpful to the company. Apparently, as a result of the deal hammered out by Murdoch and Immelt, which one employee said meant "fewer headaches on the corporate side," Olbermann discontinued his frequent criticism of both Rupert Murdoch and O'Reilly's version of journalism on June 1, 2009. Likewise, Fox News employees were told to "be fair" to GE by their bosses.[90] Olbermann had criticized O'Reilly 40 times on air from February to May 2009, and had made O'Reilly one of his "worst persons in the world" 23 times. In June and July of the same year, O'Reilly received only one negative mention (on June 1) and never made the worst-persons list. Moreover, Olbermann criticized Rupert Murdoch 25 times on his program between February and May 2009, and only once in June and July. Conversely, O'Reilly went from making 27 negative mentions of General Electric during the period from February to May 2009, to making just two such remarks in June and none in July.[91]

When the scandal broke in August, Olbermann denied being party to any deal, and announced that he had elected to stop criticizing O'Reilly independent of what Immelt and Murdoch had agreed upon, though no one denied that the CEO summit meeting took place with the resulting agreement.[92] Olbermann immediately made both O'Reilly and Murdoch "worst persons" and suggested whatever deal Immelt and Murdoch had made did not include him. But the point here is not about Olbermann or O'Reilly; it is about corporate CEOs who treat journalism as a chip to be played in the pursuit of profit. It is about the corporate environment with which journalists have to contend.

We find it difficult to avoid the conclusion reached by Glenn Greenwald. "If corporations that own media outlets engage in quid pro quos to prevent critical reporting about one another, then large corporations—which own the Congress and control regulatory agencies—have no checks imposed on them at all."[93] General Electric, the top-spending corporate lobby, is an especially striking example. "The company has spent $187 million on lobbying over the past decade, 44% more than runner-up Northrup Grumman," according to a 2009 report in the *Washington Examiner*. "Why? Because no other company is so intimately tied up with government."[94] As Greenwald concludes: "Media outlets controlled by large corporations and all of their conflicting interests, not only have proven largely ineffective at serving as an adversarial check on the government, but worse, have become mindless amplifiers of government claims."[95]

What About Professional Journalism?

The logic of much of our argument to this point might suggest we are keen to return to a purported Golden Age of journalism, say, back in the 1970s, when editorial budgets were plump, journalists ruled the roost and owners were benevolent, reasonably compensated, solely concerned with journalism and civic-minded.[96] After all, this was the era when journalists brought down a crooked president, uncovered CIA crimes and exposed the dangers inherent in the nuclear energy industry. We do admire much about this period, but it was far from perfect; at the same time the mainstream press was alarmed when the Nixon administration broke laws against the

Democratic Party in Watergate, it mostly turned a blind eye to far more egregious illegal attacks on lawful antiwar, civil-rights and socialist groups. Working journalists themselves were sometimes highly critical of the field's shortcomings, exemplified in the late 1960s and early 1970s movement for "journalism reviews."[97] The truth is that there never was a Golden Age. At any rate, it would be impossible to wave a magic wand and return young readers and advertisers to the fold even if we wanted to turn back the clock.

What people generally mean when they invoke the era in the mid–1970s when Robert Redford and Dustin Hoffman were playing newsmen in the movies is that professional standards were high, and newsrooms had considerable autonomy from the interests of owners and advertisers. Former editor Alex Jones offers this nostalgic vision of newspapers in the 1970s:

> At a newspaper, the publisher is the ultimate boss, but the editor was king in the newsroom—a place that in those days most publishers treated with caution or even awe. While the publisher had the ultimate authority, to veto an important decision by the editor would have been like the president of the United States countermanding the order of a general on the field of battle. A publisher's nightmare was that the editor might quit on principle, and editors felt their strength.[98]

This situation applied not just to print news, but to broadcast as well. We believe professionalism per se has considerable merit, and will be a necessary component of a healthy journalism going forward. But we also believe professionalism has been distorted under commercial auspices—unlike Jones, apparently, even back in the "good old days"—and the record makes clear a healthy professionalism is incompatible with corporate culture. It needs a new home, and a fresh start. As we discuss in Chapter 4, this fresh start in the United States can and should borrow from the International Federation of Journalists' Ethical Journalism Initiative, which was developed by journalists and media professionals "to restore values and mission to their profession. It aims to strengthen press freedom, reinforce quality journalism and consolidate editorial independence."[99]

It is important to understand that there is nothing inevitable or "natural" about the type of professional journalism that emerged in the United States in the last century. The professional news values that came to dominate in this country were contested; the journalists' union, the Newspaper Guild, in the 1930s unsuccessfully attempted to have a nonpartisan journalism that was far more critical of all people in power, and viewed itself as the agent of people outside of power, to "afflict the comfortable and comfort the afflicted," as Dunne's saying goes. It regarded journalism as a third force independent of both government and big business, and wanted to prohibit publishers from having any control over the content of the news. As the leading history of the formation of the Guild reports: "The idea that the Guild could rebalance the power struggle between public and publisher through a new kind of stewardship of freedom of the press became a core tenet of their mission as an organization."[100] (In our view this remains a compelling vision of journalism, worthy of being a portion of a good news system, and is still practiced today by some of our best journalists.)

This practice of journalism was anathema to most publishers, who wanted no part of aggressive reporting on their fellow business owners or the politicians they routinely worked with and relied upon for their businesses to be successful. They also were never going to sign away their direct control over the newsroom; editors and reporters had their autonomy strictly at the owner's discretion. The resulting professionalism was to the owners' liking, for the most part, and more conducive to their commercial and political needs.

The core problem with professional journalism as it crystallized was that it relied far too heavily upon official sources (i.e., people in power) as the appropriate agenda setters for news and as the "deciders" with regard to the range of legitimate debate in our political culture. This removed some of the controversy from the news, and it made the news less expensive to produce. It didn't cost much to put reporters where people in political power congregate and report on what they say—certainly a lot less than it cost to send those same reporters around the world on a mission to determine whether the officials in Washington were telling the truth. This gave the news an "establishment" tone. It made reporters careful about antagonizing those in power, upon whom they depended for "access" to their stories.[101] Chris Hedges, the former *New York Times* Pulitzer Prize-winning reporter, describes the reliance on official sources this way: "It is a dirty quid pro quo. The media get access to the elite as long as the media faithfully report what the elite wants reported. The moment that quid pro quo breaks down, reporters—real reporters—are cast into the wilderness and denied access."[102] And it meant that people outside of power had less influence, or that their influence was determined to a certain extent by how people in power regarded them.[103]

This fundamental limitation of professional journalism does not manifest itself in the coverage of those issues where there is rich and pronounced debate between or within leading elements of the dominant political parties. Then journalists have a good deal of room to maneuver and professional standards can work to assure factual accuracy, balance and credibility. There tend to be fewer problems in robust political eras, like the 1960s, when mass political movements demand the attention and respect of the powerful.

The real problem with professional journalism becomes evident when political elites do not debate an issue and march in virtual lockstep. In such a case, professional journalism is, at best, ineffectual, and, at worst, propagandistic. This has often been the case in U.S. foreign policy, where both parties are beholden to an enormous global military complex, and accept the right of the United States, and the United States alone, to invade countries when it suits U.S. interests.[104] In matters of war and foreign policy, journalists who question the basic assumptions and policy objectives and who attempt to raise issues no one in either party wishes to debate are considered "ideological" and "unprofessional." This has a powerful disciplinary effect upon journalists.[105] Among other things, the genius of newsroom professionalism is that it tends to make editors and reporters oblivious to the compromises with authority they routinely make.

So it was that, even in the glory days of 1960s journalism, our news media helped lead us into the Vietnam war, despite the fact that dubious claims from the government could in many cases have been easily challenged and exposed.[106] Such, writes journalist John Pilger, was "the insidious power of the dominant propaganda."[107] A great dissident Democrat, Oregon Senator Wayne Morse, for example, broke with both his own party and the Republicans to warn against imperialistic endeavors in places such as Vietnam. His perspective, which history has shown to be accurate, was marginalized in mainstream news media. Morse recognized the lack of critical coverage and debate in the news media were undermining popular involvement in foreign policy. "The American people need to be warned before it is too late about the threat which is arising as a result of monopolistic practices (in newspaper ownership.)"[108]

Another weakness built into professional journalism as it developed in the United States was that it opened the door to an enormous public-relations industry that was eager to provide reporters with material on their clients. Press releases and packets came packaged to meet the requirements of professional journalism, often produced by former journalists. The point of PR is to get the client's message in the news so that it looks legitimate. The best PR is that which is never recognized for what it is. Although reporters generally understood the dubious nature of PR, and never embraced it, they had to work with it to get their work done. Publishers tended to love PR because it lowered the costs of production. The dirty secret of journalism is that a significant percentage of our news stories, in the 40–50 percent range, even at the most prestigious newspapers in the glory days of the 1970s, were based upon press releases. Even then, a surprising amount of the time these press releases were only loosely investigated and edited before publication.[109] It meant that powerful interests could subtly determine what was covered in the news and how it was covered.

These weaknesses of professional journalism have only been magnified in the era of supersized corporate control. Since the late 1970s, commercial pressure has eroded much of the autonomy that professional journalism afforded journalism, and that had provided the basis for the best work done over the past 50 years. It has led to a softening of standards such that stories about sex scandals and celebrities have become more legitimate, because they make commercial sense: they are inexpensive to cover, attract audiences and give the illusion of controversy without ever threatening anyone in power. Mark Willes, the controversial publisher of the prestigious *Los Angeles Times* in the 1990s, exemplified the corporate contempt for professional autonomy. He announced his intent to tear down the "Chinese wall between editors and business staffers" with "a bazooka if necessary." He appointed a business manager to see that the editorial content would conform to the best commercial interests of the corporation.[110] Willes also authorized the *Times*'s editorial staff to formally meet with representatives of the local PR community, so reporters would not have to waste time locating the proper PR agent.[111] Willes's shenanigans may represent the most extreme, and horrific, response to the challenges faced by modern newspapers. But the power of public relations is such that the PR industry—and the powerful interests it represents—really do not need pliant editors anymore.

As editorial staffs shrink, there is less ability for news media to interrogate and counter the claims in press releases. And powerful interests will be better positioned than ever to produce self-promotional "information"—better described as "propaganda"—that can masquerade as "news." The technology actually makes it easier. A major development in the past decade has been video news releases, PR-produced news stories that are often run as if they were legitimate journalism on local TV news broadcasts. The stories invariably promote the products of the corporation which funds the work surreptitiously.[112]

Often the people who move into public relations come from the ranks of journalism, thereby muddying the waters of editorial integrity that much more. With the current collapse of newsrooms, expect much more of this in the future. Journalist Richard Wolffe, for example, left his position at *Newsweek*, where he covered the Obama presidential campaign, to become a Washington D.C.-based PR agent working for major corporations in 2009.[113] Wolffe appears as an "expert" on news programs, even guest hosting programs on MSNBC, though his fulltime employment at "Public Strategies, Inc." was never mentioned, and Wolffe refused to state which firms he was advising.[114] To MSNBC's credit, Wolffe was taken off the roster once this news was publicized. But one is left to wonder why MSNBC was unaware of Wolffe's employment prior to the negative publicity.[115] Wolffe embodies the new direction of "journalism," in an era where traditional "separation of church and state" editorial integrity seems to be increasingly

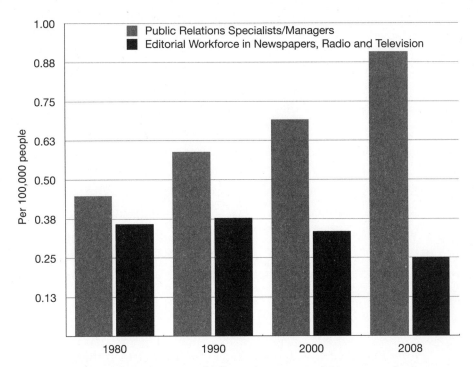

CHART 6. Estimated Employment of Editors, Reporters and Announcers in the Newspaper, Radio and Television Industries, and Public Relations Specialists and Managers Per 100,000 People, 1980–2008[116]

quaint. "The idea that journalists are somehow not engaged in corporate activities is not really in touch with what's going on. Every conversation with journalists is about business models and advertisers," Wolffe stated, recalling that, on the day after the 2008 election, *Newsweek* sent him to Detroit to deliver a speech to advertisers. "You tell me where the line is between business and journalism," he said.[117]

Chart 6 compares the number of public-relations officials with working journalists per 100,000 people from 1980 to 2008. To be clear, not all PR people work on influencing the news, but this gives a sense of the changing balance of power. And it reminds us that even as journalism shrinks, the "news" will still exist. It will increasingly be provided by tens of thousands of well-paid and skilled PR specialists ready and determined to explain the world to the citizenry, in a manner that suits their corporate and government employers.

The most important compromise is one almost never discussed: one of the central outstanding tenets of professional journalism was that it produced a product of value to the entire citizenry, that news was important to rich and poor equally and that everyone had a stake in understanding the affairs of the day. The lives of poor people and working-class people had as much value and importance as the lives of middle-class and rich people. Unless this was the case, professional journalism had at best a tenuous claim to being a democratic institution. Most people who enter journalism carry this as a core value. This value came into immediate and constant conflict with the corporate desire to create a product that appeals to the affluent consumers that are attractive to advertisers. Daily newspapers (and all of commercial journalism) have shifted decidedly to provide a product aimed at the middle and upper classes.

In the United States matters of class and race are intertwined, as people of color are found disproportionately among the poor and working class. Even at the height of the "Golden Age," the Kerner Commission highlighted how the racism of the mainstream press was a key factor in making racial segregation possible, and a peaceful resolution of legitimate grievances more difficult.[118] A constant challenge for daily newspapers has been to raise the deplorably low level of journalists of color in their newsrooms. To the industry's credit, gains had been made in the past two decades, but the present crisis threatens the recent progress. More than 42 percent of newspaper newsrooms now employ no journalists of color whatsoever.[119]

Along with commercial pressures to appeal to the middle class, a lack of class diversity, especially among those who become editors, influences decisions about what a newspaper will cover. So it is not surprising that the labor beat, a core beat in the newsrooms of midsized or large daily newspapers in the United States from the 1930s to the 1960s, had all but ceased to exist by the 1990s. Recent research by Christopher Martin demonstrates that in the 1970s coverage of labor issues shifted from an emphasis on workers to a focus on how labor-management conflicts affected "upscale" consumers.[120] Business journalism, on the other hand, skyrocketed, though the increases in resources have done little for quality, if the coverage of the financial crisis or corporate crime is any indication. The virtual blackout of coverage of the epidemic growth of prisons in the United States—putting millions of largely nonviolent offenders, mostly poor and minority, behind bars—is an indicator of where poor people register in journalism's firmament. Imagine if all those prisoners came from the upper middle class?[121] Likewise, compare coverage of the auto-industry restructuring to that of the financial industry in 2008–09.[122] Poor and working-class people are, for all intents and purposes, only newsworthy to the extent they get in the way of rich people.

Some indication of the class bias of our news media, and the basic problem before us, comes through a recent comprehensive comparative study of political knowledge by an international team of renowned scholars.[123] The rubber hits the road, so to speak, for a free press system when we measure the knowledge of its citizens. These scholars examined peer populations in Britain, Denmark, Finland and the United States, asking them a series of questions on dominant themes in the news in their nations. Their purpose was to assess how different types of media systems produce different outcomes. They found that commercial news-media systems tend to marginalize the poor and working class. We do not even need to entertain the issue of causality or correlation; the results are frightening regardless.

As Charts 7 and 8 demonstrate, the United States has an extraordinary class bias in its level of knowledge of elementary hard-news stories of import compared to the other three nations, which have much stronger public broadcasting systems.[124] If there is any consolation, it is that working-class Americans, indeed all Americans, more than hold their own when it comes to knowledge of entertainment stories and celebrity scandals.

When we put all the factors together, we are left with a situation most commentators remain reluctant to acknowledge: the general quality of journalism in the United States today is dreadful, and has been for some time. It is likely to get worse, as dire economic circumstances push commercial media firms to lessen remaining professional standards if they stand in the way of a cash infusion. There are and have been many tremendous journalists doing outstanding work over the past few decades, but

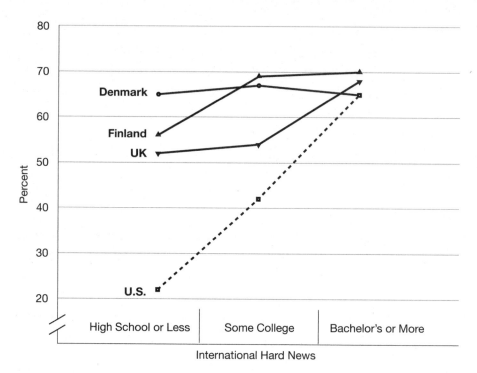

CHART 7. Comparative Survey of Political Knowledge, International Hard News[125]

they battle against a system increasingly unsympathetic, even hostile, to great journalism. The U.S. news media blew the coverage of the Iraq invasion, spoon-feeding us government lies masquerading as fact-checked verities.[126] They missed the past decade of corporate scandals in toto. They cheered on the housing bubble and genuflected before the financial sector (and Gilded Age levels of wealth and inequality) as it blasted debt and speculation far beyond what the real economy could sustain.[127] Throughout 2009 they did too little investigation into where the trillions of public dollars being spent by the Federal Reserve and Treasury are actually going, but spared not a moment to update America on the "Octomom" who gave birth to eight children. As the economy melted down and distant wars heated up, they traded in trivia in their coverage of politics and reduced everything to spin, even matters of life and death. To be frank, the list goes on and on, spurring a growth industry in media criticism. We would almost be more concerned if young people were embracing what passes for journalism today.

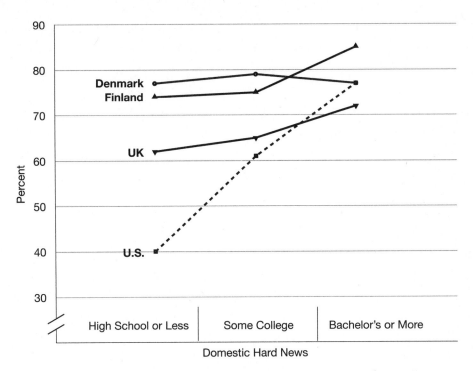

CHART 8. Comparative Survey of Political Knowledge, Domestic Hard News[128]

Now What?

If we are going to address the crisis in journalism, we have to come up with solutions that have a better chance of providing us with hard-hitting journalism that monitors people in power and who seek power; that engages all our citizens, not just the middle and upper classes attractive to advertisers; that seeks to draw all Americans into public life. Going backward is not an option nor is it desirable. The old corporate-media system choked on its own excess. We should not seek to restore or recreate it. We have to move forward to a system that promises and delivers a journalism far superior to that of the recent past. If we do, it will be a media revolution that will be part and parcel of a democratic revolution that can remake the world.

The question that should concern us is not whether we should change and improve journalism.

The question is whether we can do so with the necessary dispatch.

"What is really frightening is that newspapers appear to be dying so quickly that they may disappear, or at least disappear as a serious part of our lives, before we have a replacement for them. That's a grave danger to democracy," says Maraniss. "As flawed as journalism as practiced by newspapers is, we don't have another vehicle for journalism that picks up where newspapers leave off. That's what we should be worried about. Maybe newspapers can be replaced, probably newspapers can be replaced. But journalism can't be replaced—not if we're going to function as any kind of democracy."[129]

The very good news is that we hold the power to create exactly the great journalism our times require. We simply have to make the decision to make history rather than have it happen to us.

Kate Giammarise made the decision in the first weeks of 2009. With Angie Schmitt, another laid-off *Toledo Blade* reporter, she started rustwire.com—a "we have decided to stay" Web magazine that celebrates Toledo and the other economically battered cities of the Great Lakes "Rust Belt."

"Starting the blog was something Angie and I had talked about quite a bit before we got laid off, since we both had experiences in all these different Rust Belt cities," says Kate.

> I had grown up in Erie, lived in Pittsburgh, Cleveland, and Toledo, and my parents are from Buffalo. Angie had worked in Youngstown, and Toledo. We both saw all these cities struggling with a lot of the same problems. Yet, in a lot of ways, Rust Belt cities can be great innovators and problem-solvers. For instance, the land bank in Genesee County (Flint, Michigan) that is a national model for other areas, the shrinking city model in Youngstown, urban farming in a number of these cities, etc. So we try to share good ideas. I think we strike a good balance between being realistic about the problems our cities face, yet also being hopeful about the assets we have and optimistic about the future.[130]

Kate's being modest. The rustwire.com site she and Angie have developed is livelier, more visually appealing and more journalistic than most newspaper sites—packed with interviews, news reports and smart features on sports teams, the arts, the auto industry, buying local, local-currency movements, issues with vacant and abandoned houses, trains and old train stations, sprawl, urban farms and all things rusty and optimistic. They've interviewed *There Are No Children Here: The Story of Two Boys Growing Up in the Other America* author Alex Kotlowitz and pondered the significance of an episode of NBC's *The Office* where two of the main characters plan a wedding in Youngstown. "We've written about Milwaukee, Flint, Detroit, Toledo, Lorain, Ohio, Cleveland, Cincinnati, Erie, Braddock, and Pittsburgh, Pa, Buffalo, and also St. Louis," says Kate, who is as excited as any editor could be about the site's "Great Urban Photography Project."

Unfortunately, like most of the Web sites created by major media companies, rustwire.com is not raising enough revenue to pay the journalists. "We don't make any money on the blog," admits Kate. So she says, "My status now is still currently unemployed (since the end of December) and seeking work in the journalism field."[131]

On this one point, Kate is wrong.

Kate eventually found steady work with a trade publication, while keeping up the web site. And, whether she knows it or not, Kate *has* found work in journalism.

At rustwire.com, she's reporting and writing as well as, maybe better than, she was at *The Chillicothe Gazette*, *The Lorain Morning Journal* or *The Toledo Blade*. She is the future of journalism. Unfortunately, she's not making ends meet . . . yet. Then again, neither are the monoliths of old media.

The difference is that the old media system, the one that laid the seeds of its own destruction so long ago, the one that failed in its small-*d* democratic duties at so many turns, the one that discarded its brightest journalistic lights, is dying.

But those journalistic lights like Kate have refused to burn out. They are shining on a new media landscape that can and must be more diverse, more vibrant and more sustaining of journalism and democracy. America must find the right mechanisms for keeping those lights shining—just as it found the mechanisms to sustain the early–19th-century press that informed the citizens of a new nation. We do not diminish the difficulty of that challenge. But nor do we misjudge it. We recognize this moment as not so much one of obstacles but rather one of opportunities. Getting this right is about much more than newspapers or journalism. Getting this right is about getting America right.

America needs journalism. And it will have it in the 21st century—better and bolder than at any time since the founding of the republic.

Kate Giammarise and the tens of thousands of talented young journalists like her are committed to making it work. It is up to us to create a system where people like Kate can have a shot at being gainfully employed and Americans can have the journalism we need to be free and govern our lives.

Chapter 2

FLAWED CHOICES,
False Hopes

When Barbara Ehrenreich delivered the commencement address to the University of California–Berkeley Graduate School of Journalism Class of 2009, she did not sugarcoat things.

"You are going to be trying to carve out a career in the worst economic downturn since the Great Depression. You are furthermore going to be trying to do so within what appears to be a dying industry," she told the graduates. "You have abundant skills and talents—it's just not clear that anyone wants to pay you for them."[1]

Ehrenreich got to the nub of the crisis. It is not that newspapers and newsmagazines are imploding, nor even that traditional news bureaus and whole newsrooms are turning to dust. It is that the response to the crisis—the "where do we go from here?" message—has been so unfocused and unrealistic that the top journalism-school graduates in the nation are not even pondering how the industry they are entering can be effectively revived. They are being told by one of the ablest—and most intellectually agile—journalists of our time that she is beginning to feel "a certain kinship with blacksmiths and elevator operators."

This is not Ehrenreich's fault. Like working reporters and editors who have watched as "newspapers began to shrink within my hands or actually disappear," she's been paying attention to the various "fixes" that have been proposed. And, because journalists know what is possible and what is not, the imagined repairs inspire less in the way of hope than a "wringing of hands," a "gnashing of teeth."[2]

It is fair to say that the only thing more depressing than joining a discussion of the sorry state of American journalism is a review of the "solutions" being put forward to resolve the crisis. The use of the term *solution* to describe most of what has been proposed is misleading, or at least far too generous.

In preparing this book we made inquiries with numerous journalists and scholars from a wide range of backgrounds and political perspectives, asking for their thoughts on how journalism could be resuscitated. We read the lengthy magazine pieces, newspaper op-eds and blog postings prepared by people who, without exception, are concerned to the point of obsession with the collapse of journalism. We were struck by how flummoxed almost everyone was by the problem of journalism. There were some exceptions, generally the inveterate optimists or those promoting a personal project as the best (sometimes "only") way to get out of the woods. But few if any of the commentators are at all clear about how the current course of relying upon the market, new technologies, micropayments or macrodonations, Yankee ingenuity, volunteer labor and/or philanthropic largesse will generate a sufficient quantity or quality of journalism for self-government to survive.

This dilemma was demonstrated in 2009 when two major books were published—Alex Jones's *Losing the News* and Phil Meyer's second edition of *The Vanishing Newspaper*—that addressed the journalism crisis with the same urgency this book does. Although both books were long on astute critique and justified despair, they were short on credible solutions. Each ultimately fell back on a plaintive hope that the market would again reward people doing good journalism to replace at least some of what is being lost. "I think a commercial answer is the only enduring one," Jones concluded, arguing that as long as newspapers continue producing news they will be able to survive and possibly even prosper in the emerging marketplace. Meyer made a similar argument, saying the market will reward publishers who continue to produce news as long as they are willing to settle for less profit than they basked in during their long monopoly era. As far as we can see, their continued embrace of the market is based more on wishful thinking and a lack of alternatives they consider worthy of consideration than it is on any compelling evidence.[3] Even if some commercial news media survive (and possibly prosper) doing some aspect of journalism, that is a far cry from saying the market can provide the level and caliber of journalism our governing system requires. In their best case scenario, we remain mired in crisis.

In this chapter we review the leading ideas, as far as we can determine, being offered for rejuvenating journalism. Some, probably most, of these plans require—or, at the least, would benefit from—government policy changes, and all of them are based upon some assumption of necessary government policies. As Todd Gitlin says, "In the end, it is public policy and only public policy that will determine what kind of journalism survives."[4]

That being said, what distinguishes the proposals we will review in this chapter is that all of them, in keeping with the understood "American" position, minimize the role of government as much as possible and require no direct public funding. The shared premise of all these plans is that government involvement is bad, and significant government involvement is worse than the problem such intervention seeks to solve.[5]

The first ideas we discuss are those put forward by the corporate news media, and address ways in which their business model and their dominance can be extended into the digital era. The second group of ideas comes from those willing to concede that the "old media" are doomed, but who see the solution coming from some combination of new technologies and the market. They are from the "everything will be alright as long as we are patient" school of thought. This may well be our default approach, so we review the most promising Web-journalism ventures to see how effective a Web-journalism world looks. In our view, however, the weakness in all these approaches is the failure to appreciate journalism as a public good, so we end the chapter on that point.

Salvaging the Corporate News Media

We should repeat one point made in the previous chapter: as depressing as the corporate-news-media business model is, not everyone is going broke, at least not yet. Some daily newspapers are holding up decently, as are some weeklies. More than a few newspapers still operate in the black, and will continue to do so for years, perhaps many years, to come. "Except for some relatively special instances, newspapers are still making money that is the envy of other businesses—short of drug dealing and prostitution," Frank Denton, the vice president for journalism with Morris Communications, claimed in May 2009.[6] That's an overstatement, which could raise questions about how much Denton knows about drug dealing—or newspapering. But the veteran editor is right that, after shuttering bureaus, laying off reporters, hacking away at the physical size of publications that were once thick and rich with content and decreasing distribution in low-income and rural areas, the carcasses of many newspapers can be dragged into the black. The problem is that what remains after all the slashing and burning is not appealing enough to keep readers or attract advertisers. In fact, Denton made his comments at a conference with the not particularly hopeful title "How Newspapers Could Have Saved Themselves and How Some Still Can."[7]

There's something to the argument that a strong economic recovery could do wonders for the bottom lines of some newspapers in the near-term. But the trend line is clear, as we discussed in Chapter 1, and the rare success stories are going against the tide of history. *Slate* founding editor Michael Kinsley, an otherwise thoughtful commentator on the changing media landscape, got it precisely wrong when he claimed early in 2009 that "When the recession ends, advertising will come back" to newspapers.[8] Bob Garfield, editor at large of *Advertising Age* and cohost of NPR's *On The Media*, looked into the future of advertising in newspapers and reached the more realistic and—at least among serious observers—increasingly accepted conclusion that when all is said and done "Newspapers die, or they survive as the wispiest shadows of their former selves."[9] It is clear that those elements of traditional commercial news media that remain successful are not going to come remotely close to

providing the whole range of journalism that commercial firms once delivered, and that our society requires if it is to be even minimally democratic in character.

A news-media bailout—along the lines proposed in January 2009 by
French President Nicolas Sarkozy for his country's battered print press—
is frankly, and appropriately, in conflict with the understanding most
Americans maintain with regard to an independent news media.[10] Having
the government write checks directly to the handful of profit-driven firms
that dominate the news media is a nonstarter. And, to our view, that is
the way it should be. Pumping money into the bank accounts of media
corporations owned by speculators simply rewards the people at the helm
of a system that made irresponsible, anti-journalistic choices in the past
and is now "addressing" them by laying off reporters and editors and
shutting newspapers.

If direct bailouts, leading to permanent direct subsidies, of the corporate news media are off the table, then what are the options of those publishers that want to continue producing anything akin to journalism? The
immediate impulse of the owners of struggling newspapers has been to
beg to have existing antitrust laws waived, so that publishers can collaborate in the development of monopolistic arrangements in particular
cities and regions and set up national combines that will make it easier
to begin charging for content online. The Hearst Corporation, owner of
the ailing *San Francisco Chronicle*, got House Speaker Nancy Pelosi, who
represents the city, to advocate its interests along these lines in March
2009. In a letter to Attorney General Eric Holder, Pelosi argued that antitrust laws should not prevent rival regional newspapers from exploring
mergers and consolidations. "We must ensure that our policies enable
news organizations to survive and to engage in the newsgathering and
analysis that the American people expect," the Speaker asserted.[11] The
Justice Department was unimpressed, rejecting Pelosi's request in April:
"We do not believe any new exemptions for newspapers are necessary,"
Carl Shapiro, an assistant attorney general for economics, told a House
hearing on the subject.[12]

"Newspapers play a vital role in our society," Shapiro acknowledged
in a statement prepared for members of the House Judiciary Committee's

subcommittee dealing with competition issues, who had organized their hearing under the title "A New Age for Newspapers: Diversity of Voices, Competition and the Internet." "The Antitrust Division continues to work to protect competition in the newspaper industry," the top antitrust lawyer continued. "We believe that antitrust analysis is forward-looking and flexible enough to take into consideration the economic and technological pressures facing newspapers as we continue to make market-by-market and case-by-case factual determinations pursuant to the antitrust laws. Vigorous antitrust enforcement will guarantee that this important industry will be as competitive as possible, and that American consumers will have available to them more, rather than fewer, options for getting news and information."[13]

That's the right response to the question. If anything, the federal government has been too lax in applying classic antitrust standards to media industries. The last thing that's needed at this point is more consolidation of news gathering and delivery.

Likewise, media companies continue to push to have the ban on "cross-ownership" relaxed or eliminated.[14] This Federal Communications Commission rule prevents a single company from owning daily and weekly newspapers and broadcast stations in the same community. Despite claims by media companies that the relaxation of cross-ownership rules would make it easier to sustain news-gathering operations, all evidence indicates that this sort of consolidation leads to downsizing. Indeed, as the Benton Foundation notes in its assessment of the push by major media companies for an easing of cross-ownership constraints:

> The idea is to offer a host of avenues for advertisers to reach consumers— those consumers are surrounded by different points of contact: the radio or TV as they prepare for and get to work, billboards along the way, on the Internet as people surf instead of working, in newspaper ads as they take a coffee break, in magazines in the restroom and so forth.[15]

A number of major cities—including Chicago, where the *Tribune* owns the WGN broadcast radio and television stations—had existing cross-ownership structures "grandfathered in" when the regulations were developed, and waivers have been granted in other communities. As such, we have a good sense of the dangers inherent in this one-newsroom, company-town approach.[16] In view of the evidence that concentrated media ownership in local markets has been a significant contributing factor to the decline in the number of working journalists in these communities, relaxing local-ownership rules has been an unpopular move with the great mass of people who are not affiliated with a media company that would benefit by local monopoly.[17] As the Benton Foundation and the Social Science Research Council argued in 2006, when they released four independent academic studies on the impact of media consolidation in the United States, "These studies make clear that media consolidation does not correlate with better, more local or more diverse media content. To the contrary, they strongly suggest that media ownership rules should be tightened not relaxed."[18]

Unfortunately, sound science could not trump serious lobbying when industry-friendly Republican appointees controlled the FCC. The commission very quietly relaxed the cross-ownership rule in December 2008, during the last days of the Bush administration. The matter went to the courts, however, and the new Democratic-controlled FCC has informed the judges that it no longer supports relaxation of the cross-ownership rules.[19]

When big media firms lobbied the FCC, they argued that if one company could own the daily newspaper plus multiple radio and television stations in a community, it would have the scale and resources to provide a first-class newsroom—or perhaps even *newsrooms*—to serve all of its media outlets. At best, however, this might salvage a few jobs for a brief period, while the lack of competition would lead inevitably to strong commercial pressure to continue to reduce staffing. And broadcasters, especially broadcast news operations, are suffering almost as much as newspapers, as we discussed in Chapter 1. Even with cross-ownership, the revenues are still not there to subsidize large news operations. Thus, the relaxation of the rules in markets where they are still in place would be tantamount to giving a person with terminal lung cancer a carton of cigarettes to smoke so she can keep puffing on her deathbed. Once a high priority of the industry, efforts on behalf of these sorts of changes have become more halfhearted of late; savvy players in commercial media industries understand that scrapping antitrust laws for these purposes and relaxing cross-ownership rules, even if politically possible, will do little to solve their problems; at best, changes of this kind amount to stays of execution.

This is not a controversial point. In June 2009 Moody's Investor Service issued a report stating the traditional ink-and-paper daily newspaper was no longer commercially feasible. As Moody's pointed out, only 14 percent of the industry's budgets went to producing content, 16 percent went to advertising sales, and 70 percent went to printing and maintaining the old-media infrastructure and corporate expenses. Moody's advised newspapers to dump the old-media expenses so they could increase the portion going to content creation. In other words, to have a future, newspapers need to head online and fast. But even if that happens, Moody's is anything but optimistic, warning that there is likely to be additional downward pressure on the industry's credit ratings.[20]

Moody's reached the same conclusion as everyone else. The most proactive campaign being waged by corporate media owners now is focused on the now four-decade-long struggle to recreate a successful business model for providing journalism online.[21] Ever since the British Broadcasting Corporation (BBC) began in 1969 to test the interactive media format known as "videotext" —which transmitted text and graphics using a telephone, a modified television set and keyboard—the game has been afoot. American newspapers started going online in the summer of 1980, and San Francisco's KRON television began a report several months later with an anchor musing, "Imagine, if you will, sitting down to your morning coffee (and) turning on your computer to read the day's newspaper. Well, it's not as far-fetched as it may seem."[22] *The San Francisco Examiner*'s David Cole is quoted in the report saying, "This is an experiment. We're trying to figure out what it's going to mean to us as editors and reporters and what it means to the home user."[23]

Newspaper publishers and editors are still trying to figure out what it's going to mean. But some questions have been answered. "We're not in it to make money," explained Cole back in 1981. "We're probably not going to lose a lot, but we aren't going to make much either."[24] In fact, media companies would lose a lot. One of the biggest, Knight Ridder, would sink $50 million into Viewtron, a pioneering videotext news project that allowed subscribers to read *The Miami Herald* and other publications on their computers. It was launched in 1983 and folded in 1986, around the same time that the Times Mirror Company scrapped a similar initiative. "Viewtron's dream was very similar to the dreams of news media publishers today: new ways of communicating with customers and new ways of selling services to advertisers," recalls Howard Finberg, a veteran journalist and online pioneer who now directs the Poynter Institute's News University.[25]

The news-media publishers are still dreaming of making money online. And, for the most part, they are still, as one videotext pioneer put it, "dancing naked on the stage of history."[26] Translation: They continue to make the same mistakes, still laboring under the same misconceptions about journalism and the Web, and the same misguided motives, which fostered the failures of their predecessors a quarter century ago. And they are still experiencing "real losses" of money on a scale sufficiently "substantial" to frighten drunken sailors as they stumble around the Internet looking for sources of revenue.[27]

Even when a lesson seems to have been learned, it is unlearned in a moment of desperation. For instance, for much of the past decade it was accepted that few people would pay for content online; there was too much free material to get people to pay for anything unless it was of recognizable, perhaps even unique, value—as distinct from the genuine but less easily commodified value of the information contained in standard journalism. (Accordingly, *The Wall Street Journal* and *Consumer Reports*, with their specialized content, are among the very few old-media publications that have successfully developed Web-subscription models.) So, though many of them came to the "choice" kicking and screaming, newspapers and commercial broadcast-news organizations had learned by the mid-2000s to put much—in many instances, *all*—of their journalism online, making it available at no charge. This has allowed some U.S. newspapers to be pioneers in digital journalism—although it is generally agreed that the most important innovators have been the Web sites of British newspapers, especially *The Guardian* and *The Telegraph*, and Norwegian papers such as *Aftenposten* and *VG*—and they have done far more on the Internet than merely posting print material.[28] The hope on the part of the most sincere publishers and editors was to create Web sites of quality and then to have advertising shift over to support journalism on the Web as it had done for more than a century of old media. This project has had a small measure of success—just enough to keep the dreamers "dancing naked on the stage of history." U.S. newspaper sites had 67 million unique visitors per month, generating over $3 billion in advertising revenue in 2008.[29]

While the numbers cited with regard to newspaper advertising revenue in 2008 may sound good, the truth is that three billion dollars is a pittance for the entirety of newspaper publishing, and well below the cost of operations. Moreover, online ad sales are not growing at an appreciable rate; they even declined in the fourth quarter of 2008, and the first quarter of 2009.[30] This stagnation is due primarily to the recession, but by nearly all accounts, the future growth of advertising on news Web sites is not going to increase sufficiently to make a smooth transition from print to digital plausible. A writer for the *Columbia Journalism Review* came to the same emphatic conclusion in July 2009. "The key thing to take away from these numbers," Ryan Chittum wrote in a review of newspaper advertising data, "is this: Internet ads will not save newspapers. Say somebody cracks the code on Internet advertising in a few years, making it much more lucrative than it currently is. Great, but that will be too late for most newspapers."[31]

After digesting the many failed efforts to secure online advertising, the Project for Excellence in Journalism in early 2009 formally declared the initiative dead: "[It] is now all but settled that advertising revenue—the model that financed journalism for the last century—will be inadequate to do so in this one."[32]

Advertising was never wed to journalism per se; it used newspapers and newsmagazines and later radio and television news programs because they were the most efficient way to reach desired audiences. The relationship was simply a fluke of historical coincidence, as Clay Shirky points out:

> where Wal-Mart was willing to subsidize the Baghdad bureau ... (this) wasn't because of any deep link between advertising and reporting, nor

was it about any real desire on the part of Wal-Mart to have their marketing budget go to international correspondents. It was just an accident. Advertisers had little choice other than to have their money used that way, since they didn't really have any other vehicle for display ads.

All that has changed:

(W)hen Wal-Mart, and the local Maytag dealer, and the law firm hiring a secretary, and that kid down the block selling his bike, were all able to use that infrastructure [the Internet] to get out of their old relationship with the publisher, they did. They'd never really signed up to fund the Baghdad bureau anyway.[33]

In short, there is no particular reason or need for advertisers to support news or public-affairs Web sites to reach desired demographics. Newspaper Web sites are competing not just with each other but with all other Web sites that seek advertising; this is putting extraordinary downward pressure on ad rates, far beyond anything newspapers are accustomed to experiencing.

This competitive pressure also means businesses do not simply want exposures, they want "click-through" sales off their Web advertisements. In the world of the Internet, advertising is changing and the traditional sponsorship of editorial content is less prevalent. As one advertising executive puts it, "Are they really attracting the right customers, are the customers clicking through and providing decent leads and sales?" "If your newspaper's subscriber is so great," another advertising executive put it, "they should be able to deliver terrific marketing results for me." He added: "Let's create a revenue share agreement based on the results you produce. You get upside, we get upside, and let's all kind of walk the talk." Yet another executive said that newspapers should demonstrate that their ads work at or above industry norms.[34] Language like this suggests that even in the extremely unlikely event advertising did flood newspaper Web sites, it might exact such a high toll on the integrity of the journalism that the crisis would not go away, it would simply assume a different, and possibly more noxious, form.

This does not mean news Web sites, or any Web sites for that matter, are abandoning advertising revenues; it merely means that advertising revenues will not be sufficient to provide anywhere near the resource base for the level of journalism found in the old media, or even for a modest commercial news medium to pay its bills as it shifts online. Chris Elliott, the managing editor of Guardian News and Media in Britain, which maintains the highly regarded and highly trafficked news Web site guardian.co.uk, says advertisers have settled into patterns of paying about one-third as much for an online ad as compared with a print ad in the *Guardian* newspaper and explains, "That's just not enough to make *it* work."[35]

The "it" Elliott refers to is quality journalism, produced by experienced writers and editors who are compensated fairly—or, at least, paid a living wage—for their work. This veteran reporter who has become a cutting-edge thinker with regard to new media—and one of the Web's most respected innovators—has grown skeptical about the prospect that advertising is going to support quality, or perhaps even basic, journalism on the Web. "It's not happening," Elliott explained in June 2009. "Until about six months ago, we had people saying, 'It will. It will.' Now, that's shifting to, 'It won't. It won't.'"[36]

Why? Newspapers and television and radio stations sold access to a product people wanted. The ads fit around the news and entertainment. And advertisers wanted to get close to where the action was. The precious "real estate" of old media was limited, and could attract top dollar. There is no such scarcity on the World Wide Web. In fact, it is limitless, as are the prospects for businesses to reach consumers—often directly.

This "chaos scenario," as Bob Garfield describes it, means that old notions about linking advertising to news and entertainment are going out the window. "There is no longer a need to warn of a gathering Chaos Scenario, in which the yin of media and yang of marketing fly apart, symbiotic no more," argues Garfield. "Nudged by recession, doom has arrived."[37]

"They don't call it a digital revolution for no reason," explains the writer of *Advertising Age*'s "Ad Review" column. "A revolution leaves blood on the streets." The proliferation of Web pages—a "bazillion," by Garfield's count—makes it impossible to offer the old "precious real estate" to advertisers and creates the likelihood that they will quickly go elsewhere in search of a constantly moving audience. It's a race to the bottom and, Garfield says, the bottom line is that Internet advertising does not appear to be effective. "Have you clicked on a banner ad? Ever? In your life?" he asks. "Nobody else has."[38] In fairness, some people have so clicked, but as Mira Milosevic, deputy director of development for Press Freedom and Development Programs at the World Association of Newspapers, points out, "When they do click, they are leaving the newspaper Web site and going someplace else. They are leaving the newspaper site. And, of course, we worry about whether they will come back."[39]

The notion that they won't, and the broader notion that advertising won't pay for journalism on the Web, is beginning to dawn on enlightened—or, perhaps, just scared—publishers. The old theory about news-oriented Web sites and advertising, says Brian Tierney, who organized the purchase of *The Philadelphia Inquirer* and the *Philadelphia Daily News* by a group of local investors and is now trying to make a go of it, was "If you build it, they will come." But Tierney now admits, "I don't think it is working for media like ours ... I think we're going to have to start to find a way to charge for it and not just rely on advertising."[40]

With that in mind, many of the key players in the corporate news media suddenly reached the conclusion in 2009 that they needed to defy the culture of the Internet and charge consumers directly for their content on what most of us still imagine as a freewheeling World Wide Web. As AP president and CEO Tom Curley put it:

> The readers and viewers are going to have to pay more. Advertising is not there. Advertising will likely be contracting. So there has to be a shift. If I had tried to suggest this a couple of years ago, I'd be hollered out of the room. Last year the realization started to occur. I would say the conversation has now turned from a whisper into a roar. Media CEOs are saying, 'I've got to charge.'[41]

On May 28, 2009, the Newspaper Association of America convened a secret summit meeting in Chicago of nearly all the newspaper industry's corporate heavy hitters, including the AP's Curley, to map out strategies for selling their content online.[42]

To hear them speak, this makes perfect sense. After all, it costs money to produce their journalism, and people should be willing to pay for it if they wish to read it and use it. Otherwise, the journalism will cease to exist. Put that way, it is a no-brainer. As Frank Rich explains, "The real question is for the public, not journalists: Does it want to pony up for the news, whatever the media that prevail?"[43]

That was enough for NewsCorp's Rupert Murdoch, who announced in August 2009, that, "We intend to charge for all our news Web sites."[44] Murdoch warmed the hearts of at least some old-school journalists when he declared that: "Quality journalism is not cheap, and an industry that gives away its content is simply cannibalising its ability to produce good reporting." But there is little reason to believe that Murdoch has unlocked the secret to making money on the web. In fact, it looks as if he is making a desperate stab in the dark. Murdoch's biographer, Michael Wolff, is especially dismissive of the move, observing that, "His uphill fight is probably even greater than it might appear. Not only is he, among all media executives, the most technically disinclined (actually, totally illiterate), but his company, of all the big media enterprises, is the most technically backward and maladroit. He may now employ more reporters than anyone else in the world, but they use the oldest computers. He may have some of the world's most trafficked news sites, but they are also the slowest and most inept."[45]

Murdoch was not alone. The concept of charging for content took hold during the summer of 2009, as newspapers that had long resisted charging started to look for ways to do so. Usually, they tried to suggest that those who paid would get something more; An *Editor & Publisher* report in September, 2009, on a move by the Pittsburgh Post-Gazette to start charging, quoted editor David Shribman saying of his paper's "PG+" project: "It is like a publishing company putting out a new magazine, a new product. We were always selling chocolate and vanilla [the print and free online versions]. Now we are also selling strawberry."

"But will people pay for the extra flavor?" *E&P* asked.[46]

Don't bet on it. Despite what Murdoch, Shribman and other old media stalwarts may be telling themselves there is little or no evidence to suggest that the strategy of charging for content will work.

The corporate news media will quickly be reminded why they could not get an online pay-for-content scheme working back in the 1990s. "Somewhere at Microsoft, there is a closet packed with leftover Slate umbrellas—a monument to the folly of asking people to pay for what they read on the Internet," recalled the bemused former *Slate* editor Michael Kinsley as the talk of pay models ginned up early in 2009.

> These umbrellas—a $20 value!—were the premium we offered to people who would pay $19 for a year's subscription to Slate, the Microsoft-owned online magazine (later purchased by *The Washington Post*). We were quite self-righteous about the alleged principle that 'content' should not be free. The word itself was an insult—as if we were just making Jell-O salad in order to sell Tupperware. The experiment lasted about a year. Still, every so often the dream of getting people to pay recurs.[47]

The promoters of pay-for-content strategies face the same—and perhaps greater—challenges now than those Kinsley and the presumably Web-savvy folks at Microsoft did back in the "ancient" 1990s. For starters, unless a critical mass of newspapers and news providers participate in the proposed "paywall" scheme, their chances of success are slim or none. Why pay newspaper X for its online content if newspaper Y and TV news network Z are putting theirs up for free? But let's assume, for sake of discussion, that the promise of revenues will be enough of a lure to attract all commercial news media to adopt a "paywall" system. This is, after all, what no less an industry leader than Rupert Murdoch imagines will be the case. Murdoch says an Internet pay system for his newspaper empire will be in place by May 2010, declaring with his usual bravado: "The current days of the Internet will soon be over."[48]

Fair enough, so let's try and follow Murdoch's "logic." For the News Corp. boss to be right, media companies will have to forge a cartel that would require the mother of all antitrust exemptions to go forward. To get it will require a huge political fight. Industry lawyers and lobbyists are already priming the pump.[49] In classic form, and with no sense of irony, corporations will demand government intervention to protect their interests, all the while decrying government intervention. But the response on Capitol Hill has not been enthusiastic; indeed, when a subcommittee of the House Judiciary Committee discussed antitrust matters as they relate to newspapering and the Web in April, the two things that united dueling members—from progressive Democrat John Conyers of Michigan to conservative Republican Lamar Smith of Texas—were a frustration with existing media and a concern that media conglomerates were trying to use the current crisis as an excuse to further consolidate and harmonize their content. In other words, there was not a lot of sympathy on display. "Continuing the consolidation of newspapers may contribute to increasingly biased coverage," griped Smith. Conyers, recalling that he was arrested once while protesting cuts at Detroit's two daily newspapers, said, "Newspapers remind me of automobile corporations. [They refuse to respond to their communities and then] all of a sudden they need help—they need a lot of help, and they need it fast."[50]

The skepticism was well founded. Easing antitrust restrictions—effectively eliminating protections for consumers—is a wrong approach for newspapers and the 'Net. Indeed, as Aidan White, general secretary of the International Federation of Journalists, says, "The auto industry does not get to remove the seatbelts from cars because the numbers went bad for a quarter, or because they have to come up with new models."[51]

The genius of the Internet is that it is open and accessible to everyone, and creates a democratization of information. The last thing we should want to do is convert the Internet into cable television, and turn our computers into vending machines, defined most by the electronic barbed wire saying "Keep Out." That takes the Internet in exactly the wrong direction, aggravating class inequalities and shutting down innovation. It is a desperate and shortsighted "solution" to a problem that demands a wise and long-term solution.[52]

Moreover, there is little reason to believe that a paywall system could actually work with consumers. What the media corporations "want to do is to pretend that the last 15 years never happened, and that the survival of the industry will be found by 'protecting' content behind walled gardens," Arianna Huffington testified before the U.S. Senate in May 2009. "We've seen that movie—and consumers gave it lousy reviews."[53] And we probably don't need to mention the hackers, who would zero in on those sites that try to wall off content with a determination that would make bootleggers during the Prohibition era look like champions of the temperance movement.

Even if the paywall proponents manage to get all commercial news media to participate, there will still be a wealth of noncommercial material or unaffiliated Web sites online that will provide news and commentary at no charge. This will either undermine the paywall system, or put the paywall system in constant warfare with the non-paywall Internet. In Britain, for example, a media executive acknowledges that the presence of the BBC makes charging all but impossible: "You basically have a fully funded and publicly funded news organization on your doorstep. How can you compete with that?"[54] The answer is clear: the only option for advocates of the paywall is to lead a campaign to eliminate quality free content—i.e., smash public media or reduce it to rubble.

Even more striking, the paywall concept basically destroys the interlinked news blogosphere, where bloggers embed links to other stories and video and drive traffic to news Web sites. It is that feature of the Web that may be its most tangible and revolutionary contribution to our journalism to date, and attacking it would undermine one of the most exciting aspects of the Web for democrats: the ability of an aggregator such as CommonDreams.org to pull together articles from a variety of different perspectives at the same site and then encourage citizens to follow links out into, literally, a world of inquiry.[55] Much of this is done on noncommercial Web sites that make no profit from the material to which they link.[56] This is what works best about the Web; and to position newspaper Web sites against it would be another example of old media's long and fruitless struggle against the future. Moreover, there is the entire question of fair use, and what people are entitled to use for free without permission under copyright. To enact the "paywall" system would basically sabotage the Internet, necessitating a virtual police state to see that there are no unauthorized infringements on the content of the paywall-cartel members.[57] A few months of this living hell and most people will wish the computer had never been invented.

Experts who study the matter say that even if all of the problems we have outlined could be addressed, the paywall system still would not work. When news media charge online their traffic falls sharply and their advertising revenues plummet. There is no endgame that gets the corporate media firms anywhere near a zone where they have large newsrooms providing journalism online and are making sufficient profit to remain in the news business.[58] No matter how one does the math, there is a negative gap between revenues and expenses. Michael Kinsley breaks the numbers down with brutal precision:

> Micropayment advocates imagine extracting as much as $2 a month from readers. The Times sells just over a million daily papers. If every one of those million buyers went online and paid $2 a month, that would be $24 million a year. Even with the economic crisis, paper and digital advertising in The Times brought in about $1 billion last year. Circulation brought in $668 million. Two bucks per reader per month is not going to save newspapers.[59]

So, once again, the money is not there for journalism. The pressure to cut expenses heightens, online reporters and Web editors get laid off and the "product" declines, traffic disappears, advertisers lose interest. With micropayments, the daily-newspaper death dance simply goes digital.

The naked and uncomfortable truth is that the business model that sustained commercial news media for the past century is dying, and cannot be recreated. Former *Chicago Tribune* managing editor James Warren concludes that "attempting to create the past model, in which media entities were owned by publicly traded companies, would probably be a mistake."[60] Bob Garfield is more aggressively dismissive. As they stumble about the Internet, old-media companies keep chanting "the mantra: 'We have the audience. All we need is a business model.' As if adequate revenue were somehow guaranteed by physics or heavenly deity," writes Garfield. "It isn't. I've pored over Isaac Newton and the Ten Commandments. There is no 'Thou shalt monetize.'"[61]

That does not mean we will not have commercial media, or that we will not have advertising in our news media. It means that such media will be a diminished, perhaps unrecognizable, piece of the news-media puzzle, rather than defining the entirety of it, as has been the case for much of the past century. We can be certain that the powerful corporate-media lobbies will use their immense leverage in Washington to advance their interests regardless of the cost for society, seeking antitrust exemptions and other rule changes to benefit their bottom lines. But these are the people who have gotten almost everything wrong for the past several decades—economically, technologically, journalistically. If we try to humor the corporate chieftains, and let them remain the centerpiece of our news-media system, we will have a minuscule and pathetic journalism to show for it.

The Internet Is the Solution

A second "alternative" response to the current crisis accepts that commercial news media and their system of journalism are dying, and regards this turn of events as unavoidable and, for the most part, desirable. To this way of thinking, the same technologies that its adherents regard as so central to undermining the commercial news system will provide the basis for what replaces it. In general, this is an optimistic perspective based upon an understanding of the Internet and digital technologies as democratizing communication, lowering costs and inviting revolutionary innovations.[62] Many, though not necessarily all, of the advocates of this perspective see the role of the government as being primarily a damaging one: supporting the incumbent corporate players, to provide "bailouts," if you will, and generally mucking things up. Government is identified as a reactionary force, its interventions as destructive.

Clay Shirky, an NYU adjunct professor who is also a consultant to businesses and nonprofit groups on digital matters, has made one of the strongest and most acclaimed arguments along these lines. His 2009 essay, "Newspapers and Thinking the Unthinkable," argued that the impending demise of the newspaper industry and commercial journalism was evident by the mid-1990s.[63] "People committed to saving newspapers," Shirky notes, were "demanding to know 'If the old model is broken, what will work in its place?' To which the answer is nothing. Nothing will work. There is no general model for newspapers to replace the one the Internet just broke." "This is what real revolutions are like," he added. "The old stuff gets broken faster than the new stuff is put in its place."

Shirky concedes the importance of journalism, and believes the Internet and free markets will solve the problem, but he cautions patience:

> Nothing will work, but everything might. Now is the time for experiments, lots and lots of experiments, each of which will seem as minor at launch as craigslist did, as Wikipedia did, as *octavo* volumes did ... In the next few decades, journalism will be made up of overlapping special cases ... Many of these models will fail. No one experiment is going to replace what we are now losing with the demise of news on papers, but over time, the collection of new experiments that do work might give us the journalism we need.

This general argument cuts across the political spectrum. Author and *Nation* magazine columnist Alexander Cockburn believes the corporate news media are getting their just desserts, due to their dreadful quality more than the Internet. With no sense of irony, he evinces a faith that the market will do the necessary job of properly rewarding those news media that deserve to live. "Weep not for all of yesterday's papers, for the old Fourth Estate. The ones that deserve to will make it through– vagabonds and outlaws."[64] Arianna Huffington, cofounder of "The Huffington Post," the groundbreaking news Web site and aggregated blog founded in 2005, argues that a hybrid journalism will emerge online embracing the best of the old media and the new media.[65] On the right, Adam Thierer embraces the coming period where the market will combine with the Internet to provide the best possible solutions.[66]

This has become the dominant position, and accordingly it is someone at the heart of the mainstream who sums the position up best. "What should we do?" Michael Kinsley asked in *The Washington Post*. "How about nothing?" He explains: "But will there be a Baghdad bureau? Will there be resources to expose a future Watergate? Will you be able to get your news straight and not in an ideological fog of blogs? Yes, why not— if there are customers for these things. There used to be enough customers in each of half a dozen American cities to support networks of bureaus around the world. Now the customers can come from around the world as well."[67]

Yochai Benkler has taken this approach the furthest, suggesting that the new journalism will be so radically different from the old that traditional concerns about resource support are no longer of pressing importance. We can have a leaner journalism, and it will still be much better, thanks to the Internet. He writes:

> Like other information goods, the production model of news is shifting from an industrial model–be it the monopoly city paper, IBM in its monopoly heyday, or Microsoft, or Britannica–to a networked model that integrates a wider range of practices into the production system: market and nonmarket, large scale and small, for profit and nonprofit, organized and individual. We already see the early elements of how news reporting and opinion will be provided in the networked public sphere.[68]

The Moody's 2009 report mentioned before that indicated only 14 percent of newspaper budgets went to content creation underscored Benkler's claim that journalism could be done far more efficiently online, where the massive distribution and printing costs that are killing old print media are minimal.[69]

There are grounds for the optimism of Huffington, Shirky, Kinsley, Benkler and the rest. There have been extraordinary developments in news and public affairs online, and the one thing we can be certain of is that more is on the way. The most striking development may be the rise of the blogosphere. Although much of the blogosphere peddles off-the-cuff opinion or links to other, frequently old-media, news stories, to leave the matter there would be grossly inaccurate. Blogging has evolved, in many instances, into a vehicle for sophisticated reporting as well as commentary, with original research and links to all sorts of evidence, background material, related articles and opposing positions. It has blasted open the once-shackled doors of journalism for a number of talented people who, for whatever reason, had been locked out of the old media system. There are times we think that if the only benefit of the Internet had been to make Glenn Greenwald's blogging possible, it would justify its development. And Glenn Greenwald is just the tip of the iceberg.

We embrace the argument of Huffington and her compatriots that many of the biggest stories of the past decade—including, as an example, the questioning of former Mississippi senator Trent Lott's romanticizing of Strom Thurmond and the segregationist politics of the past that led to Lott's resignation as GOP leader in the Senate in December 2002— were nurtured into news not by old media but by bloggers. Lawrence Lessig is right when he argues that the resignation of Lott would not have occurred without blogging. After the story "disappear[ed] from the mainstream press within forty-eight hours," noted Lessig, "bloggers kept researching the story" until, "[f]inally, the story broke back into the mainstream press."[70] This pattern has played out again and again over the ensuing years, often with "The Huffington Post" and "Talking Points Memo" grabbing the sort of "scoops" on national and international stories that used to be the sole province of the now-shuttered Washington bureaus of our downsizing newspapers.

We also agree with Shirky and Benkler that there likely will be more remarkable developments that are impossible to anticipate in the coming years and decades. We are especially heartened by the development of "citizen journalism."[71] The idea that journalism is some sort of elite practice that should be restricted to professionals always struck us as dubious— after all, one of us (Nichols) started working for the local weekly newspaper in a small town in rural Wisconsin as an 11-year-old who had never taken a journalism class. Likewise we welcome the emergence of "pro-am" and "crowd sourcing" journalism, where citizens take up reporting and researching duties, often in collaboration with more experienced writers and editors. The immense labor power unleashed by "pro-am" journalism makes it possible to analyze huge amounts of research in a short period of time, as several *Talking Points Memo* projects have illustrated. And it is apparent that there is a great deal of talent that was previously lying fallow. The Wikipedia example demonstrates that "quantity can become quality if you do it right."[72]

It is also true that there is an almost dizzying array of experimentation in journalism now taking place, almost always online. "It is quite likely

that a book written on this subject today will be out of date by next week,"
the Knight Foundation's Eric Newton writes. "Things are changing so
fast, even the masters of the World Wide Web haven't figured out how to
tell the story electronically in real time." Newton is optimistic some of
the more than 150 journalism projects the Knight Foundation is affiliated
with will take off.[73] Some of this work is noncommercial, some of it is
commercial, though none of it is yet profitable or self-supporting.

There is also a push for nonprofit groups to become producers of
online journalism in the areas in which they are knowledgeable, taking
advantage of their existing resources.[74] We're genuinely intrigued by attempts to link experienced journalists with NGOs, where they can pursue stories along beats relating to the work of these oversight and
advocacy groups, even as we recognize that safeguards will have to be
constructed to maintain journalistic voices and values in this unfamiliar
territory. Even though there will be challenges, there are many more possibilities. And we embrace the general sense that this is a time to let a
thousand flowers bloom, or at least be planted, without presupposing a
structure. We think it is reasonable to presume that some of what comes
up in the months and years ahead will be more sustainable and healthier
than what it replaces.

This said, we confess to at least a trace of skepticism with regard to
some of the current Internet euphoria. We think for all the extraordinary
and revolutionary gains, there are also losses, sometimes important ones.
There are costs we pay for becoming digitized—like, possibly, the diminished ability to concentrate for sustained periods, which was encouraged by a print culture.[75] We also worry about the loss of physical
community, which was sustained in an almost intangible manner by the
old-brick newspaper office downtown, the delivery truck rumbling along
urban streets, the guy at the newsstand, the girl with a paper route and
the sense that the printed page of the local rag represented an institutional reference point for a city. We share at least some of the sentiment
of one of our favorite old-media editors turned new-media bloggers,
Dave Zweifel, who recalls with no small measure of sorrow "the days
when a newspaper was as much a part of what pulled a city together as
cheering for the baseball team."[76] But, while we can get nostalgic about

what papers were, we also understand that to a significant extent this is water under the bridge, and has as much currency as wailing about the charms of oral culture did after the invention of writing or the printing press. We aren't going to pine for the past, as doing so is a distraction from building the sort of journalism that will sustain democracy in a future where newspapers simply will not play the role they once did.

We do have concerns about the Internet and the digital revolution that fall within immediate human control. As Joseph Turow of the University of Pennsylvania puts it, the Internet is to some extent "Yochai's world," referring to the social networking and information revolution extolled by Benkler. But it is also "Martin's world," referring to Martin Sorrell, the CEO of the WPP Group, the second-largest advertising agency holding company in the world, which is steadfastly determined to convert the Internet to a primarily commercial medium. As Turow argues, those enthralled with the revolutionary implications of the technology, like Benkler, sometimes underestimate the power of existing commercial forces to permeate and extend their power online.[77] To the extent the Internet is more Martin's world than Yochai's, its democratic promise becomes less certain. In short, the technology is not magical.[78] And we always remind folks that, within the lifetimes of living Americans, radio and television were seen as transformative technologies that would steer up toward the civil and democratic high road as opposed to the commercial low road they eventually plowed. In other words, every new technology inspires a battle between those who pursue its best and brightest potential and those business interests that would colonize it for their own enrichment.

We are reminded of the words of John Adams, the second president of the United States. "Bad men increase in knowledge as fast as good men," he wrote in 1790, "and science, arts, taste, sense and letters, are employed for the purpose of injustice as well as for virtue."[79]

In the fight for the Internet's future, we should all be on the side of brilliant and optimistic theorists such as Benkler, Lessig and Cass Sunstein, who promise us that the social production of the Internet can revolutionize and democratize our societies.[80] We have seen the way the Internet has developed news stories, disseminated them, and made possible real social change for the better. And if we embrace that possibility, there is much to be hopeful about.

Similarly, we can see a new and dramatically superior caliber of journalism emerging as a result of the Internet. It will be a journalism that will overcome the great limitations of professional journalism as it has been practiced in the United States: among other things, reliance upon the narrow range of opinion of people in power as the legitimate parameters of political debate, and a bias toward seeing the world through middle-class and upper-class eyes. It will be a journalism that can truly open up our politics, in the manner democratic theory suggests. Because there are so many variables with the technology it is impossible to project exactly how this new system of journalism will work and what it will look like, but the ingredients for a genuine media revolution are in place.

One way to conceptualize this new journalism, at its best, is to imagine it as a great jazz performance. Citizen journalists, bloggers, pro-am journalists and innovators we cannot even imagine would contribute along with paid professional journalists. The former would be the improvisers who would push the implicit logic and beauty of the music to its limits. The latter, the paid journalists, would be the melody and the rhythm section. Without them the improvisers are just making noise—perhaps brilliant noise, but noise all the same. Together the players begin to feed off of each other and produce genius.[81]

There is, however, one crucial area of disagreement between our view and that of Benkler and Shirky and our other fellow optimists. For the new system to work, as we see it, there needs to be a significant body of full-time paid journalists, covering their communities, the nation, the world, in competition and collaboration with other paid journalists. There need to be independent newsrooms where journalists who are secure enough in their livelihoods to focus on their work can collaborate, and receive professional editing, fact-checking and assistance. There needs to be expertise, developed over years of trial and error, in vital areas of specialty and paid journalists accountable for those beats. We need journalists trained in languages and history and culture to work international beats, and to have the credentials to protect them from governments.

There need to be news institutions that can preserve and promote journalism. As Ben Bagdikian once put it, "great journalism needs great institutions." Institutions that can support long-term investigative work, and free up journalists to do their work, rather than having them try to hustle their next meal through shaking down an Internet micropayment or a commercial advertisement for their blog. Institutions that are respected and, yes, feared by the powerful players in business and politics. These great media institutions need to compete with other great media institutions, giving citizens muscular choices and distinct perspectives. Reporters, writers, editors and broadcast newsmen and women have to be able to make careers of this work or much of what we need will either not be done or not be done especially well.

This reality leads to three related problems with the "everything will be alright" approach that urges us all to relax and let the Internet and the marketplace work a sort of magic. First (and it is both revealing and astonishing that this point is so widely ignored): if we put Internet journalism in the driver's seat, we are writing off the roughly 40 percent of the population that does not have a broadband connection. We are effectively disenfranchising 100 million Americans, disproportionately poor, of color, rural and elderly. Anyone who proceeds with this approach, who does not have a plan for rapid transition to ubiquitous broadband connection, is not serious about journalism as a democratic undertaking. We should not be aspiring to have a level of information inequality closer to that of a feudal society than a modern democracy. The notion that this problem will magically work itself out in the mix has proven fallacious; indeed, just as the old print press underserved inner cities and poor rural areas that had little appeal to advertisers, so digital media remains more niche than general, more elite than democratic. This is a problem that requires a policy solution, as we discuss in Chapter 4.

The second problem is that the argument admits that there will be an indefinite period where the resources going to journalism are certain to decline precipitously. "We could be at a moment where the short-term negative consequences of de-monetization are felt," *Wired* editor Chris Anderson writes, "before the long-term positive effects."[82] During that interregnum, perhaps one or two decades, we apparently will have to get by on chewing gum and bailing wire. To Anderson, this is no big deal. "We'll get there. It's so early…maybe the media is going to be a part-time job. Maybe media won't be a job at all, but will instead be a hobby," Anderson says, using the term media to refer to journalism. "The marketplace will sort this out."[83] Consider the immense social, economic and foreign-policy challenges before us immediately and in the coming generation, and ask yourself if this is an especially good time to lowball the resources going to journalism. Frankly, it strikes us as suicidal.

At this point a significant percentage of the already paltry number of paid full-time journalists who work primarily or significantly on the Web are being subsidized by their affiliation with old media. There were approximately 2,300 American online journalists at the start of 2009, reporters and editors who are subsidized by daily newspapers, as they work for the unprofitable Web site side of what is still referred to as "the paper."[84] Magazines such as *Washington Monthly*, *The Atlantic*, *The Nation* and *National Review* employ correspondents who provide considerable material online, but their paychecks are attached to old-media operations. What happens if and when the old-media paymasters close down—and close their checkbooks? What happens when the income dries up for all the journalists providing material to the Web? This is the moment we are approaching. What will be left standing, besides volunteers and citizen journalists? If the present business and even not-for-profit models that are in play are all we've got to rely on, there could actually be fewer online journalists. There will not be a sufficient number of full-time paid journalists working exclusively online during this interregnum.[85] It could be years before we even replace the 2,300 newspaper online journalists, let alone make a dent in the tens of thousands of journalists' jobs we have lost over the past two decades.

When one goes down the Nielsen list of the 30 most visited news and public-affairs Web sites in the United States for March and May 2009, 26 are connected to and subsidized by newspapers and broadcasters, and three are "aggregators" of material largely coming from the Web activities of old media. Only one site, "The Huffington Post," produces original material. And even there, original journalism is a small portion of the "Huffington Post" menu. This is striking because Internet-news consumption is top-heavy; each of the three most visited sites (MSNBC, CNN, Yahoo! News) gets nearly 10 times more visitors than the Web sites ranked in the bottom five of the top 30.[86] What happens when the old-media firms can no longer subsidize their Web sites? Where will the content come from?

Third, and more to the point, where are the resources to support this new online journalism going to come from? Why should we believe that eventually the Internet and market will generate the resources to have a strong full-time force of working journalists? When one reads Shirky's list of the most promising Web-journalism ventures, they are invariably small operations that show little or no indication of ever evolving into self-supporting powerhouses. And once one gets past the first tier of digital news media, one is quickly in the frozen tundra of one-person shops and volunteer labor.

Even some of the finest Web journalists—indeed, the finest journalists, period—are struggling to get by. Consider blogger Marcy Wheeler, who made a name for herself with her nuanced coverage of the politically volatile trial of former White House aide "Scooter" Libby, and has demonstrated the potential of the Web to break big stories that cross over to old media. In April 2009, Wheeler's online scoop about Khalid Sheik Mohammed being water-boarded 183 times in one month supercharged the torture debate in the United States—causing such a stir that the blogger's groundbreaking reporting earned attention on the front page of *The New York Times*. Wheeler should have been enjoying the kudos for her innovative and important investigative reporting. Instead, she was struggling to figure out how to make a living, and facing tough decisions about whether she could continue to subsidize her own part-time work as a journalist. Author and fellow blogger Jane Hamsher, the film producer and author who founded the popular Web site firedoglake.com in late 2004, tried to get major donors and foundations to back Wheeler's work, arguing that "she's consistently demonstrated the investigative skills that show what bloggers and those using online tools are uniquely capable of doing."[87] After getting turned down again and again, Hamsher finally launched an online campaign to raise $150,000 "to support Marcy, another investigative blogger to work with her, and a researcher to help them." Two months after the launch, the campaign had raised $100,000 but remained far short of the goal for supporting one of the most pre-eminent and able bloggers in the business.[88]

This gets us to the heart of the question of where the money is going to come from to convert a proudly motley crew into the digital equivalent of the press system most democratic nations have enjoyed throughout their modern histories. Asked another way: If we can't come up with a way to support Marcy Wheeler, an online journalist who is breaking stories worthy of the front page of *The New York Times*, how are we ever going to maintain serious reporting and writing on the Web?

Greg Mitchell, the editor of *Editor & Publisher*, makes a good point:

> All these people who forecast the end of newspapers because of the de-cline in Internet advertising and users being unwilling to pay for content can't explain how the new Internet journalism websites are going to survive or even thrive—since most of them, too, need paid ads and/or subscribers. Are the ads on the new media websites cooler or less in-trusive? Do their readers respond to ads differently than readers of a newspaper website? Will users who supposedly hate to pay for web con-tent somehow decide to pay for it from online sites when there are plenty of free alternatives? I just don't get it.[89]

Some observers forecast a large increase in advertising by local small businesses on sites that develop into go-to places for news in tightly knit communities, but this is highly speculative and there is no guarantee that such local advertising will attach itself to news Web sites.[90] Heidi Sinclair predicts a digital world where major corporations like Nike will get in the media business and provide journalism directly related to their area of interest and expertise. Or celebrity journalists will become "brands" who will sell themselves individually to audiences and advertisers to sup-port their work.[91] We do not consider these options especially reassuring.

So what is left to bankroll the digital press? It looks like we're down to three options: volunteer labor, individual donations and foundation grants.

Volunteer (or grotesquely undercompensated) labor would seem ab-surd on its face, but this is the oxygen that fuels much of the prospective

Internet journalism.[92] "The blogosphere," as prominent and well-regarded blogger Chris Bowers puts it, "is giving rise to something akin to a digital sweatshop. Thousands, perhaps tens of thousands, of Americans are producing enormous amount of content for pay that is just above, or below, minimum wage and includes neither benefits nor weekends." The limitations of this approach are self-evident. People need to live, they want to have places to sleep, food to eat, health insurance, possibly even the time and resources to raise a family. Unless journalism can provide adequate compensation, it will be limited to a small number of self-selected people, either desperate for money or independently wealthy, with all the complications each of those scenarios presents. Bowers correctly concludes: This "is not a sustainable model for the people producing the content."[93]

As for individual donations, experience with public broadcasting shows people will pay, but there would be an upper limit that is far below the money needed. Individuals gave $714 million to all public and community broadcasting stations in 2007. It has not grown as a percentage of public media revenues over the past decade, and only a fraction of that went toward journalism.[94] Some of this money might be taken from Peter to pay Paul, and there might be additional money that could be shaken from the tree, but few serious analysts anticipate individual donations that can do more than supplement other sources of income. And as we've seen from the story of blogger Marcy Wheeler, the best on the Web are struggling to get the support they need. Even if the donation approach were to become viable, there is an additional concern: relying on the generosity of virtual strangers tends to extend the privileges of the upper-middle class and wealthy into the digital future because, to paraphrase the bank robber Willie Sutton, that is where the money is and bloggers seeking to survive will be inclined to follow it.

This brings us to foundations. As the newspaper meltdown unfolded in 2009, a movement was afoot to establish nonprofit newspapers and/or endowed newspapers, to be supported by philanthropy. One concept was that these would operate in conjunction with journalism Web sites that seek and receive the lion's share of their income from foundations. Vince Stehle, a visionary member of the foundation community, and Charles

Lewis, a widely respected journalist who founded the Center for Public Integrity, have been vocal advocates of this course. As Lewis puts it: "It's time for civil society, especially the nation's foundations and individuals of means, to collaborate with journalists and experts who understand the changing economics of journalism in an imaginative, visionary plan that would support our precious existing nonprofit institutions and help to develop new ones."[95]

Leaving aside the issue of whether we want foundations to have this much power—a concern that relates to the questions raised by relying on elite individual donors—how realistic is the foundation-funding model as a stable source of revenue for the next generation of journalism?

Our sense is that foundations can and should fund innovative projects, which may play a role in defining where journalism goes. And we expect that there will be individual cities where a wealthy and highly engaged foundation might keep a newspaper afloat, or develop a news-oriented Web site with reporters and editors serving a community that might otherwise go uncovered. But as a viable replacement for the broad network of commercial support of newspapers in the United States, the foundation "solution" seems to be another dead-end street.

For starters, many foundations provide only limited-term support, often for periods of three years or less, to new enterprises. Foundation boards and directors like to spawn groups, not bankroll them in perpetuity. Between 2005 and 2009, some 180 foundations provided $128 million to news and information initiatives—leaving aside public broadcasting grants—according to the most comprehensive study of the matter. And nearly half of this money went to just three investigative-journalism projects.[96] After decades of intensive efforts to attract philanthropic support, public broadcasters obtained $225 million from foundations in 2007—7.7 percent of their revenues—but only a portion of that supports journalism.[97]

It strains credulity to think that the United States is going to see a dramatic increase in funding to support journalism, especially with foundation nest eggs having been battered in the stock market—and apparently robbed by Bernie Madoff. Moreover, mass layoffs and plant closings create a greater demand for social spending along the lines that has traditionally attracted substantial philanthropic support. Lewis calculates that in 2008 $20 million in foundation money supported nonprofit publishers of investigative reporting.[98] That is less than one-tenth of the annual newsroom budget of a single newspaper, *The New York Times*.[99] Put another way: the typical pay for a veteran reporter on *The Seattle Post-Intelligencer* runs about $50,000 a year.[100] The *P-I* laid off roughly 150 reporters and editors when it ended its print edition. If we took all $20 million and spent it to get the *P-I* Web site staffed up to a level equaling what was lost—and that would be capable of covering the region in a reasonably thorough and competitive manner—provided reasonable benefits and then promoted the new project, much of the money would be gone before we filled the void in a single city.

We're fans of Chuck Lewis and his efforts to find new avenues for journalism. We've worked with him over the years. But, frankly, we would feel a lot better if Lewis's $20 million figure had a few more digits attached to it, or if there was some reasonable expectation that they might appear in our lifetimes.

Although we are enthusiastic about nonprofit media institutions, as we discuss in Chapter 4, and we welcome foundations that want to write checks, we are convinced that if the future of journalism in America is left primarily to the foundation community, it will remain small, unstable and impoverished. We have to think bigger.

Best Practices

The discussion heretofore has been by necessity somewhat abstract. Another, more illustrative way to get at these issues is to look at a handful of the most exciting and prominent new-media ventures that have emerged on the Internet over the past few years. The proliferation of Web ventures that are read by substantial numbers of Americans for their news content is evolving on literally a daily basis. The options range from a pioneering news aggregator, "The Drudge Report," recently run as a two-man shop by "conservative muckraker"[101] Matt Drudge and Andrew Breitbart, to the 24/7 news-generating site that uses all the resources of Drudge's frequent nemesis, *The New York Times*, with its 101 Pulitzer Prizes, 11 national news bureaus, 26 foreign news bureaus and nearly 1,300 print journalists and 80 "producers" and editors working exclusively for its nytimes.com site.[102]

Drudge recently bought a posh new home in Miami; the New York Times Company recently slashed its dividend and announced that it would borrow against its headquarters to avoid cash-flow problems.[103] Such are the stark outlines of journalism on the Web.

Drudge, who once joked that he had a "more than adequate curriculum vitae for a post at 7-Eleven," is anything but the model of the "Timesman" (or woman).[104] But, when it comes to defining the Web as a source of news that could compete with and often beat everyone else to the story, the man Newsweek's Michael Isikoff dismisses as "a menace to honest, responsible journalism" has been at least as significant a player as anyone at the nation's newspaper of record.[105] Eccentric, even cartoonish, Drudge modeled himself on a previously controversial journalist, gossipmonger Walter Winchell, but from the beginning in the mid-1990s he brought a hard-news sensibility to the Web. It was, admittedly, one that owed more to the tabloids of the 1920s than to the determinedly dull newspapers and news-magazines of the latter 20th century; yet, when it scooped the old media on stories such as the 1995 firing of Connie Chung as the CBS News co-anchor and 1996 Republican presidential nominee Bob Dole's selection of Jack Kemp as his running mate, "The Drudge Report" became what even the Times acknowledged was "must reading for journalists, studio executives and politicos on both coasts."[106] More importantly, Drudge was being read by tens of thousands, then hundreds of thousands, then millions of Americans each month—and not just from the conservative base that breathlessly followed his lusty revelations about the Bill Clinton-Monica Lewinsky soap opera—creating a record of page views for a self-created and self-produced Web site that began to illustrate the Web's potential.

In 2002, when "The Drudge Report" surpassed the 1-billion-views mark for a single year, its editor declared triumphantly:

In every state and nearly every civilized nation in the developed world, readers know where to go for action and reaction of news—at least one day ahead ... Free from any corporate concerns ... this new attempt at the old American experiment of full freedom in reporting is ever exciting. Those in power have everything to lose by individuals who march to their own rules.[107]

Drudge's rules were not just his own.[108] They were those of "the frontier" that was (and to some extent still is) the World Wide Web, a media no-man's-land and everyman's land where newspaper companies were losing tens of millions of dollars trying to figure out how to "do journalism on the Internet" and a conservative populist wearing a fedora was by most accounts making close to $1 million a year by 2004.[109] Old-media executives, and journalism purists, might still be mocking Drudge, but societal observers such as Camille Paglia were talking about how they "relished his take-no-prisoners bitch-slapping of the cliquish media panjandrums, snorting away in their lofty sense of false superiority," and hailing him as "the kind of bold, entrepreneurial, free-wheeling, information-oriented outsider we need far more of in this country."[110]

Ultimately, the Paglia view would prevail. And the notion of the one-man site or small shop tackling "the cliquish media panjandrums" and beating them at a digital version of their own game would take hold as a model for peddling news and views on the Web. ABC News and *TIME* magazine political analyst Mark Halperin's description of Drudge as "the Walter Cronkite of his era" was as silly—a rather typically over-the-top attempt by an old-media insider to appear 'Net-savvy—as it was inaccurate.[111] Drudge has never tried to cover all the news in an authoritative manner; in fact, he frequently neglects foreign affairs and shows little interest in economic debates. His forte has always been political gossip. And even this he tends to "report" with links to newspaper Web sites and the occasional leak from old-media reporters and journalistic hangers-on. He makes enough money to keep his small shop afloat but—perhaps wisely—has never been very interested in sharing the wealth with reporters and editors or in creating what his old-media competitors would characterize as a "serious" news operation. That said, Drudge was a pioneer who struck gold (in the form of news scoops and attention) and silver (in the form of sufficient revenue from backers and advertisers to support himself in a comfortable manner). Like most successful pioneers he attracted not just followers but imitators.

When former *American Prospect* Washington editor Josh Marshall's site, "Talking Points Memo," launched in the fall of 2000—in the midst of the *Bush v. Gore* Florida-recount fight—it evolved the model.[112] There was still a lot of aggregation from old-media news sites, but Marshall's blog featured smart analysis of what he was reading. Marshall's dogged coverage of the scandal involving Trent Lott's seeming endorsement of Strom Thurmond's old segregationist platform has, as we have noted, been broadly credited with forcing Lott to step aside as the Senate Republican Leader in 2002.[113] This was old-fashioned muckraking journalism of the classic sort, as was Marshall's aggressive-obsessive coverage of the 2005 debate over George Bush's attempt to privatize Social Security.

Like "The Drudge Report," "TPM" employs language that is more raucous and sensational than might be found in most contemporary newspaper or magazine articles—Marshall labeled Bush's speaking tour on behalf of Social Security reform "Bamboozlepalooza" and called Democrats who wavered on the issue "Mumbojumbocrats"—but the word-play would have been familiar to Upton Sinclair and the muckrakers of the previous century. And it was effective on multiple levels. During the Social Security debate, Marshall built a community of readers and contributors, a sort of journalistic social-networking operation similar to that seen on the liberal "Daily Kos" and conservative "RedState" sites, but with even more in the way of empowerment. Marshall invited readers to monitor local newspapers for comments from House and Senate members and then feed what they found into the Web equivalent of a Capitol Hill "whip list" identifying where legislators stood. "This is crowd sourcing—reporting based on the work of many people, including your readers," explains media critic Dan Kennedy, who describes these sorts of initiatives, in which "TPM" specializes, as "a different kind of journalism, based on the idea that my readers know more than I do."[114] What Marshall and his readers engage in is muscular democratic work, but it is not quite so innovative as some 'Net utopians might imagine. In fact, it is very much in the tradition of the old "reading the roll" features of *La Follette's Weekly*, the crusading magazine that would eventually evolve into *The Progressive*.[115]

"TPM" still does a lot of aggregating—borrowing from and commenting upon journalism produced by old media—but the blog has also broken more than its share of new ground. Its featuring of prominent guest bloggers—former Secretary of Labor Robert Reich, 2004 Democratic vice-presidential nominee John Edwards, economist Dean Baker—has been much copied. And its original reporting—by Marshall and journalists he has hired for an expanding set of TPM-linked sites—has earned the sort of official recognition once reserved for the nation's great newspapers and magazines. In 2008, TPM's coverage of the midterm dismissal of seven U.S. Attorneys by the Bush administration's Department of Justice earned one of journalism's highest honors, a George Polk Award for legal reporting—the first, but surely not the last, for a blog.[116] TPM was not just collecting plaudits, however; it was attracting readers—close to half a million unique visitors a month during the 2008 presidential campaign—and enough money to build a staff equivalent to that of a small magazine.[117] Through a combination of advertising revenue and online fund-raising among readers—think of it as a digital variation on the public-radio pledge drive—TPM was able to pay for specific reporting projects (for instance, covering the 2004 primary campaign in New Hampshire) and the creation of new projects. These include TPMCafe, where readers are invited to exchange ideas with politicians and specialists about issues of the day, and TPMMuckraker, where investigative reporters and crowd-sourcing readers dog officials and sort through "document dumps" by federal agencies. "The basic model is we are an ad-supported company," explains Marshall, who employed 10 reporters by 2009. "Often when we want to do some major expansion, we go to readers."[118]

Marshall is the first to admit that he is evolving a model for producing what he describes as "a combination of opinion journalism and traditional shoe-leather reporting" on the Web, and he thinks well and wisely about the struggle. "The question in my mind: Are we just in a period of tumult and we'll settle down and have the same kind of dominant entities—or is there something about the technology that has created a permanent ingrained ease of entry into the space? I think the latter is the case," he argues. "The way TPM came into existence—without any concept that it would be a company with multiple employees—simply wouldn't have been possible in any technological universe before the one that existed in the last ten years."[119]

We would agree, as we do with Marshall's view that "the more voices you have, the more takes on the news, you're just going to have a more vibrant and diverse news ecosystem—as opposed to having two or three gatekeepers that control the news."[120] But early in 2009, his lean, mean operation had just two investigative reporters and an ability to focus intensely on only a relatively narrow range of subjects—almost all of them national in character and politically "hot." TPM's "capacity" expanded substantially in July 2009, when supporters of the operation agreed to invest "$500,000 to $1 million" in support of a move "to increase the number of employees, to roughly 20, from the current 11, in the next 10 months."[121] Over the next several years, Marshall hopes to take that number to roughly 60, a significant number for a news-oriented Web site but still far fewer reporters than is currently employed by a mid-sized daily newspaper. And Marshall is attracting the readership and support of many of the most actively engaged Americans who might reasonably be expected to commit resources to this sort of work. We hope, and believe, that TPM will survive and thrive in the future. But we don't see its model as one that begins to meet the broad need for journalism that provides the great mass of citizens with the information they will require to govern themselves. Marshall has found a wellspring sufficient to support one remarkable but quite small project. However, we find it exceptionally difficult to imagine that there are enough additional wellsprings to support the hundreds of TPM-like projects that will be needed to provide the basic coverage, let alone the intensive investigative reporting, that a society of America's size demands. And we worry about the tendency of many sincere observers of the current journalistic meltdown to find individual examples of success on the Web—especially ones with a genesis so seemingly accidental as Marshall's "without any concept that it would be a company with multiple employees" process—and presume that they can fill the void.

Clearly, there must be more models—bigger, bolder, even more adventurous ones. And there must be sounder structures to support them.

Arianna Huffington is attempting to meet these challenges with "The Huffington Post" and, by virtue of her own überpersona and taste for outside-the-box thinking, she has attracted immense attention and Nielsen NetRatings (one measure of page views) that are the envy of the industry.[122] Already a multimedia personality—and former California gubernatorial candidate—before she, former AOL Time Warner executive vice president Kenneth Lerer and Massachusetts Institute of Technology Media Lab graduate Jonah Peretti launched the blog to beat all blogs in May 2005, Huffington never cloaked her desire to create a progressive variation on "The Drudge Report." "We could not have existed without Drudge," she told *Washington Post* media critic Howard Kurtz in 2007. "Drudge habituated people to going online for their news."[123] Like "The Drudge Report," "HuffPost" is hyperactive, constantly updated with an eye toward moving "sexy" items up and ditching the dull, focused not just on politics but also on entertainment and gossip. It is relaxed about the definition of what will be highlighted—anything from a one-line alert to a thoughtful rumination by actor John Cusack on the high crimes and misdemeanors of Dick Cheney. The point is to attract readers, and "HuffPost" does just that, grabbing close to 9 million unique visitors a month by 2009, as compared with 3.4 million for "Drudge" and 3.5 million for *Slate*, the ad-supported Web-only news, arts and sports "magazine" that was started by Microsoft under Kinsley's editorship before it was sold to The Washington Post Co.[124]

"HuffPost" has exceeded most of its initial expectations—especially those involving competition with "The Drudge Report." "HuffPost" is packed with blog posts from political and entertainment celebrities. One day in June 2009, Secretary of State Hillary Clinton was weighing in on combating global poverty and hunger while hip-hop entrepreneur Russell Simmons was ruminating on hate speech and *très* chic French philosopher Bernard-Henri Lévy pondered the prospects for Middle East peace. On the same page were snippets from the previous night's David Letterman show and ads for Palmolive soap, as well as aggregated news about North Korea vowing to "weaponize" its plutonium next to a video of actress Jennifer Aniston joking about her love life. Its organized chaos might be horrifying to a contemporary newspaper editor locked in the keep-it-dull-and-drab mentality of 21st-century print media but it would not unsettle any old-school "penny press" editor who measured success in millions of tabloids sold.

Huffington has figured out a lot about the Web that traditional news executives continue to struggle with. She knows, for instance, that the "paywall" schemes won't work. And she recognizes that people don't go looking for "balance," as defined by journalism-school professors but never, ever successfully achieved in print or broadcast media. Readers have always sought a best approximation of the truth—perhaps their truth, perhaps Huffington's—and she's willing to offer up her variation without apology. Ask her about bias and balance and she responds: "Very often truth is on one side or the other. That's not partisanship."[125] In this sense, Huffington "gets" what most newspaper editors still fail to recognize: that no one buys their pious pronouncements about maintaining objectivity. And that's one of the reasons why she suggests that no one—make that almost no one—is buying their papers.

But while Huffington is sometimes portrayed as being out to strangle newspapers—a prospect that a *New Yorker* cartoon famously portrayed—she is in fact a passionate believer in journalism who thinks she might yet be able to teach newspapers how to save themselves, most likely on the Web rather than in print, but Huffington is not the sort to rule anything out. And at a moment when newspapers are cutting, she's hiring. The "HuffPost" staff is small, about 60, but it includes some remarkable writers, including Tom Edsall, the veteran *Washington Post* reporter who has occupied a Pulitzer chair at Columbia University's Graduate School of Journalism. Edsall is convinced that what "HuffPost" is doing is journalism, and so are we.[126] This site does not just make news—something Huffington is very good at—it breaks news, as when one of the citizen journalists participating in "HuffPost"'s "Off the Bus" project during the 2008 presidential campaign stirred up the Democratic nomination race by publishing some not very flattering comments about Pennsylvania primary voters by front-runner Barack Obama.[127]

But is "HuffPost" really a replacement for newspapers, and does it pay for itself? The answer to each question, at least at this point, is "no." While its commentary is robust, most of the news that appears on "HuffPost" is still aggregated content from old media. Its small cadre of reporters works hard and gets scoops, but they still tend to dig in predictable fields—the White House briefing room, for instance—that downsized print operations are prone to work. But there are not enough "HuffPost" reporters and they are hard to find beyond the elite warrens of Washington, New

York and Hollywood—although Huffington is now making a sincere and potentially significant effort to highlight blogging from around the country and to get reporters on the ground in cities such as Chicago and New York. Our sense is that "HuffPost" will go from strength to strength, especially with the May 2009 hiring of CNET Networks editor in chief Jai Singh as the site's managing editor. The Web-savvy Singh's announcement that "The bottom line is the Huffington Post has figured out how new media should be" is a meaningful endorsement.[128]

Reasonable voices may still debate whether "HuffPost" really "has figured out how new media should be." But this project, for all its strengths, is not yet the replacement for old media that is necessary. It may have a reporter getting called on by Barack Obama, but it does not have full-time reporters at the Department of Agriculture, keeping daily watch on food-safety issues, let alone in the farm country of rural Iowa or arrayed along the food-processing route where Upton Sinclair, on assignment from the old socialist newspaper *Appeal to Reason*, did the muckraking that would spawn *The Jungle* and the investigative-journalism impulse of the Progressive Era.

It is not that Huffington and her compatriots are uninterested in producing the journalism that might give America a new generation of well-trained and reasonably compensated journalists ready and willing to echo the declaration allegedly made by Upton Sinclair: "Hello! I'm Upton Sinclair, and I'm here to write the Uncle Tom's Cabin of the Labor Movement!"[129] The problem is that it costs money, lots of money, to field the armies of investigative reporters that are needed to find and expose the new "inferno(s) of exploitation" that are every bit as concerning as those Sinclair uncovered a century ago. And, as Huffington admits, her project is at best "breaking even."[130]

In March 2009, "HuffPost" announced that it would assign a group of investigative journalists to start digging into economic stories. But support for the project did not come from subscription money or ad revenues. Rather, as Associated Press reported, "The popular Web site is collaborating with The Atlantic Philanthropies and other donors to launch the Huffington Post Investigative Fund with an initial budget of $1.75 million. That should be enough for 10 staff journalists who will

primarily coordinate stories with freelancers."[131] Declaring that she hoped
to make hires from the vast pool of laid-off daily-newspaper reporters,
Huffington said, "All of us increasingly have to look at different ways to
save investigative journalism."

The key phrase there is "look at different ways."

There is much to celebrate in the willingness of a journalism-oriented,
highly engaged foundation like The Atlantic Philanthropies to help "Huff-
Post" hire a handful of high-profile investigative reporters, just as there is
much to celebrate in the even more ambitious commitment of The San-
dler Foundation—in alliance with The Atlantic Philanthropies, The JEHT
Foundation and The John D. and Catherine T. MacArthur Foundation—
to provide $10 million in start-up money for ProPublica, a nonprofit in-
dependent newsroom run by former *Wall Street Journal* managing editor
Paul Steiger and former Portland *Oregonian* managing editor Stephen En-
gelberg with two dozen full-time reporters and editors.[132]

These projects and similar initiatives at the regional and state levels—
such as the New England Center for Investigative Reporting at Boston
University and the Wisconsin Center for Investigative Journalism—are
exciting, and we're delighted that they are being backed by the foundations we have mentioned, as well as the Ethics and Excellence Journalism
Foundation, the Knight Foundation and the exquisitely named Sam
Adams Alliance.[133]

We've been impressed with the take-no-prisoners approach to reporting on the financial meltdown by some of the ProPublica reporters. But
in reading the ProPublica site, we've been struck by the fact that many of
the featured articles are really just aggregations of pieces produced by
newspapers around the country. The aggregation is certainly useful, but
this is not exactly trailblazing. And it is definitely premature to suggest
that ProPublica, which attracts scant traffic to its own Web site—two days
after a compelling and well-researched piece suggesting that "buy American" provisions in the federal economic-stimulus plan might cause a
"trade war" with Canada was put up in mid-June, not a single reader had
commented on it—is developing a model that seems sustainable without
continued foundation funding.[134] The ProPublica folks aren't claiming
differently; in fact, they've launched a "Steal Our Stories" campaign to

encourage traditional news outlets to pick up the project's articles,[135] along with those of other not-for-profit journalism projects such as the Center for Investigative Reporting, the Investigative Reporting Workshop, the Investigative Fund of the Nation Institute and the Center for Public Integrity.[136]

This "partnering" between foundation-funded investigative-reporting projects at the national, regional and state levels holds promise for getting stories to broader audiences. But there are perils in the one-size-fits-all model of setting up a single investigative-reporting source for a whole state—especially at a time when newspapers that are cutting back on reporting will be all too willing to publish free "content." Instead of competition for stories by newsrooms with different perspectives, we're trending toward the single source that journalists and democrats have wisely feared across history.

If it seemed likely to us that there would be multiple newsrooms working investigative—and, frankly, local—beats in cities around the country, we'd be more encouraged. But what's developing does not appear to us like a sound model, journalistically or economically.

We are more intrigued by some of the local newsrooms that have sprung up in cities around the country, such as the *Voice of San Diego* site and *MinnPost* in the Twin Cities.[137] This is where the rubber meets the road, at the local level where newspapers are cutting back and even closing. Can these new online news operations make a go of it? At *MinnPost*—which promises "high-quality journalism for news-intense people who care about Minnesota"—the signs are journalistically encouraging; reporters such as former *Minneapolis Star Tribune* writer Eric Black are producing sharp, well-edited political reporting that challenges expectations, asks tough questions and provides real insight.[138] At *Voice of San Diego*, the coverage of city affairs is on many days at least as thorough as that found on the Web site of the city's daily newspaper, *The San Diego Union-Tribune*, which has been making deep cuts. Both *Voice of San Diego* and *MinnPost* are hiring local journalists in small but credible numbers, and they are diversifying their funding sources beyond the usual foundations by trying to build mass bases of donors—call them "subscribers" if you like, or, as *MinnPost* does, "micro-sponsors." "This year, we're projecting a massive increase in our corporate sponsorships. And the number of $1,000 to $5,000 donors is going up each week. Is it really that crazy to think that, like the opera or museum of art, we'll be able to significantly diversify our funding to sustain a $2 million organization?" says Scott Lewis of the *Voice of San Diego*, referencing the budget he hopes to establish for the digital newsroom, which now has eight reporters and a budget of roughly $800,000.[139]

Perhaps. But we'd counsel caution regarding those corporate donations. And we'd also remind our friend that his musical metaphor is not a new one. Ralph Ingersoll, the founder of the experimental ad-free New York City daily, *PM*, which was something of a journalistic sensation in the early 1940s, used to describe his generous supporters—primarily millionaire Marshall Field—as folks who compared "PM in some ways to the Philharmonic Orchestra. No one thinks of disbanding the Philharmonic merely because it doesn't now support itself."[140]

Two years after Ingersoll uttered those words, the money dried up and *PM* began a rapid decline that would within another year lead to the disbanding of what remained of its newsroom.

We don't want to rain on anyone's parade here. But we think the most accurate assessment of the many exciting and important online news, investigative-reporting and commentary projects that we've checked out comes from Stephen Janis, senior reporter for *Investigative Voice*, a terrific site in Baltimore. In its first few months, *Investigative Voice* broke major stories about city-hall corruption and was hailed by WUSA-TV reporter Scott Broom as "a wake-up call to traditional print reporters and broadcasters." Yet, Janis says, the site gets by thanks primarily to free labor by reporters who aren't making much if any of a living. "The business model," says an understated Janis, "is a challenge."[141]

How to Think About Journalism

As exciting and promising as many of the new online journalism ventures are, we believe that the only honest conclusion available to us is that the overall resources are woefully insufficient to fund a new generation of journalism institutions and practices that might satisfactorily meet the needs of the American people. While the ventures that we have examined—and that we have consulted and commiserated about with journalists, academics, activists and analysts of the media landscape—may ultimately prove more than adequate for our journalism needs, they are not so at present. And there is no reason to think they will be for quite some time, if ever. Indeed, were this any other circumstance, we suspect Americans of almost every partisan and ideological perspective would be quick to point out the absurdity of the situation and declare, "Let's get serious about cleaning up this mess or just abandon it altogether."

So what's preventing the discussion from taking a practical turn?

In our view, two false premises have prevented Americans from comprehending the truth of our journalism crisis, and realistically appraising what can be done. First, there is the assumption that journalism is naturally and appropriately an enterprise to be conducted by profit-motivated and profit-defined firms competing in the market. Because the system dominated the media spectrum and worked reasonably well—although how well is certainly debatable—for 150 years, most Americans have reached the reasonable conclusion that this was the "American Way." Markets work, and always produce rational outcomes, so the theory goes. The big problem with that line of thinking is the word *always*. We can now see that this period of profit-driven, advertising-supported journalism resulted from a constellation of factors that were historically specific. Those factors have declined in importance and the production of journalism is therefore in sharp decline. Thus, the challenge is not simply to create a business context in which producing journalism can again be profitable. This is a case where journalism as we know it, and to the extent we need it, will never be profitable again, at least for the visible future. That is the starting point for addressing the crisis.

The second false premise is that government involvement in creating journalism is, by definition, evil and should be avoided at all costs. America currently suffers from a fairy-tale understanding of the relationship of government to media that suggests that the range of possible government intervention runs from regulatory interference with press independence to the threat of direct censorship. The less government, therefore, the better. In fact, the relationship of the government to the press is far more complex and vital than the conventional wisdom allows. As we will argue in the balance of this book, the government has a range of important tools at its disposal to create, energize and where necessary subsidize a strong, pluralistic and independent press system. None of these tools entail having politicians bail out and directly fund state or private media—nor do they permit or condone censorship of media content. We can have our cake and eat it too. In fact, that is what we had, more or less, in the first few generations of our nation's history, before entrepreneurs determined they could get wealthy producing newspapers.

How should Americans think about journalism so that we can position ourselves to make wise policy? It would be comforting to imagine that merely repeating all the famous quotations from our founders and great philosophers about the importance of journalism to the survival of democracy would be enough to inspire an understanding that we cannot allow the enterprise to go down with the corporate-news-media ship. Should it not be enough to repeat Jefferson's mantra: "The only security of all is in a free press. The force of public opinion cannot be resisted when permitted freely to be expressed. The agitation it produces must be submitted to. It is necessary, to keep the waters pure."[142] Then we all just get down to the work of securing a free press and keeping the waters pure? Alas, those words have been spoken so widely in so many different contexts for so many different purposes they have lost their power, if not their meaning. The same person can invoke Thomas Jefferson, and then, incongruously and shamelessly, argue that we must allow journalism to collapse, unless rich people can make money providing it, and suggest that by some mad calculus this is the way of democracy.[143]

So let us conclude the chapter by providing four related ways to rethink journalism, which shine light clearly on the role of the government and the policymaking process. The past several decades have seen the development of significant advances in social science, economics and political theory that help us better understand the policy issues surrounding media, and that is where we turn presently.

First, and most important, in economics the notion of "public goods" has become a staple of the field. It refers to goods, often of considerable social importance, which cannot be effectively excluded from use by consumers who do not "pay" for them, and goods that can be consumed by one person without reducing their availability to be consumed by another.[144] National-defense or public-health (anti-epidemic) services are generally offered as examples of public goods. We need to be defended and we need to have measures taken to prevent pandemics, but it is impossible for individuals to purchase these, despite their importance. Moreover, few would pay for national defense voluntarily if someone else will do so; they would prefer to get the "free ride" by living in the same country. No one wants to be a chump. So no business can produce and sell this good. Either we all have it, or no one has it. Markets cannot work. It requires collective action.

The more a good or service has public-good attributes, the more appropriate it is to argue that there is a necessary role for the government to provide policies to encourage production of that good, and to share the expense equitably. That does not mean that there is not a role for commercial players and market forces, but the government plays quarterback, or the game never gets moving. It is a matter for policy deliberation and debate. Public-good theory is of value for understanding journalism in several ways.

Media content, including journalism, is not exactly a public good like national defense, but it has certain important attributes of a public good. (Hence, for the sake of discussion, most media economists characterize journalism as a public good.[145]) While journalism can be sold in a market, for example, the information and ideas (the value) contained within it can then be passed along at no charge to others. People have little incentive not to pass what they have learned along, because this process of sharing the original news article does not undermine the initial consumer's satisfaction. It is just as likely to enhance it; we get a certain satisfaction when we approach a friend or neighbor with the words: "Hey, did you see that?" People could not similarly share the same hamburger or the same pair of socks or most other commodities, which can more reasonably be thought of as "private goods."

This distinction makes for serious problems for markets in media industries.

In book publishing, for example, if people could simply republish any book they purchased themselves, the supply would increase, prices would plummet and consumers would benefit in the near-term, but authors would receive much less compensation. They would possibly have to stop writing books so they could support themselves. Copyright emerged as a policy solution to this problem, and dates to the emergence of commercial publishing. It allowed authors to have government-created monopoly rights to authorize the publication of their books for a set period of time so they could make enough money to have incentive to continue to write books.

Over-the-air broadcasting as it has been practiced is a public good. Whether three or 300 million people watch a program does not change the cost of producing that program or affect the satisfaction of individual viewers. There is no incentive to produce programs, because no one will pay you for them when they can watch them for free. Most nations solved this problem by using public money to create broadcasting content available to all. In the United States advertising emerged as the means to support content and make broadcasting viable.

The Internet, too, has strong attributes of a public good, and has undermined the "private good" attributes of old media. Internet service providers obviously can exclude people, but the actual content—the value, the ideas—once one accesses them can be shared with no loss of value for the consumer. It is also extremely inexpensive and easy to share material. This is built into the culture and practices of the Web. It has made it difficult for the "subscription" model to be effective. It explains much of the problem the film and music industries are having with the Internet, as well as firms that produce journalism. Because it is clear that advertising is not going to subsidize media content on the Internet as it did for broadcasting, we are in a situation where we may learn from public-good theory. In our view, what this suggests is we ought to be looking at ways to use public funds at the front end to produce content, and then allow it to be free on the Internet. At the most fundamental level, if we recognize the enormous changes that are reshaping how we can and will communicate, this is how we should be thinking about journalism.

This leads to the second way of thinking about journalism, a related concept to public goods, what economists call "externalities." These are the costs and benefits of market transactions that are not borne by the buyer or seller. Pollution is the classic negative externality that everyone cites. Neither the purchaser of automobiles nor the producer of automobiles has had to factor the immense environmental cost of automobiles into the price of the product, so the market cannot address pollution. Society pays these costs because they are external to the market. As a rule, markets are considered to be inefficient and inappropriate if there are large negative externalities, or potentially large and valuable positive externalities the market has no interest in generating. At the very least, markets with large negative externalities require government regulation to lessen the damage. (Consider whether automobiles would have spread so quickly if the cost of every car had included its share of the price for cleaning up the environment that we will be forced to pay if our species is to have much of a future.)

Government spending is often used in areas where it can generate large positive externalities, or where it will prevent or minimize negative developments in their absence. (This spending is often in sectors the market underdevelops, so there is a link to public-good theory, though they are a bit different.) Public education is a classic case. Good public schools will lead to a more educated society, with a higher standard of living and a more developed culture. This benefits everyone, even people who do not have children in public schools. The loss of the positive externality would produce consequences no one would want: lower economic growth, more crime, social insecurity and the like.[146] It is why people support public education, and why many of the founders of our nation put such emphasis upon it.

Journalism is chock-full of powerful externalities. If we have a tremendous journalism that informs and engages people, it will lead to more efficient and effective governance, a healthier economy and a vibrant culture. All our lives will be fuller and richer. It will benefit everyone, even people who elect not to consume journalism directly. Likewise, if the market downgrades and corrupts the production of journalism, it will lead to an ignorant citizenry with resultant corruption and misery. We will all suffer as a result. This is the scenario unfolding at present. Understanding journalism as having important externalities does not tell us what specific policy or policies to employ, but it tells us how to constructively think about the policymaking process.[147]

For economic activities that are public goods and/or that have powerful positive externalities, it can be difficult, even impossible, for people to use the marketplace to express their desires for the good or service. How does one demonstrate in the marketplace that one wants national defense or public health? What goods do you buy? It cannot be done. Along these lines, sometimes people want to have goods, and are willing to pay for them, even if they do not ever plan to use them. By market economics, this does not compute. We must confess that neither of us ever plans to take a trip to a national park in the balance of our lifetimes. If we counted our votes in the marketplace, that would mean we don't care if national parks exist. Privatize them, pave them over, who cares? Just lower our taxes, right? Wrong. In fact, we are strong supporters of national-park expansion and are more likely to vote for politicians who raise our taxes to that end. Because we like the idea that nature is being preserved, and we want to live in a country and world where there is more protected wilderness, our personal consumption choices in the market do not accurately reflect how we want society's resources allocated.

This is the situation with journalism, and a main limitation of journalism markets. Research with working-class Americans demonstrates that a striking number of them want public broadcasting, and are willing to pay taxes to support it, even if they do not plan to watch it themselves.[148] They want it for their children, or just to know there is somewhere to turn for noncommercial programming. It is a therefore a very popular use of government funds.[149] Our experience suggests the same thing is and will be true of journalism. Even people who do not regularly consume journalism like the idea that journalism exists, and that people are reporting on government, economics and the news of the day. They are willing to pay to see that journalism thrives even if they, for whatever reason, do not themselves plan to partake in it in substantial portions.

A third way to think about journalism is as a necessary part of our infrastructure. The term *infrastructure* is used primarily to refer to the roads, bridges, water systems, dams, airports, rail systems, schools, public utilities and the like that form the backbone upon which economic activity takes place. These are expenses that tend to be borne by the public sector.

Over the past three decades, the U.S. infrastructure has fallen into collapse. The American Society of Civil Engineers estimates the United States needs to spend $2.2 trillion over the next five years to get our infrastructure to the level of other economically advanced nations.[150] Financier Felix Rohatyn once told *New York Times* columnist Bob Herbert, "A modern economy needs a modern platform, and that's the infrastructure."[151] Increasingly, Americans understand that the Internet and broadband access are necessary parts of our infrastructure, as so much of our economic activity has shifted online. That the United States has fallen so far behind much of Europe and East Asia in broadband penetration and quality has proven damaging to economic growth and innovation.

We believe that we need to think of institutions producing journalism as a necessary and indispensable part of our economic infrastructure. In this book to this point and in all of our previous work, the emphasis has always been on the significance of journalism for democracy, and, conversely, the significance of democracy for journalism.[152] Arguably, the significance of journalism for markets to function efficiently and rationally is every bit as important. To work efficiently, markets depend upon consumers, workers and investors having accurate information, and such information is not generated through osmosis. It comes in large part from journalism, especially as political events and decisions go a long way toward shaping market activities. This is why we expect free market economists will rally to the cause of journalism, once they regard it as necessary infrastructure for all markets to function efficiently rather than as an area of economic importance only to the extent it can generate profits in its own right for investors.[153] It is difficult to imagine an advanced economy working well in the absence of strong journalism.

Allow us to be more concrete. If there is only one media lesson from the current economic crisis, let it be this: the global economic depression would not have taken place, or at the very least it would have been far less severe, had the United States had quality journalists in popular news media covering and investigating the financial sector and housing industry over the past dozen years. Dean Baker demonstrated that before the economy crashed the most cited expert, by far, in the major news media on the housing bubble was David Lereah, the hyperventilating chief economist of the National Association of Realtors, and author of the 2005 book *Why the Real Estate Boom Will Not Bust—And How You Can Profit From It*.[154] By Baker's count, Lereah alone received nearly one-half of the 3,600 citations in the major news media on the housing situation in 2005 and 2006.[155] It is not exactly like Lereah had any track record as an economic genius; to the contrary his expertise is at packaging pro-industry sound bites for mediocre pack reporters. His 2000 book *The Rules for Growing Rich: Making Money in the New Information Economy* promoted the idea of investing in new technologies and was published shortly before the markets for those firms crashed.[156]

Does anyone seriously think if we had a skeptical and challenging media focused on the concerns of the great mass of Americans that Congress would have voted to eliminate the Glass-Steagall banking regulations that were established to prevent precisely the sort of speculation that supercharged the current crisis? Members of the House and Senate would have told the bank lobbyists to take a hike. Instead, they quietly pocketed their campaign-contribution checks and voted to turn our financial system into a cesspool of toxic assets. Our economy is shaped to an inordinate degree by political decisions, and those decisions will be shaped by the level of press watchdogging and the degree of informed public participation that exists. Not too long ago the United States insisted that developing nations needed a viable independent free press to prevent corruption, economic stagnation, growing inequality and crony capitalism. It is time we take a dose of our own medicine. It is difficult to imagine a credible economy, not to mention a democracy, otherwise.[157]

Fourth, and finally, over the past two decades a considerable amount of American scholarship has examined the notion of the "public sphere." Drawn from the German scholar Jürgen Habermas, the core argument is that a crucial factor to the democratic revolutions of modern times has been the emergence of an independent realm, a public sphere, a commons, where citizens could meet to discuss and debate politics as equals free of government scrutiny or interference. The media has come to assume the role of the public sphere in the United States (and elsewhere). The logic of the public-sphere argument is to emphasize the importance of having a media system independent of both the state and the dominant corporate economic institutions. It has transcended much of the Left's difficulty in being critical of the government in principle and the conventional refusal to countenance the core problems brought on by corporate control and advertising. The public-sphere reasoning rejects the notion that our two choices are Rupert Murdoch or Joseph Stalin. For a generation it has provided a democratic road map and blasted open a way of thinking about a third way—an independent non-profit sector and/or small-business sector—as the necessary democratic media system. As with public-good theory, it does not tell which policies to employ, but it provides a valuable framework for thinking about appropriate policymaking.

Not surprisingly, the current critical juncture was seen clearly by only a handful of people as recently as a few years ago. "The reform of journalism will only occur when news organizations are disengaged from the global entertainment and information industries that increasingly contain them," wrote University of Illinois and Columbia professor James Carey, perhaps the dean of American journalism scholars, and no fan of government involvement with the press, in 2002. "Alas, the press may have to rely upon a democratic state to create the conditions necessary for a democratic press to flourish and for journalists to be restored to their proper role as orchestrators of the conversation of a democratic society."[158] That seems like a generation ago now, so much has happened in the intervening years. If the ensuing years have given us anything, it should be clarity. The direction is now well defined, if not yet so well understood as need be. "We are rapidly running out of alternatives to public finance," Todd Gitlin informed a conference on the crisis in journalism in May 2009. "It's time to move to the next level and entertain a grown-up debate among concrete ideas."[159]

Chapter 3

WHY THE
State

"Just as the most poisonous form of disorder is the mob incited from high places, the most immoral act the immorality of a government, so the most destructive form of untruth is sophistry and propaganda by those whose profession it is to report the news," wrote Walter Lippmann in *Liberty and the News*, his haunting meditation on the role of the press during World War I and its aftermath.

The news columns are common carriers. When those who control them arrogate to themselves the right to determine by their own consciences what shall be reported and for what purpose, democracy is unworkable. Public opinion is blockaded. For when a people can no longer confidently repair "to the best foundations for their information," then anyone's guess and anyone's rumor, each man's hope and each man's whim becomes the basis of government. All that the sharpest critics of democracy have alleged is true, if there is no steady supply of trustworthy and relevant news. Incompetence and aimlessness, corruption and disloyalty, panic and ultimate disaster, must come to any people which is denied an assured access to the facts. No one can manage anything on pap. Neither can a people.

Lippmann came to a conclusion that is even more instructive today than it was 90 years ago, when he argued that: "For in an exact sense the present crisis of western democracy is a crisis of journalism."[1] In short, the nature of journalism, and therefore the system that produces it, is a political issue of the highest magnitude.

In Chapter 1, we outlined the crisis in contemporary journalism, and provided the best explanation we could to account for the disastrous state of affairs. In Chapter 2, we chronicled the various measures, projects, innovations and new business models being developed to rejuvenate journalism, independent of government subsidies. We concluded that although many of these ventures are promising, even if they succeed we will remain far short of the resources and institutions necessary for a credible journalism. In this chapter, we continue to make the case that it is necessary for the state to institute policies to aggressively create and support journalism. By "the state," we mean all levels of government, but, in particular, the burden falls upon the federal government in Washington, D.C. We demonstrate in this chapter that while this may seem a radical notion, it is very much in keeping with great American democratic traditions. As Lippmann's prescient words remind us, the crisis we face today is not new, though it is far more severe than at any time in this country's history.

In many other democratic nations, there is no serious debate about the public interest in maintaining the public good that is journalism. Rather, there is a deep and sensible recognition that there will always be self-interested lobbies with their own agendas for state policies to suit their interests, and that they will need to be checked and balanced. But, these realities notwithstanding, the question that matters has to do with what are the best possible policies and subsidies to produce the desired results.

Many of the nations that enjoy the highest rates of voter participation, civic literacy and civil liberties maintain large direct public subsidies for journalism, through public broadcasting and, even, newspapers and magazines.[2] Countries like Holland, where Radio Netherlands is the jewel of international public broadcasting, or Norway, where a vibrant and competitive print and digital culture thrives in even the most remote regions, long ago made the discussion (and implementation) of media policies and subsidies a part of the debate about how to realize the promise of democracy.

At odds with democratic theory that had been inspired by Madison and his fellow drafters of the Constitution, and dismissing examples provided by healthy democracies around the world, the United States has gravitated toward an exceptionally constrained understanding of the role that the government might take in maintaining a democratic press system. We include this chapter, and allow it considerable length, because our argument goes against the grain of how most Americans have understood freedom of the press over the past century. In conventional parlance, as the late, great press scholar Timothy E. Cook put it, there is "a presumption that the First Amendment and the optimal public performance of journalism mandate a 'hands-off' approach from government."[3] The genius of the free press in the United States, we are told, has been that it is a function of the private sector; government involvement may work in Scandinavia, the argument goes, but it would be, well, downright un-American.

The phrase *freedom of the press*, recognized as an essential American value, has been watered down to the thin soup of protecting publishers from government censorship—i.e., the government cannot stop a medium from publishing what it wishes to publish. Indeed, if there is a common understanding of how the freedom-of-the-press provision of the Constitution works today, it is as a defense for peddlers of pornography and hateful literature. In the contemporary conventional wisdom, this is what the First Amendment is all about—keeping the fringes of discourse free from government interference.[4] If the government gets out of the way and lets the marketplace work its magic, all will be right with the Republic. After all, "Congress shall make no law ... "

Freedom of the press has been remade as a narrow protection that is virtually synonymous with freedom of speech. So thorough has the rewrite of history been that reasonable Americans might honestly wonder whether the founders—had they had access to a decent copy editor— might have eliminated any reference to the press from the Constitution. After all, under the rigid calculus of the current definitions, a freedom-of-speech protection would provide all the cover that's needed by the press and journalism. Too many scholars and journalists casually assume that the sole point of the freedom-of-the-press protection was to keep the government's hands off the press.[5] Just as the United States would not condone government interference with a person's right to stand on a soapbox and criticize the powerful, the theory goes, so it is suggested that the United States cannot condone official interference with a business or individual as it provides journalism to the market.

This relatively new article of faith has become so widely accepted that many working journalists—including some sincere, highly principled and savvy advocates for the craft—now wear it as a form of bondage. Journalist Bree Nordenson recalls that when she informed Tom Rosenstiel of the Project for Excellence in Journalism that she was writing an article for the *Columbia Journalism Review* about the ways government could support the press, he "responded brusquely, 'Well, I'm not a big fan of government support.'"

"I explained that I just wanted to put the possibility on the table," Nordenson noted.

"Well, I'd take it off the table," Rosenstiel replied.[6]

Of course, the rejection of government censorship is essential. As "small-*d*" democrats, we embrace freedom to communicate ideas and ideals—especially unpopular or controversial ones—as a basic value. As scholars of media, we find it utterly necessary for a free press. We would never advocate "reforms" that provided the slightest opening for censorious practices, and we take a backseat to no one in opposing the heavy hand of government. In fact, we have been ardent campaigners, in the United States and abroad, on behalf of journalists and journalism that is under threat from government meddling and worse.

But it will not be possible to save journalism unless all the players recognize that fretting about government interference has grown increasingly dogmatic over the past century—egged on by media moguls who have used concerns about censorship as a tool for attacking public-interest obligations that might be required in exchange for their lavish privileges. This false and self-serving construct has obscured the historical and empirical truth about the complex and necessary role of the government in our press system.

Well-intended journalists like Rosenstiel remind us of the Colonel Nicholson character in *The Bridge on the River Kwai*. Prisoner-of-war Nicholson, played by Alec Guinness in the 1957 Academy Award–winning film, held so fervently to his upper-class notion of British chivalry that he was willing to assist the Japanese military's plan to build a bridge to aid in its war with Britain. The British officer was willing to assist in the defeat of what he cherished most in order to remain true to his code of honor. When journalists and their allies allow the fantasy that government has no role in promoting and preserving a free and functional press, they become Colonel Nicholsons in the face of the most serious crisis ever for journalism.

Birthing a Free Press

A major problem with the dogma surrounding freedom of the press is that it assumes an "immaculate conception" theory of the press. Because in much of the 19th and all of the 20th centuries a viable (if far from ideal) commercial press system existed, it was taken for granted that the market was always prepared to generate satisfactory journalism as long as the government got out of the way. Accordingly, scholars and analysts looked back at the founding period of the Republic and the years that followed it with an eye toward telling the romantic tales of heroic figures like colonial printer John Peter Zenger, abolitionist editor Elijah Lovejoy and their kind—courageous journalists battling government censorship and interference with their scrappy newspapers and uncompromising journalism.[7] It became the be-all-and-end-all for examinations of freedom of the press, and the primary focus of discussions with regard to the building of a viable press system for a self-governing society.

Don't get us wrong: we're the first to show up for celebrations of Zenger and Lovejoy as heroes of journalism. History continues to prove correct Zenger's declaration that "No nation, ancient or modern, ever lost the liberty of speaking freely, writing, or publishing their sentiments, but forthwith lost their liberty in general and became slaves."[8] And our vision of what a free press can and should be is informed by our awareness of the role abolitionist newspaper editors played in advancing the anti-slavery struggle, such that we revere Lovejoy's rebuke of the taunting mobs that would eventually take his life: "But, gentlemen, as long as I am an American citizen, and as long as American blood runs in these veins, I shall hold myself at liberty to speak, to write, to publish whatever I please on any subject—being amenable to the laws of my country for the same."[9]

The struggle against censorship—by the mob or the government—was indeed a vital fight at the time the American experiment was taking shape, as it remains today; but it was hardly the only issue then, any more than it is today. Unfortunately, even serious students of the press will be excused for thinking it so. After all, we are told as much by scholars who should know better.

Consider two of the most renowned and thoughtful statements on the American tradition of freedom of the press. William Hocking's influential *Freedom of the Press*, published in conjunction with Robert Hutchins's groundbreaking Commission on Freedom of the Press in 1947, offers a glowing description of the early American press experience as one of "near-total freedom."[10] "Laissez faire was not merely a maxim for keeping government out of economic life," Hocking wrote, "it was a general principle or admonition for keeping government out of the whole range of spontaneous human nature."[11] The seminal *Four Theories of the Press*, published in 1956, informs us that the founders of the Republic "were opposed to government support since it led to domination, and they trusted the capitalist system of private enterprise to find a way."[12] Reading these writers, it is easy to imagine that the first American newspapers were brought off the presses by entrepreneurs steeped in Adam Smith's *Wealth of Nations*, rather than an industry that was, in fact, dependent upon extraordinary public subsidies.

In the past three decades a new generation of historians, communication scholars, political scientists and constitutional scholars has taken a fresh look at the Colonial and founding periods and the early Republic that has dispensed with "presentism"—i.e., reading into the past the values and conditions that are dominant today by effectively assuming them to be timeless. By dusting off long-neglected archival records of the founding era and first decades of the 19th century and engaging directly with them, these scholars have expanded our understanding of press freedom and the role journalism plays in our governing system. Their work demolishes the laissez-faire notion of old-school press history, which suggests freedom of the press is an individual right for commercial printers to do their own thing in a competitive market.[13]

Robert W.T. Martin, as much as any of the new scholars of American press history, has demonstrated that the authors of the Constitution operated under different premises and presumptions than are now generally observed. They understood newspapering in their day to operate in the context of what Martin refers to as a "free *and* open press." The words might seem synonymous. But that has never been the case. Martin explains:

> Free press doctrine lionized the press as a prime defender of public liberty in its role as a bulwark against governmental tyranny. Open press doctrine, on the other hand, stressed the individual right of every man to air his sentiments for all to consider, regardless of his political perspective or the consequences for the people's liberty.[14]

Cook agrees that "The open press model was as much in the air as the free press model approach when the First Amendment was adopted. Eighteenth-century observers did not cleanly distinguish the two."[15]

In short, freedom of the press was intended for citizens and the broader community as much as it was for printers. In early American discourse the stress was "on civic virtue and public, rather than private, good."[16] Early Americans, Martin writes,

> Clearly saw the tension between individual rights and the public good, between an open press and a free press. Even their open press discourse defended the right to press liberty not for individual expression in our current, increasingly self-indulgent sense but rather so that the community might hear and judge the merit of others' views.[17]

It is historically inaccurate to equate printers of the 18th or early 19th century with the press barons of the later 19th and 20th centuries.[18]

Printers were not considered entrepreneurs out to maximize personal profit by pursuing their naked self-interest, or even opinionated advocates of a specific viewpoint. "Printers are of the belief, that when Men differ in Opinion," Benjamin Franklin wrote in his famous essay "An Apology for Printers," "both Sides ought equally to have the Advantage of being heard by the Publick." Franklin rejected the notion that printers should only publish that with which they personally agreed: "An end would thereby be put to Free Writing, and the World would afterward have nothing to read but what happen'd to be the Opinions of Printers."[19] The job of the press, Franklin explained, was to stimulate debate, to stir the masses to action, to enlighten and, yes, to offend. "[If] all Printers were determin'd not to print anything till they were sure it would offend nobody, there would be very little printed."[20]

The press was understood as a political and in many practical senses public institution, necessary to self-government, and with obligations to serve the citizenry. "Americans generally felt," Martin writes, "that the printing presses, though legally their private property, were in some real sense public institutions that printers were obliged to manage for the public good."[21]

That service to the Republic was easily defined. But a great many practical questions about how that service might be rendered—and about how the government might encourage the process—absorbed the founders. And, as with so many of the first debates, there were genuine differences of opinion about the proper role of the press.[22] A striking degree of support developed around the importance of dissent. This was not motivated by some feel-good faith that letting wrongheaded dissenters air their fringe opinions would prove the strength of the system—of the sort now evidenced by pompous editorial writers who muse about the value of free-speech "safety valves" that let wacky outriders spout off—but because there was some sense that the great mass of citizens might benefit from the ability to assess views that, while outside the mainstream, might have validity.[23] Dissenting ideas were still ideas—some good, some bad, some backward, some so enlightened that they were ahead of their time—and they had to be made available to the broader citizenry.

Press theorist Tunis Wortman, a New York lawyer whose work one historian characterizes as "having a profound effect upon the country's attitudes," argued in the late 18th century that a genuine public opinion required a sharp and contested diversity of views, and that without such diversity genuine popular sovereignty could not effectively emerge.[24] Indeed, Wortman suggested, access to well-reasoned and well-presented dissenting views—such as the still radical notion that kings might not govern by "divine right"—could instantaneously free individuals from the bondage of old-world thinking: "In an instant the fairy spell of delusion is dissipated—the tremendous authority of this august and magnanimous despot, like the enchanted castle of the magician, vanishes for ever."[25]

Robert W.T. Martin notes that, in post-Colonial times, dissent was sometimes conflated with the notion that "the lower orders" needed to be full participants in the press system. One prominent radical democrat of the founding period, William Manning, whose work demonstrates that freedom of the press was not a matter simply debated among elites, was already suspicious in the 1790s that printers would use their privileges to "monopolize the creation and diffusion of knowledge, and to discourage popular enlightenment."[26] He argued that farmers and laborers should have their own newspapers.[27]

Jefferson recognized the necessity of the dissenting journal in the 1790s when he credited William Duane's *Aurora* newspaper with averting a totalitarian turn during the struggle over the Alien and Sedition Acts. The *Aurora*'s crusading journalism, Jefferson argued, "arrested the rapid march of our government toward monarchy."[28]

While there were rollicking disagreements about the character and content of the post-Colonial press in America, the one universally accepted premise was that the government needed to heavily subsidize the creation and development of the press if the constitutional system were to succeed. There was no notion in the early Republic, not a single solitary voice anywhere, that the press should be left to "the market" and that commercial auspices could effectively and efficiently guide journalism as long as the heavy hand of the state remained out of the way. It would be generations before the economics came together and provided the resources to make that argument plausible. The idea that Americans should roll the dice and hope rich people would find it profitable to produce the journalism required for a constitutional republic to succeed was simply unimaginable in the days when America was conceived and formed.

The premise that government subsidies were necessary for a press system was so accepted it was rarely even commented upon. To be charitable, let's assume that is why generations of 20th-century press scholars failed to notice it or address it in their many chronicles of press history. Now, however, the true history of the subsidies and of the vibrant, reforming, diverse and progressive news-media system they created is essential knowledge. Like the ancient treatment that, when rediscovered, unlocks a fresh understanding of the possibilities for healing diseases, the medicine that the founders applied offers an answer to the question of how we will support great journalism in the 21st century.

What Would Jefferson (and Madison) Do?

The very mention of the word *subsidy* provokes a reaction, not just from conservatives who may disdain any role for government in the shaping of economic affairs but from civil libertarians who are especially fearful of the heavy hand of government shaping the discourse. One reaction will be to acknowledge these subsidies but claim that the times were so dramatically different in the past, and/or the notions of the press were so unrecognizable by contemporary standards, that historical examples hold little or no relevance for us today. So before examining the subsidies of the past, and explaining their breadth and importance, let us pause for a moment and consider some of the main thoughts of Thomas Jefferson and James Madison, arguably the two founders who devoted the most attention to matters of the press. Let's see what importance they ascribed to the press, and whether those concerns hold today. If their concerns remain pressing, then surely their policy approach deserves scrutiny, particularly at a point when feasible alternatives would seem to be lacking.[29]

At a baseline level, contemporary observers recognize that both Madison and Jefferson aggressively advanced the notion that a free press was necessary to create the informed citizenry that made popular sovereignty and democracy possible. No journalism means no democracy, and no constitutional form of government based upon popular sovereignty. "To the press alone," Madison observed, "checquered as it is with abuses, the world is indebted for all the triumphs which have been gained by reason and humanity over error and oppression."[30] Leaving nothing to doubt, Jefferson delivered the most emphatic statement in his famous letter to Edward Carrington of January 16, 1787. A sentence from the middle of the letter has often been extracted: "Were it left to me to decide whether we should have a government without newspapers, or newspapers without a government, I should not hesitate a moment to prefer the latter."[31]

Jefferson went so far, during the struggle over the Alien and Sedition Acts that would frame the country's first great debate over press freedom, to suggest that, "To preserve the freedom of the human mind then & freedom of the press, every spirit should be ready to devote itself to martyrdom."[32]

Such expressions are exceptionally powerful, and give a sense across history of Madison's and Jefferson's convictions. These are not transitory stances; they stand the test of time. But they do not do justice to the power and depth of their thinking on the subject. Consider this expanded passage of Jefferson's letter to Carrington:

> The way to prevent these irregular interpositions of the people is to give them full information of their affairs thro' the channel of the public papers, and to contrive that those papers should penetrate the whole mass of the people. *The basis of our governments being the opinion of the people,* the very first object should be to keep that right; and were it left to me to decide whether we should have a government without newspapers, or newspapers without a government, I should not hesitate a moment to prefer the latter. *But I should mean that every man should receive those papers and be capable of reading them* [our emphasis].

For Jefferson, just having the right to speak without government censorship is a necessary but insufficient condition for a free press, and therefore democracy. It also demands that there be a literate public, a viable press system, and that people have easy access to this press.

In the same letter, Jefferson praises Native American societies for being largely classless and happy, and criticizes European societies in no uncertain terms for being the opposite. Jefferson also stakes out the central role of the press in stark class terms when he describes the role of the press in preventing exploitation and domination by the rich over the poor:

> Among [European societies], under pretence of governing they have divided their nations into two classes, wolves and sheep. I do not exaggerate. This is a true picture of Europe. Cherish therefore the spirit of our people, and keep alive their attention. Do not be too severe upon their errors, but reclaim them by enlightening them. If once they become inattentive to the public affairs, you and I, and Congress, and Assemblies, judges and governors shall all become wolves. It seems to be the law of our general nature, in spite of individual exceptions; and experience declares that man is the only animal which devours his own kind, for I can apply no milder term to the governments of Europe, and to the general prey of the rich on the poor.[33]

In short, to the press comes the obligation to undermine the natural tendency of propertied classes to dominate politics, reduce the masses to effective powerlessness and eventually terminate self-government.

Madison shared Jefferson's concerns and wrote about growing inequality in the context of the emergence of empire. Madison understood that the United States was going to be an extraordinarily rich and powerful nation. Indeed, this was not especially hypothetical; George Washington referred to "the rising American empire" as early as 1783.[34] Madison understood that even a democratically elected government would have strong incentives to become an imperial power, enmeshed in militarism and foreign wars:

> Of all the enemies of true liberty, war is, perhaps, the most to be dreaded, because it comprises and develops the germ of every other. War is the parent of armies; from these proceed debts and taxes; and armies, and debts, and taxes are the known instruments for bringing the many under the domination of the few. In war, too, the discretionary power of the Executive is extended; its influence in dealing out offices, honors and emolu-

ments is multiplied; and all the means of seducing the minds, are added to those of subduing the force, of the people. The same malignant aspect in republicanism may be traced in the inequality of fortunes, and the opportunities of fraud, growing out of a state of war, and in the degeneracy of manner and of morals, engendered in both. No nation can preserve its freedom in the midst of continual warfare.[35]

It is striking that the two issues Jefferson and Madison highlighted as the main threats to democracy—inequality and empire—remain arguably the central cancers for constitutional rule in our times. As we noted in Chapter 1, coverage of militarism and inequality may be the two greatest weaknesses of recent American journalism. The necessary role of the press to inform and engage those without great amounts of property or who do not benefit from these developments has not changed. The main difference is that with a global political economy and weapons of virtually unimaginable power, the stakes are vastly higher today.

In their times Madison and Jefferson were among the loudest advocates of a heavily subsidized press and had a firm commitment to seeing dissident views get a fair hearing. At the same time, they were among the most eloquent opponents of government censorship of the press. It seems only reasonable to suggest that we can learn from them and their peers how to construct a democratic press in an environment when the "free market" is insufficient or inappropriate to get the job done.

Subsidizing the Press

So what did the United States government do to spawn a press system in the early Republic and thereafter?

Long before the Revolution, under the auspices of Deputy Postmaster Benjamin Franklin, a postal service developed to serve commerce and government, and also as a means of transporting newspapers.[36] Its growth generated the "wide circulation of news throughout the colonies," according to Cook, which "made the American Revolution possible."[37] The postal system fell into disarray during the Revolution and was in tatters by 1790. Consequently, the number of newspapers fell from 37 to 20 over the course of the Revolution, but the political turbulence of the late 1780s led to a relatively strong rebirth. By 1790 there were eight daily newspapers in the nation—there were none before 1783—and there were 83 weeklies.[38]

Clarifying the postal situation was a matter of pressing concern, and the focus was almost entirely upon its role for distributing newspapers. Benjamin Rush, one of the great shapers of the American experiment and Thomas Paine's close compatriot, was a signer of the Declaration of Independence and a key champion of the adoption of the Constitution.[39] In the midst of the constitutional debates of 1787, Rush argued:

> For the purpose of diffusing knowledge, as well as extending the living principle of government to every part of the united states—every state— city—county—village—and township in the union, should be tied together by means of the post-office. ... It should be a constant injunction to the postmasters, to convey newspapers free of all charge for postage. They are not only the vehicles of knowledge and intelligence, but the centinels of the liberties of our country.[40]

No less a figure than the first president encouraged the process. "For my part I entertain a high idea of the utility of periodical publications; insomuch as I could heartily desire, copies of ... magazines, as well as common Gazettes, might be spread through every city, town, and village in the United States," observed George Washington in 1788. "I consider such vehicles of knowledge more happily calculated than any other to preserve the liberty, stimulate the industry, and ameliorate the morals of a free and enlightened people."[41]

The Constitution gave Congress the power "to establish Post Offices and post Roads." The resulting Post Office Act of 1792 was arguably one of the most significant pieces of legislation in the nation's history; as Richard R. John observes, the Post Office was "rapidly transformed into a dynamic institution that would exert a major influence on American commerce, politics, and political thought."[42] Theda Skocpol notes that "the postal system was the biggest enterprise of any kind in the pre-industrial United States."[43] In fact, it created the infrastructure of the new country. In the 1790s alone, the total mileage of "post roads," those arterials necessary for transport, increased from 1,875 to 21,000.[44] The number of post offices went from 195 in 1792 to 2,610 in 1812, to 8,000 by 1830.[45] As John puts it, "For the vast majority of Americans, the postal system was the central government." It was the largest single employer in the country. In 1831, for example, 75 percent of civilian federal employees worked for the Post Office; by 1860 the proportion had climbed to over 80 percent.[46]

What makes this crucial for our discussion, and what is striking upon review, is that the Post Office was primarily a medium of mass communication. David Henkin, the postal historian, concludes that "the extraordinary significance of the post in American public life from the 1790s at least until the 1830s lay precisely in this special relationship to the periodical press."[47] In 1794 newspapers made up 70 percent of Post Office traffic, by weight; during much of the 19th century the figure was well over 90 percent.

The crucial debate in the Congress of 1792 was what rate newspapers should be charged to be sent through the mail. All parties agreed that Congress should permit newspapers to be mailed at a price well below actual cost—to be subsidized—to encourage their production and distribution. In Congress, the range of debate was between those who wished to charge newspapers a nominal fee for postage and those who wanted to permit newspapers the use of the mail absolutely free of charge. The latter faction was supported by Benjamin Franklin's grandson (and Thomas Paine's publisher), Benjamin Franklin Bache, who argued that any postal charge would open the door to commercial pressures that would be unacceptable because they would "check if not entirely put a stop to the circulation of periodical publications."[48]

Bache was the great champion of press freedom in the early days of the Republic—he took as his motto "The Freedom of the Press is the Bulwark of Liberty"—so his understanding of the threat posed by economic barriers to the practice of journalism becomes especially instructive.[49] And Bache had powerful allies. James Madison called even a token postal fee a "tax" on newspapers and "an insidious forerunner of something worse."[50] By his fifth annual address, President Washington came out for free postage for newspapers through the mail, and even Treasury Secretary Alexander Hamilton, hardly a proponent of government deficit, conceded that the huge subsidy was necessary to spawn a viable press.[51] "Weighing all probabilities of expense as well as of income," President Thomas Jefferson stated in his first annual address to Congress in 1801, "there is reasonable ground of confidence that we may now safely dispense with ... the postage on newspapers ... to facilitate the progress of information."[52]

Those favoring completely free delivery did not quite prevail, however. One of the arguments against universal free postage, advanced by local printers, held that some graduated postal rates on newspapers traveling long distances were necessary to keep local newspapers thriving and to prevent newspaper publishing from becoming dominated by printers in the largest cities.[53] Pressure from both printers and the citizenry made the only relevant issue for Congress for subsequent generations whether to eliminate this relatively small postal rate. There were strong and passionate debates over how precisely the postal subsidy should be implemented but not over the subsidy itself. John C. Calhoun, one of the dominant political figures of the first half of the 19th century, explained: "The mail and the press are the nerves of the body politic."[54]

"There does not appear to have been a man in Congress," one writer observed in 1843, "who suspected that newspapers had not a divine right to some exclusive privilege at the post-office."[55] Abolitionists and dissident political groups (as well as printers, of course) participated in the fight to maintain and extend the postal subsidy of newspapers, arguing that the boldest publications—those advancing the radical ideas that would come to be embodied in the Republican Party that would emerge in 1854—needed the postal subsidy to survive. In 1851, Congress granted free postal privileges to weekly newspapers within their home county. Within a year, 20 percent of newspapers being mailed qualified for free postage.[56]

How extensive were these subsidies? "Between 1792 and 1845," Culver Smith, a scholar on the subject of subsidies, wrote, "the minimum charge for a letter ranged from six to twenty-five cents, depending on the distance, but the maximum postage for a newspaper for any distance was one and one-half cents."[57] All the original research by the leading scholars on the subject finds that newspapers and pamphlets accounted for around 95 percent of the weight of the mail and less than 15 percent of the Post Office revenues. Even this arguably underestimates the subsidy, because those historians like Richard John who have combed the records contend that many newspapers were mailed without being included in the official reports.

The ranks of unreported newspapers sometimes included those news-papers publishers were entitled to mail to each other at no charge. This "free exchange" of newspapers became crucial to spreading the news around the nation before the wire services, as newspapers liberally lifted material from each other's papers. "Free exchange" is estimated to have accounted for approximately 15 percent of newspaper traffic.[58] By the middle of the 19th century the consequences of the large postal subsidy—the fee was "trifling," even to Bache—had been the "almost illimitable circulation of newspapers through the mails," as one journalist remarked in 1851.[59]

The postal subsidy effectively built what became "America." During the first 75 years of the Republic, Henkin writes, "large numbers of Amer-icans subscribed to nonlocal journals, and newsprint flooded every post office in the country."[60] So significant was the role of the postal system that it became a significant, sometimes central, subject of debates about slavery.

Southern officials blocked the mail delivery of Northern publications so frequently by the 1850s that historian Elizabeth Hewitt notes, "Mail censorship increasingly became a rallying cry in both anti-southern and abolitionist literature." Congressional debates on the issue were heated, as the abolitionist press "began to include extended discussion of the fi-nancial statistics of the United States Post Office that [detailed] the precise ways in which 'the post offices of the south do not pay their way.'" Con-gressional debates touched on the question of Southern "mail robbery."[61] Hewitt notes:

The attack on southern censorship of the United States mail centered on two issues: censorship of the mail comprised yet another example of slavery's infringement on liberties and that this Draconian restriction of the post was all the more illegitimate since the postal system was largely subsidized by the north.[62]

Thus, the postal subsidy was not merely an artifact of the founding moment. It was a powerful force in forming the debates that would forge America as we know it—so powerful that it was resisted and hated by Southern slaveholders who resisted progress, so powerful that it entered into our American literary canon. Harriet Beecher Stowe, in her abolitionist novel *Dred*, features a scene in which a Southern gentleman is rebuked for obtaining "incendiary documents through the post office." The man, a Mr. Clayton, is told: "Sir, we are obliged to hold the mail under supervision in this state, and suspected persons will not be allowed to receive communications without oversight."[63]

With regard to the development of journalism, the postal subsidy was more than just powerful. It was definitional. As John concludes, the 1792 act "transformed the role of the newspaper press in American public life."[64] The number of newspapers in the United States increased from 200 in 1800 to 1,200 by 1830.[65] See Chart 1 for graphic representation.

This point was not lost on visiting Europeans, who were continually commenting on the remarkable prevalence of newspapers in American culture and politics.[66] In his *Democracy in America*, Alexis de Tocqueville wrote with astonishment of the "incredibly large" number of periodicals in the United States.[67] This had nothing to do with some notion of a laissez-faire, commercially driven newspaper market—presumed by many modern-day observers as the *sine qua non* of the founders' notion of a free press. Tocqueville wisely credited the Post Office, which, as he put it, connected the 13 million Americans spread over a rugged half continent better than the people were linked in a single province in France.[68] Timothy Cook concludes: "Public policy from the outset of the American Republic focused explicitly on getting the news to a wide readership, and chose to support news outlets by taking on costs of delivery and, through printers' exchanges, of production."[69] This was enlightened democratic policymaking, because it offered the same benefits to all newspapers regardless of their viewpoint, and it was extraordinarily successful.[70]

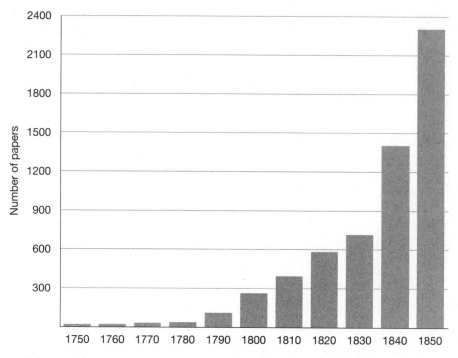

CHART 1. Daily, Weekly, Semi-weekly and Tri-weekly Papers, 1750-1850[71]

Subsidizing the Partisan Press

This summary does not do justice to the way in which the press system was consciously subsidized as a Fourth Estate in the first several generations of the Republic. In many respects, "newspaper politics" were central to all political life in the first few generations of the American experience.[72] Beginning in the 1790s, and evolving for decades thereafter, until it peaked in the 1830s and 1840s, editors were seen as politicians and were treated accordingly.[73] Ben Franklin's common carrier printer morphed into the highly partisan political operative with a printing press.[74] Many editors and publishers, including *The New York Tribune's* Horace Greeley, a serious if unsuccessful contender for the presidency in 1872, became candidates themselves. Most newspapers were funded by political parties or interests, and many of them depended not only on minuscule postal rates, but also government printing contracts to provide the revenues to subsidize their publications. These subsidies were consciously understood as an express method to generate a broad and well-funded press as well as to support political allies.

The official printing subsidies were many. The State Department, under Jefferson and Madison, the first and fifth secretaries of state, instituted subsidies of scores of newspapers, two or three in every state, to publish government laws and notices. By the time the program ended, deep into the 19th century, hundreds of papers—some of them still in existence—were the beneficiaries.[75] Each president, from Jefferson to James Buchanan, designated a Washington newspaper as "official," and gave it lucrative printing contracts to publish government documents. Jefferson arranged for printing subsidies for Samuel Harrison Smith to establish *The National Intelligencer*, which would become the *New York Times* and *Washington Post* of its day, though expressly committed to support Jeffersonian politics. Finally, the House and Senate each elected printers to receive payments for publishing congressional materials, and more important, to subsidize their newspapers. These congressional subsidies alone ran several hundred thousand dollars annually by the 1810s.[76] This was no small sum of money in a time when the defense budget totaled just $4 million.[77]

Unlike the postal subsidies, these printing subsidies were not "viewpoint neutral." The choice by a president or a senator of an "official" publication opens the door to far more political chicanery than a general postal subsidy. Yet, these subsidies offer another illustration of how the federal government contributed to the growth of a free and freewheeling, competitive and combative press in the young United States. As journalism historian John Nerone puts it, the subsidy system that produced "partisan newspapering was ideologically tolerable or attractive only because the system made it possible for competing newspapers to exist in small markets that ordinarily would have trouble supporting more than one paper."[78]

These press subsidies were very much built into the politics of the day. When Jefferson assumed office in 1801, he aggressively coordinated both federal and state printing contracts to subsidize *The National Intelligencer* and other publications to counteract the Federalists. Federalist assaults on freedom of the press during the presidency of John Adams—

which included the arrest and imprisonment of congressman/editor Matthew Lyon—had horrified Jefferson and inspired his 1800 presidential campaign. In that 1800 campaign, a significant majority of the nation's 200 newspapers opposed Jefferson and supported the Federalists, a situation Jefferson considered untenable.[79] Entering the White House in 1829, Andrew Jackson "elevated patronage of the press to a new level." He devoted $25,000 per year to the editor of his Washington-based newspaper and assigned 59 editors to "plush political appointments."[80]

The highly partisan journalism of this era would be derided by Frank Luther Mott, a leading journalism historian of the mid-20th century, as representing the "Dark Ages" of American journalism. To Mott's generation, it was best to jump from 1792 to the emergence of commercial journalism 50 years later—and the less said about the intervening Jeffersonian and Jacksonian periods the better.[81] It is common for historians of journalism to avoid attempts to reconcile the fact that the same enlightened geniuses who crafted the First Amendment also created a partisan press system subsidized by political parties and government contracts, not to mention postal giveaways. But the two pieces of the puzzle fit together if we consider the actions of these men in the context of the struggle to establish and advance a press system that fostered a raucous democratic discourse featuring participation by those who were not members of the elite.

There are important lessons here. First, not all partisan press systems need become Soviet or Nazi-style propaganda machines, producing ignorance, conformity and darkness at noon. The key to having a democratic, partisan press system is that there must be multiple competing well-funded media. If the party in power could outlaw the opposition press, it would effectively terminate its opposition. But that is not what Jefferson sought to do; indeed, he sought to strengthen journals that had been attacked by his Federalist predecessors. During the John Adams administration, the Federalists used the Alien and Sedition Acts to muzzle the Jeffersonian press. During the entire period from 1800 to 1860, federal and state subsidies were spread for the most part among all the leading parties and factions. At no point were the federal subsidies restricted to a single party. In 1832, for example, federal patronage supported three newspapers in Washington, D.C.: one for Andrew Jackson; one for Henry Clay;

and one for John C. Calhoun. The first two ran against each other for president that year while Calhoun resigned the vice presidency in 1832 to become a powerful—and frequently dissenting—voice in the Senate.

Second, far from diminishing democracy, the actions of Jefferson, Jackson and their compatriots appear by most accounts to have fostered its expansion. Ordinary Americans in these so-called dark ages, particularly in the Northern states, were unusually interested in politics compared to their counterparts in other eras. We would argue that the nature of the press system had something to do with that. Its success hinged on a variety of well-subsidized viewpoints, not just those of the party in power, and on new political groups having a chance to enter the fray with their own journalistic organs—which attracted some of the finest writers of the time. Remember that young Walt Whitman got his start on the partisan papers of Long Island and New York City.[82] The "poet of democracy" engaged in most of the excesses of the politicized press, but he also developed his personal and poetic persona at the helm of a rigidly Democratic paper, *The Brooklyn Eagle*, from which he would write of the "curious kind of sympathy ... that arises in the mind of a newspaper conductor with the public he serves. ... Daily communion creates a sort of brotherhood and sisterhood between the two parties."[83]

Partisan journalism in a democracy must appeal to independents—and even to opponents—because it is attempting to win elections; thus the demands of politics can actually provide a check on the propaganda quotient. In such a competitive partisan environment, readers can be drawn to politics, because issues tend to be put in a broader context. There is less of a threat that they will be turned off by bland, antiseptic, decontextualized reporting or duplicitous politicking. This correlates with findings in Scandinavia, where high civic literacy and voting turnout is found alongside large partisan-press subsidies, which assure multiple political perspectives.[84]

It is also worth noting that freewheeling competition on the streets of major cities meant that every view was represented—either by existing papers or, if they proved inadequate, by new publications. Inspired by the antislavery movement, Whitman began to chafe at the constraints placed upon him as editor of the *Eagle*, a paper that was not ready to break with a Democratic Party that was not ready to break with its Southern base. "The troubles in the Democratic party broke forth," he would write in *Specimen Days*, "and I split off with the radicals, which led to rows with the boss and 'the party,' and I lost my place."[85] In short order, he had found new backers for his dissident views and emerged as the editor of *The Freeman*, declaring that, "Smiles or frowns, thick or thin, we shall establish a Radical Newspaper in Kings County."[86]

The breadth and flexibility of the partisan media system of the early to mid-19th century compares favorably with our current constrained, top-down mass-media system. In fact, it had more in common with what is most appealing about the digital media of the current age. And, as with blogs and Internet journalism, as we discussed in Chapter 2, there was a range of writing and editing that invited legitimate criticism but also showed flashes of brilliance.

There has been considerable historical research and debate over the past few decades regarding the quality of the journalism produced by the partisan press, but none of it supports Mott's "Dark Ages" view. Nerone observes that the subsidized newspapers were sometimes criticized as "bought papers," and that much of the content was commentary rather than news reporting in the modern sense of the term. At the same time, he notes, an independent reform press emerged simultaneously with the partisan press because the system remained open.[87] The resulting explosion of commercial newspaper publishing was built on the foundation laid by the partisan press; it was, on balance, a complementary relationship. Journalism historian Gerald Baldasty argues that the caliber of political debate produced by the press in this era was much higher than what would soon follow.[88] The historian of *The National Intelligencer* concluded that the subsidized system produced a caliber of journalism "that in many ways has not since been equaled on an intellectual level."[89] Walt Whitman, Horace Greeley and other partisan editors would surely agree.

Although the Post Office and printing subsidies were the foundation of the government creation of the press, there were other important policies. For starters, unlike their British counterparts, American newspapers were exempt from taxation. One 1815 estimate determined that over one-half the cost of a British newspaper subscription went to the government.[90] American editors and publishers, not so burdened, could start and maintain newspapers far more easily than their old-world counterparts—a fact that led a number of British journalists to decamp for the United States.

Another crucial policy was common in state constitutions and prescribed by Jefferson and John Adams: public education. The Northwest Ordinance of 1787 provided the sentiment, even the wording, for many state constitutions concerning state-funded public education: "Being necessary to good government and the happiness of mankind, schools and the means of education shall forever be encouraged" by the state legislatures.[91] In spirit, one can see the strong link between public education and a free press as democratic institutions. Moreover, public schools formed an important market for newspapers and reading material in general by creating literate citizens. Public libraries, also funded by state government, offered another avenue for individual education. Newspapers and the commercial publishing industries would have been a shadow of themselves—with many of their greatest contributions lost—were it not for these massive public subsidies.[92]

In sum, the record of the first several generations of the Republic is clear: "Newspapers came to be regarded not strictly as a private business, but as a public service," Smith concludes. Newspapers "supplied some urgent needs; they provided the best solution to the problem of communication between government and citizen."[93] It was, therefore, the first duty of the democratic state to see that a viable journalism existed. The state nurtured a free-press system the free market showed little interest in providing; and it did so because, without state intervention on behalf of the public's right to know, constitutional rule, not to mention self-government, could not succeed. This legacy is something Americans should be deeply proud of, as it is one of our great contributions to the development of democracy not merely in the United States but in the world. Indeed, as we discuss in Chapter 4 and demonstrate in Appendix II, when the U.S. military occupiers of Germany and Japan sought to displace fascism after World War II, they carried forward the American founding commitment to intervention on behalf of a free and freewheeling press.

Journalism in the Commercial Era

As the Civil War approached, for a variety of reasons, the newspaper industry began to become commercially viable in its own right, and the great turn to a profit-driven, advertising-supported journalism commenced in earnest. The government printing contracts ended with the formation of the Government Printing Office in 1860, and the State Department ended its subsidy program in 1875.[94]

Postal subsidies remained but were of decreasing importance to the burgeoning daily-newspaper industry, which came to employ direct distribution via newsstand sales and delivery. Postal subsidies remained crucial for the massive weekly newspaper and magazine sectors, as did huge discounts for book postage, which exist to this day. As late as 1913, the postal subsidies for publications in 2009 dollars amounted to more than $5 billion.[95] Postal subsidies remained as American as apple pie— a fact that is conveniently forgotten today by the editors of publications that relied on these government handouts at crucial stages in their development. And they were handouts, even if few chose to admit the fact. During the 1910s, Richard John writes, Woodrow Wilson's postmaster general, Albert S. Burleson, faced rebuke for referring to the benefits conferred upon the press by the Post Office as a "subsidy." Burleson was chastised as one "who did not understand the fundamentals of the history of the press."[96]

During the second half of the 19th century commercial daily-newspaper publishing exploded in the United States, driven to a large extent by the rise of advertising, itself a function of the developing industrial-capitalist economy.[97] Advertising, which had been mostly a marginal phenomenon in the first few generations of the Republic, moved into the driver's seat and came over time to provide the majority of daily-newspaper revenues. Chart 2 graphs the meteoric increase in per capita print advertising in constant dollars from 1865 to 1937, which fueled the boom in newspaper production and profitability.

The mid-to-late 19th century marks the birth of the modern "free press," a press independent of government encumbrances but increasingly reliant on commercial ones. Although now fully profit-motivated

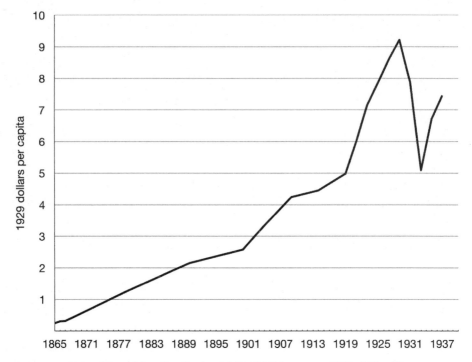

CHART 2. Print Advertising Per Capita, 1865–1937 (constant 1929 dollars)[98]

entities, and under growing commercial pressures to downplay partisanship, daily newspapers remained significantly associated with political parties and factions. Horace Greeley exemplifies this trend.

This was the era of economically competitive local commercial-newspaper markets. Between the years following the Civil War and the first two decades of the 20th century, as Chart 3 demonstrates, in any of the 12 largest cities in the United States, there were usually at least 10 daily newspapers in operation at any given time, and often many more than that. Low barriers to entry made it possible for newcomers to enter the market without onerous amounts of capitalization. Foreign-language daily newspapers serving immigrant communities proliferated. It was rare for a person to own more than one newspaper, and there was considerable turnover in the market. Prior to the 20th century it was uncommon for a single newspaper to have a circulation surpassing even 10 percent of a community's population in a major city. Even smaller towns—say Erie, Pennsylvania, or Evansville, Indiana—averaged four or five daily newspapers each during this period.[99]

The newspaper competition of this period is central to understanding how the conventional wisdom surrounding freedom of the press in the United States has crystallized. In this era, urged on by publishers, the term *freedom of the press* was narrowly redefined as protection of publishers from government interference with the newspaper business, to such an extent that press critic A. J. Liebling would eventually muse: "Freedom of the press is guaranteed only to those who own one."[100]

Private for-profit ownership with advertising support was presented as benign, or at least of no concern to the political system. Indeed, these constructs were portrayed as the American way. Government had no role to play and, in fact, should be seen as a threat, an evil that might destroy "freedom" and even democracy. The overriding concern the founders had with establishing a viable press open to a range of viewpoints, even unpopular ones, was no longer respected as necessary or appropriate, and was mostly forgotten. Nearly all viewpoints would get a fair hearing in the marketplace, the theory went, and if the existing range of viewpoints was insufficient new newspapers could be launched.

Although this understanding of freedom of the press dominates today, especially in a colloquial sense, the material conditions that spawned this understanding of a free press unraveled in short order. Competitive newspaper markets quickly begat concentrated markets with fewer and larger papers and higher barriers to entry, making it far more difficult for newcomers to enter the fray. The growth of the great chains (and massive fortunes) of the likes of Pulitzer, Hearst and Scripps only accentuated the process. The unintended effect of advertising as the main means of support for newspapers is that it tended to push local newspaper markets from oligopoly to duopoly or even monopoly, as advertisers rationally flocked to the leading newspaper(s) that could offer the best rates and the widest reach. It also made it prohibitive for newcomers to enter existing markets.

A classic sign of monopoly power: no more than a half dozen commercially successful daily newspapers were launched in existing markets after 1918, despite the fact that the industry was supremely (and to its critics, absurdly) profitable through the balance of the century and into

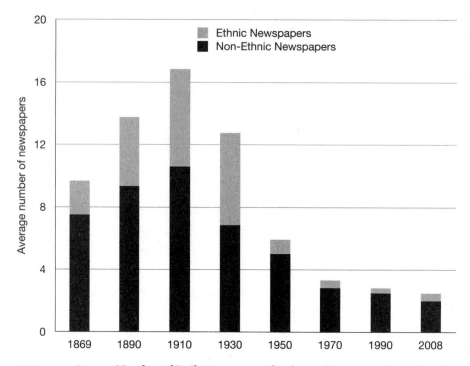

CHART 3. Average Number of Daily Newspapers for the Twelve Top Ranked U.S. Cities by Population, 1869-2008[101]

the 21st century.[102] Chart 3 demonstrates the rise and decline in the average number of daily newspapers in any of the 12 most populous cities from 1869 to 2008. Chart 4 does the same for the cities ranked 3-12, to remove the manner New York City skews the data. Chart 5 accounts for population growth, and demonstrates the number of daily newspapers in the 12 largest communities per 100,000 population from 1869 to 2008. The pattern any way you slice it is unmistakable.

As Chart 3 indicates, the total number of daily newspapers peaked by the 1920s, and only then began its great decline in the largest cities. If you approached a New York newsstand in 1924, hoping to catch up with the latest details of the three-way race for the presidency between Republican Calvin Coolidge, Democrat John Davis and Progressive Robert M. La Follette, you could choose from 15 seriously competing English-language dailies—the *Globe*, the *World*, the *Sun*, the *Mirror*, the *Graphic*, the *Telegram*, the *Mail*, the *American* and the newly established *Daily Worker*,

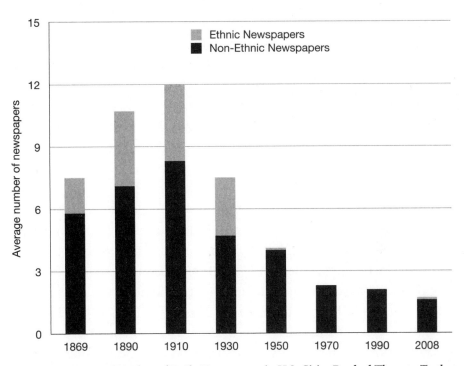

CHART 4. Average Number of Daily Newspapers in U.S. Cities Ranked Three to Twelve by Population, 1869-2008[103]

to name but a few on a list that included the *Times*, the *Post* and the *Daily News* but still anticipated the life and death of *PM*, the *Star*, the *Compass* and another *Sun*. That newsstand made room for stacks of mass-circulation dailies edited by refugee intellectuals: *Forverts*, *Freiheit* and three others in Yiddish; *New-Yorker Volkszeitung* and *Staats-Zeitung* in German; *Il Progresso Italo-Americano* in Italian; *Le Courrier des Etats-Unis* in French; *La Prensa* in Spanish; and *Al-Hoda* in Arabic.[104]

It was the same in Boston, where the *Post*, the *Daily Advertiser*, the *Evening Transcript* and the locally produced *Christian Science Monitor* jockeyed for a place on the rack with the *Herald* and the *Globe*; or San Francisco with its *Call & Post*, *Bulletin*, *Examiner*, *Chronicle*, *China Times* and *Nichibei Shimbun*, the Japanese-language paper that began publishing an English-language section in 1924.[105]

But the situation was soon to change and the consolidation that gripped smaller-town America came to our largest cities. It was not long

before many Americans realized that private ownership, profit orienta-
tion, concentrated markets and advertising had a great deal more to do
with the actual (and frequently negative) performance of the news media
than the prospect of direct government censorship, but only the latter
was considered a legitimate First Amendment or public-policy issue. During the entire era of commercial journalism there has been a trenchant
critique of the antidemocratic implications of the press structure, but it
has had almost no public-policy route to resolution.[106] In effect, the dis-
ease was identified but possible treatments were off the table. A classic
example was the 1947 Hutchins Commission on Freedom of the Press,
which delivered a blistering account of the limitations of the commercial
news media for generating the journalism a democratic society requires.[107] Nonetheless, it began its "what can be done" section by stating:
"We do not believe that the fundamental problems of the press will be
solved by more laws or by government action." Instead, in keeping with
the pattern throughout the 20th century, it recommended news-media
self-regulation.[108] The sanctity of the status quo, the dominance of commercial media, was inviolable.

In their pleas for enhanced self-regulation, critics played off the
fact that newspaper publishers consistently argued that they were not
merely profit-seeking engines of capital accumulation, willing to use
their power to advance their own political and commercial interests,
but public-service institutions, the people's advocates, and sentinels of
freedom. "Unless we can return to principles of public service," Rupert
Murdoch announced in 1961, invoking this tradition, "we will lose our
claim to be the Fourth Estate. What right have we to speak in the public
interest when, too often, we are motivated by personal gain?"[109]

The tension between commercial pressures and the public interest has
been the recurring theme of the past 120 years. By the first few decades
of the 20th century, it generated a major crisis in the commercial newspaper system. The profit motive often trumped notions of newspapers
as public servants, and sensationalism—publishing whatever generates
the most profit—became commonplace. Semimonopolistic ownership
of newspapers—initially in smaller communities, and eventually everywhere—often with conservative pro-business politics, left many Ameri-

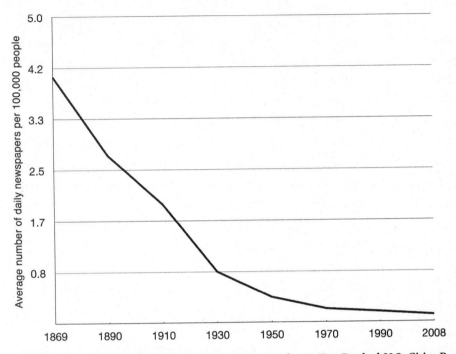

CHART 5. Average Number of Daily Newspapers in the 12 Top Ranked U.S. Cities Per 100,000 People, 1869-2008[110]

cans feeling powerless to raise an alternative voice, except on the distant margins.

The reliance on advertising did not merely give newspapers new masters, as readers accounted for a decreasing portion of the newspaper industry's revenues. It extracted a heavy toll on the content of newspapers. Advertisers wanted their products to receive favorable coverage, and the businesses that advertised had their own political viewpoints they wished to encourage.

The Progressive Era generated a tidal wave of popular press criticism, by writers like Will Irwin and Upton Sinclair, deploring the antidemocratic nature of the advertising-supported, semimonopolistic press system, as strong as anything before or after.[111] During this period voices began to call for nonprofit and/or municipal ownership of daily newspapers, and a few were actually launched.[112] A few publishers went so far as to offer "ad-less" newspapers, because they thought it would give their journalism much greater credibility.[113]

Despite social discontent, these experiments were exceptions to the rule, and structural reform was not in the offing; the power of the commercial system made it politically impossible.[114] Instead, the solution to this impasse was the rapid emergence of "professional journalism," the ultimate form of self-regulation. Professional journalism, to be clear, is a complex matter that owes to a number of factors, but it was, above all else, a frank acknowledgment that a commercially driven journalism was incompatible with a vibrant democracy.[115] For reporters and editors, professional journalism allowed them some autonomy from direct commercial pressures as they went about their work; for publishers, professionalism made their increasing market power and dependence upon advertising legitimate, and permitted them to generate extraordinary rates of return for a century.

The distinctive and crowning claim of professional journalism was that a division could be established between the owner/advertiser on the one hand and the editor/reporter on the other hand. Journalism would, it was declared, again have a public-service mission that trumped commercialism, although now under purely commercial auspices and at the discretion of the increasingly monopolistic owners. Power over the news was again in the newsroom, controlled by editors, who were educated to be neutral professionals in the newly created schools of journalism. If one avoided the editorial page, the theory went, one would have no idea what the politics of the owners (and editors) were. Likewise, because all professional journalists were to receive similar expert training, they would all select and cover news stories in a similar manner. Hence there would be no reason for a pressing concern about increasing concentration, lack of competition, even rampant monopolization in the daily-newspaper industry, since multiple papers would largely replicate each other. In an era when concerns about monopoly power were common, the American Society of Newspaper Editors was created and as its first act formally adopted a professional code for journalism in 1922.[116]

Nevertheless, it took many decades for professionalism to become the order of the day, as we chronicled in Chapter 1. So powerful has the consensus around professional journalism become in the postwar years—it still rules much of the nation's thinking—that very few Americans and perhaps even fewer journalists understand how unsettled our commercial news-media system was as recently as the 1930s. The New Deal proved to be the final battle in this struggle. There, for the last time, significant numbers of Americans, citizens and journalists, questioned whether freedom of the press was compatible with private ownership and advertising support.[117]

A press system that once fostered Whitman's "daily communion" between editor and reader had evolved toward the absurd circumstance where the overwhelming majority of the nation's newspapers endorsed Republicans Herbert Hoover and Alf Landon while the overwhelming majority of voters supported Franklin Roosevelt in 1932 and 1936.[118] After Roosevelt carried 46 states in the latter election, for the greatest popular- and electoral-vote landslide in the history of modern campaigns, *TIME* magazine observed,

> All through the land, voters thumpingly disregarded the editorial politics of an estimated 80% of the nation's daily Press. In Chicago an election night mob took direct action against the rabidly anti-Roosevelt *Tribune* by burning a truckload of its "bulldog" edition, egging its building, smashing plate glass at its Dearborn Street branch.[119]

Indeed, the battle hit fever pitch precisely as the New Deal entered its most progressive phase, following the 1936 election, finding newspaper publishers singularly hostile to President Roosevelt almost en masse. In November 1938, Roosevelt wrote to Joseph Pulitzer II, "I have always been firmly persuaded that our newspapers cannot be edited in the interests of the general public from the counting room. And I wish we could have a national symposium on that question, particularly in its relation to freedom of the press."[120] Two months later, Secretary of the Interior Harold Ickes debated press baron Frank E. Gannett on nationwide radio concerning whether the United States even had what could be called a free press because, according to Ickes, of private monopolistic ownership, the role of advertising and the exclusion of nonelite groups from adequate treatment by the press.[121] Ickes took his lecture on the road, speaking to many groups. A *Christian Science Monitor* report noted in 1938 that President Roosevelt "pointed out the annual subsidy—in below-cost postal rates—that American newspapers and magazines receive from the Government, and suggested that they clean their own houses."[122]

William Allen White, renowned editor of the Kansas-based *Emporia Gazette*, addressed the crisis in his 1939 presidential address to the American Society of Newspaper Editors:

> We must not ignore the bald fact that in the last decade a considerable section of the American press, and in particular the American daily newspaper press, has been the object of bitter criticism in a wide section of American public opinion. In certain social areas a definite minority, sometimes perhaps a majority of our readers, distrust us, discredit us.[123]

We are not claiming there was any real challenge to the newspaper system in the late 1930s, but it is striking how much political criticism the commercial structures of such a powerful institution were getting.

Professional journalism finally stabilized in the 1940s—even stridently partisan newspapers like *The Chicago Tribune* grudgingly moved toward a less partisan newsroom—and the commercial system survived the attacks on its legitimacy as stewards of the free press. The "government-hands-off," laissez-faire version of freedom of the press ruled triumphant; its rocketlike ascension fueled to some extent by a Cold War environment where anyone making structural criticism of private ownership or advertising was suspected of being squishy on the subject of whether we would be better off living under a communist dictatorship. Academics, particularly in schools of journalism, argued categorically that the existing monopolistic commercial newspaper system with professional journalism was a superior and effective system for a free and democratic society. "The newspapers have changed their roles since the rise of monopolies and chains. They are not regarded today as primarily political mouthpieces," University of Minnesota journalism professor Raymond Nixon told *TIME* magazine in 1962. "(The contemporary reader) buys newspapers for information and expects both sides of political questions. When newspapers started doing this, the need for reading two newspapers disappeared."[124]

The manner in which professional journalism developed in the United States had both strengths and weaknesses, as we discussed in Chapter 1. Publishers enjoyed the legitimacy it gave them, but also disliked it to the extent it interfered with their desire to maximize profits. It would be an enduring struggle throughout the second half of the 20th century, as we chronicled in Chapter 1. After a generation of direct and indirect commercial pressures, newsrooms are largely in tatters, and the professional code seems beside the point.

Lost in the laissez-faire mythology was the dirty secret that direct and indirect public subsidies for the newspaper industry, and for newsmagazines, continued to exist and have been of considerable importance. Though nowhere near as extensive as those of the early Republic, these subsidies include the ongoing postal discounts, as well as the underwriting of professional journalism education at colleges and universities. The government, too, has a "public information" office in nearly all of its agencies and branches to provide material to news media. In 2007, governments employed fully 23,000 people in a public-relations capacity.[125] This is, in effect, a subsidy. The government is, at times, an important purchaser of newspapers and newsmagazines. Newspapers receive a range of favorable tax breaks, and have been exempted from antitrust law when they are "economically distressed."[126] Newspapers across the country still enjoy the revenues derived from "legals," advertisements by government agencies and advertisements that are required by state governments to be placed in newspapers. In fact, some smaller publications rely on these government advertising subsidies to survive.

Even more significantly, as Inger L. Stole's work demonstrates, the government has established a series of policies to encourage advertising, and therefore increase the flow of revenues to the news media. By the mid-20th century advertising would be virtually the sole source of revenue for radio and television journalism. Advertising is not subject to state sales taxes. It is also allowed to be deducted from a business's taxable income as a legitimate business expense. These have both been contentious policy issues. The government is a major advertiser in its own right, hence contributing to the success of commercial media. Moreover, the government has countenanced what can only be called lax regulation of advertising content, thereby contributing to America's having more advertising per capita than just about any other nation in the world.[127] In sum, government policies have buttressed and encouraged at every turn the oxygen that feeds commercial news media.

The Problem of Broadcasting

The fiction of a laissez-faire media may have held for daily newspapers, evidence notwithstanding, but it was unworkable for radio broadcasting when it emerged in the 1920s. There the government selected the lucky handful of organizations that would have the privilege of a monopoly right to scarce broadcast channels. The tension was palpable between what was best for the public airwaves and the commercial aspirations of profit-seeking station owners. Most nations opted for a nonprofit and noncommercial public system, though the management models varied widely from nation to nation. The United States, instead, in the late 1920s turned over all the prime frequencies to commercial interests, linked by two national corporate networks, the National Broadcasting Company and the Columbia Broadcasting System, supported entirely by advertising.[128] The process was, by any standard, corrupt and secretive. "The whole American system of broadcasting," the British Broadcasting Corporation observed in 1932, lies "outside our comprehension" and "clearly springs from a specifically American conception of democracy."[129] The key word there is *specifically*. Just as publishers had redefined *freedom of the press* as nothing more than a protection for their business endeavors, broadcasters and their political allies imagined a "democratic" communications system in which the airwaves were owned by the people while the microphones were controlled by a handful of businessmen and their employees.

This led to what was probably the most significant uprising against commercial media in the United States in the 20th century.[130] At the center of the battle was the American Civil Liberties Union, whose radio committee debated whether the laissez-faire notion of freedom of the press applied to radio broadcasters. One member, Louis Caldwell, an attorney for the *Chicago Tribune*-owned WGN, argued that once the executive branch of the government quietly cherry-picked the corporations

that got the scarce monopoly licenses to broadcast, then those broadcasters deserved the same First Amendment relationship to the government
as newspapers enjoyed.[131] Other members, like Morris Ernst and Bethuel
Webster, said that was preposterous; that the commercial broadcasters
had proven to be far more injurious to free speech than the government
in broadcasting and their domination of broadcasting was illegitimate.
They argued that structural reform implemented by the government to
promote a more open and inclusive broadcasting system on the publicly
owned airwaves was necessary.

The debate was, at times, extraordinary, collapsing much of the tension
of the entire century of corporate media into a brief window. Caldwell
routinely invoked the Star Chamber, John Peter Zenger and the sword of
Damocles as he railed against the totalitarian logic of broadcast regulation. "I have to fight a tendency to swallow this kind of language hook,
line, and sinker, for it sounds grand and I like it," Webster explained to
another person on the ACLU radio committee. "I think that in this respect Mr. Caldwell is tilting at a windmill, and interference by network
and station owners is a daily reality, whereas the interference Mr. Caldwell
seems chiefly to oppose is a phantom."[132]

We will not keep you in suspense: the networks and advertisers won the
battle for the airwaves with the passage of the 1934 Communications Act.
The deal that was struck was that commercial broadcasters would perform
in the public interest—something they would not do if they were strictly
commercial concerns—to justify their receiving the lucrative monopoly licenses from the government at no charge. Within a decade the newly emer-
gent radio journalism became a main example of radio's public-interest
work. Even when there was grumbling about the flaws in the model—in
1945, Federal Communications Commission Chairman Paul Porter
warned that the commercial excesses on radio were such that "large and
influential sections of the public are beginning to demand that 'something be done about it'"—the owners generally headed off the threats
with pious mumblings about "broadcast freedom" and lobbying that
would grow ever more efficient and aggressive.[133]

When television and FM radio and other new technologies came
along, the corporate advertising-supported system was adopted with little

controversy and virtually no press attention or public debate. The public-interest standard for broadcasters proved to be largely toothless, and by the 1990s, goaded on by a powerful lobby, the public-service obligations were effectively nonexistent. At the same time, these industries became colossally profitable. Huge empires were built upon the back of what was in effect a massive gift of valuable public property to private interests. (The government recognized the limitations of commercial broadcasting with the adoption of public broadcasting in 1967, a topic we return to in Chapter 4.)

The case of broadcasting also points to a central issue generally overlooked in any discussion of freedom of the press or the First Amendment. Our media and communication industries, in general, are certainly profit-driven, but they are not free markets. They are *all* the recipients of significant, sometimes enormous, direct and indirect government subsidies and privileges, far beyond what nearly any other industry accrues.[134] The exact amount of these subsidies has never been determined, but the value arguably runs in the tens of billions of dollars annually.[135]

When broadcasting, telephone, satellite or cable-television companies invoke free markets to justify their wealth and power, it should be laughable. Some of these firms routinely rank high on periodic top-10 polls identifying the "most detested" businesses.[136] American communication companies in these industries won their market power as much through accumulating government monopoly licenses and pushing through industry-friendly regulation as they did by winning any victory in a competitive marketplace. Most important, major communication-technology revolutions, from the telegraph and radio to satellites and the Internet, have been developed using public subsidies.[137] Left to the private sector, they may have never developed, or certainly their development would have been very different. As Paul Starr puts it, we, the people, created our media.[138]

Like Jefferson and Madison, we approve of government policies and subsidies for media and communication. They are the price of civilization, so to speak, and the engines of democratic extension. What we disapprove of is how secretive and corrupt the policymaking process has become in the United States, as the wealth and power of media and communication industries has increased. Hundreds of thousands, even millions, of Americans have come to share our revulsion, which explains the dramatic growth of the media-reform movement over the past decade. The point of Free Press, the group we helped launch with Josh Silver in 2002, was to put the *public* back into the so-called public policies that determine and define the outlines of our media system. The movement has enjoyed great success, on issues ranging from media ownership and public broadcasting to keeping the Internet open and uncensored.[139]

Free Press now is turning to the challenge of recreating the institutions and resource base necessary for journalism. The main barrier is that the vast majority of Americans still do not understand the central role of public policy and direct and indirect subsidies in the construction of our media system. Neither are they encouraged to do so by the powerful corporate communication lobbies that rule the roost behind closed doors in Washington, or what remains of the news media. In effect, they want to maintain their ability to reap the benefits of public investment in media without having to accept the responsibilities that should go with the largesse. We argue that the spending and policies that shape our media should be advanced in the interest of the great mass of American citizens—not the handful of big media corporations that have disregarded and come close to destroying journalism.

The current collapse of journalism highlights how bankrupt the laissez-faire mythology is in addressing the real nature of our press system and the great problems before us. Imagine, for one moment, what would happen if the federal government issued an edict demanding that there be a sharp reduction in international journalism, that leading newspapers be shuttered, that statehouse bureaus be closed and that local newsrooms have their staffs and budgets slashed. Imagine, too, that the president issued an order that Washington bureaus be closed, and that news media concentrate upon celebrities and trivia, rather than investigate the economic crisis or rigorously pursue corruption in federal agencies. Had all that occurred, these official actions would have sparked an outcry that made Watergate look like a day at the beach. Yet, when quasi-monopolistic commercial interests effectively do pretty much the same thing, and leave our society as impoverished culturally as if it had been the result of a government fiat, it is met mostly with resignation, as something as unavoidable as the Rocky Mountain range when one drives from Chicago to California. Colonel Nicholson is speechless.

Does the Supreme Court Mandate the Commercial Media System?

At this point, one final set of questions remains: isn't our current media system, our current approach mandated by law? Hasn't the Constitution been interpreted as requiring us to stand to the sidelines as journalism gets slaughtered by media companies that would rather cut than create?

From our experience, even when we have scoped out the need for intervention and the prospect for doing so in smart and effective ways, there are still some who say: "No matter what evidence you produce, the Supreme Court will insist on a laissez-faire interpretation of the free-press clause of the First Amendment, so whatever reforms you might get enacted by Congress and implemented by federal agencies to renew journalism and realize its full democratic potential will eventually be found unconstitutional."

There is a certain logic to this argument. The Court tends to shade its interpretations of the Constitution to take into account broad social and economic developments. So it was that segregation was ruled constitutional at the height of Jim Crow in the 1890s, and then ruled unconstitutional after 60 years of African-American migration to the North and contributions to world wars, a nascent civil-rights movement and a Cold War in which a prominent Soviet argument to the colonial nations in Africa and Asia was that the United States was a white-supremacist society. So, it might be presumed that the Court would logically embrace the notion that freedom of the press equals the ability of media firms to maximize profit without any interference from or role for the government. After all, that has been the way that we have been told the news media have worked for at least the last century.

With this criticism in mind, we approached C. Edwin Baker, one of the leading First Amendment scholars in the nation, and probably the single greatest authority on the free-press clause, and a decorated professor at the University of Pennsylvania Law School. We asked whether the Supreme Court accepts the dominant laissez-faire press mythology that has determined that the press system is the natural province of corporations and advertisers, and that the government has little or no role to play except to let the market work its magic, regardless of what these firms do. The professor was aghast. "The court has never said that nor is it assumed," Baker replied.[140]

So how has the U.S. Supreme Court interpreted the meaning of the free-press clause of the First Amendment? A review of free-press cases reveals that there is a surprisingly small body of work, and there were no cases of note before the 1920s or 1930s. The Court has given far greater attention to free-speech cases.[141] And when it has addressed matters of the press, the Court only rarely has touched on structural issues of the role and relationship of the government and the private sector in determining the shape of the news media. But when the Court has touched on these issues, it has at all times understood the press in a manner consistent with Jefferson and Madison, rather than Wall Street and Madison Avenue.

The Madisonian notion of the central and indispensable importance of an informed citizenry, and a press system to assure the nurturing of such a constituency, has been articulated many times. (No justice has ever suggested the contrary.) In the Supreme Court's 1927 *Whitney v. California* case, Justice Louis Brandeis concluded: "Those who won our independence believed that the final end of the State was to make men free to develop their faculties; ... that the greatest menace to freedom is an inert people; that public discussion is a political duty; and that this should be a fundamental principle of American government."[142]

There has also been, at all times, a sense on the Court that the press system should not be regarded as a purely commercial undertaking, that it serves a higher calling. Baker concludes that the Court clearly recognizes the press as a unique institution distinct from individuals exercising free-speech rights, and also as distinct from other commercial enterprises.[143] Whenever a case has come forward positing the laissez-faire notion of the First Amendment—that the news media can do as they please and that none of this is Uncle Sam's business—it has been shot down. "The

Supreme Court," Baker establishes in his review of the matter, "has explicitly or implicitly rejected these premises whenever invoked by a corporate media entity."[144]

The first great case along these lines was *Associated Press v. United States*, which was decided by the United States Supreme Court in 1945. The AP argued the First Amendment prevented the government from enforcing antitrust laws against its monopoly. Consider us "absolutists" with regard to Hugo Black's magnificent majority opinion in that case, which ruled against AP:

> It would be strange indeed however if the grave concern for freedom of the press which prompted adoption of the First Amendment should be read as a command that the government was without power to protect that freedom. The First Amendment, far from providing an argument against application of the Sherman Act, here provides powerful reasons to the contrary. *That Amendment rests on the assumption that the widest possible dissemination of information from diverse and antagonistic sources is essential to the welfare of the public, that a free press is a condition of a free society.* Surely a command that the government itself shall not impede the free flow of ideas does not afford non-governmental combinations a refuge if they impose restraints upon that constitutionally guaranteed freedom. Freedom to publish means freedom for all and not for some. Freedom to publish is guaranteed by the Constitution, but freedom to combine to keep others from publishing is not. Freedom of the press from governmental interference under the First Amendment does not sanction repression of that freedom by private interests.[145] (our emphasis)

Leaving little doubt about the Court's opinion, Justice Felix Frankfurter wrote in his concurring statement: "Truth and understanding are not wares like peanuts or potatoes. And so, the incidence of restraints upon the promotion of truth ... calls into play considerations very different from comparable restraints in a cooperative enterprise having merely a commercial aspect."[146] In short, *the Court has ruled that the state has a compelling interest to see that a viable press system exists,* and there is no presumption that profit-seeking firms will necessarily deliver the goods. In his opinion in the 1994 case *Turner Broadcasting System v. FCC*, Reagan appointee Justice Anthony Kennedy concluded, "Assuring the public has access to a multiplicity of information sources is a governmental purpose of the highest order."[147]

As Ben Scott points out, what was revolutionary about the *AP* decision was that the Court could have followed precedent and simply said that applying antitrust law was permissible because it would not interfere with the press function of these firms. Instead, as Scott writes, "The affirmative right to regulate the media in the public interest was set into a Supreme Court precedent in 1945, and it has never been overturned."[148]

Black returned to these issues 26 years later in the Pentagon Papers (*New York Times v. United States*) case:

> In the First Amendment, the Founding Fathers gave the free press the protection it must have to fulfill its essential role in our democracy. The press was to serve the governed, not the governors. The Government's power to censor the press was abolished so that the press would remain forever free to censure the Government. The press was protected so that it could bare the secrets of government and inform the people. Only a free and unrestrained press can effectively expose deception in government. And paramount among the responsibilities of a free press is the duty to prevent any part of the government from deceiving the people and sending them off to distant lands to die of foreign fevers and foreign shot and shell.[149]

Equally brilliant, and instructive, is this passage from Justice Potter Stewart's opinion in the same case. Stewart, an appointee of Republican president Dwight Eisenhower, comes close to channeling James Madison:

> In the absence of the governmental checks and balances present in other areas of our national life, the only effective restraint upon executive policy and power in the areas of national defense and international affairs may lie in an enlightened citizenry—in an informed and critical public opinion which alone can here protect the values of democratic government. For this reason, it is perhaps here that a press that is alert, aware, and free

most vitally serves the basic purpose of the First Amendment. For, without an informed and free press, there cannot be an enlightened people.[150]

Radio and then television broadcasting have forced the Court to revisit its understanding of freedom of the press, and the relationship of the state to private commercial media. The commercial broadcasters wanted to get the same treatment from the government that newspapers enjoyed—i.e., a ruling that existing broadcasting regulation amounted to a violation of the First Amendment. In 1969, capitalizing on four decades of growth in their institutional and political power, the commercial broadcasters got their case before the Supreme Court. But Justice Byron White, one of the Court's most conservative members, wrote a majority opinion in *Red Lion Broadcasting Co., Inc. v. Federal Communications Commission* that rejected their claims:

> But the people as a whole retain their interest in free speech by radio and their collective right to have the medium function consistently with the ends and purposes of the First Amendment. It is the right of the viewers and listeners, not the right of the broadcasters, which is paramount. ... It is the purpose of the First Amendment to preserve an uninhibited market-place of ideas in which truth will ultimately prevail, rather than to countenance monopolization of that market, whether it be by the Government itself or a private licensee. ... It is the right of the public to receive suitable access to social, political, esthetic, moral, and other ideas and experiences which is crucial here. That right may not constitutionally be abridged either by Congress or by the FCC.[151]

The *Red Lion* decision presented an explicit rejection of the laissez-faire model for broadcasters. It was such a powerful and expansive declaration of the extent to which the First Amendment belonged to the public before private media that progressive legal minds like Jerome Barron attempted to have the *Red Lion* logic applied to the monopolistic newspaper industry. His approach returned to the critique of the 1930s and argued that "freedom of expression is meaningless if all the important means of communication—press, television, and radio—are closed."[152]

Since newspapers are in effect even more monopolistic than broadcasters, albeit for economic rather than technological reasons, and freedom of the press belongs to all of us, the argument went, the government should require newspapers to serve their communities and publish dissenting opinions. This led to 1974's *Miami Herald v. Tornillo* case, where the Supreme Court ruled 9-0 that the government could not regulate press content as it did broadcasting, despite the market dominance of newspapers in a community.

Those who have not actually read the *Miami Herald v. Tornillo* decision may assume that it is the Court's definitive endorsement of the laissez-faire notion of freedom of the press. But even a casual review of the opinions regarding the case points to a very different conclusion. To the extent it prohibited government meddling in editorial content, we concur with the opinion.[153] As Timothy Cook points out, however, the ruling was consistent with other court decisions which argued freedom of the press belonged to readers as much as to newspaper owners.[154] The Court said nothing remotely smacking of a laissez-faire notion of the press. The Court failed to distinguish between the interests of editors and owners, making the two sides identical and seemingly equal in importance. The decision was based on the presumption that the public-service editorial obligations of the press were at least the equal of the commercial needs of press owners, and it did not understand the press as a fundamentally commercial enterprise.[155]

On the heels of the *Miami Herald v. Tornillo* decision, Justice Stewart gave a rare speech on the meaning of freedom of the press at Yale Law School. "The Free Press guarantee is, in effect, a *structural* part of the Constitution." (Stewart's emphasis.) "The primary purpose of the constitutional guarantee of a free press was," he added, "to create a fourth institution outside the Government as an additional check on the three official branches." Stewart concluded: "Perhaps our liberties might survive without an independent established press. But the Founders doubted it, and, in the year 1974, I think we can all be thankful for their doubts."[156]

Stewart was speaking, it should be noted, at a point in history when the journalism of Bob Woodward and Carl Bernstein had revealed the high crimes and misdemeanors of the Nixon White House so thoroughly that, faced with the threat of impeachment, Richard Nixon would resign the presidency.[157]

Questions remain unanswered—and unasked—in the decisions we have reviewed. The Supreme Court has yet to take up the issue of what happens if the interests of owners and editors are opposed. What does that mean in monopolistic or semimonopolistic markets where it is impossible for new owners to emerge to hire new editors? What happens to freedom of the press when the right to launch effective new media is nonexistent in the market or effectively limited to billionaires, and the investors have no more interest in journalism than they do in insurance, hedge funds or producing undergarments?

Most important for the present time are these questions: What does the nation do when Wall Street and Madison Avenue have determined that there is insufficient profit in journalism to warrant investment? Does the Constitution mandate that journalism therefore must cease to exist as a viable enterprise? Is the Constitution to be regarded as a suicide pact? This was the absurd question first raised and rejected by Thomas Jefferson and Abraham Lincoln, and formally put into the legal discourse and also rejected by Justices Robert Jackson and Arthur Goldberg.[158] Is the Supreme Court now going to change course and answer that question positively?

These are the constitutional questions for our time. These are the fault lines along which we will define freedom of the press in the 21st century. The laissez-faire model, to the extent that it ever existed, has not only become irrelevant, it is downright toxic. While it may have been true that, for much of this country's history, commercial interests provided sufficient resources for the provision of journalism, this is no longer the case. Commerce is now in open conflict with journalism, and journalism is losing. The Supreme Court to date has dealt in its free-press cases with assumptions about the viability of the commercial system. Now that those assumptions no longer hold, now that journalism and democracy are threatened by a failed status quo, we can take a fresh look at the First Amendment, and how the Supreme Court has interpreted the relationship of the government to the press. Over the years, constitutional scholars like Baker have made the case for why even as the First Amendment prohibits censorship, it allows the state to play a proactive role in creating content.[159] The above opinions support their arguments.

With the current crisis in journalism at pandemic levels, with the commercial system collapsing and taking great newspapers and whole newsrooms with it, there is very good reason to believe that—acting in accordance with the Constitution and established precedent, the Court will not only condone aggressive government policies and subsidies to create viable independent journalism, it may well demand them. This prospect is as realistic as it is heartening because it offers hope that a recognition of the fact that "the present crisis of western democracy is a crisis of journalism" can be met as the founders intended—by embracing and, yes, celebrating the role government must play in maintaining and extending the promise of American journalism and democracy.

James Madison famously observed in 1822, "A popular government without popular information or the means of acquiring it, is but a Prologue to a Farce or a Tragedy or perhaps both. Knowledge will forever govern ignorance, and a people who mean to be their own Governors, must arm themselves with the power knowledge gives."[160]

In the face of the tragedy and farce that Madison imagined, we may ask and answer the essential question as patriots in tune with this country's deepest and best democratic traditions.

Why the state?

It is the American way.

Chapter 4

SUBSIDIZING
Democracy

The year 2009 did not produce many encouraging headlines about the future of newspapers in particular or journalism in general. Decades of corporate profit-taking, competition from the Internet and a scorching recession had left the landscape littered with laid-off reporters and the wreckage of once-great newspapers. But from Seattle, a city that lost one of its two daily newspapers during the season of doom and despair, came a series of shouts from the belly of the beast that seemed, well, optimistic:

"Recession Could Fuel New Era of Local Newspaper Ownership."

"Still Ready to Raise Hell and Sell Newspapers."

"Amid the Rubble, Hope for Journalism Is Stirring."

Didn't this joker get the memos? Doesn't he know that local newspapers are dead? Doesn't he know that newspapers are sacking the people who raise hell and selling their assets in an industry-wide fire sale? Doesn't he know that there is no hope for journalism?

In fact, the man responsible for those headlines did get the memos. He's been getting them from the day he was born. Ryan Blethen, the editorial-page editor of the *Seattle Times*, is a member of the fifth generation of a newspaper family that is about as old-school as you get. His great-

great-grandfather, Alden Blethen, really did promise to "raise hell and sell newspapers." And Ryan Blethen got Alden's rebel gene; indeed, he has, with his father, Frank, broken time and again with industry insiders to declare that "consolidation by huge public corporations and overleveraged private companies has endangered professional journalism." He advances the Jeffersonian notion that "Newspapers should be accountable to the communities they serve and not to Wall Street or distant corporations thousands of miles away."[1]

What's needed, Ryan Blethen says, is an openness to change, new business models and smart government interventions designed to preserve that which is essential in journalism—its link to communities, its skepticism, its independence and, above all, its determination to raise hell—in an era when it is becoming harder to sell newspapers and to maintain newsrooms capable of covering cities, states and nations. "We must start advocating for the future of professional journalism instead of lamenting what is lost," Blethen argues. "We have to consider all options and be vocal about what we believe will work. Professional journalism will not die if journalists and politicians work toward sustaining newsrooms."[2]

We agree.

So what's the plan? Or, to be more precise, what are the plans?

It should be clear by now that there is no one easy fix, no magic elixir, which will cure what ails the body politic and give us all the journalism and democracy we desire. Reasonable and well-intended people will disagree about how to get from here to there. But the openness that Blethen and other young journalists have begun to display suggests that America is finally getting ready for a serious discussion. We equate seriousness with a willingness to embrace definitional change, because there is no longer any question that such change is going to be needed to sustain journalism in the 21st century.

This is not a moment for half steps or cautious responses. It's time to be bold and, yes, radical—in the best American sense.

American radicalism is not romantic. It is all about figuring out what needs to be done and doing it. So it is that the most radical proposals we make in the coming pages are grounded not in idealism so much as a practical assessment of the current crisis.

It's time to get real.

It's time to face facts.

It's time to recognize that all the evidence available to us at this point leads inexorably to one conclusion: having anything remotely close to a satisfactory level of journalism will require a large public subsidy.[3] We know this is an unsettling notion for some, especially for journalists who have been taught to fear the heavy hand of government. But media subsidies and government intervention have taken many forms along the arc of the American experiment. And they can again. Indeed, they must.

Once we get past the fear-mongering and false premises about government subsidies, the real work begins. How much money do we need? Where does it come from? Who controls it? And who receives it? These are the daunting but unavoidable questions at the heart of any debate about government intervention to promote journalism, and these are the questions that we address in this chapter.

The broad proposal that we advance has four components: 1) immediate measures to sustain journalism, each of which transitions to a permanent subsidy if successful; 2) a plan to convert the collapsing corporate newspaper into what we term a "post-corporate" digital newspaper, with print versions at the very least until there is ubiquitous broadband; 3) converting public and community broadcasting into genuinely world-class civic and democratic media; and 4) spawning a vibrant, well-funded, competitive and innovative news-media sector on the Internet. Then we turn to the matter of how we can pay for what we propose, along with what others might propose.

Our Assumptions

For this chapter to be most effective, we must lay out our operating assumptions, offer some provisos and provide some context.

We confess at the outset that we do not have all the answers to the questions that the rapid degeneration of journalism in America has raised. Rather, we propose ideas—some with historic precedents, some fresh—that are informed by our personal and professional involvement with journalism and democracy movements. We have consulted with some of the wisest and most engaged players in mainstream and independent media in addition to leading scholars, all of whom are grappling with the urgency of the moment.

We are not presenting a fait-accompli plan for a thumbs-up or thumbs-down vote. Rather, we are advancing plausible proposals to focus and enliven a national conversation on these issues. We won't go too deep in the weeds of policy wonkery; instead, we'll attempt to provide broad outlines of sound and relevant policy initiatives in understandable terms. If these ideas are to succeed ultimately, they will need more attention from lawyers, accountants, analysts and experts of all stripes to make certain they are well structured to pass practical and official muster. To advance the process, we have anticipated potential pitfalls and problem areas and attempted to steer clear of them.

We are modest enough to recognize that a different agenda could be superior to ours. In fact, we see ourselves as being engaged in a process that relentlessly seeks superior ideas, a process that will require the embrace and abandonment of approaches, adjustments and changes in focus and function. Over the course of 2009 as we wrote this book, our thinking evolved considerably. As Christopher Warren, the federal secretary of Australia's Media, Entertainment and Arts Alliance and one of the savviest observers of journalism trends internationally, reminds us:

> Journalism as we know it is the product of hundreds of years of evolution in our thinking about how we tell our stories, and about how we pay the people who tell our stories. Disruptive technologies, the fracturing of our economic bases, these aren't new problems. We've faced this before. The issue goes beyond technology and discussions about economic models. The real question is whether we are going to be flexible enough, open enough, to take bold steps, stumble a few times and then take more bold steps. If we do, we'll have journalism in the 21st century, and it may well be better than anything we had in the 20th.[4]

We agree there's no quick fix, no single button to push that will make everything better. As frustrating as that can be in a society accustomed to instant answers, this is as it should be. A healthy news-media system must be diverse. It must have a range of institutions, structures and funding sources. We think it wise policy to have some news media that aspire to serve the entire community, even nation, and others that serve smaller segments of the population. None of the models will achieve perfection—no matter how enthusiastic the reviews from particular camps may be. But some will be better than others. Whenever there are systems of payment and institutional structures, they will influence the content of the news. It is unavoidable, whether the source is advertising and control is corporate, or the support is public and the structure is nonprofit. The task for enlightened policymakers is to recognize the dilemma and attempt to minimize the negative influences while maximizing the positive ones.

That said, we do bring some basic values and principles to this process. Our first and most fundamental purpose is to prevent any direct control by politicians over editorial content and to minimize policies that have government officials evaluating media content. We aspire in all policies and subsidies to retain the proverbial "Chinese wall" between politicians and an independent media. It is for this reason that we were never excited by the Fairness Doctrine, or other measures that required the government to determine whether broadcast programming was in the public interest. Our goal is to have policies and subsidies that create a system where it will be rational to produce good journalism, without having a government official monitoring what is written or said.

At the heart of every reform we propose is a belief that journalism is not merely needed, it needs to be better. This is not just an American challenge. We are enthusiastic about the burgeoning global movements to help journalists "to reconnect to their mission" of truth telling. The Ethical Journalism Initiative of the International Federation of Journalists, with which the American Newspaper Guild union is affiliated, speaks of a need for journalists to organize "to distance themselves from banal, superficial and cynical media." We're on board for that project, as far as it goes. But we think it should be extended. It is not just journalists but society that should seek distance from banal, superficial and cynical media. Our sense is that journalists and citizens have a common cause. The Ethical Journalism Initiative argues that journalism should be "watchful and committed to truth, alert to injustice, jealous of its own independence and, above all else, a champion of the public interest." Freeing journalists to do their jobs without fear of political or corporate masters is in the public interest, and we think the public should be actively involved in the project. That involvement begins with activism, but it can and should extend to public policies that sustain and advance quality journalism.[5]

Although the evidence suggests that the corporate, advertising-supported, profit-driven model for journalism is no longer viable, we believe in the basic right of anyone to start a media business or enterprise of any kind. We do not doubt that in specific niche areas of journalism commercial media will find a lucrative role, and we propose no policies that would undermine their prospects. For instance, if some existing commercial newspapers find success in the coming era, we'll be delighted. We do not believe that such commercial enterprises should receive any subsidies from the federal government; conversely, the government should not ask of these media businesses any more or less than it asks of other private firms.

We also believe that subsidizing strong journalism will help build an audience/readership/community for media, and this will be of value for commercial interests who wish to remain in, or enter, the field. Recall from Chapter 3 that it was the massively subsidized press of the first half of the 19th century that laid the foundation for the commercial-press explosion with which we are so familiar. It is also worth noting that British journalists tell us one of the greatest forces promoting journalism in that country's privately held newspapers is the muscular competition they face from a well-funded British Broadcasting Corporation that is committed to serving the public interest. "We have to be aggressive and cover more things in more creative ways because we aren't just competing with other newspapers, we are competing with a BBC that is serious about journalism," says Chris Elliott, managing editor of *The Guardian*.[6]

The BBC, a traditional public broadcast system, and *The Guardian*, a traditional newspaper, compete directly with one another now on the World Wide Web. There is no doubt that the future of journalism is digital, and public subsidies have to be designed to promote the creation and dissemination of material online. We are about creating a better future, not trying to pretend it does not exist. That being said, until the United States is in a situation where close to 100 percent of the population has broadband access, it is unacceptable to ignore the importance of "old media." While it may be attractive to shift all resources to exclusively digital journalism, with its much lower operating expenses, such a change would be antidemocratic in a nation where tens of millions of citizens do not have broadband, or Internet access at all.

There is another strong argument for taking steps to keep print publications functioning, at least in the foreseeable future. We believe it would be shortsighted, irrational and possibly catastrophic to permit existing newsrooms to disintegrate over the next five years, and then hope to start fresh on a scorched landscape and create a new system. We oppose bailouts or direct subsidies to existing commercial players, and we think a crucial policy objective is to convert these corporate newsrooms into viable post-corporate newsrooms. In the near-term, and in strictly controlled circumstances, arguments can be made for existing corporations getting some payoffs. These payoffs would come, however, in the form of severance packages; i.e., the government might create incentives to get bad players off the field—by selling newspapers at fair (rather than inflated) prices to more responsible owners, unions or community groups—before their layoffs and cuts destroy what remains of American newsrooms. If the media corporations that did so much to create the crisis wish to remain in the journalism business, more power to them. But they will *not* do so on the government dole.

When developing policies to promote journalism, it is important to have a set of values and a vision of what good journalism looks and sounds like.[7] We have found over the years that there is considerable consensus in democratic theory and among journalism scholars about what a healthy journalism should entail:

1. It must provide a rigorous account of people who are in power and people who wish to be in power, in the government, corporate and nonprofit sectors.
2. It must regard the information needs of all citizens as legitimate.

3. It must have a plausible method to separate truth from lies, or at least to prevent liars from being unaccountable and leading nations into catastrophes—particularly wars, economic crises and communal discord.

4. It must produce a wide range of informed opinions on the most important issues of our times—not only the transitory concerns of the moment, but also challenges that loom on the horizon. These issues cannot be determined primarily by what people in power are talking about. Journalism must provide the nation's early warning system, so problems can be anticipated, studied, debated and addressed before they grow to crisis proportions.

It is not necessarily the case that every media outlet can or should provide all these services to its community; that would be impractical. It is necessary, however, that the media system as a whole makes such journalism a realistic expectation for the citizenry. There should be a basic understanding of the commons—the social world—that all people share, so that all people can effectively participate in the political and electoral processes of self-governance.

As journalist Richard Reeves once put it, the news is "what you and I need to keep our freedom—accurate and timely information on laws and wars, police and politicians, taxes and toxics."[8] Freedom is about a lot more than being able to pick your hairstyle or decide what color shirt to wear. Freedom in the deeper civic sense involves controlling one's life, one's social environment, one's future, in collaboration with other members of the community. Even where some desires may be compromised, freedom requires that the choices be made in a democratic fashion. For instance, we might all like to keep a few more dollars from the taxman, but if we are taxed it should be for the purpose of funding initiatives that have been debated and approved by an informed people and their elected and accountable representatives.

The measure of a free press is how well a system meets these criteria of giving citizens the information they need to keep their freedom. Understood in this manner, as we discussed in Chapter 2, journalism requires resources, institutions, legal protections and people who work at the craft full-time. For great journalism to be produced, these conditions are indispensable.

The emergence of the Internet lowers costs dramatically and makes the creation of a viable democratic journalism far more plausible. The technologies are such that there will almost certainly be many innovations in the development of journalism that we cannot anticipate. Healthy policymaking will embrace this prospect, not attempt to thwart it merely to protect the turf of old media.

It is sometimes difficult to distinguish between policies to generate journalism and policies to reform the broader media system, but we will try to stick to the former while acknowledging that the latter is a legitimate and pressing issue with implications for journalism. For example, much of local commercial radio broadcasting—not just radio journalism, which has all but disappeared—has gone into the dumpster due to the relaxation of ownership and commercial regulations over the past three decades. A restructuring of radio could conceivably open the door to a new class of local stations and news programs, and these institutions could segue to the coming digital era. We're excited about this prospect. But we will leave the reform of radio alone—for now. The point to remember is that once the door is opened to broader media reform, options for journalism will grow beyond what is considered in this chapter.

We are well aware that what we propose herein is radical by recent American standards–just a few years ago, some of our proposals would have been unfathomable. But if we know nothing else, it is that these are not normal times. The United States, like much of the world, is in a critical juncture, in which the old media system is collapsing and a new one is being born.[9] The combination of revolutionary new technologies, a collapsing discredited commercial journalism and a broad economic crisis have created great danger but also considerable opportunity to begin anew. In the next few years, the range of options before us is going to be much broader than is usually the case. This moment is best seen as a founding one; a point that we might imagine as a "constitutional convention" for media. The vested corporate-media interests that usually place strict limits on the range of debate are uncertain of their future in journalism, and some are on the way out altogether. This is not the time to repair their dying system; it is the opportunity to create something much better, and much more democratic, than has ever existed before. This can be a moment of revolutionary change *and* of revolutionary importance for the Republic.

Ryan Blethen redefines *newspaper* to describe "a catchall for whatever way newspaper created content is delivered"–wisely rejecting the constraints of an increasingly pointless print-versus-digital debate. And his recognition that it is not the Internet that is destroying journalism allows him to see the current crisis in the right perspective:

> For nearly 40 years, newspapers have been acquired by publicly traded corporations or ever-expanding privately held, but highly leveraged, companies. The inexorable, greed-fueled feast might finally be coming to an end.
>
> An industry-transforming recession has exposed the decay of decades of corporate and profit-driven newspaper ownership.
>
> In the detritus comes real opportunity.[10]

This is an opportunity that, for the sake of journalism *and* democracy, we cannot afford to greet casually or cautiously. We must seize it.

What We Learn from Abroad

If we are serious about applying government policies and subsidies to create strong journalism and build a free and independent press, we can draw from more than the American traditions discussed in Chapter 3. Many European democracies, most notably the Nordic nations, have instituted significant subsidies for commercial newspapers to maintain competitive local markets and a broader range of political opinions.[11] In 2006, for example, Sweden spent more than $65 million to subsidize competing newspapers. If this same per capita rate were applied to the United States, it would be an annual subsidy of more than $2 billion to support second and third daily newspapers in American communities.[12] In Norway, a system for newspaper subsidies designed to "maintain local competition and national diversity" provides resources to the "No.

2" newspapers in communities around the country as well as to the smallest local newspapers in remote regions. The Norwegian system also provides support to national newspapers that represent dissenting and controversial political views. Imagine if *USA Today* and *The Wall Street Journal* faced competition in the marketplace of ideas from publications with socialist and libertarian perspectives. If we transferred the Norwegian system to the United States, again applying the same per capita rate, roughly $4 billion would be invested annually to foster journalistic competition and viewpoint diversity.[13]

But we are not advocating the recreation of Nordic-style press subsidies in the United States. It's not our sense that specific U.S. conditions or the nature of our crisis make the press-subsidy systems of other democracies appropriate as an American solution. What we believe can be learned from studying the European experience with subsidized newspapers, however, is that such programs do not undermine the independence of the press or make it a lackey for the political party in power. According to Daniel Hallin, arguably the leading American scholar on comparative media systems, the implementation of the subsidized newspaper system in Europe was concurrent with "a shift toward a more adversarial press. It is actually very strong evidence that press subsidies don't lead journalists to be timid."[14]

If we accept Hallin's assessment, there is something else to be learned as well: subsidizing journalism with an eye toward fostering competition and making a variety of viewpoints available creates a vibrant media culture. According to the World Association of Newspapers, Nordic countries have among the highest levels of newspaper readership in the world. In Norway, for instance, more than 625 copies of newspapers are printed daily per 1,000 people; that compares with only about 225 per 1,000 people in the United States.[15] (So much for the notion that the Internet killed newspaper readership, as Norway is among the most wired nations in the world.) And measures of democratic participation in Scandinavia— the real test of whether citizens are getting the information they need to govern themselves—are dramatically higher than in the United States.

Perhaps where we can learn the most from abroad regarding press policy might be in a comparable crisis situation when a journalism system in an advanced industrial nation had been decimated and needed to be rebuilt in order for democracy to be successful. Classic examples of such circumstances are provided by Japan and Germany following World War II. We provide the details of the extraordinary interventions and expenditures of generals Eisenhower and MacArthur to build independent news media in occupied Germany and Japan in the 1940s in Appendix II. For present purposes, what is important about this episode is that it demonstrates, again, that creating a viable free press is the first duty—or in the first tier of duties—of the democratic state.

Dealing with the Immediate Crisis

If we do indeed recognize the need for a viable press system, then the first order of business for those who would respond sufficiently to the current crisis is to stop the bleeding and keep as many journalists employed as possible. The United States needs to buy time to enact longer-term policies and subsidies. At the same time we must guard against squandering money on the failed firms and strategies of the past. In such a circumstance, the ideal programs are stopgap measures that can transition into long-term programs if they prove effective.

An immediate initiative that could be of value to a variety of journalistic endeavors that continue in print would be to dramatically lower the price of postage. It is a pleasing coincidence that this proposal resonates so deeply in the American tradition. Cutting postal rates would be of tremendous value to a broad range of publications that practice journalism and public-affairs reporting and commentary.

Unfortunately, the digital age has not been kind to journals of inquiry and opinion. Many publications are teetering as we write. At present, the lowest cost one of these periodicals enjoys for postage is around 30 or 35 cents per item. We propose that all publications with less than 25 percent advertising in their pages pay only 5 cents for postage for each of their first 300,000 copies sent to subscribers. The scale would then gradually increase from 300,000 to 500,000, where it would return to the existing postage rates. This is a classically content-neutral proposal that would benefit publications such as *The National Review* and *Human Events* on the Right and *The Nation* and *The Progressive* on the Left. In particular, it would be beneficial to intellectually and ideologically adventurous publications such as *The American Conservative*, an "old-Right" magazine that mixes distaste for big government with foreign-policy positions that are as fervently anti-imperialist—and critical of neoconservatism—as those of Left-wing periodicals. *The American Conservative* was on the verge of folding in the spring of 2009, and continues to struggle for survival; the refusal to fold is motivated by what its editors say is a determination to be a part of a moment when "the definition of conservatism is really open for debate."[16] The founders understood that when great ideological and political issues were in play, it was essential that a wide range of voices be heard. The United States can and should update that understanding to the present day by borrowing a page from Jefferson and Madison and establishing postal rates that promote—rather than constrain—a wide-ranging debate.

To avoid putting the Postal Service in the position of having to determine which magazines "do" journalism, we would make this subsidy available to all publications, commercial and nonprofit alike, regardless of content, as long as they have less than 25 percent advertising content. We concede this amounts to a subsidy for qualifying commercial magazine publishers, but it only increases the subsidy they have always enjoyed. The 5-cent fee should weed out people who just want to dump boxes of material on the post-office steps. Congressional action would be required to implement this proposal. The cost to the government would be approximately $200 million annually, according to experts in the postal community, though it is impossible to know for certain. It should come immediately so that well-written and -edited periodicals that are now making serious bids to compete in the marketplace of ideas—such as *The American Conservative* on the Right and *In These Times* on the Left—can be a part of the debate as they evolve their digital presences and explore new ownership structures and funding strategies. This will provide an invaluable service to the many millions of Americans who rely upon print as their media of choice. It will keep some of the country's finest journalists employed.

The second policy measure we recommend to stop the bleeding is the establishment of a "journalism" division of AmeriCorps, the federal program that places young people with nonprofits to get training and do public-service work.[17] The point here is to ensure that young people who love journalism will stay in the field, despite all the dire "news" of the moment and limited opportunities. As Oliver Staley noted, after reviewing the *Harvard Crimson* staff in 2009, "just three of the 16 graduating seniors who were on the Crimson executive board are seeking positions in journalism."[18] We know from personal experience the situation is the same on almost every college campus. Ken Doctor proposes young journalists in training be paid $35,000 per year, and then be assigned positions with news media that wish to employ them.[19] For a variety of reasons, it makes sense that a project of this sort would be a component of the successful AmeriCorps program, which is already working in communities across the country. Were this done with, say, 2,500 young journalists, the annual budget would be in the area of $90 million, including overhead. It strikes us as a win-win; we get more journalists covering our communities, and young journalists have a chance to gain valuable experience— even at a time when the small dailies where they might have started are laying reporters off. After three years, if the program proves to be a success, the "News AmeriCorps" could be expanded to work with as many as 5,000 young journalists. At this size, even extending the terms to two years, the cost would be around $350 million annually.

Much as the Works Progress Administration of the New Deal era trained a generation of this country's greatest authors through its Federal Writers' Project—including Saul Bellow, John Cheever, Ralph Ellison, Zora Neale Hurston, John Steinbeck, Richard Wright and Studs Terkel—we can easily imagine that a "News AmeriCorps" could produce the great investigative reporters, editors and Pulitzer Prize winners of the 21st century.

The last of the immediate policy measures we recommend would be a dramatic expansion of funding of high-school newspapers and radio stations. Comprehensive research demonstrates that young people's interest in journalism and civic involvement (and their academic performance) increases when they are personally involved in making media. And students so inspired are far more likely to follow the lead of able journalists like *Sacramento Bee* business writer Bob Shallit, who says, "I really got the journalism 'bug' in high school where we had a daily student paper that tackled a lot of meaty issues."[20]

With many school districts facing budget pressures almost as extreme as those that now batter newsrooms, over 20 percent of American high schools have no student media. In many other schools, media that now exist are being diminished and downsized.[21] The federal government could make a real investment not just in the future of journalism but also in community journalism for areas that are currently underserved by putting up the money that is required so that every public high school has a student newspaper and radio station, on the Internet if no spectrum is available. All of the material produced by these public institutions would immediately be put online and made available free to all. We imagine that as with other media, the new and expanded high-school newspaper and radio stations would gradually become indistinguishable from the student media Web sites.

Focusing on high-school media has an especially strong social component. The budget-cutting frenzy that has been clobbering school districts across the country for the better part of two decades has been especially hard on journalism education in poor, working-class and majority-minority schools. The papers in these schools—which have historically played outsized roles in surrounding neighborhoods—are now fighting for survival.[22] We can and must reinvigorate them, not merely as educational tools but also as potential sources of information for adults in rural communities and urban neighborhoods that long ago were abandoned by commercial media. And we should couple new investments in the institutions of high-school journalism with media-literacy classes for students emphasizing the civic role of journalism.

These school-media measures will require personnel to be effective. In some cases, high schools might hire veteran journalists to work with the students and to direct journalism projects. This could put an immediate dent in the surging numbers of unemployed reporters, and keep talented but currently out-of-work journalists active in their craft and contributing to their communities. We also believe that bringing in journalists from the community would get high-school reporters thinking about more than just covering school-related stories; they can get dirt under their fingernails covering local elections, city-council meetings or even statehouse debates. The fresh perspective these young journalists could bring to broader policy debates—especially with a bit of prodding from veteran reporters and editors—could be invaluable at a point when local and state government is increasingly undercovered.

Investments in high-school media will not have the immediate impact of postal subsidies and the News AmeriCorps, and they will take years to fully implement. But the positive effects should be seen within a decade—perhaps sooner where the right connections are made with a community that wants and needs a new source of journalism. And they are long overdue. Students shouldn't just be learning about freedom of the press in history classes, they should be practicing it in their schools and preparing to practice it in the Golden Age of journalism that will unfold if policymakers take the right steps.

Transitioning Newspapers to a Post-Corporate Digital Era

We believe the evidence marshaled in Chapters 1 and 2 demonstrates there is no particularly meaningful or long-term future for the corporate system of daily newspaper publishing, even in digital form. Some businesses may survive in communities as profit-making entities; but if they do, the evidence suggests they will not be doing much journalism, or they will be producing *niche* journalism, pitched at a sliver of the community. The unpleasant truth is that, for all their pious pronouncements, newspaper corporations in the 20th century treated journalism as far less important than their relationships with advertisers and investors. For a time, this business model provided enough money to produce a sufficient journalism for a democratic society. It no longer does.

If our assumption is wrong, or even if it takes time to be fully confirmed, we want to be certain that any existing or prospective commercial newspaper publisher who wishes to make a go of it has a chance to do so. None of the policies and subsidies we propose will undermine their chances.

At the same time, it would be foolish to allow still-large newspapers to be run into the ground over the next five years. It is not merely that it is smart policy to salvage the massive investment in newsrooms that still exist. We believe "newspapers" as an organizing principle for gathering and communicating information–especially information that those in power would prefer to quarantine—have a crucial role to play in a democratic society. We place the quotation marks around the word *newspapers* to emphasize that we use an evolved definition of these institutions. When we refer to "newspapers" we are talking about locally based news organizations covering the full range of political and social activities in a community, providing the news and commenting on it. For the cost reasons we outlined in Chapter 2, newspapers will be predominantly digital in the foreseeable future. And that means the rhythm will gradually change to the Web's clock of constant publishing. This will erase many of the traditional distinctions between daily and weekly newspapers, and we should emphasize that we do not believe arbitrary distinctions should be made between dailies and weeklies. Likewise, the newspaper will increasingly be audio-visual. This process is already well underway.

What will remain constant is that newspapers—the term of art we continue to employ, although we are really talking about newsrooms—will be institutions responsible for covering communities with a sense of duty that is unmatched by other media ventures. Newspapers are the place where the buck stops in a community; where people can logically expect to see coverage of what is important in their locale. And if people do not find it in their newspaper, they have a right to demand an explanation from the editors. A collection of niche Web sites covering different aspects of a community are well and good, but in combination they cannot recreate the coherence and unity a well-edited and re-sourced newspaper can deliver. We believe this remains a crucial and distinct democratic institution.

In the near-term, it's vital that at least one newspaper remain alive in every community that has traditionally had one. To this end, the federal government must intervene to aid the transition to post-corporate own-ership models for daily papers. We should state up front that we're op-posed to government-owned newspapers. There is actually a history of municipally owned newspapers in the United States, like the *Los Angeles Municipal News* nearly 100 years ago.[23] The logic for municipal ownership is clear: the newspaper is a necessary institution, much like the police and fire department or schools. It could be supported by public monies and have an elected management, accountable directly to the voters. However, due to the nature of journalism, we prefer that newspapers remain independent of municipal governments. The goal should be to have many independently owned and managed newspapers. But there is still a defining role for the government to play.

The crucial point to keep in mind is that we are dealing with a failing industry. It has no viable business model. In most cases, there are few if any commercial interests willing to invest serious money in the enterprise. That is why the government has a necessary role to play in bringing about a post-corporate future. The market is not equipped to address circumstances like this, except to let the newspapers go under. This is a crisis situation. But it is not a situation without options. The U.S. government can again, as it did in lifetimes of many living Americans but in the distant locations of postwar Germany and Japan, create the conditions where a free and independent press can be sustained through the crisis and ultimately flourish.

With an eye on those cities where no commercial interests are prepared to maintain the daily newspaper, we believe the government should establish an office to oversee and coordinate the rapid transition of failing corporate newspapers that have dysfunctional ownership structures—and, in most cases, the crushing debts that go with them—into post-corporate newspapers. (We use the term "post-corporate" recognizing that some of the models we propose are technically corporations. They are not, however, for-profit corporations in the common understanding of the term.) It should have a budget sufficient to purchase the collapsing newspapers (and then resell them to new owners), or provide low-interest loans to new ownership groups to make the deals themselves. This office could possibly be housed in the Small Business Administration, which has considerable expertise in similar operations. If the government purchases a failing newspaper outright, it will hold on to a newspaper for one year maximum—with strict controls on the official role to guard against censorship and abuses of the public trust. If a new structure is not in place at that point, the newspaper will be closed. This will give all the current and potential players incentive to get engaged, negotiate honestly and close deals.

This conversion has two distinct aspects. First, there is the process by which we get corporations to relinquish their control. In general this will have to be through a buyout of some sort, or through a managed bankruptcy. The deals may require "sweeteners." They will work best if prospective new owners are present and engage indirectly in negotiations, a circumstance we have already seen develop in some communities where newspapers are failing and wealthy individuals (such as California billionaires Eli Broad, who has stepped up several times to express an interest in buying *The Los Angeles Times*, and David Geffen, who has expressed at least a measure of interest in buying *The New York Times*), local consortiums (such as the groups that have been assembled in Philadelphia, Boston and other cities) or union and community groups have come forward.

Then the question becomes: Are there legal ownership structures that can be used to quickly, efficiently and responsibly convert corporate newspapers to post-corporate newspapers? The three most interesting options are the 501(c)(3) nonprofit model, the L3C Low-Profit Limited Liability Company model and some form of worker or community cooperative. Each of these three models, to be effective, would benefit from the enactment of fresh legislation by Congress specifically addressing their use by news media. They will also require ongoing federal resources.

But before we get into detail, let's establish that post-corporate models for operating newsrooms can and do produce great journalism. We've got examples from around the world, not only in public broadcasting but also in the newspaper business. For instance, the newspaper that is broadly seen as a world leader—perhaps *the* world leader—in getting journalism across the bridge from print to digital, London's *Guardian*, was owned from 1936 to 2008 by The Scott Trust, a charitable foundation established by its previous owner to ensure the British newspaper's editorial independence. The Scott Trust was established in 1936, when *The Guardian*'s owner at the time, John Scott, voluntarily renounced all financial interest in the business for himself and his family, putting his shares in the company, worth more than £1 million at the time, into the trust. The trust's stated "core principle" was "to preserve the financial and editorial independence of the Guardian in perpetuity, while its subsidiary aims are to champion its principles and to promote freedom of the press in the UK and abroad."[24] As a non-charitable trust, The Scott Trust had a finite lifespan, so in 2008 the trustees transferred ownership of its shares in the Guardian Media Group (GMG) to a newly established permanent limited company, The Scott Trust Limited, which became the new owner of *The Guardian*. "The change reinforces existing protections for the Guardian," the trustees explained. "The core purpose has been enshrined in the constitution of The Scott Trust Limited and cannot be altered or amended. The new company is not permitted to pay dividends, and its constitution has been carefully drafted to ensure that no individual can ever personally benefit from the arrangements." As such, said Dame Liz Forgan, the chair of The Scott Trust Limited, the new arrangement renewed "our commitment to preserve the legacy of CP Scott, further strengthen the protection afforded to GMG and the Guardian ... "[25]

The Guardian is recognized repeatedly as Britain's "Newspaper of the Year" and as the "Best Electronic Newspaper" by the British Press Awards. It was named the "World's Best-Designed Newspaper" by the Society for News Design, honored again and again as the "Best Newspaper" online at the international Webby Awards—beating *The New York Times*, *The Washington Post*, *The Wall Street Journal* and other papers. *The Guardian* keeps the faith journalistically and leads the way when it comes to innovation. Why? "Because we are owned by a trust that's profit-seeking—definitely profit-seeking, not profit-making—we were incredibly well positioned for the changes that have rocked newspapers and media over the last decade," says *Guardian* managing editor Chris Elliott.[26]

It is not just on the international stage that post-corporate papers are showing the way when it comes to maintaining journalistic standards in difficult times. In 2009, *The St. Petersburg Times* won two Pulitzer Prizes—the Florida paper's seventh and eighth such honors—for fact-checking the 2008 presidential race (national reporting) and exposing child neglect (feature writing). It was the only newspaper other than *The New York Times* to receive multiple awards. But unlike the nation's "newspaper of record," *The St. Petersburg Times* is not a classically corporate paper. The Florida paper's previous owner, Nelson Poynter, was an old-school publisher who really did believe that the newspaper business was different from all others. Instead of selling off the *Times* or willing it to his heirs, the publisher established what is now The Poynter Institute, defining for it two missions: "to teach journalists young and old, and to keep his newspaper independent and free to serve its communities."[27]

"Newspaper publishing," Poynter believed, "is a sacred trust and must always be carried out in the public's interest. Ownership by a distant corporation would make that impossible."[28] So *The St. Petersburg Times* is owned by a journalism school. And, as Andrew Barnes, who served as chairman and chief executive of the *Times* during a 15-year period from 1988 to 2004, when he had to battle to maintain the newspaper's unique ownership structure and the independence that goes with it, has written:

> The setup boils down to this: a profit-making, tax-paying publishing company owns the *St. Petersburg Times*. ... The company's earnings after taxes go to build the business and to support the Poynter Institute.
>
> That's not how it works at most newspapers. Corporate owners in distant cities all too often lack familiarity with local people and issues. They may not even know newspapers very well. As a result, the only thing that counts to the owners is dollars, and readers suffer.
>
> Some of the differences:
>
> If our owner demanded profits be twice as high as they are, it would inevitably cut into our ability to hire enough people and buy enough newsprint to really tell you what is going on in our communities. We run a nicely profitable business so we can be an excellent newspaper; all too many companies print newspapers so they can make a lot of money.
>
> The price of our paper is low. We keep it that way so all citizens can be informed, not just the well-to-do. We believe our democracy depends on informed citizens.[29]

Well said. And the strategy seems to have worked. In addition to securing its Pulitzers, the *Times* has been described by *The American Journalism Review* as a paper that "many journalists consider the nation's finest local newspaper."[30] Operating in what for many years has been one of the most competitive media markets in the nation, *The St. Petersburg Times* has emerged as the largest-circulation daily newspaper in Florida. It has, like other large newspapers, experienced circulation losses in recent years, yet it is now one of the 25 largest-circulation dailies in the United States. While home-state competitors were struggling in the spring of 2009— *The Orlando Sentinel* and Fort Lauderdale's *Sun-Sentinel* were suffering through the Tribune Company bankruptcy while the debt-hobbled Mc-Clatchy Company had reportedly offered the *Miami Herald* for sale—*St. Petersburg Times* editor and chief executive officer Paul Tash was able to wax philosophical. "The economy is especially tough if you are a public company in the stock market or if you have a lot of debt or both. *The St. Petersburg Times* is an independent, privately owned newspaper. And that allows us to focus and manage for the long term," he said. "The last 25 years was the golden age for immensely profitable newspapers. Those days are over for a long time. If you built ownership and debt on the ex-pectations that party would go on forever, this is a particularly wrenching time." Instead of fretting about debt and shutdowns, Tash was talking about digital initiatives and "figuring out how to keep that journalistic firepower in place."[31]

Other civically and democratically minded publishers have come up with strategies to keep their newspapers independent and free—and lo-cally owned and operated—after old owners slip the mortal coil. *The Capital Times* of Madison, Wisconsin, the first print daily in the country to become a primarily digital newspaper in 2008, was founded and owned from 1917 to 1970 by William T. Evjue. (John Nichols has been associated with *The Capital Times* since 1993.) A progressive reformer who through-out his lifetime was a critic of newspaper chains and complacent jour-nalism, Evjue directed at his death that all the proceeds from his controlling voting stock in The Capital Times Company be turned over to the Evjue Foundation he had formed a few years before, effectively cre-ating a post-corporate ownership structure for the paper.[32] The Evjue Foundation keeps an independent daily newspaper (now predominantly online but with a substantial newsroom and an influential role in the community) in the game while making substantial charitable donations in the community.

The Day Trust in New London, Connecticut, has a history similar to that of *The Capital Times*. Established by *The Day*'s previous publisher, Theodore Bodenwein, The Day Trust is under direction from the grave "to so manage said newspaper or newspapers as to provide liberal compensation and various forms of assistance and rewards, such as insurance, bonuses, and pensions, to its employees; to pay sufficient salaries to assure a high type of executives and skilled writers and workmen." There is more: "I believe a newspaper should be more than a business enterprise. It should also be the champion and protector of the public interest and defender of the people's rights," explained Bodenwein, in a will that outlined how he felt "his" newspaper should be operated after his passing.[33]

If every publisher left the field as Poynter, Evjue and Bodenwein did, there would be a lot less need to search for new ownership models for newspapers and strategies to preserve and promote journalism. Unfortunately, these men were the outliers in an era that saw the vast majority of local newspaper owners transfer their "properties" to chains that sold and resold them into debt and decay. As such, the precise models they developed would be difficult, if not impossible, to recreate. Writing on *The St. Petersburg Times* for *The Columbia Journalism Review* in 2008, Douglas McCollam confirmed that "given the pressures most newspapers contend with, reporters and editors at the *Times* know they have it good." But his was not a happy tale of what might be. Rather, McCollam concluded,

> The story of Nelson Poynter and his institute has become something of a soothing bed-time story for traumatized journalists. While reporters are forced to endure draconian cuts in their own newsrooms—many of them enacted (as journalists see it) by mutton-headed managers with their eyes riveted on the bottom line—they can still dream of a land not too far away where a well-tended band of scribes toils under the benevolent gaze of ownership unconcerned with trivial matters such as EBITDA (Earnings Before Interest, Taxes, Depreciation and Amortization) and online ad revenue. The reality, of course, is more complicated, and demonstrates why the Poynter model offers no easy cure for the ills that plague American journalism.[34]

McCollam's right. But that's not an argument for rejecting the search for smart, well-designed post-corporate ownership models.

Senator Ben Cardin, a Democrat from Maryland, seized the baton in March 2009, as daily newspapers seemed to be going bankrupt or closing down weekly. Cardin offered a legislative response to the news that newspapers across the country—including Maryland's dominant *Baltimore Sun*—were faltering. Cardin recognized that, despite all the talk about the Internet and the recession, what really ailed newspapers was the fact that they were being run by corporations that had as their first priority the extraction of massive returns for investors. "America is losing its newspaper industry," the senator explained.

> While the economy has caused an immediate problem, the business model for newspapers, based on circulation and advertising revenue, is broken. That decline is a harbinger of tragedy for communities nationwide and for our democracy. This is why I introduced the Newspaper Revitalization Act to help our disappearing community and metropolitan papers by allowing them to become nonprofit organizations. My goal is to save local coverage by reporters who know their communities, work their beats and dig up the stories that are important to our daily lives. Today, newspapers do that job; all other outlets—TV, radio, blogs—feed off that base. My bill would allow newspapers—if they choose—to operate under 501(c)(3) status for educational purposes, similar to public broadcasters.[35]

Cardin's Newspaper Revitalization Act proposed the necessary twists and tinkers that would make it possible for newspapers to operate as nonprofits for educational purposes under the U.S. tax code. Addressing questions about where money might come from for restructured newspapers, the senator said, "Advertising and subscription revenue would be tax-exempt, and contributions to support coverage or operations could be tax-deductible."[36]

Then he got to the touchy part. The shift from for-profit to not-for-profit status would not undermine the ability of newspapers to cover election campaigns or local, state and national affairs, Cardin claimed.

But, he acknowledged, newspapers that operated as nonprofits would not be permitted to make political endorsements.[37] The senator admitted: "This may not be the optimal choice for some major newspapers."[38]

In fact, though the senator's plan was well intended, it was not optimal for many newspapers. "Newspapers that opt for the nonprofit model leave an opening for politicians to meddle and forfeit political endorsements, a vital component to a newspaper's editorial voice and role in a community," explained Ryan Blethen, who is far more open to alternative ownership models than most newspaper executives. "Nonprofits are not allowed to make political endorsements. The same would go for nonprofit newspapers, which is unfortunate. Endorsements, especially on the local and state level, allow a newspaper to be a part of the community dialogue. Endorsements are also the framework by which an editorial board builds its identity."[39]

This concern was echoed, not surprisingly, by David Holwerk, editorial-page editor of *The Sacramento Bee* and the president of the National Conference of Editorial Writers.[40] Blethen and Holwerk are right. Editorial endorsements—or the denial of them—are among the most powerful tools that newspapers have for holding political figures to account. Trading that tool away denudes newspapers, making them even less interesting than they already are when compared with opinionated blogs. And non-endorsement policies won't shield journalists and editors from pressures by pols and interest groups. In fact, the shift could make things worse. Ask yourself this question: Can a laudatory editorial about a mayor—or even, for that matter, an article—be read as an endorsement? Can a condemnatory editorial or article about a powerful city-council member be read as an encouragement to vote for her challenger? Especially in one-newspaper towns, we can imagine that the threat of an investigation into the nonprofit status of the local daily—with all the associated prospects of legal wrangling and visits from IRS agents—would cause plenty of papers to pull their punches. And, since the scrutiny would rise at election time, newspapers would be most likely to lose their nerve at precisely the point when they are most needed as beacons in the fog of campaign spin.

Supporters of the 501(c)(3) option for newspapers respond that many nonprofit publications like *Mother Jones* and *In These Times* have had no problems making their opinions on issues and politicians known without making formal endorsements. However, those national publications are not operating in the hothouse atmosphere of a local media market, so the pressures and scrutiny they face are dramatically different. We think the endorsement issue is a serious one. We also share the concern critics have raised with Cardin's requirement for qualifying newspapers to do national and international journalism, which would preclude much ethnic and specifically local media—including weekly newspapers that provide the primary reporting in many communities—from its benefits.[41]

We are impressed that Senator Cardin has accepted the criticism and has displayed openness to tinkering with and improving his legislation. We do not rule out the 501(c)(3) model. However, the world of 501(c)(3) organizations is enormous, so any effort to change the rules to accommodate journalism could well open the door for a political food fight few politicians would welcome. It might be wise to see if we can do better, or at least develop alternative paths to a post-corporate newspaper future. The post-corporate fix that is more likely to work, on a number of levels, will borrow from but not precisely emulate existing nonprofits.

The Low-Profit Alternative

In the course of our research we have become increasingly enamored with the low-profit limited liability corporation, or L3C, model.

Robert Lang, the foundation executive who developed the L3C model, describes it as "the for-profit with a non-profit soul."[42] This new approach to an old dilemma—how to attract significant investment in projects that seek to serve charitable or community interests—is probably best understood as a hybrid of a nonprofit and a for-profit organization that builds on the strength of each. As Emily Nicole Chan explains on "Nonprofit Law Blog,"

> [This] is a new type of limited liability company (LLC) designed to attract private investments and philanthropic capital in ventures designed to provide a social benefit. Unlike a standard LLC, the L3C has an explicit primary charitable mission and only a secondary profit concern. But un-

like a charity, the L3C is free to distribute the profits, after taxes, to owners or investors.[43]

Among other things, the L3C can take investments, not merely grants, from foundations. This dramatically increases the pool of available funds. It also allows private capital to play a role. The genius of the L3C structure is its flexibility; anything but a "one size fits all" model, the L3C allows its creators to set up a specific model best suited to the community and the financial pool available to it.

The L3C model was recognized in 2008 as an official legal structure by the state of Vermont and in early 2009 by the states of Michigan, Wyoming, Utah and North Dakota, as well as the Crow Nation. This gives the L3C model "national applicability," because L3Cs formed in any of these jurisdictions can be used in other states or territories; it therefore has a flexibility traditional business and nonprofit models lack.[44] (Well-drawn federal legislation, in the form of a proposed Program-Related Investment Promotion Act that specifically mentions newspapers, would increase that flexibility. This should be a high priority.) As Chan notes, partners can "structure an L3C and adjust ownership to best fit their unique situations. By addressing these current investment challenges ... L3Cs are able to attract a greater influx of private capital from various sources of wealth in order to serve their charitable or education goals."

What this could mean for newspapers is spelled out by Bill Mitchell, the veteran newsman who leads the News Transformation program at the Poynter Institute:

> As an L3C, a news organization could rely on a wider range of financial backers than is currently possible, as long as the company and its investors share a common commitment to serving an educational or charitable public purpose beyond financial return. ... The new hybrid model makes it easier for companies to attract investors with different objectives and expectations. It also addresses a fundamental conflict of publicly traded news companies: the obligation to increase shareholder value while spending what it takes to provide communities with the journalism needed to inform civic life.[45]

The L3C approach is dramatically more flexible than a traditional nonprofit model. Plus, notes Mitchell, "A news company structured as an L3C—as opposed to a nonprofit—would avoid some of the limitations of nonprofit status, including the prohibition against political endorsements."[46]

That sounds attractive. But can anyone imagine what an L3C newsroom would look like? Well, yes. Sally Duros, a former real-estate editor with *The Chicago Sun-Times*—a newspaper that declared bankruptcy March 31, 2009—did just that in an article she wrote, appropriately enough, for *The Huffington Post*:

> Me? I am excited about the Chicago newsroom of the future, a journalist's dream come true that could rise from a floor of foundation cash and be sustained by a stream of revenue and profit. My theoretical newsroom, let's call it *The Times Democrat*, would be a new kind of company, an L3C, or Low Profit Limited Liability Company...
>
> More than ever, a newsroom must be a mission-based place. ... Let's agree that journalism must live for the future of our democracy. Let's also agree that the newsroom of *The Times Democrat* will be an amalgam of the best and most innovative practices we have online and in print, and that it will evolve to be something recognizable as newsgathering measured by a few key virtues. These include a culture of accountability and quality control that includes editors and fact checkers. And in fact, credibility and audience relevance will be the currency that moves the market of readers, or "news consumers," from news org to news org locally and nationally. ...
>
> But to get there, journalism needs one thing more than anything else to operate well: that thing is money, specifically re-birthing cash. That's what our L3C newsroom, *The Times Democrat*, is about.
>
> So, what would the business model of *The Times Democrat* look like? It would simply be a modified Limited Liability Company that has the primary goal of serving a socially beneficial purpose and as such it could accept foundation money.
>
> Americans for Community Development, a coalition sponsored by our nation's first L3C—L3C Advisors—says that the L3C is the for-profit

with a nonprofit soul. The nonprofit soul of a newspaper arises from the recognition that newspapers are the only business specifically recognized in the U.S. Constitution and that the information they provide is vital to the proper function of a democracy.[47]

Too good to be true? A modern-day alchemist's fantasy? We don't think so. And neither does Robert Lang, the foundation CEO who created the L3C model. "What we are looking at is the newspaper as a self-sufficient entity," he says. "It will not be a high-profit entity. ... I'm not saying that we can save the *Chicago Tribune* and make it what it was 10 years ago. But at least the money that's made today can go toward improving the product not paying off leveraged debt."[48]

Breaking the stranglehold of the for-profit model makes the most of what viability remains in newspapers and could help them fill the "need [for] newsgathering organizations" in cities that are losing them, says Lang. We would add that, with the right federal interventions—several of which we will discuss in short order—the L3C model could play a critical role in the transition from the print newsrooms of the past to the digital newsrooms of the future. In other words, while we generally agree with Lang, we see the possibility that Chicago might end up with a newsroom—perhaps even *newsrooms*—that are better than what *The Chicago Tribune* was 10 years ago. Maybe one of those newsrooms will be the Duros-edited *Times Democrat*.

This discussion is moving away from hypothetical status. In July 2009 Craig Whitney, the "standards editor" at *The New York Times*, acknowledged that the paper was considering "whether it would be possible to get the kind of support that NPR does from foundations for its journalism." Whitney made it clear the *Times* had no intention "to become a nonprofit corporation." It seems to us that the *Times* might want to take a hard look at L3C status. Indeed, this could be its logical trajectory if the current rulers of the Times wish to remain in journalism first and foremost.[49]

Truthfully, though, we are less worried about Manhattan and Chicago than we are about midsize cities in New York and Illinois, where historic newspapers are on the ropes and where there are fewer options for saving journalism. Could the L3C approach work in these towns? Put another way: Will it play in Peoria?

The answer, we are delighted to report, is yes! *The Peoria Journal Star*, with roots that go back more than 150 years, is a classic midsize daily that historically has provided outsize service to its downstate region. It was locally owned through most of its history, first by Peoria families and then from the mid-1980s until the mid-1990s by its employees. In 1996, after years of wrangling between managers and unions, the Employee Stock Ownership Plan (ESOP) was dissolved and the paper was sold to the California-based Copley Press chain, which in turn sold the *Journal Star* in 2007 to New York-based GateHouse Media, a publicly traded firm that paid $380 million for the Peoria paper and six other Midwestern publications. We probably don't need to explain what happened next. GateHouse paid too much for the papers. Revenues dropped. Pay cuts were announced. Buyouts. Layoffs. Downsizings.

By 2008, the union that represents journalists at the *Journal Star*, Newspaper Guild Local 86, was searching for a new ownership model that would stop the bleeding from corporate cuts, according to local president Jennifer Towery. Union members looked at cooperative models and ESOPs and nonprofit schemes, but what made the most sense was the L3C approach: "We are looking at long-term ownership that puts journalism first. [The L3C] just resonated. It has so much potential."

For Towery, the key is the requirement that newspapers organized as L3Cs must serve a social purpose—like covering the community—as opposed to merely generating profits for distant corporations. "It insists that serving the readers is your mission," the *Journal Star* editor says. "If it doesn't serve the readers to cut your newsroom staff you can't do it."

Towery is not alone. L3Cs have generated a lot of interest within the Newspaper Guild, especially at locals representing journalists on papers in or facing bankruptcy. To make the strategy work, however, Congress needs to get seriously engaged. There's been a great deal of progress at the state level; in Illinois, for instance, at the prodding of the Peoria Newspaper Guild, L3C legislation raced through the state legislature in early 2009. But there are still enough questions about how the IRS will interpret this new approach that there are vulnerabilities. Our read suggests that L3Cs have been very well designed to fit within existing IRS rules, but it would be very useful if Congress would enact federal L3C legislation that clearly mentions newspapers and news-oriented Web sites—and that guarantees the greatest possible flexibility for those seeking to "save journalism."

Necessarily, we believe that journalists will be in the forefront of this struggle. And we think they should be given as many options as possible for preserving existing newsrooms and starting new ones. It makes sense to look anew at rules governing ESOPs and cooperatives, as well as the L3C model, in each case with an eye toward making it easier for journalists—and journalists working in concert with local foundations, unions, community organizations and wealthy individuals—to buy failing newspapers and to start new newsrooms. Though these are not cure-alls, Newspaper Guild president Bernie Lunzer says, "Such changes ... would tether news organizations to the communities they serve, rather than to Wall Street."[50]

The Guild has a long history of exploring alternative ownership strategies—going back to the early 1950s, and most recently in an attempt to salvage newspapers that were being sold off by the old Knight Ridder chain—and members of Congress who are serious about building a future for journalism should keep this and other news-gathering unions at the table. Bottom line: in seeking alternative ownership models, the place to begin is with journalists and the communities they serve—not with big media companies and the investors they serve.

We are convinced that post-corporate models for newspaper ownership hold out much greater promise of success than do the corporate models for a number of reasons. And we're not alone. Ironically, the first great clarion call for a post-corporate structure for newspapers came from Harry Chandler, heir to the great *Los Angeles Times* fortune. Way back in 2006, surveying the appalling consequences of corporate ownership on newspapers, Chandler argued the future for daily newspapers needed to be based on "community ownership, like that of the Green Bay Packers football team."[51] Whether it's a community-investment scheme like that of the Packers, or some other post-corporate model, this is a fix that meets the challenges of the moment. First and foremost, it allows for a focus on journalism. Reporting and editing will no longer be an "externality." As such, the "product" will be enhanced, making it more attractive to readers and potentially to advertisers. Additionally, in a digital age, approaches that might not have worked at the height of the commercial moment—ESOPs and cooperatives, in particular—could now be far more viable. After all, digital media does not require the real estate, delivery trucks and rolls of paper that made producing a printed publication such a pricy endeavor.

At the same time, post-corporate newspapers—be they print or digital, ESOP, 501(c)(3), cooperative, L3C or some blend—will still have a difficult time making ends meet in face of the stark economics facing all journalism. Even with an L3C, nonprofit or cooperative structure, even with greatly reduced taxes, even with the ability to raise philanthropic money, many of these daily newspapers still may not generate enough advertising or sell sufficient subscriptions to sustain a viable newsroom. For that reason we believe that Lunzer and other advocates for journalism are right when they say that subsidies will be needed. The Newspaper Guild president acknowledges that "there is a reflexive antipathy by many people to the idea of tax subsidies of any kind for newsgathering." But he knows that "in fact the United States has a long history of providing such breaks, starting with subsidized mail delivery for newspapers and other periodicals."[52]

This leads to a bold plan for subsidizing journalism: University of Pennsylvania law professor C. Edwin Baker, whose insights shaped the conclusion to Chapter 3, has developed a proposal to grant newspapers a tax credit of 50 percent of the salaries of all journalistic employees, up to a maximum credit of $45,000 for each journalist. This credit would result in papers hiring (or not firing) many more journalists. A tax credit is far more valuable than a tax deduction because, among other things, the benefit does not depend on the paper's being profitable. If a firm has journalists with salaries totaling $1 million dollars, it could deduct $500,000 directly from the actual taxes it owes the government, not simply deduct $500,000 from its taxable income. If the paper does not owe taxes, the newspaper will receive a payment from the government for that amount. Baker argues that implementation issues involved in such a program are relatively simple. (There are, for example, accepted industry definitions of *journalist* that can be adapted.) Baker further argues that any newspaper or news medium, be it commercial or nonprofit, should be entitled to this tax credit. While we think that is an excellent subject to be studied and debated, we see his tax-credit plan as being, at the very least, a credible way to subsidize the new tier of post-corporate newspapers.

With that in mind, we propose keeping a version of this tax-credit principle to be used by the L3C, nonprofit or cooperative. The government will pay half the salary of every reporter and editor up to $45,000 each. Assuming most daily and weekly newspapers go post-corporate and employment returns to the high-water mark of two decades ago—the latter a very big assumption, we know—this would cost the state $3.5 billion annually.[53] If employment stayed at current levels it would run half that total. Newspapers that benefit from these subsidies would also be prime candidates for News AmeriCorps rookie journalists.

What would taxpayers and citizens get in return—aside from what Lunzer describes as "the type of journalism that protects our communities from political and corporate over-reaching, tackles systemic problems of the environment and the economy and chronicles the every-day lives of our neighbors"? Quite a bit. In exchange for accepting subsidies, post-corporate newspapers would be required to place everything they produce on the Web for free upon publication. The news, features and opinion pieces would then enter the public domain—creating vast new deposits of current and, ultimately, historic information.

For the sake of discussion, were the Baker proposal to prove successful, and therefore extend to all news media, the cost could be substantially higher—perhaps double what we have discussed. Let's talk numbers: if by 2020 we roughly doubled the number of full-time working journalists in the United States to, say, 160,000, it would require a U.S. government subsidy of $7.2 billion in 2009 dollars—roughly the same amount that it costs to occupy Iraq for a month.

It may be that this program will develop exceptional community media and revolutionize newspapering, drawing diverse communities together as never before in American history. We may then wish to expand the program to make it possible for second or even third digital newspapers to be launched in communities across the country—recreating the sort of competition not seen in many American cities since newspapers started consolidating a century ago. Or the program could prove unnecessary, and be superseded by something else, including possibly the media we discuss in the balance of the chapter. But it strikes us as a worthwhile policy risk to attempt to see if the daily newspaper can find a place in a digital world. Perhaps it is because we are old-timers, but we think the world will seem a lot emptier if there isn't something like the newspaper—as Ryan Blethen and other journalists are actively redefining it—in the 21st century.

From Public Broadcasting to Public Media

The second core policy area where government intervention can help achieve healthy journalism is in the noncommercial media sector. After decades of attacks by know-nothing politicians, it is time to restore and extend America's understanding of public-service broadcasting as a great and underutilized resource. At the same time, it is necessary to recognize that public radio and TV stations have an exceptionally important role to play in the transition to the new age of journalism. Now is the time for America to dramatically expand the existing public-broadcasting system, re-envisioning it as truly public media.

Public-service broadcasting was a radical new development in publicly subsidized media when it emerged in the early 20th century. Unlike earlier subsidies for newspapers, the plan for developing public broadcasting would use tax dollars to generate media content directly, not simply to encourage commercial entities to do work. This leap stemmed from the recognition that broadcasting presented an unprecedented problem for every nation: how to best utilize the scarce radio spectrum. There was an understanding that the emerging commercial media system, even at its very best, had inherent flaws—what in Chapter 2 we term *externalities*—that could be damaging to a self-governing or humane society. In combination, concerns about these factors inspired the belief that it was not just a right but a duty of citizens in a democratic society to subsidize and promote viable nonprofit and noncommercial broadcast media. We believe this principle holds true today for the Internet, and it holds true specifically for journalism.

Few Americans are aware of the rich history or traditions that encompass "public-service broadcasting." The term refers to nonprofit, noncommercial broadcasting directed at the entire population and providing a full range of programming. When it works as it should, public broadcasting is accountable to the citizenry, has strict independence from the dominant political powers and does not rely upon the market to determine its programming. Such a setup presents a difficult problem, although not an insurmountable one, for a free society, because it allows the state possibly to control media content far more than classical liberal theory would countenance. In authoritarian political systems, public broadcasting quickly becomes little more than state propaganda. Managing a viable public-broadcasting service can be difficult in a democracy, but the international experience shows that it can be done quite well. What is needed, as always, is a political commitment to make it happen.

The international record shows that the journalism produced by public-broadcasting services in many industrial nations is more independent of the government in power than commercial journalism.[54] Moreover, as we discussed at the end of Chapter 1, comprehensive international research demonstrates that those nations with high-quality public-broadcasting systems—e.g., Britain, Denmark and Finland—tend to have more knowledgeable and engaged citizenries. Not surprisingly, nations with significant and well-funded public-broadcasting systems tend to have considerably less information inequality along class lines than the United States, where public broadcasting has been starved financially and constrained structurally.[55]

Chart 1 demonstrates the per capita expenditures for public broadcasting in the United States compared to several other leading nations.

In most democratic nations of the world, a significant section of the spectrum is devoted to nonprofit (and usually noncommercial) radio and television. The most notable example in the English-speaking world is the British Broadcasting Corporation (BBC). These channels have proven to be successful and have maintained audiences well into the multichannel TV and Internet eras. They are demonstrating that public media can move their operations significantly to the Internet. And in so

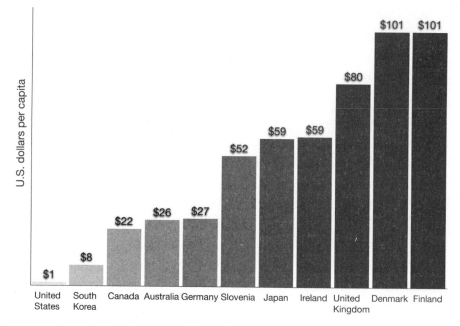

CHART 1. Global Spending on Public Media, 2007[56]

doing they are forcing newspapers and commercial broadcasters that "go digital" to do it better.[57]

Unfortunately, the United States is not enjoying the informational and social benefits that come with a strong public-broadcasting system. The American commitment to public media has been extraordinarily weak compared to nearly all other industrial nations.[58] To put the matter in context, federal spending by the U.S. government on public media is $409 million in the 2009 budget. If the United States spent at the same per capita level as Canada, our federal commitment would be $7.5 billion; if we paid at the same per capita level as Britain, our federal commitment would be $24 billion; if we paid at the same per capita level as Denmark or Finland, our federal commitment would be $30 billion annually. With that type of budget, public and community broadcasters could have multiple, high-quality newsrooms in nearly every midsize community in the nation, and even more in major metropolitan areas. (Beyond journalism, such budgets would provide an enormous spur to audiovisual production. In Europe, a huge and impressive variety of programming that is beneficial to society but that would never pass commercial muster has been produced as a result of these subsidies.[59])

This leads to the obvious question: Why is public media so weak in the United States compared to nearly every other democratic nation?

The main reason is that proponents of public broadcasting in other nations were able to get their systems established before commercial broadcasters had achieved dominance over the airwaves. The defeat of the broadcast-reform movement in 1934 quashed the hope for this caliber of public broadcasting in the United States. At the time, commercial broadcasters argued that few people would listen to their stations if they had access to advertising-free stations with quality entertainment—which they conceded that people wanted—so it was unfair to allow public broadcasting to exist and thereby undermine commercial broadcasting.[60]

The U.S. government did establish extremely well-funded noncommercial broadcasting services in the 1940s and beyond, but they were directed abroad. Indeed, the deal made with the commercial broadcasting industry was that those services—Voice of America, Armed Forces radio and television, Radio Free Europe—would not be accessible in the United States. The explanation was that explicit government propaganda should be restricted to foreigners, but a clear concern for the commercial broadcasters was that the American public not be exposed to well-funded noncommercial fare.[61]

In the late 1960s, the commercial broadcasting lobby finally relented, and a national public radio and television service started. But it was not a BBC type of operation, providing a full range of noncommercial programming to the entire population. The plan for what became the Public Broadcasting Service (PBS) and National Public Radio (NPR) did not call for such a system—the commercial dominance of the airwaves was a given—but rather for a broadcasting service that concentrated exclusively upon providing the public-service programming that commercial stations were not delivering. The commercial broadcasters laid first claim to popular programming—the big games, popular entertainment and variety shows—and public broadcasters were left with programming that had less immediate audience appeal.

At its best, as envisioned in the Carnegie Commission reports that helped birth the system, U.S. public broadcasting was seen as producing cutting-edge political and creative programming that commercial broadcasters found unprofitable and serving poor and marginalized audiences of little interest to advertisers.[62] As Senator Hugh Scott of Pennsylvania said during the congressional debates on the matter in 1967, "I want to see things on public television that I hate—things that make me think!"[63]

In the opinion of the original Carnegie Commission, this was to be a well-funded service based on an excise tax on the sale of TV sets that would eventually reach 5 percent; this money would be placed in a trust fund over which politicians would have no direct control.[64] When the Public Broadcasting Act of 1967 was passed, this key element of the Carnegie plan was dropped. Had it been fully implemented, public broadcasting would enjoy an annual subsidy approaching $4 billion in 2009 dollars—still dramatically less than the subsidies of Canada and other developed nations, but almost ten times more than is now available.[65]

The Carnegie Commission vision was doomed from the start when the independent funding mechanism was sabotaged. When PBS broadcast muckraking programs such as 1970's *Banks and the Poor*, the realization that television could question the economic status quo—as opposed to merely cheerlead on its behalf—sent politicians who supped at the table of special interests into a tizzy. President Nixon vetoed the public-broadcasting budget authorization in 1972 to express his displeasure.[66]

In response, the American Civil Liberties Union produced a 55-page report that accused the Nixon administration of attempting to "intimidate" and "starve" public broadcasting in what was described as "a cynical exercise in White House manipulation of a communications medium that threatens to reduce the medium to even worse pap than commercial television's diet."[67] The Democratic Party platform that year declared, "We should support long-range financing for public broadcasting, insulated from political pressures. We deplore the Nixon Administration's crude efforts to starve and muzzle public broadcasting, which has become a vital supplement to commercial television."[68]

PBS eventually did get funding, but the pattern of keeping public broadcasting on what the ACLU described as a "starvation diet" was established, creating a circumstance that "would leave national public affairs programming in an advanced state of poverty" while continuing to "leave the medium at the mercy of politicians."[69] Public broadcasters had received a clear signal: be careful in the coverage of political and social issues and expect resistance if you proceed outside the political boundaries that exist in commercial broadcast journalism.

U.S. public broadcasters were consigned to generate programming for which there was only a small audience; so members of Congress concluded that an underutilized service (with little popular support) did not need a lavish budget. Public broadcasters rarely dared to schedule prime-time entertainment programs with mass appeal. Such shows would have helped develop the broad audiences and public support that European public broadcasters enjoyed. But U.S. public broadcasters understood that such an approach was political suicide; the muscular commercial-broadcasting lobby would have complained to Congress that the government was subsidizing unfair competition, and thus interfering with the "free market." Public broadcasters quickly realized they could count on the federal government for only a fraction of their budgets if they were to produce anything at all. They turned away from their original commitment to experimental programming and serving marginalized and poor audiences, and instead began cultivating an upper-middle-class sliver of the overall audience with business and high-culture programming. This tactic provided a solid base for periodic "pledge drives" as well as a political constituency that commanded respect in Washington. It also made public broadcasting increasingly attractive to advertisers— or "underwriters," as they were euphemistically termed.

To be fair, public broadcasting has produced some exceptional programming over the years, and its record is all the more impressive in view of the scant resources with which it had to work. Had it been given the resources of a European public broadcaster, we're patriotic enough to believe that U.S. public broadcasting would have equaled or surpassed the BBC. Even in its constrained circumstance, public broadcasting's journalism content has been under the watchful eye of the political Right in the United States. Some conservatives use what little money Congress provides as leverage to badger public broadcasters to stay within the same ideological range found on commercial networks.[70] These conservatives are convinced that reporters and hosts are unsympathetic to the Right's ideological and political projects. Others are, in effect, obsessed with public broadcasting because in it the traditional sources of control in commercial media—owners and advertisers—are absent, so a greater possibility exists that the public system will produce critical work. Milton Friedman called for subjecting public broadcasting to "market discipline."[71] Soon after the Republican takeover of Congress in the 1994 elections, Speaker Newt Gingrich announced his plan to "zero out" public broadcasting due to its alleged liberal bias.

Ironically, while the conservative attacks on public media have created a rallying cry among some loud elements of the Right, they have never been embraced by the general population. Many conservatives like public broadcasting. In 1984, no less a conservative icon than Barry Goldwater decried cutting any government funding to public broadcasting. Goldwater argued that the rise of commercialism on public broadcasting "marks the end of the only decent source of broadcasting in this country."[72] The Republicans dropped their plan to "zero out" public broadcasting in the 1990s, when Congress was flooded with public opposition, much of it from conservatives who, presumably, enjoyed watching Bill Buckley chat with Ronald Reagan and Margaret Thatcher on the PBS program *Firing Line.*[73]

Despite the starvation diet and the political pressures imposed upon it, public broadcasting remains to this day immensely respected across broad sections of the population and is far more trusted by the public than any other branch of the news media, or the government itself, including the court system.[74] What is ironic is that for nearly two decades commentators of all stripes have predicted the eventual demise of public broadcasting due to the emergence of multichannel television and the Internet. How can the public subsidize one or two measly channels, the argument goes, when there are thousands upon thousands of choices in the new media universe?

But with the digital revolution we need public media more than ever, and people still want it. After seven decades of "competition," commercial broadcasters—and the broader commercial system—are the ones turning to narrowcasting to appease the ever-fickle advertisers obsessed with targeted demographics. It falls to public broadcasters to do in the United States what they have done in other industrial democracies for generations: serve as the medium of the entire country. The argument of choice for those who did not believe the United States needed well-funded public broadcasting was always that the service was unnecessary here, because the commercial media were doing such a bang-up job. So much for that theory, at least as far as journalism is concerned. It is the great crisis in journalism that is the main factor and concern driving this revolutionary transformation and revival of public broadcasting.

NPR has adapted to the collapse of commercial radio journalism by basically taking over the franchise, becoming indispensable as a result. NPR has doubled its national audience in the past decade, reaching 26.4 million listeners weekly.[75] The same opportunity now awaits PBS, with the demise of commercial television journalism at the local level. It is imperative that it gets the funding and green light to proceed in that direction. Public stations already air candidate debates that commercial broadcasters neglect, taking elections and public-policy differences far more seriously than for-profit media. The next step is to write budgets that permit NPR and PBS stations to build and maintain strong newsrooms at the state and local levels. The funding should extend to community radio stations, public-access TV stations and low-power FM radio stations to the extent they engage in journalism. We need to recognize the value of multiple noncommercial newsrooms competing at the local level. No one thought a single monopoly commercial news station was satisfactory for the journalism needs of a community; the case holds as we rely increasingly on nonprofit newsrooms.

But the transformation of public media entails more than simply increasing the budget. It requires a new structure, and we support the call of Free Press for a White House Commission on Public Media to address this problem directly. Among other things, this commission needs to study how nations in Europe and Asia have produced well-funded and independent public-broadcasting systems. It also requires a formal commitment to journalism and public affairs as being the raison d'être of the institution. Public broadcasting will continue do a full range of programming, like public media worldwide, but its unique and vital role will be as an authoritative source of journalism in every community and nationwide.

We realize there is considerable criticism of the journalism that is produced by the public system. There are crucial exceptions, but too often public broadcasting has adopted a staid version of conventional professional journalism, with its over-reliance on people in power—still mostly wealthy white men—to set the agenda and range of legitimate debate.[76] The plus side, and why NPR has blossomed in recent years, is that it avoids the tendency toward the sensationalism, triviality and idiocy of too much commercial TV news and it has nothing like the bombast of talk radio. In short, it regards people as if they are functionally intelligent. This is the benefit of being largely noncommercial and nonprofit. The downside is that too often it seems to be too comfortable with targeting its programming to an audience that is upper-middle class.

Public media journalism needs to get serious about becoming a news medium of relevance to poor people, minorities, the working class and young people. It has to return to its Carnegie Commission mandate and embrace controversy and dissidence. Going digital will give public broadcasters more capacity to serve diverse communities. Reimagining journalism along these lines would be made easier if "underwriting" were eliminated, hence removing much of the implicit pressure to regard the audience as well-to-do. It will also be easier when the funding is put on a more stable basis, and the ability of politicians to hector programmers about specific newscasts is lessened. That won't eliminate pressures, as anyone who is watching the current wrangling over BBC funding and programming knows.[77] But for all the frustrations across the pond, we would gladly trade our circumstance for Britain's when it comes to public broadcasting.

The experience from abroad, and to some extent here in the United States, suggests to us that public radio and television can and will seamlessly transition to the Internet so that within a decade or two these institutions will be regarded by young people as primarily digital entities, with their broadcast roots becoming the stuff of trivia. Programming will adhere to the Web sense of timing, not the old broadcast schedule. This is the process being experienced by the leading democratic public broadcasters in the world, most notably the BBC.[78]

All of these changes will cost money, quite a bit of money. The fiscal challenge will be enhanced slightly if corporate underwriting is dropped, as we believe must be the case. NPR and PBS stations received $106 million in corporate underwriting in fiscal 2009, a significant recession-induced drop from 2008.[79] The cost of wooing corporations is too high for such a paltry return.[80] Public broadcasting should be guaranteed an annual appropriation from the federal government equal, on a per capita basis, to half that of Canada, a nation with a credible public-broadcasting system that still spends much less than the European nations. Our plan would require an annual expenditure of roughly $3.75 billion in 2009 dollars. (Coincidentally, that is roughly the level of support intended for public broadcasting when it was formed in 1967. The good old days!)

Public stations would use the lion's share of this money in the near-term to ramp up their commitment to local programming. In town after town, experienced reporters are unemployed, and public broadcasters would be wise to snap them up and take advantage of their expertise. The model for this "bridge" from old media to new is already being built in St. Louis, where more than a dozen laid-off *St. Louis Post-Dispatch* reporters are working from desks at the city's public TV station, KETC, to cover the community for an online newspaper called *The Saint Louis Beacon*.[81] *The Beacon*'s Web site attracts more than 25,000 unique visits each day. That's not a bad "circulation," and the reporters are chipping in as guests on public-broadcasting programs—helping to produce especially impressive coverage of the 2008 election on broadcast and digital platforms.

A similar project is developing in Seattle, where 20 refugees from the out-of-print *Post-Intelligencer* have gathered at the city's public-television station, KCTS, to begin producing *The Seattle PostGlobe*, an online newspaper.[82] "We were doing some strategic planning at the station, looking at what public media will become, and that coincided with the closing of the paper," explains KCTS president Moss Bresnahan. "We called some of our contacts at the *P-I* and started actively exploring how to find a viable business model to support an in-depth, integrated multimedia site."[83] They haven't found the model yet. Bresnahan talks about "national foundations, local foundations and concerned citizens" as prospects for tapping—and the Knight Foundation has already coughed up $90,000 for *The Saint Louis Beacon*.[84] But if public and community broadcasting are going to truly stock newsrooms at the local level and become world-class, it will require steady sources of real money. Indeed, subsidies are essential to any serious effort to move journalism from old media platforms to new ones and to maintain it upon arrival. We turn to that in the next section.

Unleashing the Internet

The response of many casual observers of the crisis in journalism is to presume that the Internet will solve the problem, as long as the government stays out of the way. Good old Yankee ingenuity and free-market competition will lead to innovation, the theory goes, with solutions sure to follow. There's every reason to be enthusiastic about the democratic and revolutionary potential of digital technologies for journalism, but as we explained in Chapter 2, technology is not going to magically solve all our problems.

The starting point for any notion of the Internet as the solution to the challenge of producing a democracy-sustaining media is that the system must be ubiquitous and it must be open. That means that policies will have to be put in place to assure universal and inexpensive access to broadband. The dominant commercial interests have already demonstrated that this is not a high priority for their business model. Journalists and citizens need to recognize that it is a joke to talk about the Internet as democracy's "information superhighway" if tens of millions of Americans are steered onto digital dirt roads, or not allowed— for economic and technological reasons—to travel at all.

It is equally imperative that "network neutrality" be made the law of the land. This requires that internet service providers (ISPs) treat all Web sites equally and not play favorites, intrude on user privacy or exercise censorship. In a largely duopolistic or monopolistic ISP marketplace, this is a mandatory requirement.[85] Unless there is formal network neutrality, freedom of speech and freedom of the press are conditional online. Exhibit A for what it means to have a closed Internet came in June 2009, when the Iranian government demonstrated how technology and techniques (not entirely unlike what U.S. ISPs have been developing) can be used to censor and monitor Internet traffic.[86] We cannot overemphasize how important a ubiquitous and open Internet, with guaranteed privacy, is to anyone's vision of a free press or free speech in the future. Without it, nothing else is possible. To formally enshrine network neutrality, Rep. Edward Markey, Democrat of Massachusetts, and Rep. Anna Eshoo, Democrat of California, introduced the Internet Freedom Preservation Act of 2009. Its passage would be a monumental victory. Still, a ubiquitous and open Internet will not automatically produce rich and robust journalism; it is only a necessary precondition.

The proposals we have already laid out in this chapter would go a long way toward filling cyberspace with a deep and rich layer of journalism, far greater than exists at present. This would be tremendous grist for citizen journalists and bloggers to work with as they critique and develop news stories. At the same time, a great deal of innovation and promise remains unfulfilled. In Chapter 2, we chronicled the plight of online journalism, with its wealth of talented people and brilliant ideas and its poverty of resources. Even our best reporters and writers are having a hard time making a living online, and those that are able to get by must continually please funders and advertisers. There is no reason to expect this to change in the foreseeable future.

This brings us to the third core policy initiative we propose: the creation of a funding mechanism to spawn viable independent Internet journalism. The trick is to provide ample funding but not to have the government control the allocation of the funds or create a bureaucracy that doles out funds to its preferred media. We need a system that is competitive, accountable and open to innovation. Advertisers and foundations are not up to the job, and the idea of converting computers into vending machines is unappealing and impractical.

So what policy solution is there?

The strongest proposal we have seen has been developed by the economist Dean Baker and his brother Randy Baker over the past decade. Our proposal embellishes their core concept. We call it the "Citizenship News Voucher." The idea is simple: every American adult gets a $200 voucher she can use to donate money to any nonprofit news medium of her choice. She will indicate her choice on her tax return. If she does not file a tax return, a simple form will be available to use. She can split her $200 among several different qualifying nonprofit media. This program would be purely voluntary, like the tax-form check-offs for funding elections or protecting wildlife. A government agency, probably operating out of the Internal Revenue Service, can be set up to allocate the funds and to determine eligibility—according to universal standards that err on the side of expanding rather than constraining the number of serious sources covering and commenting on the issues of the day. This will lessen attempts at fraud; after all, nobody wants to mess with the IRS.

This funding mechanism is the centerpiece of our policy recommendations, and we mean for it to apply to public, community and all other nonprofit broadcasters and the new generation of post-corporate newspapers as well as Internet upstarts. For a medium that is not a post-corporate newspaper or a public broadcaster to be eligible, it would have to be a not-for-profit, although that can assume a number of legal constructs, including 501(c)(3) or cooperative structures. The medium must do exclusively media content; it cannot be part of a larger organization or have any non-media operations. Everything the medium produces must be made available immediately upon publication on the Internet and made available for free to all. It will not be covered by copyright and will enter the public domain. (This would allow, for instance, a digital outlet to sell a print version of its work.) The government will not evaluate the content to see that the money is going toward journalism. Our assumption is that these criteria will effectively produce that result, and if there is some slippage so be it.

Qualifying media ought not, in our view, be permitted to accept advertising; this is a sector that is to have a direct and primary relationship with its audience. These media can accept tax-deductible donations from individuals or foundations to supplement their income. By banning advertising from public media and this new Internet sector, the pool of advertising that exists can be divvied up between newspapers and commercial media, especially commercial broadcasters. In our view, this will give commercial media a better crack at finding a workable business model.

We would also suggest that for a medium to receive funds it would have to get commitments for at least $20,000 worth of vouchers. This will lessen fraud and also require anyone wishing to establish a medium to be serious enough to get at least 100 people to sign on. (In other words, you can't just declare yourself a newspaper and deposit the voucher in your bank account.) There will be some overhead and administration for the program, but it will not require a large regulatory body like the FCC.

So what will the Citizenship News Voucher program generate? It will have two objectives. First, it will be a means for public media organizations to dramatically increase their funding. Imagine a public TV station or a post-corporate newspaper in a metropolitan area of 1 million people managed to get 50,000 of them to donate half of their Citizenship News Voucher to the station. That would be $5 million. That goes a long way toward staffing a quality newsroom. It also means that public and community broadcasters will have to earn their support beyond the "half of Canada" base they are guaranteed.

Second, the voucher system would provide a way for Web-journalism services to become self-sufficient and even have the funds to hire a significant number of full-time paid workers. Imagine a Web site in the blogosphere right now covering national politics that produces some great content and has hundreds of thousands of regular visitors, but it depends upon low-paid or volunteer labor and praying for advertising crumbs or donations for revenue. Now the Web site goes formally nonprofit, stops obsessing over advertising crumbs and appeals directly to its readers for their vouchers. Imagine this Web site getting 20,000 people to steer their vouchers into its accounts. That is $4 million, enough to have a well-paid staff of 50 full-time journalists as well as ancillary staffers. Consider what a Web news service could do with that. And then start thinking about how motivated the reporters and editors would be to break big stories, maintain high quality and keep attracting the vouchers.

Or imagine you live in a city with deplorable news coverage of your community or neighborhood, as more and more Americans do. If someone starts a local news medium and gets 1,000 people to give her group their vouchers, that provides a nice start-up budget of $200,000. For that money a group can have several reporters covering their turf, and build up a real following. Recall Kate Giammarise and Angie Schmitt, who launched the Web site rustwire.com after being laid off from their jobs as newspaper reporters in Toledo. Think what the Citizenship News

Voucher program could mean for Kate and Angie. It could determine whether they make their careers in journalism or in some other field.

The benefits of the Citizenship News Voucher program are many. For instance, it gives the foundation community a coherent and necessary role to play. Rather than see themselves as being hit up in perpetuity to cover the operating costs of various Web-journalism ventures, foundations can do what they do best: they can help launch new ventures, fund them for three to five years, and then see if there is popular support for the venture in the form of Citizenship News Vouchers. In this model, philanthropists have much greater incentive to put money into journalism, because there is a way for their grants to lead to self-sustaining institutions.

This strategy also allows newcomers to enter the fray and hence encourages innovation. A group can raise start-up funds from donations or philanthropy, get started, and then appeal directly for voucher support. It produces intense competition because a medium cannot take its support for granted. It rewards initiative and punishes sloth. It is democratic because rich and poor get the same voucher. And the government has no control over who gets the money. It is an enormous public subsidy, but it is a libertarian's dream: people can support whatever political viewpoints they prefer or do nothing at all. We won't try and predict how effective the Citizenship News Voucher program would be. In a very real sense, the answer has to come from citizens and journalists, which is exactly as it should be.

What we do know, however, is that this approach will give public and community media as well as post-corporate newspapers an incentive to earn their support not from investors and advertisers but from the people they are trying to reach. And we also know that every struggling new online journalism outfit we talk to would love to have an opportunity to compete for these funds. We have never explained the concept—in newspaper, radio and television interviews; in speeches and at forums—without being overwhelmed by the practical questions, vibrant ideas and enthusiasm that it sparks among journalists and citizens. That makes complete sense to us, as the voucher system rebuilds the lost link between journalists and the communities that sustain their journalism. That connection, we believe, is necessary to reestablishing bonds of trust between producers and consumers of journalism that were broken by decades of top-down, one-size-fits-all media strategies that were developed not to inform citizens but to enrich investors.

The Citizenship News Voucher would, we suspect, serve as an evolutionary force in journalism. Within a few years of the program's development, we anticipate, the American people will have gravitated to the media they wish to see in place. The people will determine which institutions survive and thrive, which strikes us as both healthy and democratic. And, as long as people disagree, the systems that develop will be far more diverse in their viewpoints and perspectives than anything Americans have seen since the development of the commercial system 150 years ago.

For this program to be accepted it will require two conditions that will be hard pills for some to swallow. First, people will have to accept that some of the vouchers are going to go to media that they detest. The program requires that Americans embrace dissent in reality and not just rhetoric. Second, the program may not develop exactly the type of journalism our greatest thinkers believe is necessary. The plan requires that there be faith in the judgment of the American people. This is a risk we are more than willing to take—operating on a gut instinct that people will use their vouchers to fund serious media while reaching into their pockets to pay for copies of *The National Enquirer* at the supermarket checkout.

The annual cost to taxpayers of the Citizenship News Voucher initiative would depend upon the percentage of Americans who participate in the program. If, say, it proved wildly popular and 50 percent did so, the tab could run in the range of $20 billion.

As Dean Baker puts it, this is an economic model that recognizes in the Internet era that old-fashioned media economics no longer work. You can't produce a digital product, take it to market and sell it. And you can't get advertisers to bankroll your operation. The rational policy solution is to give media producers—journalists— money up front, and then make what they produce available to all for free online. It will fill the Web with large amounts of professional-quality journalism, and provide a genuine independent journalism sector to complement post-corporate newspapers, public media and a retooled commercial news media. Those will be the four legs of our new media table.

Ultimately, the legs may be rearranged. More weight may go on one than another. Journalists may flee commercial media and start nonprofit Web sites. Post-corporate digital newspapers might be displaced by public-media Web sites. A new generation of Web-savvy editors might leap from medium to medium, perhaps creating journalistic platforms that we cannot yet imagine. The twists and turns are inevitable and should be welcomed rather than feared. If there are sources of funding, journalists will innovate and the people will decide what works. The possibilities are endless, and endlessly democratic.

Funding Journalism

As we have presented these ideas to individual journalists and journalism groups, to community organizations and congressional panels over the course of 2009, we have noted that, regardless of how folks respond to specific measures, they are almost uniformly inclined to inquire about the cost of these subsidies. And when we mention it, there is at least initial sticker shock. By our rough calculations, the total price tag for what we propose—postal subsidies; journalist tax credits; News AmeriCorps; student media; public media; and especially Citizenship News Vouchers—could run as high as $35 billion annually. That's darned near inconceivable in a nation that has battled over whether to spend a paltry $400 million on public broadcasting.

But let's put this in context: $35 billion is close to what the much smaller nations of Finland and Denmark spend in the form of media subsidies on a per capita basis, and is considerably closer than what we currently spend to the levels seen in Britain or Japan. Finland and Denmark are nations with high civic literacy, astronomical rates of voter participation and vibrant free commercial media in addition to the subsidized sector. They rank near the top on any list of the wealthiest and freest nations in the world, with superb protection of civil liberties, and with low levels of economic inequality and government corruption.[87] These guys just might be on to something.

There is no foolproof way to make a comparison, but our sense is this level of spending would be similar to the U.S. government's commitment to subsidizing journalism in the first half of the 19th century. For example, had the federal government in 2008 devoted the same percentage of the Gross Domestic Product to press subsidies as the federal government did in the early 1840s, it would have spent some *$30 billion* to spawn journalism.[88]

We know that comparisons across 160 years are difficult, but this figure points to something we have emphasized in this book: the U.S. government from its birth and for its first several generations was devoted first and foremost to creating a viable media so people could effectively engage in self-government. This was a revolutionary contribution to democracy and world history. At the same time, European national governments were primarily engaging in military operations, and raising money to pay for war, as was the U.S. government aside from its massive commitment to subsidizing democracy.[89] No other government on earth approached the American commitment to supporting the press at this time. This devotion was seen again in the aftermath of World War II, when Generals Eisenhower and MacArthur and their staffs expended energy and resources in dangerous times to create new, democracy-sustaining media systems in formerly fascist Germany and Japan. That is the sort of commitment we need today. And if we accept this as a legitimate motivation, then $35 billion is anything but a daunting number.

The United States spends, when interest and hidden costs are taken into account, roughly $1 trillion annually on the military.[90] Chalmers Johnson makes a powerful argument that we could take a substantial portion of that money and spend it on non-military projects, with the ironic benefit of making the United States and the world a safer place.[91] Consider what we get for war spending at present and consider what we would get from spending $35 billion—just 3.5 percent of the military expenditure—on creating vibrant independent news media. Who knows? We might even get the information that's needed to avoid a few wars.

These points notwithstanding, when expensive government programs are proposed the immediate questions are, "How are you going to pay for it?" and "Where do you plan to locate the money?" We would like to believe that the importance of journalism is such that our government would simply make it a mandatory expense and allocate the money that is needed. This is the standard used for military spending and for bailing out bumbling financial institutions that have supposedly grown "too big to fail." No one dares stop the government from purchasing an expensive weapons system, for example, with the demand that the government raise taxes proportionately to cover the new costs. It is simply accepted that the importance of national defense makes such debates secondary concerns. The money must be spent and we will worry about where it comes from later.

In our view, journalism qualifies for this status as well, since the American governing system and our economy cannot prosper, or perhaps even survive, without a credible news media. What we propose would give the United States the basis for an extraordinary, diverse and competitive news culture, plus there would still be as much of a commercial news media as the market could bear. But, alas, that is a difficult argument to make today, if only because journalism does not have powerful defense contractors, financial interests and a skilled public-relations industry lobbying on its behalf. Ironically, even journalists tend not to advocate on behalf of journalism.

There is a good reason, though, for advocates of the journalism subsidies we propose to address the issues of where the money comes from. They should do so because a free press system should have its funds protected from direct inference by the government. One look at how politicians have messed with public broadcasting should make that case clearly enough. In addition, it is important that the funds that go to Citizenship News Vouchers come from a dedicated fund generated for that purpose. Otherwise some people will understandably say, "Hey, give me my $200 back to spend as I please." This way people are given the privilege of allocating funds generated from sources other than federal income taxes, and if people elect not to exercise their privilege to use a voucher, the funds remain in the account.

The United States can and should establish a distinct Citizenship Media Fund. And we should aspire to a larger fund that can pay for the balance of the journalism subsidies, as well. A sound argument can be made that the appropriate way to locate the funds would be to increase tax rates on the wealthy and corporations to where they were in the 1950s and 1960s. Were the United States to do that, more than enough money would be freed up to pay for everything we propose—and we'd get the added bonus of introducing greater fairness to the tax code. But, alas, raising taxes on the wealthy and corporations is very difficult in the United States for reasons that ought to be self-evident by now, and that are intricately related to the state of our news media, as we discussed in Chapter 1.

Who should pay, then? There are two groups that are logically called upon to subsidize nonprofit and noncommercial media. These are the commercial interests that benefit from being granted privileges in media by the government, and the people who use the media and should therefore be willing to pony up to subsidize noncommercial content. On principle, we lean more toward taxing those who enjoy the greatest privileges rather than consumers, since a progressive tax on the wealthy is invariably fairer and more functional than a regressive tax that falls disproportionately upon low- and middle-income people.

With that in mind, we have located several possible sources of revenue to fund the Citizenship News Vouchers, and possibly the entire journalism program. We offer them here not so much in the form of a budget as for the purposes of illustrating where the money might be found.

1. Tax on broadcast spectrum. Commercial radio and television broadcasters are given monopoly rights to extremely lucrative spectrum at no charge. This has been a massive public subsidy of commercial broadcasting. In return, in theory, the commercial broadcasters are ostensibly broadcasting in the "public interest"; i.e., doing something they would not do if they were purely profit-maximizing firms. The National Association of Broadcasters, the trade association of the commercial broadcasters, places the value of this public-interest work by commercial radio and television broadcasters at more than $10 billion in 2008.[92] Most consumer and public-interest groups place the figure much closer to zero. Much of consumer activism for the past 60 years has been attempting to get the commercial broadcasters to actually do public-interest programming. A key part of that has been public affairs and journalism.

It is time to end this fight. We take the NAB at its word that it produces $10 billion annually in public service. We have good news for them: they can stop doing so, and return to what they have always done best: maximize their profits. In exchange, the government will tax the revenues the broadcasters generate from their spectrum at a rate of 7 percent. The commercial broadcasters are in the process of locating lucrative new revenue streams from their spectrum, and the public should get a cut of the action. We anticipate in the not-so-distant future annual funds in the $3 to $6 billion range. If the commercial broadcasters don't like the deal, they can return their monopoly broadcast licenses to the government or sell them. But they will probably be delighted to be relieved of the onerous public-interest obligations. By their calculations, they will come out ahead with our proposal.

We hope that commercial television broadcasters continue to produce news programs, though indications are that they are just a year or two behind newspapers on the gangplank. Were their newsrooms more substantial, it might be worth an effort to salvage them, as with newspapers. If commercial broadcasters continue to do news, it will be for the same reason they have done it in the recent past and the same reason corporate newspaper publishers remain in the business: to make money. We wish them luck.

2. Tax on consumer electronics. This is a long-standing model for supporting noncommercial content. The notion is that people who pay for consumer electronics also put some money toward paying for quality noncommercial content to be accessed on that equipment. A German household with a TV and DVD player pays as much as $280 per year to support public media by this system. The initial Carnegie Commission suggested an excise tax of 5 percent on television sets, which would be below the rate Germans, for example, are accustomed to paying. If we put the tax on consumer electronics at 5 percent, it would generate $4 billion annually.[93]

3. Spectrum auction tax. The government has been auctioning off valuable spectrum to commercial communication firms for many years. There are going to be more auctions in the next decade. There should be a tax on the auction sales prices, with the proceeds going to the public-media pot. It is impossible to predict this flow in advance, but it is not likely to be as large a pot as any of the other sources.

4.Advertising taxes. Advertising has a privileged role in our media and our economy. Much of our broadcast spectrum has been turned over to its dissemination, for example. If we placed a 2 percent sales tax on advertising, it would generate in the range $5 to $6 billion annually. Most people do not realize that businesses can deduct the cost of advertising from their taxable income. Merely changing the ability of businesses to "write off" all of their advertising as a business expense in one year, and extending it to a five-year write-off, could generate another $2 billion per year. This makes sense because much of advertising is about brand building and having influence beyond a single year. It should be treated accordingly by the IRS.

5.ISP-cell phone tax. The principle here is the same as with consumer electronics. Consumers pay a small tax on their monthly ISP-cell phone bills and they fund content to access on their digital services. A tax of 3 percent on the monthly fees would net $6 billion annually.[94] This is not a source of funds to be encouraged because demand for these services is what economists call "elastic," meaning a slight price rise will cause many people, almost always low-income, to drop the service.

The above revenue streams could generate as much as $25 billion annually. We readily accept there may be superior alternatives. We offer these specifics with the intent of illustrating that there are effective ways to solve the revenue puzzle. And, it bears repeating, merely returning to a tax structure for business and the wealthy similar to that of the 1950s to 1970s would instantly produce the necessary amount of revenue—and then some.

Conclusion

Tom Paine wrote about the price of freedom in 1777: "Those who expect to reap the blessings of freedom, must ... undergo the fatigues of supporting it."[95]

The privations of Valley Forge and the battlefields of the Revolutionary War were a good deal greater than what we ask our fellow citizens to consider as today's price of freedom. But, make no mistake, what is at issue here is a question of how free Americans will be in the 21st century.

In a democracy, an informed citizenry is not *governed*. An informed citizenry *governs*. This distinction is what makes democracy real, and what allows citizens to be free. If like the founders of the American experiment we believe that popular information and the means to acquire it allow us to avert tragedy and farce, if like General Eisenhower we believe that a free and independent press must be nurtured and sustained at every critical juncture, then surely we must recognize that the current crisis of journalism—and democracy—requires a response sufficient to the task.

Freedom comes with a price tag. Those who would conspire to be free do not fret about it. They do not haggle, hoping that liberty can be obtained on the cheap; or that, with a little less expenditure, they might get by with fewer (or "a couple fewer") rights. They make the commitment, as Jefferson and Madison and their compatriots did at the opening of the American experiment. They pursue that commitment even when it requires creating new systems, new institutions and new understandings, as Eisenhower and MacArthur did in the heady days after World War II. It is that commitment, and that determination to pursue it, that we ask of Americans who would be not merely the consumers that advertisers seek but the citizens that the founders anticipated—Americans who believe that the knowledge that surely is power belongs to all.

This country can have great journalism in the 21st century, greater journalism than it has ever known. And from that can come a richer democracy and a truer freedom than we have yet experienced. But Paine was right. "What we obtain too cheap, we esteem too lightly: it is dearness only that gives every thing its value."[96] Getting serious about journalism and democracy requires a recognition that America cannot wait for the market to spring a solution to the crisis of journalism upon us. We need to forge the policies and make the expenditures that are necessary to create the free and independent press that has always been and shall always be the guardian of liberty.

Conclusion

THE AGE OF THE
Possible

This book takes as its elementary premise the certainty that President Barack Obama was right when he declared in May of 2009: "Government without a tough and vibrant media is not an option for the United States of America."[1] But we have argued that an understanding of the necessity of a "tough and vibrant media" is not a destination for policymakers but rather a point of embarkation. If government without watchdogs is not an option, then the question is begged: How do we assure that there will be watchdogs roaming the remade media landscape of the 21st century? And how do we assure that they will be up to the challenges of an era when the public and private powers that be have available to them a propagandistic arsenal so vast and sinister that it would have shocked the most ardent totalitarians of historian Eric Hobsbawm's "age of catastrophe"?[2] Those questions will not be answered with rhetoric—not even rhetoric that reasserts the most enlightened values of the American experiment—but with action.

The quality of that action will go a long way toward determining whether this will be another age of catastrophe, or whether it is one of those ages of the possible that Americans have historically seized upon to make real the promises of freedom and democracy.

It is with an eye toward prompting action that is at once transformational in scope and progressive in character that we have made six fundamental claims in this book. First, as the president suggests, a strong independent journalism is mandatory for the self-governing society envisioned by our founders and extended by the abolitionists, suffragettes and civil-rights campaigners of the past two centuries; in fact, in a restless time of economic and social turmoil such as ours, it is more necessary than ever. Second, the commercial system of journalism that has defined and dominated our discourse for the past 150 years has entered a rapid process of decline that will not be reversed. Third, the notion that free markets and new technologies will solve the problem and magically produce the commitment to journalism the nation requires is baseless. Fourth, the government has played an essential and enormous role at key points in American history by creating and subsidizing the news-media system. Fifth, the government needs to again play a creative and sustaining role, and soon, or the current crisis in journalism will only grow with consequences that are as frightening as they are entirely unacceptable. Sixth, there are viable strategies for the government to subsidize a free press without threatening America's ardent and long-standing opposition to official censorship.

Journalists and academics—the authors of the first and latter drafts of history—always hope that the words and the evidence they marshal to support specific claims will be deemed convincing by readers. We are no different. But if that is as far as this book goes, we will be disappointed. This book is not written as a reflection on the zeitgeist. Rather, our purpose is to contribute to a radical shift in policymaking that will see the embrace of a necessary agenda of major policies and subsidies in the foreseeable future.

The final question we have to ask ourselves is whether the sort of reform we envision is politically realistic. Can the United States actually have a media revolution that would, in effect, begin the world again?

Here we cannot write with the same confidence that marked the four chapters of this book. But we can write with more than a little authority, as we have actively studied and engaged in media-reform politics for many years, and with at least a modicum of success.

The grounds for pessimism are ample and ever-present. We hear the comments every time we raise these issues, often from people who agree with us in principle, if not in spirit. They tell us that the commercial interests that dominate the news media have massive political lobbies and always get their way. They tell us that politicians and government officials have no incentive to generate a strong independent journalism, as they are the first beneficiaries of a euthanized watchdog. They tell us that the American people for the most part are apathetic and depoliticized, and that even the engaged few are so disappointed with our current news media that they cannot be rallied to the cause of journalism. Even if the inclination to act could be found, we are warned, the more pressing entanglements of economics and foreign policy will always take precedence—forever putting off until another day the work of democratic renewal.

The pessimism becomes paralyzing and self-fulfilling. It is unquestionably the greatest obstacle to fundamental and successful reform of our media system.

Yet, for all its power, the pessimism is in every meaningful sense bogus.

Perhaps pessimism would be credible—if still pointless—were we living in normal times. In normal times, the entrenched interests generally rule the roost and policy debates are tangential and of minimal interest to the general population. Corporate special interests can and do take advantage of general disengagement to carve up the pie behind closed doors, shaping government policies to their benefit. That is a challenge for democracy that ought not be underestimated, and that we have in our work over the years sought to address. But we have always recognized that the greatest openings for reform of any kind come at those moments where a collapse of the status quo and the ensuing chaos leads everyone to start talking about what to do.

That is the point we are at. National newsmagazines tell us "the crisis in journalism has reached meltdown proportions." House and Senate hearings on the future of newspapers and journalism have already been held, and more are in the offing. Even the president is addressing the matter. And, most importantly, in cities across the country, in coffee shops and classrooms, church basements and union halls, citizens are talking about the decline and in some instances the disappearance of publications they have known all their lives.

As observers of the American political discourse who have made it our mission to monitor and motivate debates about media, who know from frustrating experience how hard it is to get a serious discussion regarding these issues going in elite circles, we recognize that these are anything but normal times. We are in what we described in Chapter 4 as a "critical juncture," a period in which the entrenched media interests are disintegrating and losing their power. This is due to a revolutionary technology that has undermined the old media business models, an exceptionally unstable economy and a reckoning that comes after years, even decades, of declining commitment to journalism. It is a perfect-storm moment. In historical instances of this nature, the range of alternatives grows dramatically broader; policies that were unthinkable suddenly move into play. People who normally pay no attention get drawn into the debate because the severe nature of the crisis and the broad range of possible outcomes attract their attention.

These media critical junctures grow ever more intense when they occur in conjunction with turmoil in the broader economic and social order. In times like these, as in the 1930s and 1960s, people begin to take a greater interest in journalism. It is no longer remotely optional. There is a recognition that journalism is necessary; that, indeed, it is required if democracy is to survive.

Citizens, so inspired, are dramatically more open to structural changes because it is so very clear that the society is not functioning as it should. There is reason to believe the United States is entering such an era of broader turmoil now, in view of the gravity of the social, environmental and economic challenges confronting the Republic and its people. In such moments, the hunger for credible journalism increases exponentially. People who were willing to put up with stories about Britney Spears shaving her head and Madonna adopting a child suddenly want to know everything that can be known about the accelerating process of deindustrialization that could leave them permanently unemployed, about a mortgage crisis that could leave them without a home, about a financial meltdown that sucked in their retirement accounts.

In the absence of a sufficient journalism, citizens will be inclined to demand more.

Make no mistake, our journalism—even before it was bought out, laid off, downsized and shuttered—was insufficient. Now, however, it is indefensible.

This creates the potential for the sort of "political prairie fire" moment that the rural radicals of the early 20th century celebrated, a point at which a citizenry that is suddenly engaged calls clearly and loudly for changes that will provide more and better journalism, and where there is at least a measure of willingness on the part of political elites to consider reforms that were previously off the table.[3]

That's the definition of a critical juncture, and we welcome it. Unfortunately, merely having reached such a point does not guarantee positive change or a progressive outcome. Our friend Tony Benn, the British parliamentarian and former government minister who looks back on a life in which he met Gandhi as a precocious anticolonialist, fought the Nazis as a young man, joined the transformational Labour Party governments of the postwar era, imagined and embraced the digital age as Britain's minister of technology, identified and battled the rising ideological tides of neoliberalism and neoconservatism and remains an ardent campaigner in his mid-80s, always reminds us of the lessons of history in this regard:

> The global economic turbulence of the 1920s and 1930s gave us Franklin Roosevelt, and we are thankful for that, but it also gave us Mussolini, Hitler and the fascist and totalitarian regimes and movements of that era. It was clear that nations needed to act, but that did not mean that they acted in consort. There were moves to the left, lurches to the right. Chaos and crisis produce change. The reason that we must be more active in turbulent times, more serious and determined, is because we know that change is in the offing but that we must make it a good change.[4]

Fast forward to this moment and think about where the downsizing and shuttering of newspapers, the disappearance of radio news, the withering of television news and all the other collapses of the underpinnings of contemporary journalism might leave us. In the absence of commercial media institutions with the capacity and the authority to hold the powerful to account, information about our political and governmental processes could become exceptionally disorganized. Surely, blogs and public media would attempt to fill the void, and some aggregators might do an especially good job of it. But don't doubt that in so unstable a moment the elites might decide to meet the demand for information in a manner that serves their needs more fully than the commercial media that is now collapsing did; after all, they have the resources and access to brilliant new technologies. It is easier than ever to package information in appealingly "newsy" forms and to distribute it. The penchant of the powerful to employ public-relations talent is well established, and the growth in marketed "news" has been exponential. We discussed the striking growth of PR—in direct relation to the collapse of journalism—in Chapter 1. So what's to stop government agencies and big businesses from producing their own media—video news releases, "fake news" productions, have permeated our broadcast news in recent years, dressing up propaganda and marketing in a form that looks like independent reporting—in dramatically more insidious yet aggressive forms?[5]

We're not worrying here about the clumsy propaganda of the past, which was so bumbling in presentation that it tended to remind people of precisely what they were not being told. We're talking about detailed information packaged in attractive, usable forms that just happens to favor the interests of those doing the packaging. This would be the ultimate triumph of what Australian sociologist Alex Carey referred to as the dangerous "ideal of a propaganda-managed democracy," where anything akin to a freewheeling journalism and the genuine democratic discourse that it fosters is replaced by official "messaging" and an equally official "debate" that is so constrained as to be meaningless.[6] If information packaged by political and corporate elites were to become the dominant "news" sources for Americans—hardly an unimaginable prospect—there would still be critique. Bloggers would blog, activists would gripe. And conspiracy theorists would go wild, as they always do in such circumstances. It would be their Golden Age. Ultimately, those who choke on the strangled discourse would move to the extremes, creating polarization that is ever more volatile. And we might well revisit Eric Hobsbawm's age of catastrophe.

It bears repeating that aspects of this dystopian turn are already evident. "Never before have we had so many tools to learn and to communicate," writes Maureen Dowd. "Yet the art of talking, listening and ascertaining the truth seems more elusive than ever in this Internet and cable age, lost in a bitter stream of blather and misinformation."[7]

Faced with the fact of a critical juncture, and the unsettling prospect that it could produce something worse than what we now have, the charge of democrats is clear. We must throw ourselves into the fight for something better. The opening exists for fundamental changes that will give us a greater journalism than we have ever known. We must seize it, with an understanding not merely of what is at stake but of what is possible.

In journalism history the first great critical juncture came in the revolutionary and constitutional era, when the need for a credible press led to the massive subsidies of the early Republic. The second great critical juncture came with the crisis surrounding monopolistic commercial control over news media in the first half of the 20th century; the solution to this crisis was the emergence of professional journalism. We are now deep into the third great critical juncture surrounding journalism.

The current crisis has been growing over the past three decades, although it has escalated since 2000. Some sense of the changing dynamic is indicated by the history of Free Press, the media-reform organization we cofounded with Josh Silver in 2002–03. When Free Press was launched, with the basic idea that citizens should have a voice in the crucial media-policy decisions that are made in the public's name, but usually without the public's awareness or informed consent, we were told, to be blunt, that we were insane. After all, for decades a small handful of earnest and dedicated media-policy activists had battled for the public interest with little impact and even less popular awareness or support. The accepted wisdom was that media reform was a nonstarter as a popular political issue. It would never, we were told, rank in the top 50 of anyone's list of social or political priorities.

But we were not proceeding in normal times. Free Press exploded, organizing national conferences that attracted thousands, signing up more than 500,000 members and hiring 35 full-time organizers and staffers in just five years. Even in the unsympathetic political climate of Washington,

D.C., in the period of its initial development, Free Press was able to ally with groups that had traditionally been engaged with media issues and others that had never been so involved to win extraordinary coalition victories. These include the campaigns against media monopoly and government propaganda, and for public media and an open and uncensored Internet.[8] In at least two of these campaigns, Free Press and its allies were able to mobilize millions of Americans. The Free Press experience has reaffirmed Saul Alinsky's dictum: the only way to defeat organized money is with organized people. What Free Press also established was that media reform was an issue that could not only attract broad popular support, media reform roamed the ideological spectrum; nearly every major campaign gained support from those on the Left and the Right, as well as those with no discernible political philosophy or commitments.

Free Press was founded with the current crisis in mind. It was created to help lead the public-policy debates to reform and rejuvenate our system of journalism, to create a free press. That is what has driven public support for the group. So the public does not enter this critical juncture ill-equipped. At the same time, the forces of reaction are weakened. The strongest traditional opponents to media reform, the media corporations, are in an ambiguous position. Once-powerful newspaper chains and their investors are abandoning the field, having determined that journalism is no longer a smart investment. Even the most old-school of old-school journalists are stepping up to say, as did former CBS News anchorman Dan Rather recently, not only that "traditional journalism is under siege" but that media reform must be an "immediate national priority."[9] All of this makes the political challenge at least somewhat less daunting.

No, this does not mean that we're anticipating a cakewalk. There are still those dead-enders who hold to the belief that any government involvement in fostering and maintaining free and independent news media is improper—they are the Colonel Nicholsons of Chapter 3, if you will. But these people are not the enemy; rather, they are true believers in a particular order who cling to its orthodoxies even as it collapses. The overwhelming majority of Colonel Nicholsons are principled and honest, and we are convinced that once they encounter the actual history of the government's role in creating and sustaining American journalism in its most vibrant era, and digest the consequences of doing nothing, they will abandon their dogma. Recall that in *The Bridge on the River Kwai*, Colonel Nicholson finally did recognize the folly of his ways, too, shortly before he was killed by the Japanese.

The great majority of Americans, including the journalists and politicians who are most deeply concerned about this issue, will be ready to consider some or even most of the radical interventions and policy shifts we propose for a very simple reason: the tepid and self-serving proposals advanced by old- and new-media fabulists fail to offer even remotely plausible solutions to the crisis. When it becomes "put up or shut up" time, people lose interest in tinkering around the margins and start looking for what might actually work.[10] When this happens, the ideas we have outlined will move to the fore, as debates begin with the recognition— the essential recognition—that the magnitude of this crisis will require action by the government. Newsman Rather came to that conclusion in the summer of 2009, suggesting at an Aspen Institute event that President Obama should establish a White House commission on public media and independent reporting as part of a response designed "to help the slipping media and aid the new."[11] We do not doubt that others will soon be making the same demand.

Rather is not arguing that the government is the only answer, and neither are we. There are significant roles to be played by private enterprise, foundations and nonprofit organizations. But we no longer have any doubt that without the government providing subsidies comparable to what other leading democratic nations provide, and to what this nation routinely provided in its first century, the initiatives of these other actors will have limited effect. To be blunt, on their own they can achieve nothing more than the guy with the shopping bag standing in front of the tanks at Tiananmen Square. We can and should respect their determination, celebrate their ingenuity, perhaps entertain the fleeting hope for a miracle. But we cannot wait for the miracle. And we must not deceive ourselves into imagining that a real crisis requires anything less than a real response.

There are two critical constituencies that will not be immediately disposed to favor public policies and subsidies designed to nurture into being a powerful and diverse independent news media. They are, as already mentioned, powerful politicians and government officials, on the one hand, and the corporate special interests they work with closely, on the other hand. It is pretty much an iron rule that the greater the authority of government executives, the greater their preference for operating in secrecy. This is true regardless of their party or their ideology. Legislators, too, prefer minimal public attention to their affairs, especially when we're talking about affairs with special interests. This is one of the reasons an ideological conservative, General Douglas MacArthur, was so adamant about using the authority and resources of the U.S. military to establish an independent free press in Japan after World War II. MacArthur explained that it would be necessary to the development of an open and democratic society. This is why we believe that sincere political conservatives, with their innate skepticism toward the government, can and should be crucial actors in the campaign for journalism in the United States. We mention conservatives—and we'll mention them again in a moment—because it is our view that a broad consensus will be developed in favor of reform, and that this consensus can overcome the uncertainty of individual representatives and caucuses about the need for congressional action.

In effect, we are betting on a renewal of the relationship between a majority of our elected leaders and their better angels, and we do not think this is an unreasonable expectation. Members of Congress have egos. They like the limelight. Whether they admit it or not, the gaggle of microphones, the favorable editorial, the interested interviewer is a part of what drew them to the public stage. As hometown newspapers shutter Washington bureaus—and stop showing up for town-hall meetings and forums in their districts—representatives and senators recognize that the democratic infrastructure is crumbling. Despite the usual skepticism about the elected, it is our experience that many members of the House and Senate sincerely worry about that crumbling. Yes, there are some autocrats in Congress. But there are also representatives of the people who are alarmed, not encouraged, by the disintegration of journalism in their districts and states in particular and the nation as a whole. They actually want to have a credible relationship between citizens and elected officials;

and they may even recognize that they need questions, challenges and pushes from savvy journalists to avoid making very big mistakes.

Our experience on Capitol Hill, which is considerable, leads us to believe that there are a sufficient number of honest players who will be receptive to sound arguments, especially if they are encouraged to do so by an avalanche of voters. We see the spring 2009 House Judiciary and Senate Commerce committee hearings on the crisis in journalism as evidence of this; indeed, the House committee even invited one of us to testify.[12] In both the chambers, key players on relevant committees—Congressman John Conyers, a Democrat from Michigan, and Senator John Kerry, a Democrat from Massachusetts—have indicated that these hearings were the beginning of what they see as a serious search for real repairs. The Congressional Research Service released a report for members of Congress on the crisis with daily newspapers in July, which should serve to push debate and even legislation going forward.[13]

The action is not restricted to Capitol Hill. In his parting shot as Acting Chair of the Federal Communications Commission, Michael Copps circulated a "notice of inquiry" into the state of journalism in July 2009. Such notices begin the process that leads ultimately to changes in rules and regulations. Copps' internal document on journalism specifically said the inquiry should address the role of media conglomerates and new media upon the state of journalism. Copps has been concerned about the decline of journalism, especially at the local level, for years. "How about journalism?" he asked in a speech in May 2009. "Will anyone figure out a business model to support in-depth, investigative journalism – or must we develop something completely new, perhaps based on philanthropy, non-profit models or public media?"[14] His successor, Julius Genachowski, announced his support for the journalism inquiry upon assuming the chairmanship. "I have real concerns, as many Americans do, about what is going on in America with respect to newspapers, local news and information. It has been an area of ongoing interest at the FCC from the beginning. Local news and information has been a core pillar of the Communications Act and remains that," Genachowski said in an interview. "I respect the leadership the commissioner has taken. The commission will be tackling this topic."[15]

Federal Trade Commission Chairman Jon Leibowitz announced in May 2009 plans to launch a formal FTC study on the matter of "Can the News Survive the Internet Age?" The FTC examination, Leibowitz said, will be "much, much broader" than simply whether an antitrust exemption is needed. The agency will look into other reasons for the current problems. People in a democracy "need to be informed, and sources of news are enormously important. I think as we all know, [those sources] are incredibly embattled," Leibowitz said. "We are going to have economists and journalists and bloggers and people from different parts of the news media, and we are going to think through [what is occurring] and what the future will look like and whether that future—which might be a handful of newspapers and [TV] networks that don't have nearly as much reach as they once did and 5 million bloggers— is a good thing for American democracy." The work will begin in December 2009 with the aim, among other things, of providing ideas for legislation. "We are going to invite a lot of smart people on different sides of this issue to educate us," Leibowitz said. "This is a really important public policy issue, and we think we can add, as we have in a lot of other areas, an objective voice that can point industry or lawmakers in the right direction."[16]

In short, there is already widespread attention to the crisis in journalism in Washington, attention of a sort that has never existed in the lifetimes of any Americans. The better angels are indeed emerging. There is every reason to believe this is the beginning of of a new era of reflection on not just the crisis of the journalism that was but the promise of the journalism that will be.

The barriers to reform that most concern us will be erected by powerful players who will be more difficult to address than elected officials. These are the well-funded and well-placed special interests, generally corporate, that benefit so massively from an ignorant and apathetic populace—and that would prefer to manage that ignorance and apathy to their own ends in a post-journalism future. As Paul Krugman notes, there has been a "vast expansion of corporate influence" over our political system over the past three decades, and, as a result, "reform of any kind has become extremely difficult." "(T)urning this country around," Krugman concludes, "is going to take years of siege warfare against deeply entrenched interests, defending a deeply dysfunctional political system."[17]

The last thing these corporate plutocrats want is a watchdog with sharp teeth that might bite into their bottom lines. The notion of a rich and diverse journalism engaging people from all walks of life and drawing previously discouraged and disenfranchised citizens into public life is anathema to these power players. They won't speak honestly about why they really oppose federal policies and public subsidies that enhance journalism—at least not outside the boardrooms and country clubs. But they are more than capable of warping the debate with false premises and fear-mongering, and as such they are likely to be difficult adversaries.

Because the political Right has been so closely attached to these special interests in recent decades, this position is sometimes characterized as "conservatism." It is nothing of the sort. Most rank-and-file conservatives we know are appalled by corruption and welcome a vibrant and dynamic journalism. That's because they remain confident, like William F. Buckley, that their political ideas can win in a fair competition with other viewpoints.[18] They do not fear democracy. Indeed, at a time when they have lost control of the executive and legislative branches of government, they are among the loudest advocates for in-depth investigations and aggressive questioning of those in power.

The special-interest campaign against journalism, at least on its face, will as well be advanced by those dogmatic "free market" economist types who have for decades been telling us that government can't do anything right, except, perhaps, organize wars, lock people up and manage prisons. As the debate about the future of journalism develops, we are already hearing from the most shameless of these fabulists about the infallible genius of free enterprise and the despicable nature of government. These are the people who have spent the past generation attacking the very notion of public goods. They are having a harder time peddling this line since the reckless deregulation mania their crackpot theories prescribed for the financial sector collapsed the global economy.[19] Their political influence is at the lowest level it has been in at least a generation. But they retain a strong institutional half-life in academia and think tanks—owing in part to massive financial support from wealthy individuals and big business—

and they will be in this fight. The threat that their ideas might face serious scrutiny from a more vibrant and diverse free press is one they will take seriously.

The interests that oppose journalism can also count on those loud-mouthed propagandists who currently proliferate on commercial radio and cable television. These pundits thrive in an era where there is little actual reporting. They can provide their self-serving take on the day's events as gospel "truth," confident that their audience will rarely be exposed to news media where their often half-baked and opportunistic claims are exposed. This crowd will be certain to oppose reform, and distort the issues beyond recognition, because ignorance is their best friend—and because they make a lot of money spinning scary stories of blood-sucking taxmen, deadly Canadian health care and moderate Republicanism. Expect to see any call for public subsidies equated with direct government takeover of the editorial functions of all media, invariably leading to a totalitarian dungeon. You know, like in Britain and Denmark. Or the United States in the Jeffersonian and Jacksonian eras.

But if this is the best that the forces of reaction can do, we're optimistic: If the crisis generates an open and honest debate, the cause of journalism will win. As a rule, we like to be in this position in a political fight. When people really are engaged, it is not so hard to turn the discussion from the tiresome repetition of old and discredited dogmas regarding government subsidies to the heart of the matter: what form should smart, democratically inclined subsidies take; and what sort of journalism institutions and practices are we going to make viable?

Don't get us wrong. We have no illusions about the power of special interests in the United States. We know this is why, in debates over health care, it is so difficult to challenge the hegemony of the insurance industry. We know this is why military spending is off-limits as a political issue. We know this is why the very speculators who grew obscenely wealthy by wrecking our economy play a central role in drafting the proposals to reform the financial sector. We know this is why our tax code has reduced the burden placed on the wealthy and corporations for four decades.

But we also know this is why the battle for journalism is necessarily part of a broader struggle for democratic renewal. This is a fight that gets beyond the narrow confines of standard policy debates. It's not about just newspapers, by whatever definition they may attain in an era of reformation. Not just newsrooms, be they print or digital. Not just journalism. This is a fight about whether Americans will have available to them in the 21st century that intangible yet essential mix of honestly assembled information and sincerely advanced ideas that makes us something more than mere consumers, that makes us citizens. If it is true that knowledge equals power, then democratized knowledge—vital information made available to all, immediately and through multiple channels, from diverse perspectives, without compromise or apology—is what makes we the people powerful. And it is that power that sets us free, enabling us to be the masters of governments.

In the pursuit of what in other struggles and in other lands has been described as "people power," all Americans who would topple the appalling corruption of our governing system can be united. It is to this end that we imagine Americans rising up, shedding the lethargies of manufactured consent and saying "No more." And if we are right to believe that such a coalition will materialize, there is every reason to believe that it will prove as powerful as the unlikely alliance of plantation owners and freemen, shopkeepers and farmers, federalists and republicans who all bought copies of *Common Sense* and determined that, yes, "We have it in our power to begin the world over again."[20]

In the course of the past year, as we turned our attention more and more seriously to the crisis of journalism, we came to truly understand what Paine meant with that phrase.

When our *Nation* magazine cover story, "The Death and Life of Great American Newspapers," appeared in April 2009, we were not surprised by the overwhelming response from citizens, journalists and policymakers in the United States—although we were definitely heartened.[21] What blew us away was the flood of e-mails, calls, letters and invitations from around the world. We had known that the crisis of journalism was a global phenomenon, and that, while things were certainly worse in some countries than others, serious democrats on every continent were worried. Our friend Aidan White, the general secretary of the International Federation of Journalists, says, "The capacity of media, of journalism, is under threat around the world."[22] What we had not known was the extent to which journalists and policymakers around the world were watching the United States for a sense of how the crisis would be managed in the nation that exported both the ideal of a free press *and* the pathologies of a corporate mass-media system to so many countries. "It's very important to a lot of people in other countries that we understand the U.S. experience, not just of what's gone wrong but of what is being done about it," explains Granville Williams, whose work with Britain's Campaign for Press and Broadcasting Freedom inspired so much of our activism.[23] Williams and other experts in global media do not look to America because they presume that this country has all the answers, especially when it comes to media policy. But they rightly recognize that the severity of the American media meltdown will require responses that are more immediate, and potentially bolder, than those seen in other countries. And, frankly, they're casting about for ideas.

To our view, many of the best ideas come from countries other than the United States. This book has sampled liberally from them, urging Americans to borrow from the experience and wisdom of Canada, Britain, Denmark and all the other countries that have invested more aggressively and extensively in public media than has the United States; from the Scandinavian countries that have used subsidies to promote media competition and to assure that diverse ideas and ideologies have forums in which to communicate; from the Japanese newspapers and broadcasters that have maintained their long-term commitment to large newsrooms with substantial staffs of journalists as the essential building blocks of responsible and serious media. But we are more than ready to believe—perhaps because the crisis in the United States is more immediate and severe, perhaps because the United States has the right government at the right time, but mostly because the United States has a rich tradition of supporting meaningful journalism and a free and independent press—that our country could lead in a moment when everything we know about media is changing. The old order is collapsing, brought down by its own compromises and corruptions. There will be a new order, but it need not be a reflection of that which caused the crisis. We can grab what is good and necessary from the crumbling edifice—

serious journalism, with its scope, skepticism and strength—and raise it up on a new platform that is freer, faster and fiercer in its determination to communicate the whole story to all the people.

America has been here before. We have responded in a time of crisis not with tinkering reforms but with revolution. And we have not merely rebelled; we made real the promises of the revolution by subsidizing and sustaining a free press, providing popular information and a means of acquiring it as the essential building blocks of democracy. Our deep history, our oldest experience offers the best antidote to the current crisis of journalism—and our best counsel to the anxious democrats of other countries. These are perilous times that we are going through. But America was founded in perilous times, and the wisest of our founders recognized that peril as opportunity.

Thomas Paine saw the struggle of his day as "not local, but universal." He rejected the momentary relief of reform, arguing that posterity itself was "virtually involved in the contest, and will be more or less affected, even to the end of time." He wanted a reformation that would toss aside that which had failed and establish the framework for that which could not fail. It was in this context, and with this understanding, that Paine declared on the eve of America's first Independence Day, "The birthday of a new world is at hand. ... "[24]

We take America's first great journalist at his word. We believe that Americans still have it in our power to begin the world again. And we propose to use that power not merely to save journalism but to provide America—and the world—with a greater journalism than any of us has ever known.

Appendix 1

Founding Principles

The founders believed that the United States needed a free and independent press to maintain liberty and to make real the promise of democratic governance. They understood, as well, that it was essential for the national and state governments to act to facilitate the establishment of newspapers and to assure that they could easily and widely circulate. To this end, they supported a variety of postal and printing subsidies.

Thomas Jefferson, James Madison and their compatriots were not casual revolutionaries. They saw it as their duty to go beyond merely outlining theories about what might make a republic. They were committed to the practical work of making that republic functional.

As such, the founders did not merely promise a free press, they used the authority of the government to establish the policies and subsidies that would sustain a free press.

The words of the patriots, so often neglected by contemporary media and political players who have allowed the infrastructure of democracy to decay and crumble, remain as resonant and clear in the 21st century as when they were put to paper in the days of revolution and nation building.

On the Press as the Guarantor of Liberty

The question before the Court and you, Gentlemen of the jury, is not of small or private concern. It is not the cause of one poor printer, nor of New York alone, which you are now trying. No! It may in its consequence affect every free man that lives under a British government on the main of America. It is the best cause. It is the cause of liberty. And I make no doubt but your upright conduct this day will not only entitle you to the love and esteem of your fellow citizens, but every man who prefers freedom to a life of slavery will bless and honor you as men who have baffled the attempt of tyranny, and by an impartial and uncorrupt verdict have laid a noble foundation for securing to ourselves, our posterity, and our neighbors, that to which nature and the laws of our country have given us a right to liberty of both exposing and opposing arbitrary power (in these parts of the world at least) by speaking and writing truth.

Andrew Hamilton, the attorney who argued in defense of New York printer John Peter Zenger, who in 1735 was charged with publishing "seditious libels" against the British governor of New York state. The jury, ignoring the instructions of the judge, accepted Hamilton's argument that a free press was an essential check on arbitrary power.[1]

The trial of Zenger in 1735 was the germ of American freedom, the morning star of that liberty which subsequently revolutionized America.

Gouverneur Morris, the great-grandson of Lewis Morris, the New York politician who hired Zenger to publish articles critical of the colonial governor. Gouverneur Morris was a key author of the Constitution of the United States and a prime advocate for what he described as "a vigorous government" that backed the founding document's words up with policies and expenditures.[2]

The liberty of the press is the great bulwark of the liberty of the people: It is, therefore, the incumbent Duty of those who are constituted the Guardians of the People's Rights to defend and maintain it.

Massachusetts House of Representatives, resolution passed March 3, 1768, in response to a request by the British governor of the colony that it support an effort to prosecute the *Boston Gazette*, a radical newspaper that featured the writings of outspoken patriot Joseph Warren, for seditious libel. The resolution was advanced by Samuel Adams and his allies in the chamber.[3] Colonial legislatures enacted state constitutions that frequently referred to liberty of the press as "one of the blessings of a free people," "the chief bulwark and support of Liberty in general" and the "great bulwark of our Constitution."[4]

I am no friend of licentiousness, but the liberty of the press must be preserved sacred, or all is over.

The Rev. Andrew Eliot, April 18, 1768, leading Boston patriot, writing during the *Boston Gazette* struggle.[5] Argued Eliot (May 13, 1767): "Nothing is of greater importance than to secure the entire freedom of publishing, without fear, any censures upon public measures. The liberty of the press is the palladium of English liberty. If this is gone, all is gone."

The last right we shall mention, regards the freedom of the press. The importance of this consists, besides the advancement of truth, science, morality, and arts in general, in its diffusion of liberal sentiments on the administration of Government, its ready communication of thoughts between subjects, and its consequential promotion of union among them, whereby oppressive officers are shamed or intimidated, into more honourable and just modes of conducting affairs.

Continental Congress, "To the Inhabitants of the Province of Quebec," resolution enacted in 1774.[6]

There is no declaration of any kind for preserving the Liberty of the Press ...

George Mason, delegate to the Constitutional Convention of 1787, explaining why he would not sign the document he had played an essential role in crafting. With delegates Elbridge Gerry and Thomas Pinckney, he tried to include language in the original document that read: "the liberty of the press should be inviolably observed."[7]

The framers of it; actuated by the true spirit of such a government, which ever abominates and suppresses all free enquiry and discussion, have made no provision for the liberty of the press, that grand palladium of freedom, and scourge of tyrants; but observed a total silence on that head. It is the opinion of some great writers, that if the liberty of the press, by an institution of religion, or otherwise, could be rendered sacred, even in Turkey, that despotism would fly before it.

Centinel, "To the Freemen of Pennsylvania," October 5, 1787. The Centinel letters, a series of 24 articles, appeared in the *Philadelphia Independent Gazetteer* and the *Freeman's Journal* between October 5, 1787, and November 24, 1788. Historians believe they were written by Samuel Bryan and Eleazer Oswald, both ardent advocates of a strong free press as an essential check on tyranny that needed to be protected and supported by the new republic. Campaigning for the liberty of the press was central to the push for adoption of a Bill of Rights.[8]

On the 23d, Mr. Madison made a report to the House of Representatives on the subject, which was taken up for consideration on the 24th; whereupon …

Provided, That the two articles which by the amendments of the Senate are now proposed to be inserted as the third and eighth articles, shall be amended to read as followeth:—

Article the third. Congress shall make no law respecting an establishment of religion, or prohibiting the free exercise thereof; or abridging the freedom of speech, or of the press; or the right of the people peaceably to assemble, and to petition the government for a redress of grievances

Senate Journal, September 24, 1789, reflecting the final stages of the debate on the first amendment to the Constitution of the United States.[9]

To preserve the freedom of the human mind then & freedom of the press, every spirit should be ready to devote itself to martyrdom; for as long as we may think as we will, & speak as we think, the condition of man will proceed in improvement.

Thomas Jefferson, 1799. Jefferson wrote these words in the midst of the first great battle over freedom of the press in the United States, when the administration of President John Adams and its Federalist allies in Congress were using the Alien and Sedition Acts to jail critical editors such as the Vermont printer, newspaper editor and politician Matthew Lyon. Jefferson battled Adams in 1800, making liberty of the press a central issue. Lyon, elected to Congress while serving in jail, cast the deciding vote for Jefferson when the election went to the U.S. Congress following an Electoral College tie.[10]

The press (is) the only tocsin of a nation …
> **President Thomas Jefferson**, 1802. Even as he objected, often passionately, to negative newspaper coverage, Jefferson held to the founding view that "The only security of all is in a free press."[11]

In an instant the fairy spell of delusion is dissipated—the tremendous authority of this august and magnanimous despot, like the enchanted castle of the magician, vanishes for ever.
> **Tunis Wortman**, 1800. This New York lawyer and political activist gave voice to the Enlightenment faith that knowledge was transformational and that a free and widely circulated press was essential to America's democratic experiment. While Jefferson and others saw the press as a guardian of liberty, Wortman recognized it also as a champion of freedom.[12]

The most informed and judicious of our nation, believe that such a press would go further to remove ignorance, and her offspring superstition and prejudice, than all other means … Such a paper, comprising a summary of religious and political events, &c. on the one hand; and on the other, exhibiting the feelings, disposition, improvements, and prospects of the Indians; their traditions, their true character, as it once was and as it now is; the ways and means most likely to throw the mantle of civilization over all tribes; and such other matter as will tend to diffuse proper and correct impressions in regard to their condition—such a paper could not fail to create much interest in the American community, favourable to the aborigines, and to have a powerful influence on the advancement of the Indians themselves.
> **Elias Boudinot**, editor of *The Cherokee Phoenix*, appealing for support of the newspapers in 1826. Boudinot, a Cherokee Indian, was a pioneering Native American editor who did much to advance an understanding of newspapers as a tool for communal empowerment and

education of the broader populace. Among other things, he argued that a newspaper could challenge bigotries and ignorance directly. "We shall also feel ourselves bound to correct all misstatements," he argued in the pages of the *Phoenix*.[13]

We wish to plead our own cause. Too long have others spoken for us. Too long has the publick been deceived by misrepresentations, in things which concern us dearly, though in the estimation of some mere trifles; for though there are many in society who exercise towards us benevolent feelings; still (with sorrow we confess it) there are others who make it their business to enlarge upon the least trifle, which tends to the discredit of any person of color; and pronounce anathemas and denounce our whole body for the misconduct of this guilty one . . . The civil rights of a people being the greatest value, it shall ever be our duty to vindicate our brethren, when oppressed, and to lay the case before the publick. We shall also urge upon our brethren, (who are qualified by the laws of the different states) the expediency of using their elective franchise; and of making an independent (use) of the same.

Samuel Cornish and John Russwurm, 1827, introducing their publication *Freedom's Journal*, the first African American–owned and – operated newspaper published in the United States. Cornish and Russwurm, writing less than a year after the death of Jefferson and almost a decade before the death of Madison, expanded the understanding of the vital role that a diversely owned and operated free press would have in a democratic state.[14]

In the First Amendment the Founding Fathers gave the free press the protection it must have to fulfill its essential role in our democracy. The press was to serve the governed, not the governors. The Government's power to censor the press was abolished so that the press would remain forever free to censure the Government. The press was protected so that it could bare the secrets of government and inform the people. Only a free and unrestrained press can effectively expose deception in government. And paramount among the responsibilities of a free press is the duty to prevent any part of the government from deceiving the people and sending them off to distant lands to die of foreign fevers and foreign shot and shell. In my view, far from deserving condemnation for their courageous reporting, the New York Times, the Washington Post, and other newspapers should be commended for serving the purpose that the Founding Fathers saw so clearly. In revealing the workings of government that led to the Vietnam war, the newspapers nobly did precisely that which the Founders hoped and trusted they would do.

Hugo Black, 1971, from the U.S. Supreme Court's decision in *New York Times Co. v. United States*, the Pentagon Papers case.[15]

On the Use of Government Policy and Subsidies to Sustain a Free Press

For the purpose of diffusing knowledge, as well as extending the living principle of government to every part of the united states—every state—city—county—village—and township in the union, should be tied together by means of the post-office. This is the true non-electric wire of government. It is the only means of conveying heat and light to every individual in the federal commonwealth. Sweden lost her liberties, says the abbe Raynal, because her citizens were so scattered, that they had no means of acting in concert with each other. It should be a constant injunction to the postmasters, to convey newspapers free of all charge for postage. They are not only the vehicles of knowledge and intelligence, but the centinels of the liberties of our country.

Benjamin Rush, "Address to the People of the United States," 1787. Rush made the linkage of liberty and a free press–conveyed to the people via the subsidy of free postage–a part of his campaign to secure adoption of an American constitution.[16]

The way to prevent these irregular interpositions of the people is to give them full information of their affairs thro' the channel of the public papers, and to contrive that those papers should penetrate the whole mass of the people. The basis of our governments being the opinion of the people, the very first object should be to keep that right; and were it left to me to decide whether we should have a government without newspapers, or newspapers without a government, I should not hesitate a moment to prefer the latter.

But I should mean that every man should receive those papers and be ca-
pable of reading them.

> **Thomas Jefferson**, 1787, arguing both for a free press and for the
> postal subsidy that would mean that "every man should receive those
> papers."[17]

For my part I entertain a high idea of the utility of periodical publications;
insomuch as I could heartily desire, copies of ... magazines, as well as common
Gazettes, might be spread through every city, town, and village in the United
States. I consider such vehicles of knowledge more happily calculated than
any other to preserve the liberty, stimulate the industry, and ameliorate the
morals of a free and enlightened people.

> **George Washington**, 1788, arguing not just for a free press but for sys-
> tems to guarantee that "magazines, as well as common Gazettes, might
> be spread through every city, town, and village in the United States."[18]

Public opinion sets bounds to every government, and is the real sovereign in
every free one ...

The larger a country, the less easy for its real opinion to be ascertained,
and the less difficult to be counterfeited; when ascertained or presumed, the
more respectable it is in the eyes of individuals. This is favorable to the au-
thority of government. For the same reason, the more extensive a country,
the more insignificant is each individual in his own eyes. This may be un-
favorable to liberty.

Whatever facilitates a general intercourse of sentiments, as good roads,
domestic commerce, a free press, and particularly a circulation of news-
papers through the entire body of the people, and Representatives going
from, and returning among every part of them, is equivalent to a contrac-
tion of territorial limits, and is favorable to liberty, where these may be
too extensive.

> **James Madison**, 1791. Arguing for postal subsidies, the father of the
> Constitution recognized that the free-press protection in the Bill of
> Rights was made real by policies that promoted "a circulation of news-
> papers through the entire body of the people."[19]

I can not forbear to recommend a repeal of the tax on the transportation of public prints. There is no resource so firm for the Government of the United States as the affections of the people, guided by an enlightened policy; and to this primary good nothing can conduce more than a faithful representation of public proceedings, diffused without restraint throughout the United States.

George Washington, 1793. In his fifth address to the nation as its first president, Washington sided with those who supported the free distribution of news reports on government affairs "without restraint throughout the United States."[20]

Weighing all probabilities of expense as well as of income, there is reasonable ground of confidence that we may now safely dispense with . . . the postage on news papers . . . to facilitate the progress of information.

Thomas Jefferson, 1801, from his first annual message as president to the Congress and the American people. Eliminating postage costs was seen by democrats as an essential guarantee that a free press would be available to all.[21]

(We have become) a nation of newspaper readers.

Portfolio, 1801. This prominent Philadelphia newspaper celebrated the growth in American publishing that resulted from postal and governmental subsidies. In this time, "Under the fostering arm of the government, the press enjoyed special privileges accorded to no other genre of print . . . in the United States news was potentially accessible to all."[22]

Appendix 2

Ike, MacArthur and the Forging of a Free and Independent Press

The U.S. government has played a critical role in the creation and nurturing to strength of some of the most vibrant media systems on the planet—media systems that are adjusting to threats from the Internet and surviving the global financial meltdown relatively intact. The only problem is that they aren't operating in the United States. Confused? So were we, until we made the acquaintance of a certain General Dwight David Eisenhower. Historian Stephen Ambrose called Eisenhower to our attention some years ago, suggesting, "Ike started more newspapers than William Randolph Hearst."[1] Ambrose hinted at what he was talking about in one of his most compelling books on the supreme commander of Allied forces, writing of how, in the summer of 1945, Eisenhower "called in German reporters and told them he wanted a free press. If he made decisions that they disagreed with, he wanted them to say so in print. The reporters, having been under the Nazi regime since 1933, were astonished that the man who had directed their conquest could invite such criticism."[2]

In fact, Eisenhower did a lot more than invite such criticism. He facilitated it, as did General Douglas MacArthur during the period when he served as supreme commander of the Allied powers in Japan.

Let's put this in context: imagine if the invasion and occupation of Iraq had been a genuinely international endeavor that had broad support and clearly defined goals. Then, imagine if, instead of being guided by neoconservative fantasists with their haphazard schemes and corrupt cronies, the occupation of Iraq had been organized by people who really were serious about creating a vibrant and fully functional democracy. Imagine if teams of Arab and Muslim democrats had been given the structural support and resources to start new media with a charge to tell it like it is, rather than L. Paul Bremer's edicts—which one Iraqi editor interpreted as: "In other words, if you're not with America, you're with Saddam"—and you can begin to get the picture.[3]

Our point here is not to compare occupations. Rather, it is to suggest that the story of how Eisenhower and MacArthur used the power of the U.S. military to develop free and freewheeling press systems in post–World War II Germany and Japan offers useful insights about the prospect for successful government interventions in times of crisis for the purpose of creating media that encourage and sustain democracy. We would not suggest that the generals in Germany and Japan did everything right (there is much to criticize in any occupation by one land of another), and we are especially conscious of the excesses of censorship.[4] Indeed, as the Cold War developed in the late 1940s it led to unwarranted U.S. abuses against the Left, especially in Japan.[5] Nor would we attempt to suggest that circumstances in the United States today are comparable with those in Germany and Japan in the tenuous days after the fall of Adolf Hitler and Hideki Tôjô —fascists whose tenures illustrated the ease with which a free press can become a propaganda tool. But we think it is more than merely instructive that within the lifetimes of many living Americans (and virtually all of our parents and grandparents), the United States successfully initiated what one of Ike's top aides correctly referred to as "the biggest newspaper enterprise in the world."[6]

At a critical juncture, when American officials were faced with the daunting task of building functional democracies in occupied lands that had seen their civic and political infrastructures obliterated by fascist regimes, Dwight Eisenhower and Douglas MacArthur—with muscular encouragement from Harry Truman—used the authority and resources of the U.S. government to establish media systems with competitive, at times combative, newspapers and independent broadcasting networks.

At the heart of the project was an understanding that a free press and broadcasting system were essential to the renewal and maintenance of a healthy democracy, and that at the core of that system had to be independent, well-trained and well-compensated journalists who understood their communities and countries, responded to the concerns of their readers and listeners and were prepared to challenge official and commercial propaganda and censorship. Nothing was left to chance. Ike and Mac did not wait for "the market" to come up with fixes; the work of establishing "a free and independent press" was too vital a task for that. [7]

These lessons are vital to the current debate over the future of journalism in the United States, which occurs at another critical juncture. We think it is important to reflect on them in detail—not merely for instruction on what the United States has done in the past but also in hopes of tapping into the spirit of the initiative. Our task is different from that undertaken by Eisenhower and MacArthur. But we employ their story with the purpose of getting Americans thinking more seriously about the role of the state in fostering the sort of robust journalism that is as necessary today as it was in the postwar moment.

In the years following World War II, the United States essentially governed a portion of Germany (other sections of the defeated nation were controlled by the British, French and Soviets) and all of Japan. These occupations had as their stated purposes the "reconstruction" of formerly fascist states "on a democratic basis."[8] Essential to the project, Eisenhower and MacArthur both understood, was the establishment not just of constitutional protections for a free press but of an actual free press.

So vital was the link between the establishment of a functional press system and democratic renewal that, well before VE Day, as U.S. troops battled their way into Germany, they came with orders to preserve printing plants and to move immediately to help anti-Nazi Germans establish local newspapers. That process began when *Aachener Nachrichten* rolled off the presses in January 1945, in Aachen, the first German city to be captured by the advancing Allied forces. Four thousand Germans had defied Nazi evacuation orders and remained in the city, which for months after the arrival of the U.S. troops was such a dangerous place that the lawyer who was appointed as the city's first non-Nazi mayor in more than a decade, Franz Oppenhoff, was murdered by a team of SS men and Hitler Youth parachuted in under orders from Heinrich Himmler to kill "collaborationists."[9] Aachen was so violent and unstable, in fact, that the name of the anti-fascist publisher of *Aachener Nachrichten* was for a time kept secret in order to protect him from assassination.[10] Yet, the publisher and his small team of reporters and editors knew their mission as they put the four-page paper out each week and rapidly built a circulation of 20,000 in the region along the Dutch and Belgian borders. "The attempt was to establish real news, not Military Government gazettes, since otherwise the papers would soon discredit themselves with the German people," explained an official report by the U.S. military overseers of the project. "They are German newspapers and the publishers from the first have been told that they were working toward the time when Germany would have a completely free press."[11]

The roots of this initiative—and of the notion that a United States that wanted to advance President Franklin Roosevelt's "four freedoms" in a postwar world would have to take a hands-on approach to the development of the sort of free and independent media that nurtures democracy—had been planted years earlier by Kent Cooper, the longtime general manager of the Associated Press.[12] Cooper was one of America's highest-profile newsmen, a genuinely "dominant figure in world journalism" from the 1920s to the 1950s.[13] In the aftermath of World War I, as an AP manager, Cooper was in Paris when the Versailles Treaty was being crafted. He argued aggressively for inclusion of a clause guaranteeing worldwide freedom of the press and actually earned the support of Colonel Edward M. House, who at the time was President Woodrow Wilson's foreign-policy adviser.[14] Cooper's codicil was left out of the final peace agreement, but the AP man kept pressing the point.

During World War II, Cooper penned a series of essays on what he saw as the necessity of promoting free and independent media in the postwar era as part of any broader initiative to maintain peace and spread democracy.[15] "The deep night that blotted out the truth need not fall on any country again, nor need there be maintained in most countries a murky twilight as far as knowledge of other peoples is concerned. Since it has been proved that poisoned news can generate a war, its antithesis, truthful news, should have a chance to prove that it can maintain the peace," wrote Cooper shortly before VE Day. "Truthful news and a free press can do more than anything to avert war, but the acceptance of both must be real and sincere, not lip service paid to the ideals of a free press in countries which pride themselves on democratic institutions."[16] Translation: This is going to take some heavy lifting on the part of the Allies.

The man who was often described as a "no-nonsense journalist" and a "hard-headed realist" met with presidents, prime ministers, cabinet secretaries and generals, as well as editors and publishers, to promote the vision.[17] He had considerable success in shaping the ideas of Roosevelt, with whom he corresponded regularly, and Secretary of State Cordell Hull.[18] It was Hull who got the 1943 Moscow conference on post-fascist Italy to agree to this statement: "Freedom of speech, of religious worship, of political belief, of press and of public meeting shall be restored in full measure to the Italian people."[19] That move led Edwin L. James, the managing editor of *The New York Times*, to declare: "The matter of a free press is now on the peace table agenda."[20]

But what made this commitment "real and sincere, not lip service" was the determination of key players at the highest levels of government. Generals Eisenhower and MacArthur, in particular, were given remarkable leeway in their commands to commit energy and resources to the development of newspapers, magazines and radio networks at points when Allied forces were still battling for control of Germany and Japan. The linkage between journalism and democracy was well understood, and official involvement in the development of free and independent media was recognized as necessary to the work of establishing the infrastructure of democratic renewal. "The program planned in the field of press before V-E Day was based on the fact that the Nazis had crushed the opposition press; forced democratic editors, journalists and publishers into exile, retirement or concentration camps; acquired financial control of newspapers and press facilities; dictated the make-up of content of papers, and channeled all news through governmental or semi-official press agencies," the Americans observed. Hence the first step was to "wipe out the propaganda press which the Nazis had set up and to suspend or abolish the approximately 1,500 Nazi newspapers still being published up to V-E Day."[21]

Then came the hard part. Eisenhower and his lieutenants—like MacArthur and his lieutenants in Japan, who referred to their work as "nursing Japanese newspapers"— were not about to leave the restructuring of old media and the development of new media to the market.[22] They were not going to roll the dice and hope some rich guys would think it profitable to start establishing new newspapers and radio stations; after all, the rich guys had in many cases been willing collaborators with the fascists.[23]

In Japan, MacArthur found newsmen in his ranks, like Major Daniel Imboden, a former reporter and editor from California, and sent them into the newsrooms of existing papers. Their mandate was to "[lecture] Japanese editors and reporters three times weekly on how to run an honest newspaper"—lesson one: don't "follow the leader"; question, challenge and prod officials.[24] The lessons took when, after an autobiography of MacArthur became a runaway best seller and letter writers began to describe the general as "a living god," the *Nippon Times* editorialized in 1946:

> If the conception of government is something imposed upon the people by an outstanding god, great man or leader is not rectified, democratic government is likely to be wrecked. We fear the day after MacArthur's withdrawal, that some living god might be searched out to bring the sort of dictatorship that made the Pacific War . . . The way to express the gratitude of the Japanese people toward General MacArthur for the wisdom with which he is managing post-war Japan and for his efforts to democratize the nation is not to worship him as a god but to cast away the servile spirit and gain the self-respect that would not bow its head to anybody.[25]

In Germany, where the Nazis had integrated their propaganda network far more deeply into the old newspapers and radio networks than in Japan, the work of creating a new media system required a more ambitious intervention. Thus, "expert teams began the search for democratically-minded editors, journalists and publishers and seized Nazi printing plants, newsprint and news facilities."[26]

At Aachen, a socialist printer named Heinrich Hollands who had re-sisted the Nazis was given the license to publish the first post-Nazi news-paper.[27] He was assisted by a team of European journalists and intellectuals, many of them with Jewish backgrounds, who had fled to the United States in the 1930s or 1940s and returned as U.S. Army officers or aides. Chief among these was Major Hans Habe, a former Austrian newspaperman who had been briefly imprisoned by the Germans before escaping, making his way to the United States. In exile Habe penned an account of the German invasion of France, *A Thousand Shall Fall*, which sold more than 3 million copies and was made into a Hollywood film. Habe hit the ground running in Germany, with a theory about the im-portance of staffing the country's new newspapers with writers and edi-tors who would not lecture Germans on how to be democrats but would rather make real the promise of democratic life by publishing diverse and dissenting ideas in competing journals.[28] Habe rallied refugee journalists, many of them socialists and communists, and survivors of the concen-tration camps to staff his "chain" of newspapers that within a year after VE Day would number 18.

The Austrian Jewish journalist Ernest Landau recalled Habe showing up at the displaced-persons camp at Feldafing and declaring: "You have nothing more to lose in this camp. We're starting a newspaper in Munich. That's where you belong. We need people like you." Within days, Landau was effectively employed—thanks to the U.S. military—as a journalist, restarting a career that would eventually see him become editor in chief of the newspaper *Neue Welt* and then an editor at Bayerische Rundfunk (Bavarian Radio)[29]—both projects developed by the U.S. authorities.

Landau became one of the thousands of German and Japanese jour-nalists who were given jobs in some cases and kept in jobs in others by what *TIME* magazine referred to in a headline about the project as: "Uncle Sam, Publisher."[30] Staffs on the papers in Germany and Japan were described by U.S. journalists as "astonishingly" large. Though newsprint shortages often restricted the number of pages in the editions of German papers to four or six—and sometimes of Japanese papers to just one—the numbers of reporters and editors hired onto the new papers in Germany and the restructured old papers of Japan were massive by

U.S. and British standards. The theory was that, particularly at so contentious a moment, when both countries were in the thick of definitional debates over constitutional matters and the run-up to initial free elections, papers needed massive staffs to cover every side of every story.[31]

Some of the greatest German journalists, who had lost their jobs under the Nazis, got them back under Uncle Sam. They found themselves working out of the same buildings and using the same presses that they had before their papers were first censored, then sanctioned and finally shuttered by Hitler. Now they were under explicit orders to "build an objective, free democratic press."[32]

The American plan, from the start, was to evolve a free and independent press that would be owned by Germans. But in the immediate aftermath of World War II, in an exceptionally unstable country with millions of displaced people, a ruined economy and varying occupying powers competing for turf, the Americans ran newspapers as what General Lucius Clay referred to as "quasi-public institutions." Initial plans to tightly censor and control the press were abandoned so that, in Clay's words, "there should be a free flow of information to the people of Germany, particularly on matters connected with the building of democratic government."[33] This cost a great deal of money—the Americans secured printing plants and newsprint and set up distribution networks and then got about the work of establishing independent radio stations in the various German states under U.S. control.[34] The State Department authorized establishment of a revolving capital fund of $3.5 million to provide loans to German papers—and a number of other financial and structural supports were put in place to help the free and independent newspapers consolidate their positions and guard against financial takeover by neo-Nazis.[35] Some newspapers, such as Hans Habe's *Die Neue Zeitung*, were directly subsidized.

The Americans were explicit about their mission. As in Japan under MacArthur, in Germany it was: "To use the authority of Military Government to strengthen the economic and community position of the democratic press and safeguard it as far as possible against attempts to destroy it in order to revive a press more to the liking of Nazis, militarists, racists and nationalists, and groups whose special interests demand a subservient press."[36] To insure diversity of opinion was represented, the Americans chose several newspaper licensees in a given community so Germans had access to "varying political points of view rather than a single licensee with a single point of view." In Aachen, a year after the first license went to a socialist, U.S. authorities authorized the establishment of a second newspaper by the more conservative burghers of the community.[37]

Perhaps most important, financial structures were developed to assure that the newspapers could become and remain self-sustaining. From 1945 on, all newspapers were required to pay 20 percent of their gross receipts into a dedicated fund. This fund eventually contained RM 58,000,000 when payments were stopped. At that point, the fund began making grants to individual newspapers and to a cooperative that had been established to help newspapers acquire printing plants and equipment. This was all part of a strategy—in which the U.S. military intervened frequently to force owners of printing plants who had in many cases obtained their concessions from the Nazis to negotiate fair long-term agreements to publish newspapers and magazines offering a range of political and ideological perspectives.[38]

In the area of broadcasting, it was determined that the best way to protect against the return of the old *Reichsrundfunk* ("Imperial Broadcasting") propaganda model was to develop public radio and later television networks in the various German states. This decentralized model fostered the creation of strong individual broadcasting agencies for most German states—so that there would be no one-size-fits-all control of content from the national capital—and protected them from government interference and economic dependence on advertisers by assuring that most of the funding came from license fees from radio and TV owners. The funding scheme owed much to structures set up to develop Britain's BBC and reflected the influence of the British occupation forces in Germany on their American counterparts.[39]

There were disputes about censorship, access to newsprint and a thousand other issues in Germany, as there were in Japan.[40] Even as the U.S. authorities put editors on their "own responsibility," there were still clashes, some of them journalistic, some of them extensions of the broader political tensions associated with the occupations.[41] But several of the greatest challenges came from Washington, where officials who favored "hard occupations"—rigorously controlling the discourse—bristled at the tendency of German and Japanese newspapers to criticize U.S. officials and policies.

The first great test came just weeks after VE Day, when Elmer Davis, the Washington-based director of the Office of War Information, issued an order imposing a news blackout on Germany. "The reason is very simple," said Davis. "Germany is a sick man. He now can have only what the doctors prescribe." General Eisenhower cabled the White House immediately to object, and several days later President Truman opened a press conference by saying that the first issue of the day would be the vital matter of press freedom in Germany. "General Eisenhower has advised me that he has issued no policy or order (restricting communications). The general has expressed the personal opinion that a free press and a free flow of information and ideas should prevail in Germany," said Truman, who concluded, "I agree with General Eisenhower."[42]

So, it appears, did a great many Germans. Within a year after VE Day, Major Hans Habe was in Washington celebrating the "terrific response" of the Germans to the paper he was editing at the time, *Die Neue Zeitung*. Habe delighted in noting his paper was being printed on the formerly Nazi-controlled presses that published the first editions of his arch nemesis Hitler's *Mein Kampf*. The Munich-based *Die Neue Zeitung* had achieved a circulation of 1.6 million and was receiving an average of 1,100 letters to the editor each day—some critical of the U.S. occupation, some supportive, most reflecting on the day-to-day challenges of shaping the new Germany. "It was the objectivity of the American-controlled newspaper, reflected in the release of news not necessarily favorable to the Allies that made the deepest impression on the German readers," Habe told *The New York Times*.[43]

There would be additional battles, especially when Cold War sentiments gave rise to objections from Washington about the U.S. military putting communists and socialists in the news business. By 1950, as tensions heightened on the Korean Peninsula, MacArthur was aggressively cracking down on the Japanese Communist Party newspaper, *Akhata (Red Flag)*, with the general effectively acknowledging that his actions were "violative of the broad philosophy which has guided the development of the free press in Japan."[44] In 1953, U.S. Senator Joe McCarthy crusaded generally against aid to German papers and specifically against what he alleged was a $3 million annual allocation for Hans Habe's old paper, *Die Neue Zeitung,* complaining in a letter to Secretary of State John Foster Dulles that "one of the most heavily subsidized papers is as of today run by a Communist editor." As with many of McCarthy's charges, this one was unfounded. But *Die Neue Zeitung* did criticize U.S. policies, treat dissenting and dissident political views with respect and, at its best, operate like the sort of "free and independent" newspaper Eisenhower had said he wanted. Responding to McCarthy, *The New York Times* would editorialize that the project "to help a really free press strike firm roots in German soil . . . has been a good investment."[45]

In other words, Joe McCarthy's griping aside, by the time the United States military dialed down the occupations of Germany and Japan in the early 1950s, remarkably vibrant free and independent media systems were in place—along with functioning democracies. "West Germany, a nation without a single operating newspaper at war's end, last week boasted 1,497 dailies and greater press freedom than at any other time in its history," observed *TIME* magazine in 1957. "As newspapers throughout the country noted their tenth anniversaries, they reported that circulation (total: 17.3 million) and advertising revenues were also at record peaks."[46] By the 1960s, U.S. publications were profiling Japanese newspapers as the most successful print publications in the world.

The media systems developed by the United States proved to be flexible enough to grow and evolve along democratic lines—with commercial sectors sufficiently vibrant to excite the most ambitious free marketer and space for cooperative and public-service ventures. Some of the newspapers and magazines created with assistance from the U.S. forces failed, and many new publications were created in the years after the "German Treaty" of 1955 officially ended the occupation. For example, Berlin's respected Left-leaning daily newspaper, *Die Tageszeitung (taz),* was launched in 1978 and remains a muscular player in the local and national discourse, a scenario virtually unimaginable in the United States. Then there is the remarkable story of *Berliner Zeitung,* an old East German newspaper that after the fall of the wall transformed itself into a popular national daily that styles itself as "Germany's *Washington Post.*"

The durability of the institutions and the structures the United States put in place in the late 1950s is easily observed—*Aachener Nachrichten*, the first paper started by the Americans, is still going strong, as are dozens of others. The systems were so durable, in fact, that in 2008 and 2009, when U.S. reporters went looking for models of media systems where newspapers were surviving—and in some cases even thriving—they found them in Germany and Japan. In the summer of 2008, as American newsrooms were imploding, *Business Week* headlined a story from Germany: "Where Newspapers Are Thriving." And from Japan came headlines like "Newspapers: Still Big in Japan." A *Washington Post* foreign correspondent explained:

Japanese newspapers are acting surprisingly spry, especially compared with their woebegone peers in the United States, where relentless declines in readership, circulation, advertising and profits have triggered buyouts, layoffs, hiring freezes and cutbacks in reportorial ambition.

Nearly all of this unpleasantness is on hold in Japan, at least for the time being.

While the circulation of U.S. newspapers has dropped more than 15 percent in the past decade, it has slipped just 3.2 percent here. Japan's five big national dailies have kept nearly all their readers.

The Japanese remain the world's greatest newspaper buyers, with 624 daily sales per thousand adults. That's 2 1/2 times greater than in the United States, according to a 2008 estimate by the World Association of Newspapers. Slightly more than one daily newspaper, on average, is delivered to every household in this country. The Yomiuri newspaper, with a circulation of more than 10 million, is the world's largest daily.

About one in 10 newsroom jobs in the United States has disappeared in the past decade, according to the American Society of Newspaper Editors. The *Washington Post* has reduced its news staff in recent years by almost a quarter. But in Japan, large-scale layoffs and buyouts of reporters and editors are unheard of. "That is sacred ground," said Megumi Tomita, director of management and circulation at the Japan Newspaper Publishers & Editors Association. "We haven't seen any decrease in the number of journalists.[47]

Remarkably, most of the reports from Germany and Japan, while frequently noting the distinctive journalism ethics of those countries—including a higher regard for keeping reporters and editors on the job—as well as distinctive ownership structures, generally failed to mention the role of the U.S. government in establishing those ethics, structures and approaches.

As Americans wrestle with the question of how to renew and extend journalism that sustains democracy in the 21st century, however, we think it is more important than ever to recognize that our government has experience when it comes to establishing new media systems—and that this experience was forged in crisis. The U.S. government has intervened where the market could not be trusted to produce a free and independent press and a broadcasting system that was neither propagandistic nor deferent to economic special interests. The U.S. government has provided resources and established financial and ownership structures for media that were designed to be both self-sustaining and responsible to the mission of providing citizens with the information they need to be their own governors. Of course, there were missteps and stumbles along the way, indefensible deviations and boneheaded bumbles. But the willingness to intervene in bold and creative ways succeeded because, at the most fundamental level, there was an understanding that the mission could not fail. Kent Cooper, the old AP man, was right then and he's still right now: truthful news and a free press remain as essential today as ever. What we need today, as was needed in 1945, is a recognition, extending from the grassroots to the highest levels of government, that, "the acceptance of both must be real and sincere, not lip service paid to the ideals of a free press in countries which pride themselves on democratic institutions."

There are critical junctures where getting beyond "lip service" for the purpose of "help[ing] a really free press strike firm roots" requires an engaged and active government that respects that there will be times when journalism must be supported and sustained by official policies. At a critical juncture in 1945, General Eisenhower understood this, and so did General MacArthur. And they acted upon it. At a critical juncture today, we need to renew that understanding. And we need to act upon it with the same sense of purpose and recognition that, like Germany and Japan and every other democratic state, America needs a free and independent press.

Appendix 3

Sources for the Book's Charts

The charts contained in this book provide mostly original evidence of the extent of the current crisis and its roots. For that reason, we determined that it would be wise to add a detailed appendix outlining the sources of the information contained in the charts. We thank our research assistant R. Jamil Jonna of the University of Oregon for guiding our work in this area and preparing this appendix.

CHAPTER 1, CHART 1. Estimated Workforce in Radio and Television
Broadcast Media Per 100,000 People, Selected Years 1982–2008

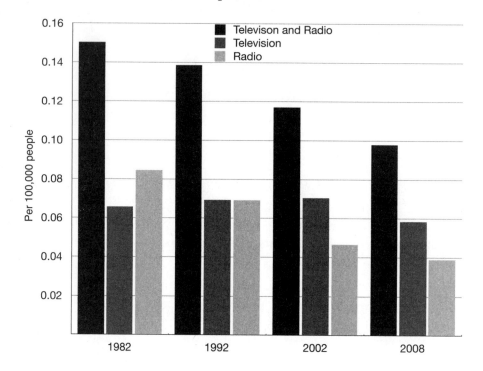

Sources: **1982–2002**: David H. Weaver, Randal A. Beam, Bonnie J. Brownlee, Paul S.
Voakes and Cleveland G. Wilhout, *The American Journalist in the 21st Century: U.S.
News People at the Dawn of a New Millennium* (Mahwah, NJ: Lawrence Erlbaum,
2007), p. 2; **2008**: Estimated based on Weaver et. al. (2007) and employment trends
of Announcers, Editors and Reporters in the Radio and Television Broadcasting Industry (NAICS 515100), Bureau of Labor Statistics, U.S. Department of Labor, Occupational Employment Statistics, http://bls.gov/oes/ (accessed 12 June 2009);
Population Division, U.S. Census Bureau, "Annual Estimates of the Population for
the United States," various releases, http://census.gov/.

CHAPTER 1, CHART 2. Total Circulation of Daily Newspapers Per 100,000 People, 1950–2008

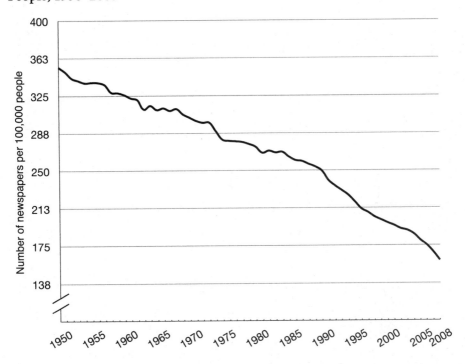

Sources: Business Analysis and Research, Newspaper Association of America (NAA), "Trends and Numbers," http://www.naa.org/ (accessed May 29, 2009); Population Division, U.S. Census Bureau, "Annual Estimates of the Population for the United States," various releases, http://census.gov/.

CHAPTER 1, CHART 3. **Percentage of All Media Advertising Going to Newspapers, 1950–2009**

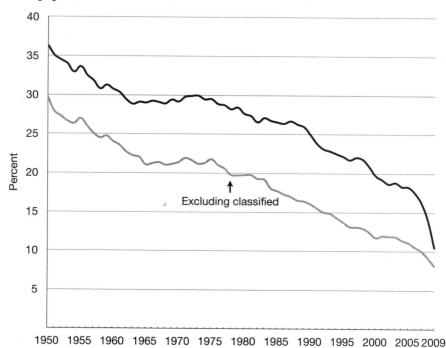

Sources: Newspaper advertising spending: Business Analysis and Research, Newspaper Association of America (NAA), "Trends and Numbers." Available at http://www .naa.org (accessed May 29, 2009). After 2003, total includes both print and online advertising spending. This is estimated based on the first two quarters; *Total advertising spending*: **1950–1998**: Daniel M. G. Raff, "Advertising expenditures, by medium: 1867–1998," in Susan B. Carter et al. (eds.), *Historical Statistics of the United States, Earliest Times to Present: Millennial Edition* (New York: Cambridge University Press, 2006); **1998–2007**: Universal McCann, "Historical Cross-Media Ad Expenditures" (Television Bureau of Advertising: TVB Online), http://www.tvb.org/ (accessed June 13, 2009); **2008–2009**: forecasted data from *Magna Global*, "Insider's Report: Robert Coen Presentation on Advertising Expenditures," December 2008, p. 3.

CHAPTER 1, CHART 4. Ratio of Average Salaries of CEOs in Leading News Media Firms to Average Salaries of Editors and Reporters, 1970–2009* (Five-year Averages, except 1970†)

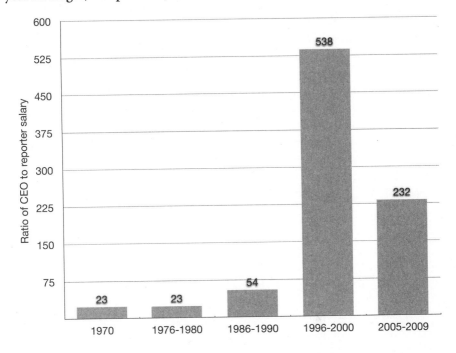

*All data is for the previous fiscal year except for 1970, which is for FY 1970.

†Editor and Reporter salaries are for single years: 1970–2000 from the U.S. Census; 2007 data from the American Community Survey (ACS) is used as a proxy for 2009. Mean wage includes only full time, privately employed editors and reporters.

Sources: *Editor and reporter salaries*: S. Ruggles, Matthew Sobek, Trent Alexander, Catherine A. Fitch, Ronald Goeken, Patricia Kelly Hall, Miriam King and Chad Ronnander, "Integrated Public Use Microdata Series (IPUMS): Version 4.0 [Machine-readable database]." (Minneapolis, MN: Minnesota Population Center [producer and distributor], 2008). *CEOs*: **1970–1999**: "The Dimensions of American Business: A Roster of the Country's Biggest Corporations," *Forbes*, May 15, 1971; "The Dimensions of American Business: A Roster of the U.S.'s Biggest Corporations," *Forbes*, May 15, 1976; "The Dimensions of American Business: A Roster of the U.S.'s Biggest Corporations," *Forbes*, May 15, 1977; "The Boss' Paycheck: Who Gets the Biggest?" *Forbes*, May 29, 1978; "How Much Does Your Boss Make?" *Forbes*, June 11, 1979; "It Ain't Hay, but is It Clover?" *Forbes*, June 9, 1980; "How Much the Bosses Earned in 1985," *Forbes*, June 2, 1986; "The People in Power," *Forbes*, June 15, 1987; "Corporate America's Most Powerful People," *Forbes*, May 30, 1988; "Corporate America's Most Powerful People," *Forbes*, May 29,

1989; "Corporate America's Most Powerful People: The Pay," *Forbes*, May 28, 1990; "The People at the Top of Corporate America," *Forbes*, May 20, 1996; "Spoils of Success," *Forbes*, May 19, 1997; "How They Got There," *Forbes*, May 18, 1998; "The Scorecard," *Forbes*, May 17, 1999; "The Top Paid 800 CEOs," *Forbes*, May 15, 2000; **2005–2008**: Forbes.com (accessed June 24, 2009).

Aside from the U.S. Census, there is no consistent data on the average salaries of editors and reporters from the 1970s to present. Weaver et. al. (2007, Table 3.15, p. 101) provide data from 1970 to 2001, and while they report the median annual salaries of journalists, *average* salaries are required for this comparison. Incidentally, the census numbers track Weaver et. al. very closely. With some qualifications—see the explanation on 'estimating the editorial and public relations workforce' given in chart 6—we believe data from the U.S. census is adequate. Table 3 summarizes our results and compares them with those of Weaver et. al.

TABLE 3. Detail of Reporter Pay by Year

Year	Average Reporter Pay	N	Median Reporter Pay, Weaver et. al.*
1970	$9,966	358	10,699
1980	$19,952	2,199	18,226
1990	$34,740	2,580	29,145
2000	$49,205	2,647	46,254
2007	$57,198	569	—

*Average of all mediums except the category "News Magazine."

Thirteen major public media companies were used as a starting point to gather CEO compensation data: CBS, Cox Enterprises, Disney, E. W. Scripps, Gannett, McClatchy, NBC (General Electric), New York Times, News Corp, Time Warner, Tribune Company, Times Mirror, Washington Post. These companies represent the media industry in its most concentrated form, having merged or taken over numerous other companies. Such extinct companies—when they appeared in the *Fortune* lists—were used when data was available. For example, Times Mirror and Time Inc. were distinct companies for much of this period, until the formation of Time Warner. Similarly, Disney was not included until it had media interests, even thought it has been a Fortune 500 company for many years. According to the time periods used in this study, Disney was included for the first time in 1996, by which time it had purchased Capital Cities Communications/ABC (prior to their merger, each of the latter companies' data were used).

What links all of these companies together over time is that they had newsrooms. While it is impossible to obtain CEO compensation data for significantly large private companies, such as Hearst and Advance Publications, we believe this survey is sufficient for our purposes. The actual years surveyed, number of companies used and average CEO pay are detailed in table 3.

TABLE 3. Detail of CEO Pay by Year

Year	Average CEO Pay	Number of Companies
1970	$231,610	5
1976	$304,616	8
1977	$385,281	8
1978	$445,500	8
1979	$535,050	11
1980	$615,063	9
1986	$1,028,600	10
1987	$1,620,818	11
1988	$3,014,000	11
1989	$2,248,083	12
1990	$1,551,000	12
1996	$3,398,667	12
1997	$5,808,417	12
1998	$8,375,417	12
1999	$74,348,645	12
2000	$40,318,600	10
2005	$8,427,000	10
2006	$11,400,000	9
2007	$14,018,750	8
2008	$17,002,857	7
2009	$15,590,000	7

CHAPTER 1, CHART 5. **Number of Top 500 Firms with Interests in Broadcast News, Newsmagazines or Daily Newspapers, 1960–2008 (Five-year moving averages)**

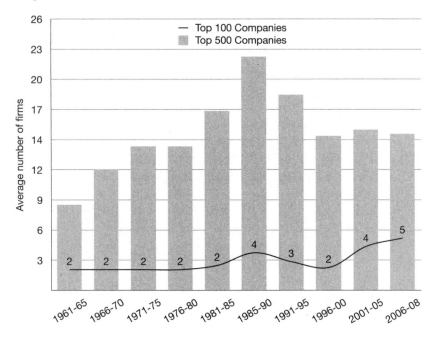

'All data is for the previous fiscal year.

Sources: *Publicly held firms*: Fortune 500 listings; Securities and Exchange Commission (SEC) 10-K Filings; *Privately held firms*: "The Private Enterprisers: The U.S.' 60 Largest Private Companies," *Forbes*, February 1, 1965; "Private: Keep Out," Forbes, May 15, 1969; "S.I. Newhouse and Sons: America's Most Profitable Publisher," *Business Week* (Industrial Edition), January 26, 1976; "After Years of Hoarding Cash, Hearst is Spending Big," *Business Week*, September 15, 1976; "In Privacy They Thrive," *Forbes*, November 1, 1976; William H. Jones and Laird Anderson, "Newhouse Sprawling, Rich, Private." *Washington Post*, July 28, 1977, p. D13; "ABC's Profit Grows 6.7%." *New York Times*, July 23, 1982; Martha M. Hamilton, "Inside the Newhouse Empire: Newhouse Outbid Competitors; Newhouse Revenue, Profit Revealed," *Washington Post*, October 16, 1983; "RCA Net Rose 45% In Fourth Quarter On 17% Sales Gain" *Wall Street Journal* (Eastern edition), Jan 24, 1984, p. 1; Stephen Grover, "CBS Profit Fell 53% in Quarter," *Wall Street Journal*, February 13, 1985; "The Largest Private Companies in the U.S.," *Forbes*, November 18, 1985; "The Largest Private Companies in the U.S.," *Forbes*, November 17, 1986; "The Largest Private Companies in the U.S.," *Forbes*, December 14, 1987; "The 400 Largest Private Companies in the U.S.," *Forbes*, December 12, 1988; "The 400 Largest Private Companies in the U.S.," *Forbes*, December 11, 1989; "The 400 Largest Private Companies in the U.S," *Forbes*, December 10, 1990; "The 400 Largest Private Companies in the U.S," *Forbes*, December 9, 1991; "The 400 Largest Private Companies in the U.S," *Forbes*, December 7, 1992; "The 400 Largest Private Companies in the U.S," *Forbes*, December 6, 1993; "The 500 Largest Private Companies in the U.S," *Forbes*, December 5, 1994; "The 500 Largest Private Companies in the U.S," *Forbes*, December 4, 1995; "America's Largest Private Companies," *Forbes*, 1996–2008 (available online; accessed August 6, 2009); "Gannett Soars 30%; Scripps Net Up 22%," *Financial Post* (Toronto, Canada), July 15, 1998.

Media company ownership data were compiled from *Forbes* or *Fortune* profiles, Hoover's Company Profiles, the "Funding Universe" website (http://www.fundingu-niverse.com/), individual company websites, and various news sources. The Top 500 firms were determined by revenue, using the *Fortune* listings as a basis. *Forbes*' "largest private companies" lists started in 1985. For previous years, estimates are based on revenue data from scattered sources (cited above); where no data was available, revenue was estimated based on available dates.

CHAPTER 1, CHART 6. Estimated Employment of Editors, Reporters and Announcers in the Newspaper, Radio and Television Industries, and Public Relations Specialists and Managers Per 100,000 People, 1980–2008

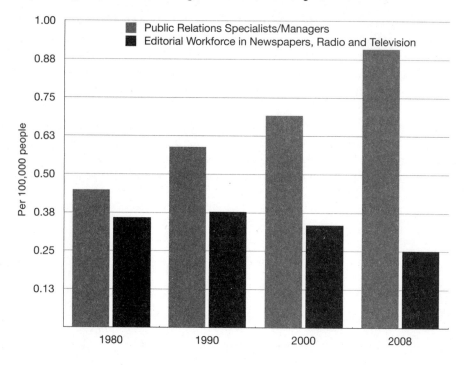

*Estimates for the editorial workforce in radio and television are for the years 1982, 1992 and 2002.

Sources: **1980–2007**: *Radio-Television*: Weaver et. al. (2007) (for radio and television only; see chart 1); *All other editors and reporters and PR persons*: S. Ruggles, et. al, "IPUMS" (editors and reporters only); **2008**: *Editorial Workforce*: Estimated based on employment trends reported in Jon Morgan (ed.), "The State of the News Media 2009" (Washington, DC: Pew Research Center, Project for Excellence in Journalism, 2009), http://www.journalism.org (accessed 12 June 2009); **2008**: *PR*: Estimated based on employment trends of "Public Relations Specialists" (SOC 27–3031) and "Public Relations Managers" (SOC 11–2031), Bureau of Labor Statistics, U.S. Department of Labor, Occupational Employment Statistics, http://bls.gov/oes/ (accessed 12 June 2009); Population Division, U.S. Census Bureau, "Annual Estimates of the Population for the United States," various releases, http://census.gov/.

Estimating the editorial and public relations workforce: Estimates of the editorial workforce of the U.S. News Media outside of radio and television, as well as those employed in public relations, were made using occupational and industry data recorded in the U.S. Census from 1960 to 2000. We used the following samples: 1960,

TABLE 1. Occupation and Industry Variables for Each Census Year

Year	Occupation	Industry
1960	Editors and Reporters	Newspaper publishing and printing
1960	Public Relations Men and Publicity Writers	None or Public Administration
1970	Editors and Reporters	Newspaper publishing and printing
1970	Public Relations Men and Publicity Writers	None or Public Administration
1980	Editors and Reporters	Newspaper publishing and printing
1980	Public Relations Specialists	None or Public Administration
1990	Editors and Reporters	Newspaper publishing and printing
1990	Public Relations Specialists or Public Relations Managers	None or Public Administration or Active Duty Military
2000–07	Editors or News Analysts, Reporters and Correspondents	Newspaper publishers
2000–07	Public Relations Specialists or Public Relations Managers	None or Public Administration or Active Duty Military

"1% sample"; 1970, "Form 2 Neighborhood sample"; all subsequent years, "5% sample." 2001–2009 estimates are based either on the Bureau of Labor Statistics' Occupational Employment Statistics (OES) or American Community Survey (ACS) data (2000–2007). Census data was retrieved from the IPUMS database published by the Minnesota Population Center (as cited above). Occupation and industry titles, variable names and variable descriptions are taken directly from the IPUMS online codebooks (see table 1).

To get an accurate estimate of the number of editors and reporters in the newspaper industry it was necessary to add certain conditions to narrow the focus to those employed by major media companies. For example, a census respondent might have reported that they were an "Editor" or "Reporter" in a given year but they might also have been unemployed, part-time, working for the government or a non-profit, or receiving very low pay (and thus unlikely to be working in the mainstream news industry). By controlling for these characteristics, it is possible to estimate the full-time editorial workforce. Similarly, controls restricted public relations specialists to those that were employed full time (see table 2).

TABLE 2. Variables Used to Estimate the Full Time Editorial Workforce

Variable	Description	Condition (controls)	Assumption
OCC	Occupation	Variable	
IND	Industry	Variable	
INCWAGE	Wage and salary income	≥ 25,000 in constant $2008	Part of a major media company
CLASSWKR	Class of worker	"Wage/salary, private"	Working in the private sector
EMPSTAT	Employment status	≠ "Unemployed"	Employed
WKSWORK2	Weeks worked last year (interval)	≥ 27 weeks	Fully employed
HRSWORK2	Hours worked last week (interval)	≥ 35 hours	Full time
UHRSWORK	Usual hours worked per week	≥ 35 hours	Full time

A major benefit of utilizing census data is that many additional characteristics are available for each case or respondent. For example, the INCWAGE variable was used to determine the average wage of reporters in chart 4 of chapter 1, in addition to being a control variable. Given the large number of cases that the census provides, narrowing the sample by industry, occupation, and non-response to controls, was not an issue. Indeed, our figures correspond closely with other researchers who have made estimates of the editorial workforce in the U.S. (e.g., Weaver et . al. [2007]).

CHAPTER 1, CHART 7. Comparative Survey of Political Knowledge, International Hard News

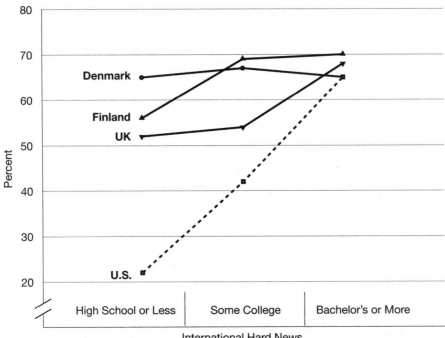

CHAPTER 1, CHART 8. Comparative Survey of Political Knowledge, Domestic Hard News

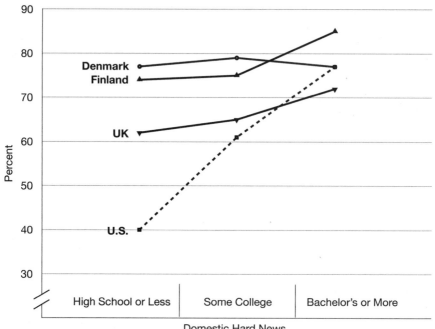

Sources: The charts appear in an unpublished ms: Shanto Iyengar, Kyu Hahn, James Curran, Anker Lund and Inka Morin, "Cross-National Versus Individual-Level Differences in Political Information: A Media Systems Perspective." Unpublished ms, (Department of Communication, Stanford, 2008).

CHAPTER 3, CHART 1. Daily, Weekly, Semi-weekly and Tri-weekly Papers, 1750–1850

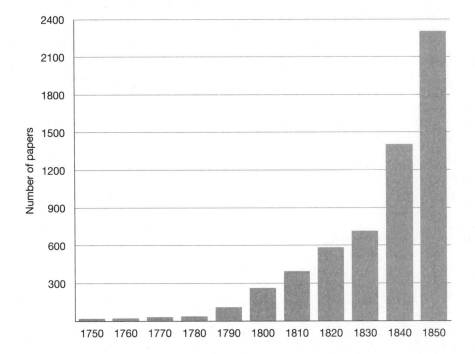

Sources: **1830–1850**: Alfred McClung Lee, *The Daily Newspaper in America* (New York: Macmillan, 1937), 718, Table VIII (for 1830 there is no data for semi-weeklies and tri-weeklies so only weeklies and dailies make up "all papers"); **1750–1820**: Jeffrey L. Pasley, *"The Tyranny of Printers": Newspaper Politics in the Early American Republic* (Charlottesville: University of Virginia Press, 2001), 403, Chart 2 (figures are rough estimates based on the chart).

CHAPTER 3, CHART 2. Print Advertising Per Capita, 1865–1937 (constant 1929 dollars)

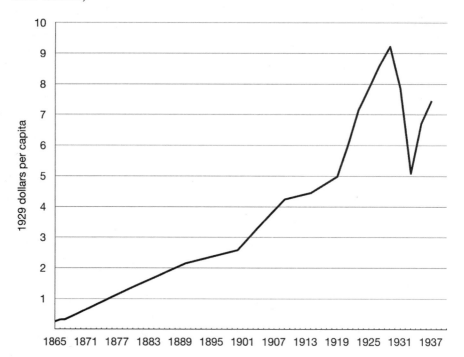

Sources: Neil H. Borden, *The Economic Effects of Advertising* (Chicago: Richard Irwin, Inc., 1942), 48, Table 1; "The Inflation Calculator." http://www.westegg.com/inflation/ (accessed February 28, 2009). Figures for total U.S. advertising expenditure become most reliable starting in 1935, when complete census data is available. Before this, analysts have made estimates based on various industry sources.

CHAPTER 3, CHART 3. Average Number of Daily Newspapers for the Twelve Top Ranked U.S. Cities by Population, 1869–2008

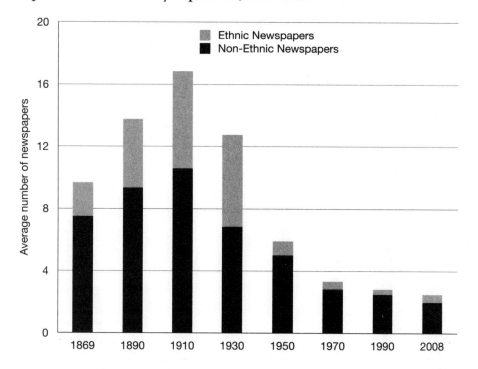

CHAPTER 3, CHART 4. Average Number of Daily Newspapers in U.S. Cities Ranked Three to Twelve by Population, 1869–2008

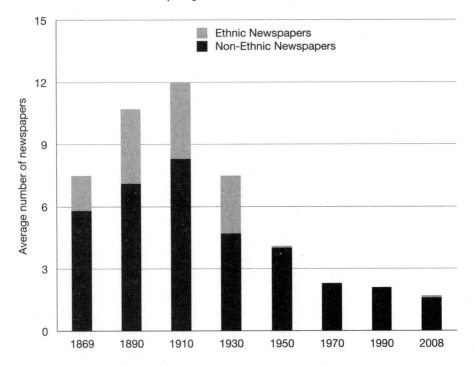

Sources: Newspapers: **1869**: *Geo. P. Rowell and Co.'s American Newspaper Directory* (New York: Geo. P. Rowell & Co., 1869); **1890–1930**: *N.W. Ayer & Son's American Newspaper Annual*, (Philadelphia: N.W. Ayer and Son, 1890, 1910 and 1930); **1950–2008**: *Editor & Publisher International Year Book*, (New York: Editor & Publisher Co., published annually) *Population*: **1869–1990**: Michael R. Haines, "Population of Cities with at Least 100,000 Population in 1990: 1790–1990, "Table Aa832–1033 in Susan B. Carter et. al. (eds.), *Historical Statistics of the United States* (New York: Cambridge University Press, 2006); **1990–2008**: Population Division, U.S. Census Bureau. "Table 1: Annual Estimates of the Population for Incorporated Places Over 100,000, April 1, 2000 to July 1, 2007" (released July 10, 2008).

Only daily newspapers were counted and if morning and evening editions differed they were counted separately. For 1930, only newspapers with paid circulation (weekly or Sunday) greater than 10,000 were counted; for 1950, the cutoff was 30,000; and for 1970–2008, the cutoff was 35,000. All specialty papers, such as those covering the bond market, legal or agricultural news, were excluded. For New York, all boroughs (Bronx, Brooklyn, Manhattan, Queens, and Staten Island)—if they appeared separately—were combined to correspond with census figures.

By the 1950s, most "foreign language" and "ethnic" newspapers were printed in English or were bilingual but became weeklies or monthlies. In *Editor & Publisher*, the titles of the sections listing these papers changed and split over time as a consequence. Only daily newspapers in the following sections were counted: in 1950, "Principle Foreign Language Dailies in the United States"; in 1970, "Principle Foreign Language Dailies in the United States"; in 1990: "Ethnic Newspapers Published in the United States"; and in 2008, "Ethnic," "Hispanic," and "Jewish" sections.

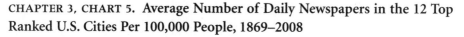

CHAPTER 3, CHART 5. Average Number of Daily Newspapers in the 12 Top Ranked U.S. Cities Per 100,000 People, 1869–2008

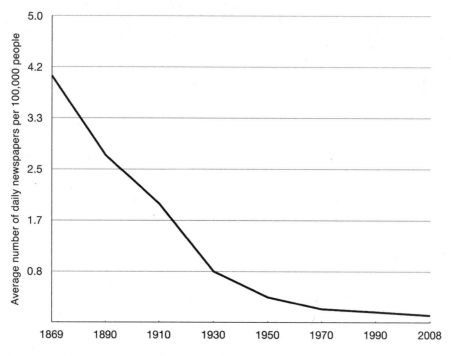

Sources: See source notes to Chapter 3, Charts 3 and 4.

CHAPTER 4, CHART 1. Global Spending on Public Media, 2007

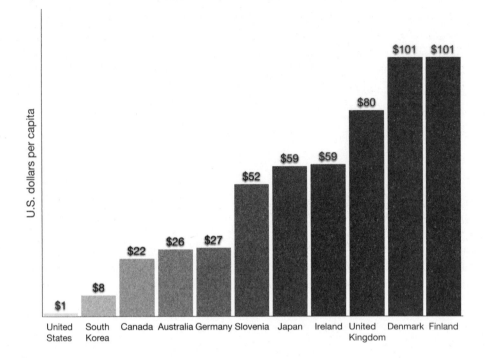

Source: *Changing Media: Public Interest Policies for the Digital Age* (Washington, D.C.: Free Press, 2009), p. 267.

Notes

Preface

1. Michael O'Brien, "Obama Open to Newspaper Bailout," *The Hill*, September 20, 2009; http://thehill.com/blogs/blog-briefing-room/news/59523-obama-open-to-newspaper-bailout-bill.

2. See The Knight Commission on the Information Needs of Communities in a Democracy, *Informing Communities: Sustaining Democracy in the Digital Age* (Knight Foundation, 2010), http://www.report.knightcomm.org/foreword; Leonard Downie Jr. and Michael Schudson, "The Reconstruction of American Journalism," *Columbia Journalism Review*, issued online October 19, 2009. http://www.cjr.org/reconstruction/the_reconstruction_of_american.php?page=all.

Introduction

1. Thomas Paine, *Common Sense*, 1776.

2. Thomas Paine, *Liberty of the Press*, 1806.

3. Thomas Paine, *The Necessity of Taxation*, 1782.

4. What did Madison mean by the term "information," which is so widely used today in a variety of contexts? "In the early republic," Richard John, arguably the leading historian of the subject, writes, "it denoted the time-sensitive 'intelligence' about public affairs and market trends that was commonly called news. Information was news for a spatially dispersed population that would never meet face-to-face; its circulation presupposed the establishment of institutional arrangements to keep this population well informed." See Richard R. John, *Network Nation: Inventing American Telecommunications* (Cambridge: Harvard University Press, forthcoming, 2010).

5. "Kerry Statement on the Future of Journalism," Senator John Kerry's office, press release, May 6, 2009, http://kerry.senate.gov/cfm/record.cfm?id=312584.

6. Michael Calderone, "John Kerry on Journalism: 'Brave New World'," *Politico*, May 6, 2009, http://www.politico.com/news/stories/0509/22204.html.

Chapter 1

1. The great Chicago journalist of the late 19th and early 20th centuries, who wrote satirical columns in the Irish brogue of his alter ego, Mr. Dooley, once opined: "Th newspaper does ivrything f'r us. It runs th' polis foorce an' th' banks, commands th'

milishy, controls th' ligislachure, baptizes th' young, marries th' foolish, comforts th' afflicted, afflicts th' comfortable, buries th' dead an' roasts thim aftherward." The afflicts-the-comfortable line has been in circulation ever since, employed perhaps most famously by Gene Kelly (as *Baltimore Herald* newsman E. K. Hornbeck) in Stanley Kramer's 1960 film about the 1925 Scopes "Monkey" Trial," *Inherit the Wind.* Confronting a prominent lawyer and politician who objected to his reporting style, Hornbeck declared, "Mr. Brady, it is the duty of a newspaper to comfort the afflicted and afflict the comfortable."

2. Written and directed by Richard Brooks and released in 1952, *Deadline USA* is a classic old-school American newspaper story, where heroic journalists announce: "The newspaper is always published in the public interest."

3. Kate Giammarise e-mail to John Nichols, December 13, 2008. Giammarise, who was recommended for several of her jobs by Nichols, has regularly corresponded through her career with him.

4. Walter Isaacson, "How to Save Your Newspaper," *Time*, February 5, 2009.

5. Mark Potts, "How Low Can Newspaper Stocks Go," *Recovering Journalist*, March 15, 2009, http://recoveringjournalist.typepad.com/recovering_journalist/.

6. John F. Sturm, "The Reality About Newspapers," Newspaper Association of America advertisements in major daily newspapers, May 2009.

7. David B. Wilkerson, "Newspaper Circulation Declines 7 Percent in Last Six Months," *MarketWatch*, April 27, 2009.

8. Tim Arango, "Fall in Newspaper Sales Accelerates to Pass 7%," *New York Times*, April 27, 2009.

9. Source: Newspaper Association of America, http://www.naa.org/TrendsandNumbers/Advertising-Expenditures.aspx.

10. Erik Sass, "AP: Newspapers Cut Young Employees," MediaDailyNews, September 1, 2009. www.mediapost.com.

11. Oliver Luft, "Gannett Confirms 1,400 More Job Cuts at US Local Newspapers," *The Guardian*, July 2, 2009. Gannett Blog's terrific coverage of the cuts can be found at: http://gannettblog.blogspot.com/2009/07/urgent-dickey-says–1400-job-cuts-most.html.

12. Material taken from *Changing Media: Public Interest Policies for the Digital Age* (Washington, D.C.: Free Press, 2009), pp. 193–94.

13. Alex Crippin, "Buffett Wouldn't Buy Most U.S. Newspapers 'At Any Price'," *CNBC*, May 2, 2009, http://www.cnbc.com/id/30535393/.

14. See, for example, Robert W. McChesney, *Rich Media, Poor Democracy: Communication Politics in Dubious Times* (New York: The New Press, 2000).

15. Michael Winerip, "Looking for an 11 O'Clock Fix," *New York Times Magazine*, January 11, 1998, p. 33.

16. "Midwest Local TV Newscasts Devote 2.5 Times As Much Air Time To Political Ads As Election Coverage, Study Finds," Midwest News Index (a project of the University of Wisconsin's NewsLab) analysis, released November 21, 2006.

17. David Zurawik, "Recession Redrawing Local Media Landscape, With No End in Sight," *Baltimore Sun*, June 7, 2009, http://www.baltimoresun.com/entertainment/tv/bal-ae.zontv07.1jun07,0,1149975.story.

18. Brian Stelter, "Ad Losses Put Squeeze On TV News," *New York Times*, May 11, 2009, pp. B1, B8.

19. See, for example, Glenn Greenwald's treatment of how the blogosphere was able to call Jeffrey Rosen on his coverage of Sonia Sotomayor. *Salon*, May 31, 2009, http://www.salon.com/opinion/greenwald.

20. For sources see Appendix III.

21. See Alex S. Jones, *Losing the News: The Future of the News that Feeds Democracy* (New York: Oxford University Press, 2009), p. 4.

22. "U.S. Newsroom Employment Declines," American Society of Newspaper Editors, survey, published April 16, 2009.

23. Kristen Henman, "The Post-Dispatch Is Shedding News Pages and Slashing Editorial Staff—and There's No End in Sight," *Riverfront Times*, September 9, 2008.

24. Erica Smith, "Paper Cuts," http://graphicdesignr.net/papercuts.

25. Erica Smith e-mails with John Nichols, May 2009.

26. Thadeus Greenson, "Eureka Reporter to Close Doors Saturday," *Eureka Times-Standard*, November 6, 2008.

27. See Ben Bagdikian, *The Media Monopoly* (Boston: Beacon Press, 1983), for a cogent analysis of this episode.

28. See, for example, Charles L. Klotzer, "The Newspaper Preservation Act Legitimized 'Criminal Conduct' and Turned St. Louis into a One-Newspaper Town," *St. Louis Journalism Review*, May 1, 2002.

29. Kirk Johnson, "Part of Denver's Past, The Rocky Says Goodbye," *New York Times*, February 27, 2009.

30. Christine Tatum, "In Denver, Residents Lament the Closing of a Newspaper," *The New York Times*, March 1, 2009.

31. Dan Barry, "In Seattle, the World Still Turns, a Beacon in Memory of a Lost Newspaper," *The New York Times*, March 16, 2009.

32. Ibid.

33. Erica Smith, "Paper Cuts."

34. Joe Strupp, "SPECIAL REPORT: As Cuts Trim News Pages and Newsrooms—What Gets Lost?" *Editor & Publisher*, May 31, 2007.

35. Jones, *Losing the News*, p. 7.

36. Tim Arango, "Death Row Foes See Newsroom Cuts as Blow," *New York Times*, May 21, 2009.

37. Adam Liptak, "In Shrinking Newsrooms, Fewer Battles for Public Access to Courtrooms," *New York Times*, September 1, 2009, pp. A10, A17.

38. Chris Mooney and Sheril Kirshenbaum, "Unpopular Science," *The Nation*, August 17, 2009. For a longer treatment of the issue, see their book: Chris Mooney and Sheril Kirshenbaum, *Unscientific America: How Scientific Illiteracy Threatens Our Future* (New York: Basic Books, 2009).

39. Richard Perez-Pena, "Big News in Washington, but Far Fewer Cover It," *New York Times*, December 18, 2008.

40. Belinda Luscombe, "As Newsrooms Cut Back, Who Covers the Statehouse?" *Time*, May 7, 2009.

41. Jennifer Dorroh, "Statehouse Exodus," *American Journalism Review*, April/May 2009.

42. Ibid.

43. "Old and New Media Go to Washington," *On the Media*, National Public Radio, May 8, 2009. The transcript is online at http://www.onthemedia.org/transcripts/2009/ 05/08/01. See also: David Simon, "Death of the Newspaperman," *In These Times*, July 2009, pp. 15–17.

44. Paul Starr, "Goodbye to the Age of Newspapers (Hello to a New Era of Corruption)," *The New Republic*, March 4, 2009.

45. For a striking assessment of our situation, see Sheldon S. Wolin, *Democracy Incorporated: Managed Democracy and the Specter of Inverted Totalitarianism* (Princeton: Princeton University Press, 2008). A similar argument is made by Pulitzer Prize-winning journalist Chris Hedges in his sobering analysis of America circa 2009. See Chris Hedges, *Empire of Illusion: The End of Literacy and the Triumph of Spectacle* (New York: Nation Books, 2009).

46. Robert Weisman, "What Went Wrong? Secure in Their Profits, the Globe and Other Newspapers Underestimated the Impact of the Web," *Boston Globe*, April 12, 2009.

47. Source: http://www.naa.org/TrendsandNumbers/Advertising-Expenditures.aspx

48. Thomas E. Patterson, *Young People and the News* (Cambridge, Mass.: Joan Shorenstein Center on the Press, Politics, and Public Policy, 2007), p. 8.

49. The problem of attracting young readers is only exacerbated by the fact that a disproportional percentage of the laid-off reporters in 2008-09 were under the age of 35. These results from an Associated Press survey of 95 editors led one reporter to characterize the lay-offs as "in effect constituting a purge of people under 35 from the newspaper business." See Erik Sass, "AP: Newspapers Cut Young Employees," MediaPostNews, September 1, 2009, www.mediapost.com.

50. Jeff Jarvis, "My Testimony to Sen. Kerry," *Buzz Machine*, April 21, 2009, http:// www.buzzmachine.com/.

51. Ryan Chittum, "Circulation Revenue Only Thing Growing at Newspapers," *Columbia Journalism Review* online, July 23, 2009, www.cjr.org.

52. Ryan Chittum, "NYT Now Gets As Much Money from Circulation as from Ads," *Columbia Journalism Review* online, July 23, 2009, www.cjr.org.

53. Shira Ovide and Russell Adams, "Hearst Plans to Slash, Sell or Shut Paper in Bay Area," *Wall Street Journal*, February 25, 2009.

54. Steven Syre, "Will Times Company Close the Globe? Will They Pull the Trigger?" *Boston Globe*, April 24, 2009.

55. Eric Pfanner, "The Outlook is Murky for Media Advertising," *New York Times*, September 2, 2009, p. B2.

56. Joe Garofoli, "Chronicle to cut 25% of jobs in newsroom," *San Francisco Chronicle*, May 19, 2007; John Geluardi, "San Francisco Chronicle to Cut 125 Positions," *SF Weekly*, Aug. 1 2008; Howard Kurtz, "Under Weight of Its Mistakes, Newspaper Industry Staggers," *Washington Post*, March 1, 2009; "More Job Cuts Coming at SF Chronicle," *Editor & Publisher*, August 31, 2009.

57. For a discussion of the radical restructuring of the music industry, see Greg Kot, *Ripped: How the Wired Generation Revolutionized Music* (New York: Scribner, 2010).

58. Juliet Schor, *Born to Buy* (New York: Scribner, 2004), p. 28.

59. Sarah Ellison, "Newspapers Try New Math of Circulation," *Wall Street Journal*, November 6, 2007. See also: "The State of the News Media," *Project for Excellence in*

Journalism, at www.stateofthemedia.org for details on the average circulation of daily newspapers, 1940–2000.

60. For sources see Appendix III.

61. One of us, as a teacher of media and journalism at universities since the early1980s, can attest to the on-going decrease in newspaper reading and general news consumption by students over this entire period. Daily newspaper reading was not overwhelming in the 1980s, either.

62. Thomas E. Patterson, "Young People Flee From the News," *Television Quarterly* 38:2 (Winter 2008), p. 35.

63. Mirjana Milosevic, deputy director for Press Freedom and Development, World Association of Newspapers (WAN), discussion with John Nichols, June 3, 2009. See also: "World Press Trends 2008," World Association of Newspapers.

64. For sources see Appendix III.

65. Leonard Downie and Robert Kaiser did an experiment along these lines for somewhat later years and reached the same conclusion we did. Leonard Downie and Robert G. Kaiser, *The News About the News: American Journalism in Peril* (New York: Alfred A. Knopf, 2002).

66. David Simon, "Hearing on the Future of Journalism," testimony given before the Senate Committee on Commerce, Science, and Transportation, Subcommittee on Communications, Technology, and the Internet, May 6, 2009.

67. John H. McManus, *Market-Driven Journalism: Let the Citizen Beware?* (Thousand Oaks, CA.: Sage, 1994); Penn Kimball, *Downsizing the News: Network Cutbacks in the Nation's Capital* (Woodrow Wilson Center, 1994); James D. Squires, *Read All About It! The Corporate Takeover of America's Newspapers* (New York: Random House, 1995); Doug Underwood, *When MBAs Rule the Newsroom: How Marketers and Managers Are Reshaping Today's Media* (New York: Columbia University Press, 1993).

68. David Weaver, et al, *The American Journalist in the 21st Century* (Mahwah, NJ: Lawrence Erlbaum Associates, 2007), p. 3.

69. See, for example, Gene Roberts (ed.), *Leaving Readers Behind: The Age of Corporate Newspapering* (Fayetteville: University of Arkansas Press, 2001); William Serrin (ed.), *The Business of Journalism: 10 Leading Reporters and Editors on the Perils and Pitfalls of the Press* (New York: New Press, 2000); Davis Merritt, *Knight Ridder and How the Erosion of Newspaper Journalism Is Putting Democracy at Risk* (New York: Amacom, 2005).

70. Gilbert Cranberg, Randall Bezanson, and John Soloski, *Taking Stock: Journalism and the Publicly Traded Company* (Ames: Iowa State University Press, 2001).

71. Mooney and Kirshenbaum, "Unpopular Science."

72. See Downie Jr. and Kaiser, *The News About the News: American Journalism in Peril*. Downie and Kaiser have offered variations on this line frequently in interviews and speeches, and it is one of the most valuable insights from these two veteran editors.

73. Pamela Constable, "Demise of the Foreign Correspondent," *Washington Post*, February 18, 2007, p. B01, http://www.washingtonpost.com/wp-dyn/content/article/ 2007/02/16/AR2007021601713_pf.html; Tom Fenton, *Bad News: The Decline of Reporting, the Business of News, and the Danger to Us All* (New York: HarperCollins, 2005).

74. "The State of the News Media 2006," Project for Excellence in Journalism. This material comes from the introduction to the report, which can be found online at http://www.stateofthemedia.org/2006/narrative_overview_intro.asp.

75. John Nichols, "Newspapers and After," *The Nation*, January 12, 2007.

76. Howard Gardner, Mihaly Csikszentmihalyi and William Damon, *Good Work: When Excellence and Ethics Meet* (New York: Basic Books, 2001), ch. 7.

77. Deborah Potter, "Pessimism Rules in TV Newsrooms," *Columbia Journalism Review*, November/December 2002, p. 90.

78. Nichols, "Newspapers and After." See also: John Nichols, "Remembering Molly Ivins," *The Nation*, February 1, 2007.

79. Philip Meyer, *The Vanishing Newspaper: Saving Journalism in the Information Age*, second edition (Columbia, Mo.: University of Missouri Press, 2009), p. 2.

80. Ibid, p. 2.

81. Lawrence R. Mishel, Jar Bernstein and Heidi Shielholz, *The State of Working America, 2007/2008* (Armonk, N.Y.: M.E. Sharpe, Inc., 2008), Figure 3ae, p. 221.

82. For sources see Appendix III.

83. A comprehensive 2009 study concluded that media cross-ownership had a negative impact on local journalism. See Danilo Yanitch, "Cross-Ownership, Markets, and Content on Local TV News," Report of the Local TV News Media Project, University of Delaware, May 2009.

84. For sources see Appendix III.

85. Nichols, "Newspapers and After."

86. Dan Rather sued Viacom as a response to his treatment by CBS (which was owned by Viacom at the point when he wrangled with and then left the network) after his much-criticized 2004 report on George W. Bush's National Guard record. The lawsuit was dismissed in September, 2009, by a New York state appellate court. For details see Matea Gold, "Dan Rather's Lawsuit Against CBS Dismissed," *Los Angeles Times*, September 30, 2009. Despite the dismissal, there was always reason to believe (and released documents have confirmed) that Viacom was concerned about how a critical report on the sitting president might damage its commercial interests in Washington. As Viacom CEO Sumner Redstone had put it, in a discussion of his company's 2004 presidential preference: "From a Viacom standpoint, we believe the election of a Republican administration is better for our company." See John Nichols and Robert W. McChesney, *Tragedy and Farce: How the American Media Sell Wars, Spin Elections and Destroy Democracy* (New York: New Press, 2005), p. 155.

87. The classic example is MSNBC's treatment of Phil Donahue, whose program was cancelled after being harassed by corporate executives for being insufficiently deferential to the Bush administration. See Jeff Cohen, *Cable News Confidential: My Misadventures in Corporate Media* (Sausalito, CA: PoliPoint, 2006) for a discussion of this and several other similar episodes.

88. Ben Bagdikian pioneered much of the exposure of this corruption of journalism. See *The Media Monopoly*. The group Fairness & Accuracy In Reporting has chronicled these scandals of corporate interference since the group began operations in the late 1980s. Go to http://www.fair.org/index.php?page=7&issue_area_id=6. Also see McChesney, *Rich Media, Poor Democracy*, for numerous examples of this corporate influence over news values and content. In desperate economic times the problem only grows worse.

89. Their programs placed a high emphasis upon entertainment values similar to the pattern at other commercial television news channels.

90. Brian Stelter, "Voices From Above Silence a Cable TV Feud," *New York Times*, August 1, 2009, pp. A1, A3. It should be added that PBS journalist Charlie Rose chaired the meeting between Murdoch and Immelt. It was left to Glenn Greenwald, again, to note the grand irony of Rose helping broker the deal. It was Rose who lectured Amy Goodman in 2003 that: "I promise you, CBS News and ABC News and NBC News are not influenced by the corporations that may own those companies." See Glenn Greenwald, "GE's silencing of Olbermann and MSNBC's sleazy use of Richard Wolffe," *Salon*, August 1, 2009, http://www.salon.com/opinion/greenwald/2009/08/01/ge/. For excellent treatment of this episode, see also David Sirota, "Taboo-Alert: The Real—and Most Disturbing—News in the Olbermann-O'Reilly Feud," *OpenLeft*, August 3, 2009, http://openleft.com/diary/14439/taboo-alert-the-real-and-most-disturbing-news-in-the-olbermannoreilly-feud.

91. Factiva search conducted on August 3, 2009 using the date range February 1, 2009 to July 30, 2009. For MSNBC's *Countdown*, the source was restricted to "MSNBC: *Countdown*" and the search terms were "O'Reilly" (46 hits) and "Rupert Murdoch" (27 hits); for Fox's *O'Reilly Factor*, the source was restricted to "Fox News: *O'Reilly Factor*" and the search term was "General Electric" (36 hits). The hits are slightly higher than the totals of negative comments because brief, insubstantial references were not counted.

92. Specifically, on June 1—the last time Olbermann mentioned O'Reilly on his program, until the scandal broke on August 3—Olbermann stated at the end of his broadcast he would cease referring to O'Reilly in the future because ignoring him (and "quarantining" Fox) would supposedly help get O'Reilly off the air ("So as of this show's end, I will retire the name, the photograph, and the caricature.") See Greenwald, op. cit. Olbermann was provoked to this dismissal of O'Reilly by what he regarded as O'Reilly's irresponsible attacks on Dr. George Tiller, the women's health physician and abortion doctor, which contributed to a culture where to some it was fair game to murder Tiller. O'Reilly routinely called Tiller a killer who was willing to kill babies for $5,000 and who had blood on his hands. Olbermann did not explain why Murdoch was removed from critical analysis at the same time, if Olbermann had no awareness of the Immelt-Murdoch deal, or of GE's growing concerns that his attacks on O'Reilly were counterproductive for GE's corporate success. See also: http://www.msnbc.msn.com/id/3065420/ns/msnbc_tv-countdown_with_keith_olbermann/.

93. Glenn Greenwald, "The scope—and dangers—of GE's control of NBC and MSNBC," salon.com, August 3, 2009, http://www.salon.com/opinion/greenwald/2009/08/03/general_electric/index.html.

94. The statistics are from the Center for Responsive Politics. Timothy P. Carney, "General Electric is once again the lobbying champion," *Washington Examiner*, July 21, 2009, http://www.washingtonexaminer.com/opinion/blogs/beltway-confidential/General-Electric-is-once-again-the-lobbying-champion–51338342.html?c=y.

95. "Izzy Award Winners," *ICView*, vol. 1, 2009, p. 10.

96. See William L. Rivers, *The Other Government: Power and the Washington Media* (New York: Universe Books, 1982).

97. See: http://sjreview.org/Aboutus.htm. Claude-Jean Bertrand has done the most work on this subject. See, for example, *An Arsenal for Democracy* (Cresskill, NJ: Hampton Press, 2003). For some sense of the criticism of professional journalism in the "golden age," see Glen Feighery, "Two Visions of Responsibility: How National Com-

missions Contributed to Journalism Ethics, 1963-1975," *Journalism and Mass Communication Monographs*, Vol. 11, No. 2, Summer 2009, pp. 167-210.

98. Jones, *Losing the News*, p. 22.

99. Ethical Journalism Initiative, International Federation of Journalists. IFJ general secretary Aidan White has written an excellent book on the campaign, *To Tell You the Truth: The Ethical Journalism Initiative*, which is available from the federation at http://ethicaljournalisminitiative.org/en.

100. Ben Scott, "Labor's New Deal for Journalism: The Newspaper Guild in the 1930s," PhD dissertation, University of Illinois at Urbana-Champaign, 2009, ch. 7.

101. See John Nichols and Robert W. McChesney, "Bush's War on the Press," *The Nation*, December 5, 2005.

102. Hedges, *Empire of Illusion*, p. 170.

103. For a long discussion of the reliance on official sources and other problems built into the professional code for journalism, see Robert W. McChesney, *The Problem of the Media* (New York: Monthly Review Press, 2004), ch. 2, ch. 3.

104. For a variety of treatments of this issue, see Howard Friel and Richard A. Falk, *The Paper of Record: How the New York Times Misreports U.S. Foreign Policy* (New York: Verso, 2004); Edward S. Herman and Noam Chomsky, *Manufacturing Consent* (New York: Pantheon, 1989); Jonathan Mermin, *Debating War and Peace: Media Coverage of U.S. Intervention in the Post-Vietnam Era* (Princeton: Princeton University Press, 1999).

105. For a superb treatment of this issue, see W. Lance Bennett, Regina G. Lawrence and Steven Livingston, *When the Press Fails: Political Power and the News Media from Iraq to Katrina* (New York: Cambridge University Press, 2007).

106. It is ironic that in popular mythology the American news media sometimes are regarded as having been an anti-Vietnam War force. It is true that the news media became less supportive of the war, and at times quasi-oppositional, but that was only after significant elements of elite opinion began to question the war in late 1968, 1969 and into the 1970s; i.e., when the official sources began sending mixed messages. Many years into the war, in early 1968, with tens of thousands of American soldiers already dead and millions of Americans actively opposed to the war, and the factual arguments for the war barely credible, the February 18 *Boston Globe* published the results of its survey of the editorial positions on the war of 38 leading U.S. daily newspapers, which had a combined circulation of 22 million. It determined that not a single one of these newspapers was calling for the withdrawal of U.S. troops from Vietnam. (Even later, as the press became somewhat more open to antiwar positions, it was on tactical grounds. The news media never questioned whether the United States had a moral right to invade a nation like Vietnam, only whether the invasion was an effective use of resources and a prudent policy option to support American interests.) See Martin A. Lee and Norman Solomon, *Unreliable Sources* (New York: Carol Publishing Group, 1990), p. 107.

107. John Pilger, *Heroes* (London: Jonathan Cape, 1986; New York: Vintage, 2001), p. 178.

108. "The Press: The Newspaper Collector Samuel Newhouse," *TIME*, July 27, 1962.

109. Ronald D. Smith, *Strategic Planning for Public Relations* (Mahwah, N.J.: Routledge, 2004), p. 191; Norman Solomon, *Unreliable Sources: A Guide to Detecting Bias in News Media* (New York: Carol Publishing Group, 1992), p. 66; Trevor Morris and Simon Goldsworthy, *PR—A Persuasive Industry? Spin, Public Relations and the Shaping of the*

Modern Media (UK: Palgrave Macmillan, 2008). See also: http://www.nku.edu/~turney/prclass/readings/media_rel.html.

110. Iver Peterson, "At Los Angeles Times, A Debate on News-Ad Interaction," *New York Times*, November 17, 1997, pp. C1, C11.

111. "PR Day at the L.A. Times," *Extra! Update*, August 1998, p. 4. This period and these developments are covered at length in Robert W. McChesney, *Rich Media, Poor Democracy: Communication Politics in Dubious Times* (New York: New Press, 2000).

112. See Diane Farsetta and Daniel Price, "Fake TV News: Widespread and Undisclosed," Center for Media and Democracy, April 6, 2006, http://www.prwatch.org/fakenews/execsummary.

113. See Richard Wolffe, *Renegade: The Making of a President* (New York: Crown Books, 2009).

114. On August 1, 2009 the MSNBC Web site had numerous references to Wolffe and his valuable role on the program "Countdown with Keith Olbermann," but there was no mention of his fulltime employment as a corporate PR person. He was characterized as a journalist.

115. After examining his record and determining Wolffe had not used his position at MSNBC to advance the concerns of his corporate clients, MSNBC allowed Wolffe to return to the air as an expert commentator in October 2009, as long as he did not comment on affairs related to the corporate clients he advised as a full-time PR executive.

116. For sources see Appendix III.

117. Wolffe quotations cited in Glenn Greenwald, "GE's silencing of Olbermann and MSNBC's sleazy use of Richard Wolffe," *Salon*, August 1, 2009, http://www.salon.com/opinion.greenwald/2009/08/01/ge/.

118. In National Advisory Commission on Civil Disorders, *Report of the National Advisory Commission on Civil Disorders* (Kerner report) (Washington, D.C., 1968), http://historymatters.gmu.edu/d/6553.

119. Sally Lehrmann, "The Danger of Losing Ethnic Media," *Boston Globe*, March 5, 2009.

120. Christopher Martin, "'Upscale' News Audiences and the Transformation of Labour News," *Journalism Studies*, vol. 9, no. 2, April 2008, pp. 178–194.

121. Hannah Holleman, Robert W. McChesney, John Bellamy Foster and R. Jamil Jonna, "The Penal State in an Age of Crisis," *Monthly Review*, June 2009. http://www.monthlyreview.org/090601holleman-mcchesney-foster-jonna.php

122. See Eamonn Fingleton, "How the U.S. Press Helped Destroy the Auto Industry," *CounterPunch*, May 16–30, 2009, pp. 1, 4–8.

123. James Curran, Shanto Iyengar, Anker Brink Lund and Inka Salovaara-Moring, "Media System, Public Knowledge and Democracy: A Comparative Study," *European Journal of Communication*, vol. 24, no. 1 (2009): pp. 5–26.

124. The charts appear in an unpublished manuscript: Shanto Iyengar, Kyu Hahn, James Curran, Anker Lund and Inka Morin, "Cross-National Versus Individual-Level Differences in Political Information: A Media Systems Perspective." Unpublished manuscript, Department of Communication, Stanford University, 2008.

125. For sources see Appendix III.

126. Gilbert Cranberg, "Cranberg Wants a Serious Probe of Why the Press Failed in Its Pre-war Reporting," *Nieman Watchdog*, February 7, 2007, http://www.niemanwatchdog

.org/index.cfm?fuseaction=ask_this.view&askthisid=00261. See also John H. Cushman Jr., "Web Site Assembles U.S. Prewar Claims," *New York Times*, January 23, 2008, p. A12. Several authors have assessed the news coverage of the Iraq invasion and occupation. Our analysis can be found in Nichols and McChesney, *Tragedy and Farce*. See also Jeff Cohen, *Cable News Confidential: My Misadventures in Corporate Media* (Sausalito, CA: PoliPoint Press, 2006); Robin Andersen, *A Century of Media, A Century of War* (New York: Peter Lang, 2006); Norman Solomon, *War Made Easy* (Hoboken, NJ: John Wiley & Sons, 2005); Frank Rich, *The Greatest Story Ever Sold: The Decline and Fall of Truth from 9/11 to Katrina* (New York: Penguin Press, 2006); Sheldon Rampton and John Stauber, *The Best War Ever: Lies, Damned Lies, and the Mess in Iraq* (New York: Penguin Books, 2006); Michael Isikoff and David Corn, *Hubris: The Inside Story of Spin, Scandal, and the Selling of the Iraq War* (New York: Crown Publishing Group, 2006); Bill Katovsky and Timothy Carlson, *Embedded: The Media At War in Iraq* (Guilford, CT: Lyons Press, 2003); Norman Solomon, et al., *Target Iraq: What the News Media Didn't Tell You* (New York: Context Books, 2003); Philip M. Seib, *Beyond the Front Lines: How the News Media Cover a World Shaped by War* (New York: Palgrave MacMillan, 2004); Ralph D. Berenger (ed.), *Global Media Go to War: Role of News and Entertainment Media During the 2003 Iraq War* (Spokane, WA: Marquette Books, 2004); Ralph D. Berrenger (ed.), *Cybermedia Go to War: Role of Converging Media During and After the 2003 Iraq War* (Spokane, WA: Marquette Books, 2006); Michael Massing, *Now They Tell Us: The American Press and Iraq* (New York: New York Review Books, 2004); Howard Tumber, *Media at War: The Iraq Crisis* (London: Sage, 2004); Alexander G. Nikolaev and Ernest A. Hakanen, *Leading to the 2003 Iraq War: The Global Media Debate* (New York: Palgrave MacMillan, 2006); David Miller, *Tell Me Lies: Propaganda and Media Distortion in the Attack on Iraq* (London: Pluto Press, 2004); David Dadge, *The War in Iraq and Why the Media Failed Us* (Westport, CT: Praeger Publishers, 2006); Danny Schechter, *When News Lies: Media Complicity and the Iraq War* (New York: Select Books, 2006).

127. See the special issue of the *Columbia Journalism Review*, May/June 2009, for excellent coverage of this point.

128. For sources see Appendix III.

129. Nichols, "Newspapers and After."

130. Kate Giammarise e-mail to John Nichols, May 12, 2009, and May 28, 2009.

131. Ibid.

Chapter 2

1. Barbara Ehrenreich, "Welcome to a Dying Industry, J-School Grads," commencement address to the University of California–Berkeley Graduate School of Journalism Class of 2009, May 16, 2009.

2. Barbara Ehrenreich in discussion with John Nichols, May 23, 2009.

3. See Jones, *Losing the News*, pp. 212-213; Meyer, *The Vanishing Newspaper*, pp. 231-232.

4. Todd Gitlin, "A Surfeit of Crises: Circulation, Revenue, Attention, Authority, and Deference," keynote address to "Journalism in Crisis" conference, University of Westminster, London, England, May 19, 2009.

5. To its great credit, the *Columbia Journalism Review* has led efforts to develop alternative means to salvage and sustain journalism over the past few years, with a general (though not exclusive) emphasis on locating commercially viable models. See the special issue of July-August 2009, for example. It includes a piece by David Simon—yes, the David Simon of Chapter 1—calling for an Internet paywall for journalism content. See David Simon, "Build the Wall," *Columbia Journalism Review*, July-August 2009, http://www.cjr.org/feature/build_the_wall_1.php.

6. Kevin Anderson, "US Newspapers: Print still pays the bills," *The Guardian*, June 12, 2009.

7. The mini-conference, part of a pattern of urgent gatherings of frightened managers and journalists organized by universities, foundations and think tanks, was held at the Donald W. Reynolds Journalism Institute of the University of Missouri, May 18 to 19, 2009.

8. Michael Kinsley, "You Can't Sell News by the Slice," *New York Times*, February 9, 2009.

9. Tom Gantert, "Newspapers Aren't the Only Form of Media Struggling," *Ann Arbor News*, March 23, 2009.

10. Sarkozy announced in a January 23, 2009, speech that "It is indeed [the state's] responsibility . . . to make sure an independent, free and pluralistic press exists." The president then announced a detailed plan to increase the French government's annual support for newspaper and magazine deliveries, dramatically increase spending for official advertisements in print publications and eliminate some fees the publications face. Sarkozy also proposed a pilot program to give teenagers celebrating their 18th birthday a free, yearlong subscription to any general news daily of their choice—with the state paying for delivery of the papers to the teens. Sarkozy portrayed the bailout as a temporary measure intended to stabilize newspapers while publications restructured their finances, embraced new technologies and trained journalists to work in multiple forms of media. For an extended description of Sarkozy's response, see Laurent Pirot's Associated Press report from Paris, "Sarkozy Gives French Print Media a Serious Boost," which was distributed January 23, 2009.

11. Oliver Burkeman, "US House speaker urges easing competition laws for newspapers," *The Guardian*, March 17, 2009.

12. Laurie Kellman, "Newspaper Reps Seeking Antitrust Relief Find Opposition," *Editor & Publisher*, April 22, 2009, http://www.editorandpublisher.com/eandp/news/article_display.jsp?vnu_content_id=1003964934.

13. Carl Shapiro, "A New Age for Newspapers: Diversity of Voices, Competition and the Internet" testimony given before the Subcommittee on Courts and Competition of the U.S. House Judiciary Committee, April 21, 2009.

14. See "Dereg is Key to Local TV's Survival: Executive Session with Gene Loving," TVNewsCheck.com, August 4, 2009.

15. "Chicago's Media," The Benton Foundation, http://www.benton.org/node/7186.

16. Mark Lloyd, "Media Maneuvers: Why the Rush to Waive Cross-Ownership Ban?" Center for American Progress, December 5, 2007.

17. See, for example, the following 2002 report of the Project for Excellence in Journalism: http://www.journalism.org/node/225. For excellent FCC filings on this matter, see Further Reply Comments of Consumers Union, Consumer Federation of America and Free Press, 2006 Quadrennial Regulatory Review—Review of the Commission's Broadcast Ownership Rules and Other Rules Adopted Pursuant to Section 202 of the

Telecommunications Act of 1996; 2002 Biennial Regulatory Review—Review of theCommission's Broadcast Ownership Rules and Other Rules Adopted Pursuant to Section 202 of the Telecommunications Act of 1996; Cross-Ownership of Broadcast Stations and Newspapers; Rules and Policies Concerning Multiple Ownership of Radio Broadcast Stations in Local Markets; Definition of Radio Markets, MB Docket Nos. 06-121, 04-228, 02-277; MM Docket Nos. 01-317, 01-235, 00-244, Nov. 1, 2007; Ex Parte Letter of Consumers Union, Consumer Federation of America and Free Press, Nov. 14, 2007, pp. 21–27.

18. "Does Bigger Media Equal Better Media? Four Academic Studies of Media Ownership in the United States," Benton Foundation/Social Science Research Council, October 2006.

19. John Eggeton, "FCC: Still Deciding on Newspaper/Broadcast Crossownership Rules," broadcastingcable.com, May 6, 2009.

20. Mark Fitzgerald, "Get Out of the Printing Business, Moody's Tells Newspapers," *Editor & Publisher*, June 4, 2009, http://www.editorandpublisher.com/eandp/news/article_display.jsp?vnu_content_id=1003980461.

21. See David Shedden, "New Media Timeline," *Poynter Online*, http://poynter .org/content/content_view.asp?id=75818; Shedden, the library director for the Poynter Institute, has done remarkable, almost archaeological, work in this area.

22. View the KRON report on YouTube at http://www.youtube.com/watch?v= 5WCTn4FljUQ.

23. Ibid.

24. Ibid.

25. Howard I. Finberg, "Before the Web, There Was Viewtron," *PoynterOnline*, October 29, 2003, http://www.poynter.org/content/content_view.asp?id=52769.

26. Ibid.

27. Frank Aherns, "Washington Post Newspaper Facing Losses in 2009, Chairman Says," *The Washington Post*, March 26, 2009. The *Post*, an industry leader, maintains what has been considered to be one of the most successful newspaper Web sites in the United States. For more on this, read Ahern's "Washington Post Co. Swings to First-Quarter Loss," May 1, 2009, which notes that "revenue at The Post's online properties—chiefly washingtonpost.com—dropped 8 percent in the quarter, the first decline in ad revenue at the online unit since at least 2004." Of course, this was a recessionary moment, but it is notable that ad revenues did not shift from the more expensive print "product" to the cheaper Web site; they disappeared. It is also important to note that, even if online ad revenues had continued to rise, they would not have been sufficient to offset losses on the print side; in other words: the Web is nowhere near a point where it might produce sufficient revenue to sustain the *Post* or, for that matter, other major newspaper operations.

28. See Mark Sweney, "Guardian Wins Three Webby Awards," *The Guardian*, May 5, 2009; and Eric Pfanner, "While Others Struggle, Norwegian Newspaper Publisher Thrives on the Web," *The New York Times*, February 19, 2007.

29. Martin Langeveld, "Paying for online news; Sorry, but the math just doesn't work," *Nieman Journalism Lab*, April 3, 2009.

30. Walter Isaacson, "How to Save Your Newspaper," *TIME*, February 5, 2009.

31. See Ryan Chittum, "Circulation Revenue Only Thing Growing at Newspapers," *Columbia Journalism Review* online, July 23, 2009, www.cjr.org.

32. "The State of the News Media 2009," Project for Excellence in Journalism. This quote comes from the introduction to the report. Examine the document online at http://www.stateofthemedia.org/2009/index.htm.

33. Clay Shirky, "Newspapers and Thinking the Unthinkable," shirky.com, March 2009.

34. All quotations from David B. Wilkerson, "Newspapers face pressure in selling online advertising. Ads need to be cheaper and more closely tied to performance, buyers say," *MarketWatch*, May 18, 2009.

35. Chris Elliott discussion with John Nichols, June 3, 2009.

36. Ibid.

37. Bob Garfield, "Future May Be Brighter, But It's Apocalypse Now," *Advertising Age*, March 23, 2009.

38. Gantert, "Newspapers aren't the only form of media struggling."

39. Mira Milosevic, discussion with John Nichols, June 3, 2009.

40. Brian Tierney reviewed concerns when he appeared with John Nichols before the House Judiciary Committee in April 2009. Said Tierney: "We're starting to realize that a lot of the assumptions that we were relying on just aren't going to play out that way we thought on the Web. That doesn't mean we're giving up. But we are being forced to explore very different approaches."

41. Langeveld, "Paying for online news; Sorry, but the math just doesn't work."

42. Mark Fitzgerald and Jennifer Saba, "NAA Leads Meeting of Newspaper Execs to Discuss Charging for Online Content," *Editor & Publisher*, May 28, 2009, http://www.editorandpublisher.com/eandp/search/article_display.jsp?vnu_content_id=1003977470.

43. Frank Rich, "Why the Press Is on Suicide Watch," *New York Times*, May 13, 2009.

44. See Yobie Benjamin, "Murdoch man who owns the news goes pay-per-view," SFGate,com, August 6, 2009.

45. Michael Wolff, "This is Rupert's Last Stand: Making You Pay," www.newser.com, August 6, 2009.

46. Joe Strupp, "'Post-Gazette' Editor: New 'Paid' Site is Whole New Flavor," *Editor & Publisher*, September 1, 2009.

47. Michael Kinsley, "You Can't Sell News by the Slice," *New York Times*, February 9, 2009.

48. Andrew Clark, "News Corp Will Charge for Newspaper Websites, Says Rupert Murdoch," *The Guardian*, May 7, 2009.

49. Bruce W. Sanford and Bruce D. Brown, "Laws That Could Save Journalism," *Washington Post*, May 16, 2009.

50. John Nichols, notes from "A New Age for Newspapers: Diversity of Voices, Competition and the Internet," hearing of the Subcommittee on the Courts and Competition Policy and the Internet, House Judiciary Committee, April 21, 2009. Nichols was among those testifying at the hearing. For details and links, visit http://judiciary.house.gov/hearings/hear_090421.html. Also, consider a snarky article by Dana Milbank that captured the sentiments of committee members, "In Congress, No Love Lost for Newspapers," *Washington Post*, April 22, 2009.

51. Aidan White to John Nichols, June 3, 2009.

52. For a cogent critique of paywalls, see Steve Buttry, "Seven reasons charging for content won't work," *Gazette*, stevebuttry.wordpress.com, May 29, 2009.

53. Arianna Huffington, "The Paywall Is History," *The Guardian*, May 11, 2009.

54. Chris Tryhorn, "Leading the Charge," *The Guardian*, May 11, 2009.

55. CommonDreams.org, a pioneering and innovative new aggregator site, was created by Craig Brown and his late wife, Lina Newhouser, more than a decade ago. It is just one example of what news aggregators do, but we think it's one of the best, and it has built a broad, loyal and supportive audience that would be the envy of many old-media operations. Veteran journalist Bill Moyers says, "CommonDreams.org is a must in my life and work." Visit the site at www.commondreams.org.

56. For an example of how the industry is attempting to crack down on commercial online "piracy" of news stories, see Saul Hansell. "Start-Up Plans to Make Journalism Pirates Pay Up," *New York Times*, July 27, 2009, p. B4.

57. See Art Brodsky, "Oh, the Hypocrisy: First Amendment Lawyers Would Destroy the Internet to Save Newspapers," *Huffington Post*, May 18, 2009, http://www.huffingtonpost.com/art-brodsky/oh-the-hypocrisy-first-am_b_204809.html.

58. Martin Langeveld, "Paying for online news; Sorry, but the math just doesn't work," *Nieman Journalism Lab*, April 3, 2009.

59. Kinsley, "You Can't Sell News by the Slice."

60. James Warren, "When No News Is Bad News," *The Atlantic Online*, January 2009.

61. Garfield, "Apocalypse Now."

62. For a discussion of the Internet's democratizing effect upon media, see Dan Gillmor, "Toward a (New) Media Literacy in a Media Saturated World," in Zizi Papacharissi, ed., *Journalism and Citizenship: New Agendas in Communication* (New York: Routledge, 2009), p. 1.

63. All quotations are from Shirky, "Newspapers and Thinking the Unthinkable." See also, Clay Shirky, "The Revolution Will Not Be Published," *Utne Reader*, July-August 2009, pp. 44-47.

64. Alexander Cockburn, "Who Needs Yesterday's Papers," *Creators Syndicate* column, May 15, 2009, www.creators.com.

65. Huffington, "The Paywall Is History."

66. Adam D. Thierer, "Socializing Media in Order to Save It," *City Journal*, March 27, 2009. www.city-journal.org.

67. Michael Kinsley, "Life After Newspapers," *The Washington Post*, April 6, 2009.

68. Yochai Benkler, "A New Era of Corruption?" *The New Republic*, March 4, 2009, http://www.tnr.com/story-print.html?id=c84d2eda-0e95-42fe-99a2-5400e7dd8eab. We agree that many costs have plummeted in online journalism, but we hardly think that obviates the need for extensive material resources for journalism, particularly labor costs; it just means we can get more bang for the buck.

69. Mark Fitzgerald, "Get Out of the Printing Business, Moody's Tells Newspapers," *Editor & Publisher*, June 4, 2009, http://www.editorandpublisher.com/eandp/news/article_display.jsp?vnu_content_id=1003980461.

70. Lawrence Lessig, *Free Culture: How Big Media Uses Technology and the Law to Lock Down Culture and Control Creativity* (New York: Penguin, 2004).

71. Scott Gant, *We're All Journalists Now* (New York: Free Press, 2007).

72. Amanda Michel, "Get Off the Bus," *Columbia Journalism Review*, March/April 2009, pp. 42-45.

73. Eric Newton to Robert W. McChesney, email, April 27, 2009.

74. Carroll Bogert, "Old Hands, New Voice," *Columbia Journalism Review*, March/April 2009, pp. 29-31.

75. Arnie Cooper, "Computing the Cost: Nicholas Carr on How the Internet Is Rewiring Our Brains," *The Sun*, March 2009, pp. 4-11. There is an important body of work that argues media technologies have important effects upon individuals and society, and that our enthusiasm for new technologies—often pushed by those that profit by them—can blind us to the negative consequences. Most important along these lines is Neil Postman, *Amusing Ourselves to Death: Public Discourse in the Age of Show Business* (New York: Penguin Books, 1985). Our sense is that Postman's arguments about the negative effects of television transitions well to a critique of the Internet. A recent book that takes this up is Andrea Batista Schlesinger, *The Death of Why? The Decline of Questioning and the Future of Democracy* (San Francisco: Berrett-Koehler, 2009).

76. Dave Zweifel discussion with John Nichols, April 1, 2008. Zweifel is the longtime editor of *The Capital Times* newspaper in Madison, Wisconsin, which shifted in the spring of 2008 from a daily print paper to an online publication with a weekly print publication. Nichols is an associate editor of *The Capital Times*.

77. As an example of "Martin's world," see Stephanie Clifford, "Ads Follow Web Users, and Get Deeply Personal," *New York Times*, July 31, 2009, pp. A1, A3. The extraordinary loss of privacy that the successful commercialization of the Internet apparently requires may well become one of the important to policy issues of the coming generation. We hope so. An encouraging sign is the newfound interest of the Bureau of Consumer Protection at the Federal Trade Commission in the matter. See Stephanie Clifford, "Fresh Views At Agency Overseeing Online Ads," *New York Times*, August 5, 2009, pp, B1, B5.

78. Comments of Joseph Turow, International Communication Association annual conference, Chicago, Illinois, May 22, 2009. In fairness to Benkler, although he is captivated by digital technology, he is not of the "magic" school, and he understands that for the Internet to be a democratic agency it requires policies to encourage that part of its potential. Peter Dahlgren makes a related argument that understands the promise of new technologies if the right policies are pursued in Peter Dahlgren, *Media and Political Engagement: Citizens, Communication, and Democracy* (New York: Cambridge University Press, 2009). Likewise, the case is made persuasively in Stephen Coleman and Jay G. Blumler, *The Internet and Democratic Citizenship: Theory, Practice and Policy* (New York: Cambridge University Press, 2009).

79. Cited in C. Wright Mills, *The Power Elite* (New York: Oxford University Press, 1956), p. 352.

80. Cass R. Sunstein, *Infotopia: How Many Minds Produce Knowledge* (New York: Oxford University Press, 2006); Yochai Benkler, *The Wealth of Networks: How Social Production Transforms Markets and Freedoms* (New Haven: Yale University Press, 2006); Lawrence Lessig, *Remix: Making Art and Commerce Thrive in the Hybrid Economy* (New York: Penguin, 2008).

81. In a manner of speaking it would be similar to the relationship between entertainers and artists and journalists. Many people learn about the world through art, culture, music and entertainment, as much as or more than they learn about it through journalism. But for artists and entertainers to make powerful statements on current events, they need to have a viable journalism to draw from and to play off of. They must make assumptions about a certain sufficient level of political knowledge in their audience or the community at large.

82. Chris Anderson, *Free: The Future of a Radical Price* (New York: Hyperion, 2009), p. 133.

83. Frank Hornig, "Who Needs Newspapers When You Have Twitter? Chris Anderson, Wired's editor in chief discusses the Internet's challenge to the traditional press," *Salon*, July 28, 2009.

84. See American Society of Newspaper Editors, 2009 Newsroom Employment Census, http://www.asne.org/index.cfm?id=7323.

85. In 2009 the Online News Association partnered with the Project for Excellence in Journalism to survey online journalists, producing a report based on responses from 292 members of the ONA from the United States and around the world, http://journalists.org/news/24401/ONA-News—Resources-Survey-results-Online-journalists-optimistic-about.htm.

86. Jennifer Saba, "Exclusive: Top 30 Global News Sites, by Unique Visitors," *Editor & Publisher*, April 17, 2009; Jennifer Saba, "Top 30 Global News Sites See Drop in Time Spent," *Mediaweek* online, June 25, 2009.

87. For a profile of Hamsher as a blogosphere innovator, see, "The Insider: Jane Hamsher," *The Washingtonian*, August 13, 2008.

88. Learn more about Wheeler's work and Hamsher's campaign at http://firedoglake.com/2009/04/21/go-organic-no-artificial-blogging-support-marcy-wheeler.

89. Greg Mitchell to Robert W. McChesney, e-mail, May 21, 2009.

90. Claire Cain Miller and Brad Stone, "News Without Newspapers," *New York Times*, April 13, 2009, pp. B1, B4.

91. Heidi Sinclair, "Media and Brand Supremacy: Why the New Media Brand Could Be Nike," *Huffington Post*, May 11, 2009.

92. Chris Anderson, in *Free*, makes the point that many bloggers are not motivated by money and are driven by the pleasure of writing, the prospect of having people read their work and getting a measure of recognition. We agree that salary is not the only factor that motivates people, and this has tended to be a weakness in conventional economic analysis. When time permits, one of us blogs extensively on professional basketball—under a nom de plume—and does so precisely for the reasons Anderson advances. The experience was made possible by the Internet and is a source of profound pleasure. But the quality of this blogging depends to some extent on the existence of professional basketball writers who have the time and access to get information unavailable to the amateur blogger. It also depends upon having a "day job" to pay the bills, which limits the amount of blogging dramatically. For example, the blogging stopped during the course of writing this book. One can only wonder what the quality and quantity of Anderson's uncompensated blogging would be if he had no income and no savings and he had young mouths to feed and a pile of bills staring him in the face. It may be fine to have our coverage of the National Basketball Association run on volunteer labor; there is still not a shred of evidence that

this could possibly work for journalism. We do know that when the volunteer bloggers have to turn to their day jobs to pay their bills, the good folks working for PR firms will be at the ready with their very sophisticated material to flood cyberspace.

93. Chris Bowers, "Do We Need To Save Newspapers, Or Just Unionize Bloggers?" *OpenLeft*, March 26, 2009. http://www.openleft.com/showDiary.do?diaryId=12498.

94. Public Broadcasting Revenue Reports, Corporation for Public Broadcasting, http://www.cpb.org/stations/reports/revenue.

95. Charles Lewis, "The Non-Profit Road," *Columbia Journalism Review*, September/October 2007; Vince Stehle, "It's Time for Newspapers to Become Nonprofit Organizations," *The Chronicle of Philanthropy*, March 18, 2009.

96. The three groups are ProPublica, the Center for Public Integrity and the Center for Investigative Reporting. The report: Jan Schaffer, *New Media Makers: A Toolkit for Innovators in Community Media and Grant Making* (Washington, D.C.: American University, June 2009). The report was funded by the John S. and James L. Knight Foundation.

97. Public Broadcasting Revenue Reports, Corporation for Public Broadcasting, http://www.cpb.org/stations/reports/revenue.

98. Charles Lewis, "A Social-Network Solution," *Columbia Journalism Review*, March/April 2009, p. 27.

99. Richard Perez-Pena, "New York Times Plans to Cut 100 Newsroom Jobs," February 14, 2008.

100. The Newspaper Guild-CWA, "TNG Salary Database."

101. Saul Hansell, "The Associated Press to Set Guidelines for Using Its Articles in Blogs," *New York Times*, June 16, 2008.

102. "NYTimes.com Masthead." http://www.nytimes.com/ref/membercenter/help/webmasthead.html.

103. James Surowiecki, "News You Can Lose," *The New Yorker*, December 22, 2008.

104. Matt Drudge with Julia Phillips, *Drudge Manifesto,* (Penguin, 2004).

105. Todd Purdum, "The Dangers of Dishing Dirt in Cyberspace," *New York Times,* August 17, 1997.

106. Ibid.

107. Matt Drudge, "Over One Billion Served," *The Drudge Report*, November 12, 2002.

108. Purdum, "The Dangers of Dishing Dirt in Cyberspace."

109. Philip Weiss, "Watching Matt Drudge," *New York*, August 27, 2007.

110. Camille Paglia, "Ask Camille," *Salon*, September 1, 1998, http://archive.salon.com/col/pagl/1998/09/01pagl2.html.

111. Mark Halperin and John F. Harris, *The Way To Win* (New York: Random House: 2006).

112. See http://www.talkingpointsmemo.com.

113. To get a feel for Marshall's style and effective approach to the Lott scandal, check out archived TPM material at http://www.talkingpointsmemo.com/archives/week_2002_12_01.php.

114. Noam Cohen, "Blogger, Sans Pajamas, Rakes Muck and a Prize," *New York Times,* February 25, 2009. Follow Dan Kennedy's work at http://medianation.blogspot.com.

115. Matthew Rothschild (ed.), *Democracy in Print: The Best of The Progressive Magazine, 1909–2009* (Madison: University of Wisconsin Press, 2009).

116. The Center for Public Integrity received a Polk Award for Internet reporting in 2003, but TPM's was the first for an Internet-only news operation.

117. Mark Walsh, "Huffington Post, Politico Top Political Sites," *Online Media Daily*, October 23, 2008.

118. Cohen, "Blogger, Sans Pajamas, Rakes Muck and a Prize."

119. Josh Marshall, "The Growth of Talking Points Memo: A Case Study in Independent Media," inaugural address, Park Center for Independent Media, September 15-16, 2008.

120. Ibid.

121. Noam Cohen, "New Hiring At Talking Points Memo," *New York Times*, July 12, 2009.

122. See www.huffingtonpost.com.

123. Howard Kurtz, "A Blog That Made It Big: The Huffington Post, Trending Up and Left," *Washington Post*, July 9, 2007.

124. *Slate*, online home to the brilliant legal writer Dahlia Lithwick, and *Salon*, home to the equally brilliant legal writer Glenn Greenwald, are a pair of high-profile projects that have struggled to unlock the mysteries of the Internet. Both contain smart mixes of original reporting and commentary and offer commendable models for Web magazines, except when it comes to the economics. In its first decade, *Salon* lost more than $80 million, although it has found some success in recent years by peddling content via "premium subscriptions" and a "hybrid subscription" model that requires visitors to the site to view a 15-second full-screen advertisement in order to earn a "day pass" and read the article they are interested in.

125. Arianna Huffington, D: All Things Digital conference, panel discussion that also featured Washington Post Media's Katharine Weymouth, May 28, 2009.

126. Kurtz, "A Blog That Made It Big: The Huffington Post, Trending Up and Left."

127. James Rainey, "Barack Obama Can Thank 'Citizen Journalist' for 'Bitter' Tempest," *The Los Angeles Times*, April 15, 2008. For an excellent review of this episode and the entire role of the blogosphere in politics and political reporting, see Eric Boehlert, *Bloggers on the Bus: How the Internet Changed Politics and the Press* (New York: Free Press, 2009), ch. 10.

128. Kara Swisher, "Huffington Post Hires CNET Vet Jai Singh as Managing Editor," *Wall Street Journal Digital Network*, April 28, 2009.

129. Anthony Arthur, *Radical Innocent: Upton Sinclair* (New York: Random House, 2006), p. 43.

130. Huffington, D: All Things Digital conference.

131. David Bauder, "Huffington Post Launches Investigative Journalism Venture," Associated Press, March 29, 2009.

132. "New Non-Profit Investigative News Organization to Be Led by Paul Steiger," ProPublica, October 15, 2007.

133. Interviews with Andy Hall of the Wisconsin Center for Investigative Journalism and other reporters by John Nichols, spring 2006. For the best analysis of these projects, keep an eye on David Westphal's "Online Journalism Review" blogging at the Knight Digital Media Center site: http://www.ojr.org/ojr/people/davidwestphal.

134. See http://www.propublica.org.

135. "AP to Publish Investigative Stories From Nonprofits," Associated Press, June 13, 2009.

136. As an example of the challenges faced by even the top projects of this sort, it should be noted that the Center for Public Integrity—which *Slate* media critic Jack Shafer described as having "broken as many stories as almost any big-city daily in the last couple of decades"—experienced serious economic turmoil after founder Chuck Lewis stepped down as executive director in early 2005. By the end of 2006, according to Lewis, the full-time staff had been reduced by a third and the annual deficit was over $1.5 million. The center survived, but only after going through what David Westphal describes as "a near-death experience."

137. See http://www.voiceofsandiego.org and http://www.minnpost.com.

138. John Nichols discussions with Eric Black, February 2009.

139. David Westphal, "New Grassroots Life for Investigative Reporting?" *Online Journalism Review*, Knight Digital Media Center, April 9, 2009, http://www.ojr.org/ojr/people/davidwestphal/200904/1693/.

140. "The Press: Who's Pushing?" *TIME*, April 22, 1946.

141. Westphal, "New Grassroots Life for Investigative Reporting?"

142. Thomas Jefferson, letter to Lafayette, *The Writings of Thomas Jefferson, Memorial Edition* (Washington, D.C.: 1903-04), vol. 15, p. 491.

143. Thierer, "Socializing Media in Order to Save It."

144. The classic statement is Paul A. Samuelson, "The Pure Theory of Public Expenditure," *Review of Economics and Statistics* 36 (4) (1954): pp. 387–389. Another classic work from that period is John Kenneth Galbraith, *The Affluent Society* (Boston: Houghton Mifflin, 1958), especially chapters 18-22.

145. James Hamilton, *All the News That's Fit to Sell* (Princeton: Princeton University Press, 2006), pp. 8-9. See also, for example, the work of leading media-policy expert Mark Cooper: "The Future of Journalism Is Not in the Past," *Huffington Post*, April 14, 2009.

146. For a good discussion of externalities and media, see Edward S. Herman, "The Externalities Effects of Commercial and Public Broadcasting," in Kaarle Nordenstreng and Herbert I. Schiller (eds.), *Beyond National Sovereignty: International Communication in the 1990s* (Norwood, NJ: Ablex, 1993), pp. 84-115.

147. Ben Scott has provided a way to use externalities to rethink the relationship of journalism to advertising and commercial media. Rather than think of the relationship between media owners and journalism consumers as the primary industry, think of the primary industry as the relationship between media owners and advertisers, since this produces the lion's share of revenue for most major news media. Media owners make their profits by selling space and time to advertisers. They produce whatever editorial content they think will appeal to the audience that generates the most advertising revenues. (As Scott points out, this is not an inaccurate way to regard most newspaper publishers in the 1920s, his period of research, and it certainly captures the modern media corporation.) Advertisers purchase ad time and space where they think they will get the most bang for their buck, sell the most of their products. They, too, are indifferent

to the content as long as it sells products. Journalism, in this context, is the externality to the market relationship between media owners and advertisers. It simply was the content that produced the best commercial results.

Journalism is both a positive and negative externality. To the extent it creates ample quality content that makes our governing system work and people generally happier, freer and more engaged with their communities and the world, it is very much a positive externality. To the extent the market process warps journalism and produces sensationalism, propaganda and dubious content, it can have the opposite effect. This has been the great debate over commercially supported journalism for the past century.

But what is important in Scott's formulation is that the journalism itself is external to the central market transaction. And now that media owners have decided to lowball or redirect the production of journalism and advertisers have decided to look elsewhere to better achieve their commercial goals, there is simply much less journalism to be found. It was always a dependent variable on commercial goals that had no intrinsic interest in journalism or democracy. This explains our current crisis. We are back to the public-good scenario: what do we do when the market cannot make a profit producing something we desperately need?

148. The conclusion: "Public broadcasting was hailed by most respondents as a wonderful resource that avoided virtually all of the pitfalls of commercial media. Its news programs are viewed as objective and informative with no sensationalism, its commercial-free format is widely appreciated, and it offers quality educational content for children and adults alike. And yet, aside from a handful of passionate advocates, the vast majority acknowledged that they rarely, if ever, watch public broadcasting (except with their children) or tune in NPR, saying they simply do not think of it as an option on a daily basis and feel it is perhaps too dry. For all of their complaints about sensationalism, some grudgingly acknowledge they want to be entertained by their news." Gerstein Agne Strategic Communications, "Media Reform Focus Groups: Understanding Public Attitudes and Building Public Support for Media Reform," June 1, 2005, http://www.freepress.net/files/focus_groups.pdf.

149. Roper Public Opinion Poll on PBS, January 2009.

150. See http://www.infrastructurereportcard.org.

151. Bob Herbert, "Risking the Future," *New York Times*, February 2, 2009.

152. See Robert W. McChesney, *The Political Economy of Media: Enduring Issues, Emerging Dilemmas* (New York: Monthly Review Press, 2008), ch. 5, for a discussion of this point.

153. See Justin Fox, *The Myth of the Rational Market: A History of Risk, Reward, and Delusion on Wall Street* (New York: HarperBusiness, 2009).

154. See Dean Baker, *Plunder and Blunder: The Rise and Fall of the Bubble Economy* (Sausalito, Cal.: PoliPoint Press, 2009), p. 3; David Lereah, *Why the Real Estate Boom Will Not Bust – And How You Can Profit From It: How to Build Wealth in Today's Expanding Real Estate Market* (New York: Broadway Business, 2005).

155. Dean Baker, "Midsummer Meltdown: Prospects for the Stock and Housing Markets," Center for Economic and Policy Research, Washington, DC, August 2007, p. 5, table 2, http://www.cepr.net/documents/publications/DB_Midsummer%20Meltdown %20Final.pdf.

156. David Lereah, *The Rules for Growing Rich: Making Money in the New Information Economy* (Crown Books, 2000).

157. In his final book, the great John Kenneth Galbraith sounded the alarm for precisely the sort of corrupt crony capitalism that results from unchecked corporate power over the government, a power that results from and perpetuates a hollowed out journalism, especially on economic matters. See John Kenneth Galbraith, *The Economics of Innocent Fraud: Truth for Our Time* (Boston: Houghton Mifflin, 2004).

158. James Carey, "American Journalism on, before, and after September 11," in Barbie Zelizer and Stuart Allan (eds.), *Journalism After September 11* (New York: Routledge, 2002), p. 89.

159. Todd Gitlin, "A Surfeit of Crises: Circulation, Revenue, Attention, Authority, and Deference," keynote address to Journalism in Crisis conference, University of Westminster, London, England, May 19, 2009.

Chapter 3

1. Walter Lippmann, *Liberty and the News* (Princeton: Princeton University Press, 2007). For more on this, see Sidney Blumenthal's thoughtful afterward in which he writes, "The gap between Lippmann's ideals and present realities is one of the major reasons why *Liberty and the News* remains so pertinent—and so troubling—nearly ninety years after its publication."

2. See Henry Milner, *Civic Literacy: How Informed Citizens Make Democracy Work* (Medford, MA: Tufts University Press, 2002).

3. Timothy E. Cook, "Freeing the Presses: An Introductory Essay," in Timothy E. Cook (ed.), *Freeing the Presses: The First Amendment in Action* (Baton Rouge: Louisiana State University Press, 2005), p. 2.

4. When drafted and ratified, the Bill of Rights and First Amendment were primarily concerned with protecting the majority from the few, and providing structural support to make that possible. See Akhil Reed Amar, *The Bill of Rights: Creation and Reconstruction* (New Haven: Yale University Press, 1998).

5. See, for one example, M. L. Stein, *Freedom of the Press: A Continuing Struggle* (New York: Julian Messner, 1966), p. 18. Many, perhaps most, studies of freedom of speech and freedom of the press concentrate overwhelmingly on the former, and extend the lessons from speech cases to the press with little or no qualification.

6. Bree Nordenson, "The Uncle Sam Solution," *Columbia Journalism Review*, September/October 2007.

7. See Rutherfurd Livingston, *John Peter Zenger: His Press, His Trial and a Bibliography of Zenger Imprints* (New York: Dodd, Mead & Company, 1904) and Paul Simon, *Freedom's Champion: Elijah Lovejoy* (Carbondale: Southern Illinois University Press, 1994) as compelling examples of this trend.

8. "The Trial of John Peter Zenger," The Historical Society of the Courts of the State of New York. Materials can be found online at http://www.courts.state.ny.us/history/zenger.htm.

9. Horace Greeley, *The American Conflict: A History of the Great Rebellion in the United States of America, 1860-64: Its Causes, Incidents, and Results: Intended to Exhibit Especially*

Its Moral and Political Phases, with the Drift and Progress of American Opinion Respecting Human Slavery from 1776 to the Close of ... (Chicago: O.D. Case & Company, 1864), p. 135.

10. See, for the best treatment of this topic, Victor W. Pickard, "'Whether the Giants Should Be Slain or Persuaded to Be Good': Revisiting the Hutchins Commission and the Role of Media in a Democratic Society," *Critical Studies in Media Communication,* forthcoming, 2009; Victor W. Pickard, "Media Democracy Deferred: The Postwar Settlement for U.S. Communications, 1945-1949," Ph.D. dissertation, University of Illinois, 2008, pp. 350-439.

11. William Ernest Hocking, *Freedom of the Press: A Framework of Principle* (Chicago: University of Chicago Press, 1947), pp. 11-12.

12. Fred S. Siebert, Theodore Peterson and Wilbur Schramm, *Four Theories of the Press* (Urbana: University of Illinois Press, 1956), p. 52.

13. The term "laissez-faire" has been loaded up with a greater meaning than it had in the late 18th and early 19th centuries, as Richard John observes. It meant at the time "open entry" and nothing more. Richard John to Robert W. McChesney, email communication, July 8, 2009. See also Ronald E. Seavoy, "Laissez-Fairre: Business Policy, Corporations, and Capital Investment in the Early National Period," In Jack Greene, ed., *Encyclopedia of American Political History* (New York: Scribner's, 1984).

14. Robert W.T. Martin, *The Free and Open Press: The Founding of American Press Liberty, 1640-1800* (New York: New York University Press, 2001), pp. 4-5.

15. Cook, *Freeing the Presses*, p. 8.

16. Martin, *The Free and Open Press*, p. 8.

17. Ibid., p. 168.

18. See Charles E. Clark, *The Public Prints: The Newspaper in Anglo-American Culture, 1665-1740* (New York: Oxford University Press, 1994).

19. Cited in Cook, *Freeing the Presses*, p. 8.

20. Benjamin Frankin, *The Pennsylvania Gazette*, June 10, 1731, quoted in Richard Rosenfeld, *American Aurora: A Democratic Republican Returns* (New York: St. Martin's Press, 1997). Rosenfeld's book provides an essential link to the era. Rosenfeld refers to his book as "The suppressed history of our nation's founding and the heroic newspaper that tried to report it." John Nichols reviewed the book on its publication and wrote, "This is heady stuff, filled with monumental intrigues and twists of fate on which turned the very idea of America as we know it." But, of course, we cannot "know it" as completely as we should without leaping over contemporary misinterpretations and getting to the reality of the roots of our free press.

21. Personal correspondence, Robert W.T. Martin to Robert W. McChesney, April 24, 2009.

22. Our point is not to exaggerate the commitment of the founding generation to informed self-government. One can find practices and attitudes in this era that would raise the eyebrows of any democrat, then and now. The importance of the founders is not that they were perfect and their words need to be hung on to like biblical prophecy. It is, rather, that they went about the very real business of building a nation on a constitution, and how they regarded the role of the press and its relationship to government is of tremendous value as we understand how we got to where we are today, and what

our options are going forward. Even if the founders had messed up the task of building a free press, we would need to study the period.

23. See Philip S. Foner (ed.), *The Democratic-Republican Societies, 1790-1800: A Documentary Sourcebook of Constitutions, Declarations, Addresses, Resolutions, and Toasts* (Westport, CT: Greenwood Press, 1976).

24. Louis Edward Inglebart, *Press Freedoms: A Descriptive Calendar of Concepts, Interpretations, Events, and Court Actions, from 4000 B.C. to the Present* (Westport, CT: Greenwood Press, 1987), p. 152; Robert W.T. Martin, "Between Consensus and Conflict: Habermas, Post-Modern Agonism and the Early American Public Sphere," *Polity* (Vol. 37, No. 3), July 2005, pp. 380-381.

25. Tunis Wortman, *A Treatise Concerning Political Enquiry and the Liberty of the Press* (New York: George Forman, 1800), available through the American Imprint Collection (Library of Congress), pp. 23-24.

26. Cited in Martin, "Between Consensus and Conflict," p. 383.

27. Michael Merrill and Sean Wilentz (eds.), *The Key of Liberty: The Life and Democratic Writings of William Manning, "A Laborer," 1747-1814* (Cambridge, MA: Harvard University Press, 1993).

28. Thomas Jefferson, letter to James Monroe, October 19, 1823, in Paul Leicester Ford (ed.), *The Works of Thomas Jefferson*. Federal Edition. (G.P. Putnam's Sons, 1904-5), 12 vols., XII, p. 316. This point has been made convincingly in Michael Schudson, *Why Democracies Need an Unlovable Press* (Cambridge, UK: Polity Press, 2008), chapter 5.

29. Madison and Jefferson were hardly naïve about the press in practice and both were capable of being quite critical of it during their lifetimes. Jefferson was especially appalled by the press during his presidency, once writing: "The man who reads nothing at all is better educated than the man who reads nothing but newspapers." But that point did not deter Jefferson from his commitment to the necessity of a vibrant press system. Quotation from Jones, *Losing the News*, p. 52.

30. Cited in Ralph Ketcham, *James Madison: A Biography* (Charlottesville: University of Virginia Press, 1990), p. 401.

31. As more than one wag has commented, in 2009, Jefferson's worst nightmare may indeed come true.

32. Thomas Jefferson, letter to William Green Munford, June 18, 1799, from Dumas Malone, *Jefferson and His Time* (Boston: Little, Brown, 1948-1981), vol. III, p. 418.

33. *Papers of Thomas Jefferson*, vol. 11: 48-49.

34. Cited in Richard W. Van Alstyne, *The Rising American Empire* (New York: Quadrangle Books, 1960), p. 1.

35. Cited in John Nichols (ed.), *Against the Beast: A Documentary History of American Opposition to Empires* (New York: Nation Books, 2005), p. 14.

36. Eric Burns, *Infamous Scribblers: The Founding Fathers and the Rowdy Beginnings of American Journalism* (New York: PublicAffairs, 2006), pp. 26-27. See also Ian Kenneth Steele, *The English Atlantic, 1675-1740: An Exploration of Communication and Community* (New York: Oxford University Press, 1986).

37. Timothy E. Cook, "Public Policy Toward the Press: What Government Does for the News Media," in Geneva Overholser and Kathleen Hall Jamieson (eds.), *The Press*

(Oxford and New York: Oxford University Press, 2005), p. 252. See also Bernard Bailyn and John B. Hench, eds., *The Press and the American Revolution* (Boston: Northeastern University Press, 1980).

38. Benno C. Schmidt Jr., *Freedom of the Press vs. Public Access* (New York: Praeger, 1976), p. 38.

39. Craig Nelson, *Thomas Paine: Enlightenment, Revolution and the Birth of Modern Nations* (New York: Penguin, 2006), pages 65-66, 78-80. It was Rush who suggested the title *Common Sense* for Paine's revolutionary pamphlet.

40. See Benjamin Rush, *Address to the People of the United States* (1787), available at http://teachingamericanhistory.org/library/index.asp?document=1779.

41. George Washington, letter to Mathew Carey, found in Earl Lockridge Bradsher, *Mathew Carey, Editor, Author and Publisher: A Study in American Literary Development* (New York: Columbia University Press, 1912).

42. Richard R. John, *Spreading the News: The American Postal System from Franklin to Morse* (Cambridge, MA: Harvard University Press, 1995). John's research has been of singular importance to our argument. See also Richard R. John, "Post Office," in Paul Finkelman, ed., *Encyclopedia of the New American Nation, Vol. 2* (Detroit: Charles Scribner's Sons, 2006), pp. 575-578; Richard R. John, "Governmental Institutions as Agents of Change: Rethinking American Political Development in the Early Republic, 1787-1835," *Studies in American Political Development*, Vol. 11 (Fall 1997): pp. 347-380.

43. Theda Skocpol, "The Tocqueville Problem: Civic Engagement in American Democracy," *Social Science History* 21(4) (1997): 455-79.

44. Christopher W. Shaw, *Preserving the People's Post Office* (Washington, D.C.: Essential Books, 2006), p. 8.

45. Culver H. Smith, *The Press, Politics, and Patronage* (Athens: University of Georgia, 1977), p. 9.

46. Kelly B. Olds, "The Challenge to the U.S. Postal Monopoly, 1839-1851," *Cato Journal*, vol. 15, no. 1 (Spring-Summer 1995).

47. David M. Henkin, *The Postal Age: The Emergence of Modern Communications in Nineteenth-Century America* (Chicago: University of Chicago Press, 2006), p. 42.

48. Cited in Richard B. Kielbowicz, *News in the Mail: The Press, Post Office, and Public Information, 1700–1860s* (Westport, CT: Greenwood Press, 1989), p. 35.

49. *Aurora General Advertiser*, October 2, 1790, quoted in Richard Rosenfeld's *American Aurora: A Democratic Republican Returns* (New York: St. Martin's Press, 1997), p. 524.

50. Cited in Kielbowicz, *News in the Mail*, p. 35.

51. This is discussed in Mark Lloyd, *Prologue to a Farce: Communication and Democracy in America* (Urbana: University of Illinois Press, 2007), pp. 30-31.

52. Thomas Jefferson, "First Annual Message to Congress," in *A Compilation of the Messages and Papers of the Presidents Prepared under the direction of the Joint Committee on printing, of the House and Senate Pursuant to an Act of the Fifty-Second Congress of the United States* (New York: Bureau of National Literature, Inc., 1897).

53. See Kevin G. Barnhurst and John Nerone, *The Form of News: A History* (New York: Guilford, 2001), chapter 2.

54. Ithiel de sola Pool, *Technologies of Freedom* (Cambridge: Harvard University Press, 1983), p. 77.

55. Quotation from Timothy E. Cook, "Public Policy Toward the Press: What Government Does for the News Media," in Geneva Overholser and Kathleen Hall Jamieson (eds.), *The Press* (Oxford and New York: Oxford University Press, 2005), p. 253.

56. Cook, *Governing with the News*, pp. 40-44.

57. Smith, *The Press, Politics, and Patronage*, p. 6.

58. Ibid., p. 8.

59. John, *Spreading the News*, chap. 2.

60. Henkin, *The Postal Age)*p. 42.

61. Elizabeth Hewitt, *Correspondence and American Literature, 1770-1865* (Cambridge, UK: Cambridge University Press, 2004), p. 115.

62. Ibid., p. 115.

63. Harriet Beecher Stowe, *Dred: A Tale of the Great Dismal Swamp* (Boston: Phillips, Sampson and Company, 1856), as noted in Hewitt, *Correspondence and American Literature, 1770-1865*, p. 115.

64. John, *Spreading the News*, chapter 2.

65. Ian C. Friedman, *Freedom of Speech and the Press* (New York: Facts On File, 2005), p. 23.

66. See, for example, Jeffrey L. Pasley, *"The Tyranny of Printers": Newspaper Politics in the Early American Republic* (Charlottesville: University Press of Virginia, 2001), p. 202.

67. Alexis de Tocqueville, *Democracy in America* (New York: Signet Classics, 2001), p. 93.

68. Cited in Mark Lloyd, *Prologue to a Farce: Communication and Democracy in America* (Urbana: University of Illinois Press, 2006), p. 33.

69. Cook, *Governing with the News*, p. 44.

70. This is a subtle point. Subsidies obviously favored those without the resources to survive otherwise, so they favored those without means. And specific subsidies could favor one class of newspapers over another, and that would possibly have indirect consequences for favoring certain groups of people and political viewpoints. But at no point were postal subsidies capable of specifying which viewpoints were eligible and which were not. A complete subsidy—free postage for all publications—would have eliminated the concern, except for those who thought those without means should not participate in the press.

71. For sources see Appendix III.

72. See Pasley, *"The Tyranny of Printers."*

73. See Kevin G. Barnhurst and John Nerone, *The Form of News: A History* (New York: Guilford, 2001), chapter 2.

74. Marcus Daniel, *Scandal and Civility: Journalism and the Birth of American Democracy* (New York: Oxford University Press, 2009).

75. Smith, *The Press, Politics, and Patronage*, pp. 256-274.

76. Ibid., pp. 250-254.

77. *Bicentennial Edition: Historical Statistics of the US, Colonial Times to 1970.*

78. John Nerone to Robert W. McChesney, e-mail, May 18, 2009.

79. Louis Edward Inglebart, *Press Freedoms: A Descriptive Calendar of Concepts, Interpretations, Events, and Court Actions, from 4000 B.C. to the Present* (Westport, CT: Greenwood Press, 1987), p. 157.

80. Cook, *Governing with the News*, pp. 26-32.

81. Frank Luther Mott, *American Journalism* (New York: The Macmillan Company, 1962), chapter 9.

82. See Thomas L. Brasher's *Whitman as Editor of the Brooklyn Daily Eagle* (Detroit: Wayne State University Press, 1970) and a collection edited by Emory Holloway and Vernolian Schwarz, *I Sit and Look Out: Editorials from the Brooklyn Daily Times* (New York: Columbia University Press, 1932).

83. Brasher, *Whitman as Editor*, p. 6.

84. See Henry Milner, *Civic Literacy*.

85. Floyd Stovall (ed.), *Prose Works 1892* (New York: New York University Press, 1963–1964), vol. 1, p. 288.

86. Jerome Loving, *Walt Whitman: The Song of Himself* (Berkeley: University of California Press, 1999), p. 145.

87. John Nerone to Robert W. McChesney, e-mail, May 18, 2009.

88. Gerald J. Baldasty, *The Commercialization of News in the Nineteenth Century* (Madison: University of Wisconsin Press, 1992).

89. William E. Ames, *A History of the National Intelligencer* (Chapel Hill: University of North Carolina Press, 1972), p. 345.

90. Smith, *The Press, Politics, and Patronage*, p. 8.

91. Harry G. Good and James D. Teller, eds., *A History of American Education*, 3rd ed. (New York: Macmillan, 1973), p. 85.

92. See Sarah Mondale and Sarah B. Patton, *School: The Story of American Public Education* (Boston: Beacon Press, 2001).

93. Smith, *The Press, Politics, and Patronage*, p. 11.

94. Smith, *The Press, Politics, and Patronage*, p. 245.

95. Research conducted by C. Edwin Baker. Baker took information for the 1913 subsidy from the Supreme Court's report on what was said in the government's brief in *Lewis v. Morgon*, 229 US 288 (1913) at 304. He then factored in inflation and population growth.

96. Personal communication, Richard John to Robert W. McChesney, April 2, 2009.

97. See Robert W. McChesney, John Bellamy Foster, Inger L. Stole and Hannah Holleman, "The Sales Effort and Monopoly Capital," *Monthly Review*, vol. 60, no. 11, April 2009, pp. 1-23.

98. For sources see Appendix III.

99. Source: Newspapers: 1869: *Geo. P. Rowell and Co.'s American Newspaper Directory* (New York: Geo. P. Rowell & Co., 1869; 1890–1930: *N.W. Ayer & Son's American Newspaper Annual* (Philadelphia: N.W. Ayer & Son, annual directories.

100. Abbott Joseph Liebling, "Do You Belong in Journalism?" *The New Yorker*, May 4, 1960.

101. For sources see Appendix III.

102. This point was explained well by Ben H. Bagdikian in his classic *The Media Monopoly* (Boston: Beacon Press, 1983). The book has enjoyed numerous updated editions.

103. For sources see Appendix III.

104. "Timeline: NYC Newspapers of General Circulation, 1900–1967," New York Public Library (Research Guides: New York City Newspapers), http://www.nypl.org/research/chss/grd/resguides/newspapers/nyc.html.

105. See "Chronicling America: Historic American Newspapers," The Library of Congress (in conjunction with the National Endowment for the Humanities as part of the National Digital Newspaper Program).

106. See Robert W. McChesney and Ben Scott (eds.), *Our Unfree Press: 100 Years of Radical Media Criticism* (New York: The New Press, 2004).

107. Victor W. Pickard, "'Whether the Giants Should Be Slain or Persuaded to Be Good': Revisiting the Hutchins Commission and the Role of Media in a Democratic Society," *Critical Studies in Media Communication,* forthcoming, 2009.

108. Robert D. Leigh (ed.), *A Free and Responsible Press: A General Report on Mass Communication: Newspapers, Radio, Motion Pictures, and Books by the Commission on Freedom of the Press* (Chicago: University of Chicago Press, 1947), p. 80. The report did condone the use of government antitrust power to break up media monopolies.

109. Cited in Julianne Schultz, *Reviving the Fourth Estate: Democracy, Accountability and the Media* (Cambridge, UK: Cambridge University Press, 1998), p. 230.

110. For sources see Appendix III.

111. See McChesney and Scott, *Our Unfree Press.*

112. See *Changing Media: Public Interest Policies for the Digital Age* (Washington, D.C.: Free Press, 2009), p. 215. We return to this topic in Chapter 4.

113. See Duane C. S. Stoltzfus, *Freedom from Advertising: E. W. Scripps's Chicago Experiment* (Urbana: University of Illinois Press, 2007).

114. See Linda Lawson, *Truth in Publishing: Federal Regulation of the Press's Business Practices, 1880-1920* (Carbondale: Southern Illinois Press, 1993).

115. See David T. Z. Mindich, *Just the Facts: How "Objectivity" Came to Define American Journalism* (New York: New York University Press, 1998).

116. See Paul Alfred Pratte, *Gods Within the Machine: A History of the American Society of Newspaper Editors, 1923-1993* (Westport, CT: Praeger, 1995).

117. Among academics, only the most visionary of 1930s observers expressed concern about consolidated newspaper ownership, and even then gently. "What are the social implications of dailies printed in a relatively few, closely-held plants?" inquired the young sociologist Alfred McClung Lee in his book, *The Daily Newspaper in America,* which noted that the mergers by the time Lee was writing in the mid-1930s were leaving more and more communities that had once known vibrant journalistic competition with just one newspaper. "Does a single newspaper continue to serve the various minorities of a community sufficiently well to stave off demands for governmental tampering? Can a single newspaper adjust to the changing needs of a majority of people in its field? Does a more and more closely-integrated industry meet the demands of changing economic, political and social conditions as well as the more loosely bound together, competing dailies of a century or even fifty years ago?" See Arthur McClung Lee, *The*

Daily Newspaper in America: The Evolution of a Social Instrument (New York: Macmillan, 1937), p. 95.

118. "The Press: Editors Line Up," *TIME*, September 2, 1940.

119. "The Press: Editor's Afterthoughts," *TIME*, November 16, 1936.

120. Joseph Pulitzer (ed.), *St. Louis Post-Dispatch Symposium on Freedom of the Press* (St. Louis: St. Louis Post-Dispatch, 1938). We found this material in Ben Scott, "A New Deal for Journalism," PhD dissertation, University of Illinois at Urbana-Champaign, 2009.

121. "Ickes Charges News Distortion By Press in Air Debate," *Editor & Publisher*, January 21, 1939, p. 4.

122. "President Hits Press Subsidy Of Low Mail Rates," *Christian Science Monitor*, January 8, 1938, p. 3.

123. William Allen White, "Don't Indulge in Name-Calling With Press Critics," *Editor & Publisher*, April 22, 1939, p. 14.

124. "The Press: The Newspaper Collector Samuel Newhouse," *TIME*, July 27, 1962. Note the assumption that there are exactly two and only two legitimate sides to an issue.

125. Bureau of Labor Statistics, U.S. Department of Labor, Occupational Employment Statistics, http://bls.gov/OES (accessed June 12, 2009).

126. Timothy E. Cook, "Public Policy Toward the Press: What Government Does For the News Media," in Geneva Overholser and Kathleen Hall Jamieson (eds.), *The Press* (Oxford and New York: Oxford University Press, 2005), p. 257.

127. Inger L. Stole, *Advertising on Trial: Consumer Activism and Corporate Public Relations in the 1930s* (Urbana: University of Illinois Press, 2006). See also Inger L. Stole, *A War on Many Fronts: Advertising, Its Critics and the Government during World War II* (Urbana: University of Illinois Press, forthcoming, 2011).

128. NBC was split into two and the American Broadcasting Company was born in the early 1940s.

129. "American Broadcasting," in *B.B.C. Year-book* (London: The British Broadcasting Corporation, 1932), p. 47.

130. This episode is described in detail in Robert W. McChesney, *Telecommunications, Mass Media, and Democracy: The Battle for the Control of U.S. Broadcasting, 1928-1935* (New York: Oxford University Press, 1993).

131. Caldwell insisted the selection of the lucky firms that got the broadcast licenses should be secret, even from members of Congress, because they would not grasp the subtleties of the technology as well as the engineers and lawyers who came from the commercial broadcasting industry. See McChesney, *Telecommunications, Mass Media, and Democracy*, chapter 9.

132. See McChesney, *Telecommunications, Mass Media, and Democracy*, pp. 245-246.

133. "Threat," *TIME*, September 17, 1945.

134. The industries that may top the communication sector for government support that come to mind are agri-business, armaments and the financial sector.

135. See McChesney, *Communication Revolution*, chapter 3.

136. See Karen Aho, "2009 Customer Service Hall of Shame," MSN Network, June 10, 2009, http://articles.moneycentral.msn.com/SmartSpending/ConsumerActionGuide/the-customer-service-hall-of-shame-2009.aspx.

137. Timothy E. Cook, "Public Policy Toward the Press: What Government Does for the News Media," in Geneva Overholser and Kathleen Hall Jamieson (eds.), *The Press* (Oxford and New York: Oxford University Press, 2005), p. 254.

138. Paul Starr, *The Creation of the Media: The Political Origins of Modern Communications* (New York: Basic Books, 2004).

139. See www.freepress.net.

140. See, for example, C. Edwin Baker, *Media Concentration and Democracy: Why Ownership Matters* (New York: Cambridge University Press, 2006).

141. This may contribute to an explanation of why some of the best critical work on the First Amendment in recent years has also dwelled upon free speech to the exclusion of free-press issues. See, for example, David M. Rabban, *Free Speech in Its Forgotten Years* (Cambridge, UK: Cambridge University Press, 1997); Steven H. Shiffrin, *The First Amendment, Democracy, and Romance* (Cambridge, MA: Harvard University Press, 1990); Laura Stein, *Speech Rights in America: The First Amendment, Democracy, and the Media* (Urbana: University of Illinois Press, 2006).

142. *Whitney v. California*, 274 U.S. 357 (1927), cited in Gene Kimmelman, "Deregulation of Media: Dangerous to Democracy," text of speech given at University of Washington Law School, Seattle, Washington, March 6, 2003.

143. C. Edwin Baker, "The Independent Significance of the Press Clause Under Existing Law," presentation to the Reclaiming the First Amendment: Constitutional Theories of Media Reform conference, Hofstra University, Hempstead, New York, January 19, 2007.

144. Baker, *Media Concentration and Democracy*, p. 159.

145. *Associated Press v. United States*, 326 U.S. 1 (1945). For easy access to this important ruling, go to: http://supreme.justia.com/us/326/1/index.html

146. Cited in Donald R. Simon, "Big Media: Its Effect on the Marketplace of Ideas and How to Slow the Urge to Merge," *The John Marshall Journal of Computer and Information Law* 20, no. 2 (Winter 2002): 273.

147. Simon, "Big Media," p. 273.

148. Moreover, as he notes, "this expansive legal precedent has never been truly enforced or acted upon." Ben Scott, "Labor's New Deal for Journalism," chapter 7.

149. *New York Times Co. v. United States*, 403 U.S. 713 (1971). For easy access to this important ruling, go to: http://caselaw.lp.findlaw.com/scripts/getcase.pl?court=US&vol=403&invol=713.

150. *New York Times Co. v. United States*, 403 U.S. 713 (1971). Ibid.

151. Opinion located online at http://www.epic.org/free_speech/red_lion.html. The opinion also includes a reference to a related opinion from 1964: "Speech concerning public affairs is more than self-expression; it is the essence of self-government." *Garrison v. Louisiana*, 379 U.S. 64, 74-75 (1964).

152. Jerome A. Barron, *Freedom of the Press for Whom? The Right of Access to the Mass Media* (Bloomington: Indiana University Press, 1973). Quotation from the back cover.

153. Ed Baker adds another crucial point about *Miami Herald v. Tornillo*: "The Court has since repudiated, in Turner Broadcasting I, even that view that government involvement with content is improper. In Turner, the Court said the evil of government action in Tornillo was not mandating inclusion of content but mandating the inclusion as a penalty for having

said something negative about a candidate. In other words, according to Turner, the basis of Tornillo was not that Florida told the editor what to publish (the law upheld in Turner involved telling the cable operators, whom the Court said had full first amendment rights, what to carry, e.g., publish) but that the evil in Tornillo was that government censored/punished what the paper decided to publish on its own—a criticism of a candidate." Personal communication, C. Edwin Baker to Robert W. McChesney, May 30, 2009.

154. Cook, *Freeing the Presses*, p. 7.

155. Baker, *Media Concentration and Democracy*, p. 136.

156. Potter Stewart, "Or of the Press," *Yale Law Report*, vol. 21, no. 2, (Winter 1974-75), pp. 9-11.

157. See "The Watergate Story," *Washington Post*, at http://www.washingtonpost.com/wp-srv/politics/special/watergate.

158. See http://en.wikipedia.org/wiki/The_Constitution_is_not_a_suicide_pact.

159. For an excellent argument along these lines, see Marvin Ammori, "Beyond Content Neutrality: Understanding Content-Based Promotion of Democratic Speech," *Federal Communications Law Journal*, vol. 61, no. 2 (2009): pp. 273-324. See, in particular, the discussion on pp. 286-287. Much of this work is inspired by the work of Alexander Meiklejohn. See his *Free Speech and Its Relation to Self-Government* (New York: Harper Brothers, 1948).

160. John Nichols and Robert W. McChesney, *Tragedy and Farce: How the American Media Sell Wars, Spin Elections and Destroy Democracy* (New York: The New Press, 2005).

Chapter 4

1. Ryan Blethen, "Negotiating the Storm in the Newspaper Industry," *Seattle Times*, May 15, 2009, and "Making Newspapers Accountable to Their Communities, Not Distant Investors," *Seattle Times*, April 23, 2009. Also, conversations between John Nichols and Ryan Blethen, June 2008.

2. Ryan Blethen, "Amid the Rubble, Hope for Journalism Is Stirring," *Seattle Times*, March 26, 2009. In this article, Blethen examined some of our ideas and added perspectives of his own, noting with regard to one of our pieces for *The Nation* magazine, "They argue government intervention is needed. In the past, such a suggestion would encourage a heap of righteous indignation from journalists. I doubt that is the case today because of the sorry state of the industry. Before the purists get too riled, they should read Nichols and McChesney. They point out that the United States government did much to foster the press in the early years of the republic, with postal subsidies and printing contracts, and is still influencing the press: 'The truth is that government policies and subsidies already define our press system. The only question is whether they will be enlightened and democratic, as in the early Republic, or corrupt and corrosive to democracy, as has been the case in recent decades.'"

3. The notion of investing in democracy is gaining currency in academia. It is time to throw journalism into the mix. See Carmen Sirianni, *Investing in Democracy: Engaging Citizens in Collaborative Governance* (Washington, D.C.: Brookings Institution Press, 2009).

4. Christopher Warren to John Nichols, June 3, 2009.

5. Aidan White, *To Tell You the Truth: The Ethical Journalism Initiative.* The initiative is an ongoing project, with substantial web resources that can be found at: http://ethicaljournalisminitiative.org/en/. We especially appreciate their analysis of the current crisis, their recognition that it differs between countries but is global in its reach, and their focus on the link between journalism and democracy. "The role of media in helping to build democracy has never been more important, but how will journalism in future deliver the service people need?" they argue. "Traditional private and public sector models of media are under reconstruction as markets adapt to historic changes taking place in the way people communicate with one another. Unfortunately, quality journalism has been a casualty as media managers and owners have cut editorial budgets, reduced investment in journalism and created a precarious work environment for hundreds of thousands of media staff. Journalists and their unions and associations say we need to invest in quality information and quality journalism. Our stories, on whatever platform they are distributed, will have impact and build public trust when they have style and relevance and when they nourish and enhance the values that make journalism an integral part of democracy. This is why the Ethical Journalism Initiative has been launched by the International Federation of Journalists and its member organisation across the globe."

6. Chris Elliott to John Nichols, June 3, 2009.

7. See, for example, Clifford G. Christians, Theodore L. Glasser, Denis McQuail, Kaarle Nordenstreng, and Robert A. White, *Normative Theories of the Media: Journalism in Democratic Societies* (Urbana: University of Illinois Press, 2009).

8. Richard Reeves, *What the People Know: Freedom and the Press* (Cambridge, MA: Harvard University Press, 1998), pp. 61, 118.

9. The notion of critical junctures in media is developed in Robert W. McChesney, *Communication Revolution: Critical Junctures and the Future of Media* (New York: New Press, 2007).

10. Ryan Blethen, "Recession Could Fuel New Era of Local Newspaper Ownership," *Seattle Times,* June 12, 2009.

11. For a discussion of these, see Bree Nordensen, "The Uncle Sam Solution," *Columbia Journalism Review,* September-October 2007.

12. We draw from the excellent evaluation of Sweden in *Changing Media: Public Interest Policies for the Digital Age* (Washington, D.C.: Free Press, 2009), chapter 8.

13. "Media Landscape—Norway," European Journalism Centre, http://www.ejc.net/media_landscape/article/norway.

14. Cited in Ezra Klein, "The Truth—So Long As It's Profitable," *The American Prospect,* October 4, 2007, http://www.gmgplc.co.uk/ScottTrust/Formationandpurpose/tabid/189/Default.aspx. See also, for a similar set of findings, Rodney Benson and Daniel C. Hallin, "How States, Markets and Globalization Shape the News," *European Journal of Communication,* Vol. 22, No. 1 (2007): pp. 27-48.

15. "World Press Trends," World Association of Newspapers. We use figures here from 2006, prior to the steep decline in U.S. newspaper circulation and the closures of a number of U.S. papers, for purposes of fair comparison. Readers can find the details of these studies at: http://www.wan-press.org/article11185.html.

16. Daniel Strauss, "The American Conservative's Next Step," *Campus Progress,* May 29, 2009.

17. This idea originated, as far as we can tell, with Eric Klinenberg, Craig Aaron, Victor Pickard and Josh Silver in the spring of 2009, calling it a "Journalism Jobs Program."

18. Oliver Staley, "Harvard Crimson Editors Fleeing Ravaged Profession," *Bloomberg News*, May 18, 2009, http://www.bloomberg.com/apps/news?pid=newsarchive&sid=ar7ZDZn2bvZY.

19. Ken Doctor, "It's Time for a News Corp," *Content Bridges*, May 26, 2009, http://www.contentbridges.com/2009/05/its-time-for-a-news-corps.html. We are sympathetic to the argument that News AmeriCorps journalists should be limited to public and nonprofit media down the road, but we believe it best to make them available to all news media during the present crisis.

20. Shallit is active with the American Society of Newspaper Editors' impressive High School Journalism Initiative, which readers can learn more about at http://my.hsj.org. We are, as well, huge fans of American University law professor Jamin Raskin's great work with high-school journalists, and his book *We the Students: Supreme Court Cases for and About Students* (Washington, D.C.: CQ Press, 2000).

21. Kenneth Dautrich, David A. Yalof and Mark Hugo Lopez, *The Future of the First Amendment: The Digital Media, Civic Education, and Free Expression Rights in America's High Schools* (Lanham, MD: Rowman and Littlefield, 2008), chapter 3.

22. Ibid., p. 123.

23. Nikki Usher, "New Business Models for News Are Not That New," *Online Journalism Review*, December 17, 2008.

24. "The Scott Trust: Formation and Purpose," Guardian Media Group. Details available online at http://www.gmgplc.co.uk/ScottTrust/.

25. Tara Conlan, "Guardian Owner The Scott Trust to Be Wound Up After 72 Years," *The Guardian*, October 8, 2008.

26. Chris Elliott discussion with John Nichols, June 3, 2009.

27. Andrew Barnes, "Who Owns *The St. Petersburg Times*? Why It Matters to Readers," *The St. Petersburg Times*, December 26, 1999.

28. Ibid.

29. Ibid.

30. James V. Risser, "Endangered Species," *American Journalism Review*, June 1998.

31. Robert Trigaux, "Q&A: Newspapers Prove Worth in Tough Economy," *The St. Petersburg Times*, April 28, 2009.

32. "The Evjue Foundation Story," The Capital Times, http://www.madison.com/tct/.

33. "Bodenwein Will" and "About Us," http://www.theday.com/theday/bodenwein.aspx.

34. Douglas McCollam, "Somewhere East of Eden: Why the St. Pete Times Model Can't Save Newspapers," *Columbia Journalism Review*, March/April 2008.

35. Benjamin Cardin, "A Plan to Save Our Free Press," *Washington Post*, April 3, 2009.

36. Ibid.

37. "U.S. Bill Seeks to Rescue Faltering Newspapers," *Reuters*, March 24, 2009.

38. Ibid.

39. Ryan Blethen, "Nonprofit Model Double-Edged for Newspapers: It's a Solution—But One That Would End a Key Editorial Role in the Community," *Minneapolis Star-Tribune,* April 15, 2009. (An earlier version of the piece appeared in Blethen's newspaper, *The Seattle Times.*)

40. Ibid.

41. Another concern with Cardin's proposal was voiced by *The Atlantic*'s Conor Clarke ("Can't a Website Be a Newspaper?" *The Atlantic,* March 26, 2009), who said of the legislation that "on balance it's a good idea" but found it "strange" that the senator had excluded news-oriented Web sites: "The cost of printing a physical newspaper isn't an ineluctable burden that must be shouldered by a free press. It's a historically limited delivery mechanism for the news. The idea of delivering news on a bundle of dead trees hasn't been around forever and it won't be around forever. (If anything, there is widespread consensus within and without the industry that physical product won't be around for much longer.) Don't we want a law that subsidizes the news gathering and not the physical newspaper? In the long run, subsidizing the physical product might make the news-gathering harder, because it raises the cost of innovation. Why build a website when you can build a tax-free newspaper?" Clarke asks: "Can't a website be a newspaper?" We would answer that newspapers are going to have to be Web sites, just as news Web sites are going to have to be newspapers. The crisis facing journalism is not going to be resolved by defining repairs so narrowly that they create unintended yet destructive consequences. We think the solution is to work to create a post-corporate newspaper as well as a healthy tier of Internet news services, which may evolve into newspapers.

42. Lang is CEO of the Mary Elizabeth and Gordon B. Mannweiler Foundation. He has worked closely with the group Americans for Community Development, which is promoting the L3C model in alliance with the Council on Foundations and other groups. The Americans for Community Development Web site is at http://americans-forcommunitydevelopment.org and provides detailed background and up-to-date information on legislative initiatives relating to L3Cs.

43. Emily Nicole Chan, "L3C—Low-profit Limited Liability Company," "Nonprofit Law Blog." "Nonprofit Law Blog" is a rich resource, featuring detailed yet accessible definitions and discussions. It is published by attorney Gene Takagi, a leading nonprofit attorney in California, who contributes to it along with Chan.

44. Ibid. For details of the other states that have adopted L3C structures or that are in the process of doing so, see Emily Nicole Chan, "L3C-Developments & Resources," "Nonprofit Law Blog," http://www.nonprofitlawblog.com/home/2009/03/l3c-developments-resources.html.

45. Bill Mitchell, "L3Cs a 'Low-Profit' Business Model for News," *Poynter Online,* March 2, 2009, http://www.poynter.org/column.asp?id=131&aid=159320.

46. Ibid.

47. Sally Duros, "Newsrooms Must Die, Long Live Newsrooms," *The Huffington Post,* February 26, 2009. Duros, who has also worked for *The Wall Street Journal* and a number of other publications, has significant experience in journalism and government—she was an aide to Chicago Mayor Richard M. Daley. Check out her savvy blog at http://www.sallyduros.com.

48. Ibid.

49. See Bill Mitchell, "*New York Times* Considers Foundation Funding for News," *Poynter Online*, July 17, 2009.

50. Bernie Lunzer, "Senate Testimony," May 5, 2009, The Newspaper Guild-CWA Web site, Also, Bernie Lunzer to John Nichols, April 23, 2009.

51. Harry Chandler, "A Chandler's Advice for the L.A. Times," *The Los Angeles Times*, November 12, 2006.

52. Lunzer, "Senate Testimony."

53. David H. Weaver, et al., *The American Journalist in the 21st Century* (Mahwah, NJ: Lawrence Erlbaum, 2007), p. 2.

54. See, for example, Jay Blumler and Michael Gurevitch, "'Americanization' Reconsidered: U.K.-U.S. Campaign Communication Comparisons Across Time," in W. Lance Bennett and Robert M. Entman (eds.), *Mediated Politics* (Cambridge, UK: Cambridge University Press, 2001), pp. 380-403.

55. To be clear, the authors of the study do not necessarily regard the nature of the broadcasting system as the only or even most important variable that determines political knowledge. James Curran, Shanto Iyengar, Anker Brink Lund and Inka Salovaara-Moring, "Media System, Public Knowledge and Democracy: A Comparative Study," *European Journal of Communication*, vol. 24, no. 1 (2009): pp. 5-26.

56. For sources see Appendix III.

57. Chris Elliott to John Nichols, June 3, 2009. "Our competition is not just other newspapers, it's the BBC, and that means we have to do more."

58. See Hugh Richard Slotten, *Radio's Hidden Voice: The Origins of Public Broadcasting in the United States* (Urbana: University of Illinois Press, 2009).

59. See Kristin Hohenadel, "Where Television Sponsors the Film Industry," *New York Times*, June 11, 2000.

60. See Robert W. McChesney, *Telecommunications, Mass Media, and Democracy: The Battle for the Control of U.S. Broadcasting, 1928-1935* (New York: Oxford University Press, 1993).

61. One of us had the opportunity to listen to American Forces radio a great deal in the late 1960s and early 1970s. We can say unconditionally that had that commercial-free programming of sports, entertainment and news been available to domestic audiences in the United States, it would have been extremely popular.

62. See Carnegie Commission on Public Television, *Public Television: A Program for Action* (New York: Harper & Row, 1967).

63. Roger Smith, "Public Broadcasting as State Television," TomPaine.com, March 11, 2003.

64. Carnegie Commission, *Public Television*, p. 8.

65. Barnhart, "In Public TV We Trust," *Electronic Media*, July 22, 2002, p. 10.

66. Laura R. Linder, *Public Access Television: America's Electronic Soapbox* (Wesport, Conn.: Praeger, 1999), p. 2.

67. "Nixon Administration Public Broadcasting Papers; Summary of 1972," *Public Broadcasting PolicyBase*, http://www.current.org/pbpb/nixon/nixon72.html.

68. "Democratic Platform 1972," in Donald Bruce Johnson, compiler, *National Party Platforms, Volume 2: 1960-1976* (Chicago: University of Illinois Press, 1978), pp. 718-743.

69. Ibid.

70. Jerry Landay, "Failing the Perception Test," *Current*, June 2001; David Hatch, "PBS Decision Irks Tauzin," *Electronic Media*, May 15, 2000, p. 4.

71. Quotes from Lawrence Jarvik, *PBS: Behind the Screen* (Rocklin, CA: Forum, 1997), back cover.

72. "ANA '84: Washington Update, Cost Concerns," *Broadcasting*, November 19, 1984, p. 66.

73. Tom McCourt, *Conflicting Communication Interests in America: The Case of National Public Radio* (Westport, CT: Praeger, 1999), pp. 2–3; William F. Buckley, *On the Firing Line: The Public Life of Our Public Figures* (New York: Random House, 1989). Buckley, in sharp contrast to "conservative" hosts on commercial media today, sometimes hosted left-wing guests and treated them with respect. It produced some of the best television in our memories. Socialist economist Robert Lekachman, for example, appeared five times on *Firing Line*, in an era when he was almost never to be found on commercial network television. We suspect that had Buckley been on a commercial station, his ability to host a Lekachman and take a program to discuss the state of socialism or growing economic inequality would have been undermined. See http://hoohila .stanford.edu/firingline/guestList2.php?letter=L.

74. See research in *Changing Media: Public Interest Politics for the Digital Age* (Washington, D.C.: Free Press, 2009), p. 264.

75. Anya Kamenetz, "Can NPR Save the News?" *Fast Company*, March 18, 2009.

76. Steve Rendall and Julie Hollar, "Are You on the NewsHour's Guest List? PBS Flagship News Show Fails Public Mission," *Extra!* September/October 2006.

77. Maggie Brown, "BBC Television Networks Face New Round of Cuts," *The Guardian*, June 19, 2009.

78. See "Digital Britain," *The Guardian*, .

79. "CPB: System revenue may drop $418 million in fiscal 2009," *Current*, February 17, 2009.

80. There are reasons to believe public media face the same difficulties attracting advertising as do commercial media. All the more reason to abandon the area altogether, rather than get in a race to the bottom attempting to lure underwriting.

81. See http://www.stlbeacon.org.

82. See http://www.seattlepostglobe.org/

83. Dru Sefton, "Not-Too-Strange New Bedfellows: Print Refugees," *Current*, March 30, 2009.

84. Ibid.

85. For details of the battle for network neutrality and examples of how ISPs have attempted to violate it, go to http://www.freepress.net or http://www.savetheinternet .com.

86. Christopher Rhoades and Loretta Chao, "Iran's Web Spying Aided by Western Technology," *Wall Street Journal*, June 22, 2009.

87. See the results of the annual survey by *The Economist* on the state of global democracy: "Off The March," economist.com, October 29, 2008. What is striking is that the top six positions in *The Economist*'s rankings all are nations with massive subsidies of media and journalism.

88. To estimate what the federal subsidy of the press would amount to in today's political economy entailed two distinct tasks. First, we needed to determine the size of the subsidy in the 19th century. Second, we needed to determine how best to translate it to the contemporary economy. We determined the subsidy for the five-year period of 1840 to 1844, so we would not pick an anomalous year. For the postal subsidy of newspapers, the data we needed was in the *Historical Statistics of the United States from Colonial Times to 1970* and in the *Annual Reports of the Postmaster General, 1840-1844*. The subsidy is a combination of other postal customers paying higher rates to subsidize the newspapers (cross-subsidy) and the Post Office running a deficit.

We also consulted the two postal historians who had worked in the archival records of the period as well as several public-policy experts and economists. The historians agreed that the assessment of the Postmaster General in 1840, made after a detailed study of the five largest cities, was correct throughout this period: newspapers accounted for at least 95 percent of the weights of the mails, and no more than 12 percent of the revenues the Post Office needed to pay its bills. (Source: *Report from the Postmaster General* (John M. Niles), U.S. Senate, 26th Cong., 2d sess. [1840], p. 484.) Newspapers also accounted for two-thirds of all mailed items. The experts thought weight was the most important determinant of cost of postage–especially in the pre-railroad era–but that all items entailed a certain amount of labor. Thus we decided to give the percentage of overall weight twice the importance as the percentage of items in determining the subsidy. By this calculus, newspapers put up 12 percent of the revenues between 1840 and 1844 and accounted for 85 percent of the costs. The total amount of the subsidy was $16,954,852.25.

The printing subsidies provided by Congress and the State Department were made available for these years in Culver H. Smith, *The Press, Politics, and Patronage: The American Government's Use of Newspapers, 1789-1875* (Athens: University of Georgia Press, 1977), Appendix II, Appendix V. The leading living historian on the printing subsidies stated that at least 40 percent of these printing contracts went toward subsidizing newspapers, so that is the figure we used. The federal printing subsidies for these five years equaled $398,314.40.

The combined amount of the subsidies from 1840 to 1844 was therefore $17,353,166.65. It is worth noting that there were other subsidies, like state printing contracts, which we could not collect and therefore did not include. So our figure errs on the conservative side. At this point we had two choices: First, we could determine what percentage the press subsidies accounted for in federal spending from 1840 to 1844 and then apply that percentage to federal spending in 2008. The problem there was that the federal government has taken on vast new functions over the past 160 years and plays a much larger role in the economy. The postal and printing subsidies accounted for 15.7 percent of all federal spending during the period from 1840 to 1844. (It is worth noting that military spending is well over 50 percent of federal spending in each of those five years.) To have the same percentage of federal spending go to journalism subsidies in 2008 would have called for spending in the area of $450 billion. That struck us as a tad extreme; although it does not seem to raise eyebrows that military spending has stayed close to its 1840s percentage of federal spending.

We opted for the second choice: to take the press subsidies of 1840 to 1844 and determine them as a percentage of the Gross Domestic Product for those five years, and then apply that percentage to the GDP for 2008. GDP figres were taken from: http://www.measuringworth.org/usgdp/. This is not a flawless approach, because the translation of GDPs across time is not perfect, but it gets around the issue of federal-government growth. It also avoids the issue of changes of price levels altogether. Press subsidies were 0.216 percent of the GDP of 1840 to 1844. When that percentage is applied to the 2008 GDP it leads to a total subsidy of $30.8 billion.

89. The classic work is John Brewer, *The Sinews of Power: War, Money and the English State, 1688-1783* (New York: Alfred A. Knopf, 1989). See also: Christopher Storrs (ed.), *The Fiscal-Military State in Eighteenth-Century Europe* (London: Ashgate, 2009).

90. John Bellamy Foster, Hannah Holleman, and Robert W. McChesney, "The U.S. Imperial Triangle and Military Spending," *Monthly Review*, October 2008, http://monthlyreview.org/081001foster-holleman-mcchesney.php.

91. Chalmers Johnson, "Three Good Reasons to Liquidate Our Empire and 10 Ways to Do It," TomDispatch.com, July 31, 2009. Obviously the Pentagon is mostly off-limits to legitimate political debate and to sustained journalistic inquiry at present. The best work on it is done by the freelance community, and bloggers. See Nick Turse, *The Complex: How the Military Invades Our Everyday Lives* (New York: Metropolitan Books, 2008).

92. "National Report on Broadcasters' Community Service," National Association of Broadcasters, http://www.broadcastpublicservice.org/2008_National_Report.pdf.

93. "Consumer electronics in the United States: Industry profile," *Datamonitor Report*, September 2008, Reference Code 0072-2033.

94. "Wireless Telecommunication Services Industry Profile: United States," *Datamonitor Report*, August 2008, Reference Code 0072-2154; "Internet access in the United States: Industry profile," *Datamonitor Report*, June 2008, Reference Code 0072-2284.

95. Tom Paine, *The American Crisis*, 1776.

96. Ibid.

Conclusion

1. "Obama's White House Correspondents Dinner Speech," *Huffington Post*, May 10, 2009. http://www.huffingtonpost.com/2009/05/09/full-video-obamas-white-h_n_201264.html.

2. Eric Hobsbawm, *The Age of Extremes: The Short Twentieth Century, 1914-1991* (New York: Vintage, 2002). Hobsbawm referred to the period from 1914 to 1947, which saw the rise and fall of totalitarian regimes in Europe and Asia, as the age of catastrophe.

3. See Robert L. Morlan, *Political Prairie Fire: The Nonpartisan League, 1915-1922*, Minnesota Archive Editions edition (Minneapolis: University of Minnesota Press, 1955).

4. Tony Benn to John Nichols, March 12, 2005.

5. See "Fake TV News: Widespread and Undisclosed," Center for Media and Democracy, April 6, 2006, and a series of related studies and reports by CMD, such as "Still Not the News: Stations Overwhelmingly Fail to Disclose VNRs." CMD has campaigned

with Free Press to encourage inquiries by the Federal Communications Commission into abuses, which are ongoing.

6. Alex Carey, *Taking the Risk Out of Democracy: Corporate Propaganda versus Freedom and Liberty* (Champaign: University of Illinois Press, 1997).

7. Maureen Dowd, "Toilet-Paper Barricades," *New York Times*, August 12, 2009, p. A21.

8. For some history of Free Press and the media-reform movement in the 2000s, see Robert W. McChesney, *Communication Revolution: Critical Junctures and the Future of Media* (New York: New Press, 2007).

9. Rick Carroll, "Dan Rather Laments Journalism's Rapid Decline in Aspen Appearance," *Aspen Times*, July 29, 2009.

10. See, for example, the thoughtful writings of Ezra Klein. Ezra Klein, "Should Newspapers Be Funded by the Government?" *Washington Post*, July 2, 2009. http://voices.washingtonpost.com/ezra-klein/2009/07/should_newspapers_be_funded _by.html.

11. Carroll, "Dan Rather Laments Journalism's Rapid Decline."

12. John Nichols, "Saving Journalism Crucial to Saving Democracy," *The Capital Times*, April 29, 2009. See also: John Nichols, "Public Firms' Greed Fueled Papers' Woes," *Providence Journal*, May 18, 2009.

13. Suzanne M. Kirchoff, "The U.S. Newspaper Industry in Transition," report of the Congressional Research Service, July 8, 2009. http://www.fas.org/sgp/crs/misc/ R40700.pdf.

14. Matt Cover, "FCC Commissioner Circulates Document on 'The State of Media Journalism'," cnsnews.com, July 09, 2009. http://www.cnsnews.com/public/Content/Article.aspx?rsrcid=50761.

15. John Eggerton, "Genachowski: FCC Still Justified in Regulating Broadcast Content: New FCC chairman confirms commission will conduct inquiry into state of journalism industry," *Broadcasting & Cable* online, July 30, 2009, http://www.broadcastingcable .com/article/326051-Genachowski_FCC_Still_Justified_in_Regulating_Broadcast_ Content.php.

16. Ira Teinowitz, "FTC May Ease Anti-Trust Laws to Save News," *The Wrap*, July 31, 2009, http://www.thewrap.com/article/ftc-chief-may-ease-anti-trust-laws-save-news_4744; See also, Pradnya Joshi, "F.T.C. to Assess Business of News," *New York Times*, August 24, 2009, p. B6.

17. Paul Krugman, "Missing Richard Nixon," *New York Times*, August 31, 2009, p. A17.

18. See Ben Adler, "Heresy on the Right: A Handful of New Web Sites Try to Rewire Conservative Media," *Columbia Journalism Review*, May/June 2009.

19. See Richard Posner, "Is the Conservative Movement Losing Steam?" May 10, 2009, The Becker-Posner Blog, http://www.becker-posner-blog.com/archives/2009/05/is_ the_conserva.html.

20. Tom Paine, *Common Sense*, 1776.

21. John Nichols and Robert W. McChesney, "The Death and Life of Great American Newspapers," *The Nation*, April 6, 2009, pp. 1, 11-20. To give some sense of how rapidly the ground—and our thinking—have changed, from the beginning of 2009 to when we completed this book ten months later, we revamped our reform proposals dramat-

ically. In particular, in the *Nation* piece, we had called for allowing people a $200 tax credit for daily newspaper subscriptions. Upon receiving critical feedback to the article, we became convinced that the subscription tax-credit was not a good idea.

22. Aidan White to John Nichols, June 3, 2009.

23. Granville Williams e-mail to John Nichols, March 31, 2009.

24. Paine, *Common Sense.*

Appendix 1

1. See Burton Alva Konkle, *The Life of Andrew Hamilton: The Day Star of the American Revolution* (Freeport, NY: Books for Libraries Press, 1972), and William David Sloan and Julie Hedgepeth Williams, *The Early American Press, 1690-1783* (Westport, CT: Greenwood Press, 1994).

2. See Gouverneur Morris, *Observations on the American Revolution* (a pamphlet published in 1780), as referenced in James J. Kirschke, *Gouverneur Morris: Author, Statesman, and Man of the World* (New York: Macmillan, 2005).

3. See Richard Frothingham, "Connection with the Press," in *Life and Times of Joseph Warren,* (Boston: Little, Brown & Co., 1865), p. 43.

4. See Paul Finkelman, *Encyclopedia of American Civil Liberties* (New York: Routledge, 2006), vol. I, p. 137.

5. Frothingham, *Life and Times of Joseph Warren,* p. 45.

6. "Continental Congress to the Inhabitants of the Province of Quebec," October 26, 1774, *Journals of the Continental Congress, 1774—1789,* edited by Worthington C. Ford et al., 34 vols (Washington, D.C.: Government Printing Office, 1904—37), vol. 1:105—13.

7. Finkelman, *Encyclopedia of American Civil Liberties,* p. 139.

8. See *The American Republic: Primary Sources,* edited by Bruce Frohnen (Liberty Fund, 2002). The full article can be read online at.

9. Senate Journal, September 24, 1789, History of Congress 169—70. This can be viewed online at the *The Founders' Constitution,* which is edited by Philip B. Kurland and Ralph Lerner.

10. See *The Papers of Thomas Jefferson, Volume 31: 1 February 1799 to 31 May 1800* (Princeton: Princeton University Press, 2004), pp. 126-30.

11. Thomas Jefferson to Thomas Cooper, November 29, 1802, found in *The Writings of Thomas Jefferson,* Memorial Edition (Lipscomb and Bergh [eds.]), 20 Vols., Washington, D.C., 1903-04, vol. 10, p. 341.

12. Tunis Wortman, *A Treatise Concerning Political Enquiry and the Liberty of the Press* (New York: George Forman, 1800), available through the American Imprint Collection (Library of Congress), pp. 23-24.

13. Elias Boudinot, "An Address to the Whites Delivered in the First Presbyterian Church, on the 26th of May, 1826, by Elias Boudinott, A Cherokee Indian," found in Theda Perdue's *Cherokee Editor: The Writings of Elias Boudinot* (Athens: University of Georgia Press, 1996), p. 65.

14. Samuel Cornish and John Russwurm, "TO OUR PATRONS," *Freedom's Journal,* March 26, 1827. See Wisconsin Historical Society: African-American Newspapers and

Periodicals: *Freedom's Journal*, http://www.wisconsinhistory.org/libraryarchives/aanp/freedom.

15. U.S. Supreme Court, *New York Times v. United States*, 403 U.S. 713 (1971).

16. Benjamin Rush, "Address to the People of the United States," delivered at the American Museum, Philadelphia, in January 1787. Found in *Friends of the Constitution: Writings of the "Other" Federalists, 1787-1788*, edited by Colleen A. Sheehan and Gary L. McDowell (Liberty Fund, 1998).

17. Thomas Jefferson to Edward Carrington, January 16, 1787, found in *The Papers of Thomas Jefferson*, edited by Julian P. Boyd et al. (Princeton: Princeton University Press, 1950), papers 11:48–49.

18. George Washington, letter to Mathew Carey, found in Earl Lockridge Bradsher, *Mathew Carey, Editor, Author and Publisher: A Study in American Literary Development* (New York: Columbia University Press, 1912).

19. James Madison, "Public Opinion," *The National Gazette*, December 19, 1791, found in *The Writings of James Madison*, ed. Gaillard Hunt, 9 volumes (Putnam's, 1900-1910), vol. 6, p. 70.

20. George Washington, "Fifth State of the Union Address," December 3, 1793, found in *The Writings of George Washington*, ed. Worthington Chauncey Ford (New York: G.P. Putnam's Sons, 1891), p. 355.

21. Thomas Jefferson, "First Annual Message," December 8, 1801, found in *The Writings of Thomas Jefferson*, Memorial Edition (Lipscomb and Bergh [eds.]) 20 Vols., Washington, D.C., 1903-04, vol. 3, p. 331.

22. Simon Eliot and Jonathan Rose, *A Companion to the History of the Book* (Hoboken, NJ: Wiley-Blackwell, 2007), p. 317.

Appendix 2

1. Stephen Ambrose to John Nichols. As an editor at *The Capital Times* in Madison, Wisconsin, Nichols maintained a long relationship with Ambrose, interviewing the historian frequently about his books on Eisenhower and World War II. Ambrose, a Wisconsin native, wrote frequently for *The Capital Times*. See John Nichols, "Ambrose Left Without Writing Memoir," *The Capital Times*, October 15, 2002.

2. Stephen Ambrose, *Eisenhower and Berlin, 1945: The Decision to Halt at the Elbe* (New York: W. W. Norton, 2000), p. 5.

3. Irene Pusher, "In Volatile Iraq, U.S. Curbs Press," *The Christian Science Monitor*, June 19, 2003. See also: "Exporting Censorship to Iraq," Project Censored, "Top 25 Censored Stories for 2005" (http://www.projectcensored.org/top-stories/category/y-2005/); "War in Iraq," *Reporters Without Borders* (http://arabia.reporters-sans-frontieres.org/special_iraq_en.php3); Stephen Schwartz, "Free the Iraqi Press," *The Weekly Standard*, May 17, 2004; and "Staffers Quit At U.S.-Backed Paper," *The Washington Post*, May 4, 2004, which reported on the mass resignations of reporters and editors on a U.S.-backed newspaper, *Al-Sabah*, where it was alleged by the editor that "American overseers had threatened their future editorial independence." The editor, Ismael Zayer, told the *Post*, "We thought that Americans were here to create a free media," but "instead, we were being suffocated." The *Post* observed, "The exodus from

al Sabah is the latest setback in U.S. efforts to shepherd Iraq into a new media era. The effort has faced allegations of wasted funding and uninspired programming. Many Iraqis view the outlets created as mouthpieces of the occupation, not independent voices."

4. See, for instance, Manfred Malzahn, *Germany, 1945–1949: A Sourcebook* (New York: Routledge, 1991) for a smart assessment of the many missteps of the U.S. occupiers and their allies. Malzahn examines the challenges that arise whenever an occupying force tries to "teach democracy" and dwells at considerable and insightful length on the legitimate concerns of Germans, including the "mistrust of this new press by the German population (which assumed) that it was not presenting the honest opinions of licensed publishers and editors but a reading matter shaped by military control," p. 170. Critical assessments of the occupation and its approach to freedom-of-the-press issues can be found in Detlef Junker, *The United States and Germany in the Era of the Cold War: A Handbook* (Cambridge, UK: Cambridge University Press, 2004).

5. See Junker; see also John W. Dower, *Embracing Defeat: Japan in the Wake of World War II* (New York: W. W. Norton, 2000). The latter offers especially important insights in the chapter "Censoring Democracy: Policing the New Taboos," pp. 405–442.

6. Major General Robert Alexis McClure, quoted in Colonel Alfred H. Paddock Jr. (USA Retired), "Major General Robert Alexis McClure: Forgotten Father of U.S. Army Special Warfare," *The United States Army Special Operation Command News Service* (http://news.soc.mil). In July 1946, McClure wrote C. D. Jackson, a vice president of Time-Life Inc., a letter in which the general suggested to his longtime friend that they shared avocations: "We now control 37 newspapers, 6 radio stations, 314 theatres, 642 movies, 101 magazines, 237 book publishers, 7,384 book dealers and printers, and conduct about 15 public opinion surveys a month, as well as publish one newspaper with 1,500,000 circulation, 3 magazines, run the Associated Press of Germany (DANA), and operate 20 library centers . . . The job is tremendous."

7. Clinton Green, "Japan Told to Set Press, Radio Free: Editors and Officials Warned by U.S. on Concealing and Distorting News," *The New York Times*, October 25, 1945.

8. United States Department of State, "U.S. Directive to General Eisenhower on Military Rule of Germany," October 17, 1945. This document can be found online at: http://www.ibiblio.org/pha/policy/post-war/451017a.html

9. Klaus Schwabe, "American Occupation Experiences in Aachen before Germany's Surrender, Aachener Geschichtsvereins (Aachen Historical Society, 2000). These materials can be found online at http://www.histinst.rwth-aachen.de.

10. Sydney Gruson, "Allies Set Up Free Press in Aachen But Find Non-Nazi Germans Scarce," *New York Times*, February 19, 1945.

11. Military Governor, "The German Press in the U.S. Occupied area: 1945–1948; special report; November 1948," German Reconstruction Collection, online at images .library.wisc.edu/History/EFacs/GerRecon/SpecialReport/reference/history.specialreport .i0009.pdf.

12. In his January 6, 1941 State of the Union Address to the Congress, Roosevelt declared: "In the future days, which we seek to make secure, we look forward to a world founded upon four essential human freedoms. The first is freedom of speech and expression—everywhere in the world. The second is freedom of every person to worship God in his own way—everywhere in the world. The third is freedom from

want—which, translated into universal terms, means economic understandings which will secure to every nation a healthy peacetime life for its inhabitants—everywhere in the world. The fourth is freedom from fear—which, translated into world terms, means a world-wide reduction of armaments to such a point and in such a thorough fashion that no nation will be in a position to commit an act of physical aggression against any neighbor—anywhere in the world. That is no vision of a distant millennium. It is a definite basis for a kind of world attainable in our own time and generation. That kind of world is the very antithesis of the so-called new order of tyranny which the dictators seek to create with the crash of a bomb." Though a war-time president who would die before the fighting was done, Roosevelt devoted a great deal of attention to the question of how to foster democracy in the postwar era and was exceptionally aware of the need to help develop a free press in formerly fascist and formerly occupied countries, as is detailed in Robert Dallek's *Franklin D. Roosevelt and American Foreign Policy, 1932–1945* (New York: Oxford University Press, USA, 2nd edition, 1995).

13. Associated Press, "Kent Cooper Dies, Former A.P. Chief," *New York Times,* January 31, 1965.

14. "Free Press v. War," *TIME*, November 22, 1943.

15. See, for example, Kent Cooper, "To Prevent War—No News Blackout," *New York Times*, March 11, 1945.

16. Ibid.

17. "Free Press v. War," *TIME*.

18. Betty Houchin Winfield, *FDR and the News Media* (Champaign: University of Illinois Press, 1990), p. 186.

19. "Joint Four-Nation Declaration," The Moscow Conference, October 1943. Source: *A Decade of American Foreign Policy: Basic Documents, 1941–49, Prepared at the request of the Senate Committee on Foreign Relations By the Staff of the Committee and the Department of State* (Washington, D.C.: Government Printing Office, 1950).

20. "Free Press v. War," *TIME*.

21. Military Governor, "The German Press in the U.S. Occupied area: 1945–1948; special report; November 1948." This remarkably detailed document can be found online at: http://digicoll.library.wisc.edu/cgi-bin/History/History-idx?id=History.SpecialReport.

22. Major Daniel C. Imboden, "Japan's Free Press," U.S. Army, http://www.army.mil/-news/1950/02/01/4636-japans-free-press.

23. Military Governor, "The German Press in the U.S. Occupied area: 1945–1948; special report; November 1948."

24. "Old Japanese Customs," *TIME*, August 19, 1946.

25. Dower, *Embracing Defeat: Japan in the Wake of World War II*, p. 406.

26. "The German Press in the U.S. Occupied area: 1945–1948; special report; November 1948."

27. For an account of the creation of the Aachen paper, see Eugene Jolas, *Man From Babel* (New Haven: Yale University Press, 1998) p. 215—the autobiography of the co-founder of the Parisian literary magazine *Transition*, a publisher of James Joyce, a pal of Ernest Hemingway and a member of the team of European intellectuals assembled to establish newspapers in Germany.

28. For a detailed account of Habe's ideas, successes and failures, see Jessica C. E. Gienow-Hecht, *Transmission Impossible: American Journalism as Cultural Diplomacy in Postwar Germany 1945–1955*, Eisenhower Center Studies on War and Peace (Baton Rouge: Louisiana State University Press, 1999).

29. Landau's account is contained in Michael Brenner, *After the Holocaust: Rebuilding Jewish Lives in Postwar Germany* (Princeton: Princeton University Press, 1999), pp. 85–86.

30. "Uncle Sam, Publisher," *TIME*, November 29, 1948.

31. "Old Japanese Customs," *TIME*. Despite the fact that MacArthur and his commanders were facilitating the publication of Japanese newspapers, the magazine reported, "The U.S. so far has done nothing about the size of Japanese newspaper staffs, except to be astonished at them. Tokyo's biggest paper, Asahi Shimbun ("Rising Sun Newspaper"), which has a 3,350,000 circulation, is only a two-page paper now—but has an editorial staff of 1,100, of whom 500 are reporters. Prewar Asahi had a fleet of 80 automobiles, 40 gliders, 20 airplanes. Now it is down to seven wheezy cars, and insists that one reason it needs a big staff is that its men take so long to get around. Reporters start at a meager 255 yen a month ($14), get frequent bonuses to help them break even. Asahi has 26 photographers, keeps six reporters at Tokyo police headquarters, sends a task force of 40 to cover a session of the Japanese Diet. About one-fourth of Asahi's reporters sometimes go a week at a time without breaking into print. Even so, Asahi thinks it needs more reporters for the day paper gets more plentiful, has scheduled September exams to pick them."

32. Military Governor, "The German Press in the U.S. Occupied area: 1945–1948; special report; November 1948."

33. Ibid.

34. The actual amount spent on this project is difficult to ascertain, as much of the work was carried out as part of military operations and programs to aid refugees and displaced peoples. For instance, Hans Habe, who helped start a score of newspapers and edited a number of them, did so as a U.S. Army officer.

35. "Free Press in Germany," *New York Times*, April 28, 1953.

36. Military Governor, "The German Press in the U.S. Occupied area: 1945–1948; special report; November 1948."

37. Information about the development of postwar newspaper competition can be found on the Web site of the International Newspaper Museum in Aachen at http://www.izm.de.

38. Military Governor, "The German Press in the U.S. Occupied area: 1945–1948; special report; November 1948." Office of the Military Government for Germany (U.S.) (http://onlinebooks.library.upenn.edu/webbin/book/browse?type=lccn&key=PN5208 %20%2eA53)

39. For more information on the development of Germany's *Lander* broadcasting laws and networks, check out the extensive materials available in German and English from the Arbeitsgemeinschaft der öffentlich-rechtlichen Rundfunkanstalten der Bundesrepublik Deutschland (ARD). A very good Web site is maintained at http://www.ard.de.

40. See "Censors Restrict Japanese Papers," *The New York Times*, January 10, 1946, for a classic example of the sort of disputes that developed. Japanese editors clashed

with U.S. military officials over the issue of speculation over possible arrests of accused war criminals. There were also disputes, in Germany and Japan, over the portrayal of occupation forces and individual officials, including Generals Eisenhower and MacArthur, although the generals frequently went out of their way to urge reporters to question them.

41. Lindesay Parrott, "Press Censorship Ends in Japan; Editors Put on Own Responsibility," *New York Times*, July 16, 1948.

42. "Truman Lifts News Curb on Reich; Backs Eisenhower Against Davis," *New York Times*, May 16, 1945.

43. "U.S. German Paper Reaches 1,600,000," *The New York Times*, April 10, 1945.

44. Lindesay Parrott, "MacArthur Extends His Ban to 17 Heads of Red Paper," *New York Times*, June 8, 1950.

45. "Free Press in Germany," *New York Times*, April 28, 1953.

46. "The First Decade," *TIME*, January 14, 1957.

47. Blaine Harden, "Japan's Papers: Doomed But Going Strong," *Washington Post*, October 25, 2008.

Index